Institute of Judicial Administration
American Bar Association

Juvenile Justice Standards

Annotated

A Balanced Approach

Robert E. Shepherd, Jr., editor

Foreword by Hon. Patricia M. Wald

Introduction by Barbara Flicker

Criminal Justice Section American Bar Association

The materials contained herein represent the opinions of the authors and editors and should not be construed to be the action of either the American Bar Association or the Criminal Justice Section unless adopted pursuant to the bylaws of the Association.

Nothing contained in this book is to be considered as the rendering of legal advice for specific cases, and readers are responsible for obtaining such advice from their own legal counsel. This book and any forms and agreements herein are intended for educational and informational purposes only.

01 00 99 98 97   5 4 3 2 1

The ABA juvenile justice standards, annotated / Robert E. Shepherd,
    Jr. [editor] ; foreword by Patricia Wald ; introduction by Barbara
    Flicker.
        p.   cm.
    Includes index.
    ISBN 1-57073-326-0 (pbk.)
    1. Juvenile justice, Administration of—United States.
    2. Juvenile corrections—United States. 3. Children—Legal status,
    laws, etc.—United States.   I. Shepherd, Robert E., 1937–   .
    KF9779.A1A23   1996
    345.73'08—dc20
    [347.3058]   96-14510
                                                                  CIP

Discounts are available for books ordered in bulk. Special consideration is given to state bars, CLE programs, and other bar-related organizations. Inquire at Publications Planning & Marketing, American Bar Association, 750 North Lake Shore Drive, Chicago, Illinois 606111.

Contents

Foreword   xi

Introduction   xv

Editor's Introduction   xxiii

About the Authors   xxvii

STANDARDS RELATING TO ADJUDICATION
Robert O. Dawson, Reporter

Part I:	Requisites for Adjudication Proceedings to Begin	1
Part II:	Standards Applicable to Uncontested and Contested Adjudication Proceedings	2
Part III:	Uncontested Adjudication Proceedings	4
Part IV:	Contested Adjudication Procedures	8
Part V:	The Adjudication Decision	9
Part VI:	Public Access to Adjudication Proceedings	11

STANDARDS RELATING TO APPEALS AND COLLATERAL REVIEW
Michael Moran, Reporter

Part I:	The Nature of the Appellate Structure	13
Part II:	Reviewability	13
Part III:	The Right to Counsel and Records	15
Part IV:	Procedures	15
Part V:	Stays of Orders and Release Pending Appeal	15
Part VI:	Collateral and Supplementary Proceedings	16

STANDARDS RELATING TO ARCHITECTURE OF FACILITIES
Allen M. Greenberg, Reporter

Part I:	Definitions	19
Part II:	Values and Purposes	21
Part III:	Architectural Program and Design	21
Part IV:	Group Homes	23
Part V:	Secure Corrections Facilities	24
Part VI:	Secure Detention Facilities	25

STANDARDS RELATING TO CORRECTIONS ADMINISTRATION
Andrew Rutherford and Fred Cohen, Reporters

Part I:	General Principles	29
Part II:	Jurisdiction of the Department Responsible for the Administration of Juvenile Corrections	30
Part III:	Organizational Structure and Personnel	32
Part IV:	Required Features of All Programs	36
Part V:	Modification of Dispositions	44
Part VI:	Nonresidential Programs	45
Part VII:	Residential Programs	48
Part VIII:	The Disciplinary System	58
Part IX:	Accountability	63

STANDARDS RELATING TO COUNSEL FOR PRIVATE PARTIES
Lee Teitelbaum, Reporter

Part I:	General Standards	69
Part II:	Provision and Organization of Legal Services	70
Part III:	The Lawyer-Client Relationship	75
Part IV:	Initial Stages of Representation	80
Part V:	Advising and Counseling the Client	81
Part VI:	Intake, Early Disposition and Detention	82
Part VII:	Adjudication	84
Part VIII:	Transfer Proceedings	88
Part IX:	Disposition	89
Part X:	Representation after Disposition	91

STANDARDS RELATING TO COURT ORGANIZATION AND ADMINISTRATION
Ted Rubin, Reporter

Part I:	Organizational Structure of Courts of Juvenile Jurisdiction	95
Part II:	Judicial and Chief Administrative Personnel Performing Court Functions	96
Part III:	Court Functions	96
Part IV:	Responsibility of the Family Court Division to Effectuate Its Duties and Orders	98

STANDARDS RELATING TO DISPOSITIONAL PROCEDURES
Fred Cohen, Reporter

Part I:	Dispositional Authority	101
Part II:	Dispositional Information	101
Part III:	Parties Present	104
Part IV:	Custody Awaiting Disposition	105
Part V:	Predisposition Conference and Disposition Agreements: Experimentation Suggested	105
Part VI:	Formal Disposition Hearing	106
Part VII:	Imposition and Correction of Disposition	107

STANDARDS RELATING TO DISPOSITIONS
Linda R. Singer, Reporter

Part I:	General Purposes and Limitations	109
Part II:	Dispositional Criteria	110
Part III:	Dispositions	111
Part IV:	Provision of Services	114
Part V:	Modification and Enforcement of Dispositional Orders	116

STANDARDS RELATING TO INTERIM STATUS: THE RELEASE, CONTROL AND DETENTION OF ACCUSED JUVENILE OFFENDERS BETWEEN ARREST AND DISPOSITION
Daniel J. Freed and Timothy P. Terrell, Reporters

Part I:	Introduction	119
Part II:	Definitions	119
Part III:	Basic Principles	123
Part IV:	General Procedural Standards	124
Part V:	Standards for the Police	127
Part VI:	Standards for the Juvenile Facility Intake Official	129
Part VII:	Standards for the Juvenile Court	133
Part VIII:	Standards for the Defense Attorney	138
Part IX:	Standards for the Prosecutor	139
Part X:	Standards for Juvenile Detention Facilities	140
Part XI:	General Administrative Standards	143

STANDARDS RELATING TO JUVENILE DELINQUENCY
AND SANCTIONS
John M. Junker, Reporter

Part I:	Preliminary Principles	147
Part II:	Jurisdiction	148
Part III:	General Principles of Liability	149
Part IV:	Sanctions	151
Part V:	Limits on Type and Duration of Delinquency Sanctions	152

STANDARDS RELATING TO THE JUVENILE PROBATION
FUNCTION: INTAKE AND PREDISPOSITION
INVESTIGATIVE SERVICES
Josephine Gittler, Reporter

Part I:	Definitions	155
Part II:	Juvenile Court Intake	156
Part III:	Predisposition Investigations and Reports	164
Part IV:	Organization and Administration of Juvenile Intake and Predisposition Investigative Services	166
Part V:	Intake and Investigative Personnel	167

STANDARDS RELATING TO JUVENILE RECORDS
AND INFORMATION SERVICES
Michael L. Altman, Reporter

Section I:	General Standards	
Part I:	Definitions	171
Part II:	General Policies Pertaining to Information	172
Part III:	Collection of Information	175
Part IV:	Retention of Information	177
Part V:	Dissemination of Information	180
Section II:	Specific Standards for Juveniles' Social and Psychological Histories	
Part VI:	Definition	185
Part VII:	Preparation of Social Histories	185
Part VIII:	Retention of Social Histories	186
Part IX:	Dissemination of Social Histories	187
Part X:	Destruction of Social Histories	187

Section III: Specific Standards for the Records of Juvenile Courts
    Part XI: Legislation   188
    Part XII: Records of Juvenile Courts   189
    Part XIII: Records of Legal Proceedings   189
    Part XIV: Probation Records   191
    Part XV: Access to Juvenile Records   192
    Part XVI: Correction of Juvenile Records   196
    Part XVII: Destruction of Juvenile Records   196
    Part XVIII: Use of Juvenile Records   198
Section IV: Standards for Police Records
    Part XIX: General   199
    Part XX: Access to Police Records   202
    Part XXI: Correction of Police Records   203
    Part XXII: Destruction of Police Records   203

STANDARDS RELATING TO MONITORING
Stephen R. Bing and J. Larry Brown, Reporters

    Part I: General Standards   205
    Part II: Monitoring Focal Points   209
Specific Monitoring Mechanisms
    Part III: Defense Counsel or Counsel for Private Parties   212
    Part IV: State Commission on Juvenile Advocacy   213
    Part V: Community Advisory Councils   215
    Part VI: Legislature-Based Monitoring   215
    Part VII: Ombudsman-Based Monitoring   216
    Part VIII: Private-Sector Activities   217
    Part IX: Court-Based Monitoring   218
    Part X: Self-Monitoring by Juvenile Justice Agencies   220

STANDARDS RELATING TO PLANNING FOR JUVENILE JUSTICE
Suzanne and Leonard Buckle, Reporters

    Part I: General Principles for Juvenile Justice Agencies   223
    Part II: Organization of the Juvenile Justice Planning
                    Network   224
    Part III: Functions of the Juvenile Justice Planner   227
    Part IV: Roles for External Participants in the Juvenile
                    Justice Planning Process   230

STANDARDS RELATING TO POLICE HANDLING OF JUVENILE PROBLEMS
Egon Bittner and Sheldon Krantz, Reporters

Part I:	Introduction	233
Part II:	Role of the Police in the Handling of Juvenile Problems	233
Part III:	The Authority of the Police to Handle Juvenile Delinquency and Criminal Problems	235
Part IV:	Implications of the Police Role for Police Organization and Personnel	237
Part V:	The Need for Incentives and Accountability: Directions for Needed Improvements and Further Research	241

STANDARDS RELATING TO PRETRIAL COURT PROCEEDINGS
Stanley Z. Fisher, Reporter

Part I:	Report, Petition, and Summons	243
Part II:	Notification of Rights; Initial Appearance	246
Part III:	Discovery	247
Part IV:	The Right to a Probable Cause Hearing	253
Part V:	Respondent's Right to Counsel	253
Part VI:	Waiver of the Juvenile's Rights; the Role of Parents and Guardians *ad Litem* in the Delinquency Proceedings	255
Part VII:	Juvenile Court Calendaring	261

STANDARDS RELATING TO PROSECUTION
James P. Manak, Reporter

Part I:	General Standards	263
Part II:	Organization of the Juvenile Prosecutor's Office and Qualifications of the Juvenile Prosecutor and His or Her Staff	263
Part III:	Relationships of the Juvenile Prosecutor with Other Participants in the Juvenile Justice System	265
Part IV:	The Preadjudication Phase	267
Part V:	Uncontested Adjudication Proceedings	269
Part VI:	The Adjudicatory Phase	270
Part VII:	Dispositional Phase	272
Part VIII:	Postdisposition Proceedings	273

STANDARDS RELATING TO RIGHTS OF MINORS
Barry Feld and Robert J. Levy, Reporters

Part I:	Age of Majority	275
Part II:	Emancipation	275
Part III:	Support	276
Part IV:	Medical Care	277
Part V:	Youth Employment	280
Part VI:	Minors' Contracts	283

STANDARDS RELATING TO TRANSFER BETWEEN COURTS
Charles Whitebread, Reporter

Part I:	Jurisdiction	285
Part II:	Waiver	286

STANDARDS RELATING TO YOUTH SERVICE AGENCIES
Judith Areen, Reporter

Part I:	Establishment of Youth Service Agencies	293
Part II:	Objectives	293
Part III:	Decision Structure	294
Part IV:	Access to the Youth Service Agency	294
Part V:	The Service System	298
Part VI:	Monitoring and Assessment System	299
Part VII:	Organization and Administration	301

CASES CITING TENTATIVE JUVENILE JUSTICE STANDARDS VOLUMES THAT WERE NOT APPROVED

Abuse and Neglect	303
Standards Relating to Noncriminal Misbehavior	305

Index to the *ABA-IJA Juvenile Justice Standards*   307

FOREWORD

George Santayana's warning that "those who cannot remember the past are condemned to repeat it," is by now a truism, and nothing could be truer of the history of juvenile justice reform in the United States. Throughout most of this century, we have ricocheted between benevolent rehabilitation and get-tough remedies as leitmotifs in treating our miscreant youth. Neither works for long, and today—twenty years after the pathbreaking Institute of Judicial Administration–American Bar Association *Juvenile Justice Standards*—we are told that "numbed by teenage killers and unable to rehabilitate youthful offenders, the juvenile justice system is [again] turning to get-tough measures to halt a new generation of crime." One commentator adds wistfully, "The answer to all of our troubles may be a program out there somewhere in some small town that we don't know about yet." Don't count on it.

I was an original participant in the ten-year effort inaugurated in 1971 by Judge Irving Kaufman to distill the very best of the research, thought, and experience of all relevant disciplines in the juvenile justice field and incorporate them into usable standards for social service personnel, juvenile judges, probation officers, correctional administrators and legislators. The roster of three hundred experts who devoted over a decade to the project—many of them, like Judge Kaufman, no longer living, others, like Janet Reno, currently leading the country's law enforcement agencies—could not be reassembled nowadays; in the intervening years, too many have lost faith in the value of comprehensive planning or rational remedies as antidotes to the scourge of mindless violence that plagues our cities and infects our children. A retrospective of the *Juvenile Justice Standards,* however, persuades me that it was a most worthwhile effort, still viable, and not susceptible to facile characterizations as "too hard" or "too soft" on violent-prone youth. Indeed, I recall the strenuous debates and anguished criticisms from more traditionally oriented juvenile experts that accompanied the *Standards'* adoption in the mid-seventies of norms of finite sentencing proportional to the severity of the offense. The *Standards'* stress on more systematic but carefully controlled information-sharing between child-caring agencies deserves revisiting as we enter the age of information, though it was considered by many overly innovative at the time. The notion of discrete time limits to pretrial detention, paralleling Speedy Trial Act guarantees for adult offenders, seemed downright revolutionary to others, as did the concept that teenaged youths had certain legal rights as well as duties in critical choices as to their future. The unifying thread to all twenty-three volumes was that we—the adult world—had the right to judge and to punish youthful wrongdoers, but we also had responsibilities for adjudicating children fairly, for intervening in families in ways that would be salutary, not punitive and destructive, and for treating youths who must be removed from society in a manner which did not derogate their humanity and guarantee them a pass to the nearest penitentiary. No community thus far has chosen to make that trade-off, and so we continue to repeat our rhetoric and poignantly to scan the landscape in search of a cure for our fast metastasizing social cancer. Reducing the age limit for the death penalty, allowing waiver to the adult criminal system at successively earlier ages—do we really think those will do the job?

Ironically, the number of juvenile offenders in our midst has mounted perceptibly in the twenty years since the *Standards* were issued. And the nature of their crimes has unmistakably worsened. If we are to believe the interviews with these alienated teenagers that flood our newspapers daily, their desperation, their distancing from all normal adolescent aspirations or feelings of empathy or compassion for others has intensified almost beyond human comprehension. Over half of their vicious crimes are committed against each other. Over one hundred thousand of them are already shut away in junior jails, and many in adult prisons. What happens when they emerge?

No doubt some of the standards in this compendium could benefit from things learned in twenty years. But what little new learning there is, in most cases, simply reinforces the basic truths that were already there. A recent listing by the Office of Juvenile Justice Delinquency and Prevention of the most effective juvenile offender programs in the country mirrored the same essential components we mandated back then: early intervention, accurate needs assessment, small group programs in the community, intensive staff supervision and follow-up, education on individual responsibilities and the consequences of violent behavior. No juvenile boot camps have yet proved there are short cuts.

As in times of past crises, the future of the entire juvenile justice system as an entity separate from adult justice is again befogged. Americans have a tendency to demand swift results and to change course often and sharply when they are not achieved. It bears noting, however, that the *IJA-ABA Standards* still represent the most comprehensive, balanced vision of a just and potentially effective system for dealing with youthful offenders that exists. They have not been given a fair chance; implementation where it has occurred has been piecemeal and, in the main, they have taken second place to fads, slogans and quick fixes. One can only hope that before the nation turns on end again, its leaders will pause long enough to look at what a dedicated and knowledgeable group of experts thought would work twenty years ago, and if they can, build on that foundation to do even better. If that happens, the republication of the *Standards* in this one accessible volume will be well worth the candle.

Patricia M. Wald
Judge, United States Court of Appeals
Washington, D.C.

INTRODUCTION

The Standards and Changing Times

During the ten-year period in which the Juvenile Justice Standards Project of the Institute of Judicial Administration (IJA) and the American Bar Association (ABA) was engaged in producing the twenty-three volumes of the *IJA-ABA Juvenile Justice Standards*, the project was governed by numerous well-articulated policies and guidelines. The most fundamental working principle was that the standards were designed to establish the best possible juvenile justice system for our society, not to fluctuate in response to transitory headlines or controversies.

Ironically, public acceptance of the *Standards* has been as variable as the political climate. The only constant has been the demand for reform of a glaringly deficient juvenile justice system. The current alarm over juvenile crime is exemplified by a recent article in the *New York Times*, preceded by the query, "What Can Be Done About the Scourge of Violence Among Juveniles?" It reflects the popular view that the juvenile justice system should somehow protect the public, punish and rehabilitate the offenders, and prevent future crimes.

"New age" politicians, journalists, and other barometers of public opinion have embraced the position that since poverty, abusive parents, and dysfunctional families are the best predictors of criminality, draconian proposals to remove and institutionalize children through the welfare system are justified. They dispense with such formalities as detecting crimes or pursuing due process of law. The Child Savers are back, orphanages are in, and early intervention to salvage the children of poor parents is the answer for our new intellectual leaders.

These views are not consonant with the principles underlying the *IJA-ABA Juvenile Justice Standards*. The standards were drafted in the 1970s, a period of burgeoning individual rights. But they were published in 1980 and 1981 and their implementation was not a priority of the Reagan and Bush administrations. In 1992, the Juvenile Justice Committee of the ABA Section of Criminal Justice responded to the apparent promise of more progressive policies in Washington by forming a subcommittee to review and revive the standards. The incoming administration was expected to support the standards that many of its leaders had participated in adopting. Attorney General Janet Reno had been an active member of the IJA-ABA Joint Commission on Juvenile Justice Standards. First Lady Hillary Clinton had served on one of the four substantive task forces that supervised the drafting of the volumes.

The members of the subcommittee reviewed the volumes and reported that the black letter *Standards* remained fundamentally relevant and sound and that the commentaries accompanying the *Standards* were illuminating but should be updated to cover changes in the law and literature during the intervening years. At the 1994 ABA Annual Meeting, the committee presented a Presidential Showcase Program on "Taking the ABA *Juvenile Justice Standards* to the 21st Century: Juvenile Justice Reform for the '90s." The audience was enthusiastic and plans were made to publish this volume of annotated standards to spearhead the committee's efforts towards widespread implementation of the *Standards*. That was in August 1994, a mere three months before the national midterm elections once again shifted the political balance of power.

Although the sheer mass of the volumes of *Standards* conveys a sense of the monumental work performed by the hundreds of juvenile justice specialists who were involved in the Juvenile Justice Standards Project, it does not show the meticulous scholarship and intense debate over the implications of every detail of policy and practice that characterized the lengthy process by which the *Standards* were drafted and finally adopted. As a former director of the project, executive editor of the final published version, and author of the summary volume, *Standards for Juvenile Justice: A Summary and Analysis*, I feel qualified to describe that process.

Development of the Standards

The Juvenile Justice Standards Project was initiated in 1971 at the Institute of Judicial Administration, a nonprofit research and educational national court organization located at the New York University School of Law. It began as an afterthought to the ABA Project for *Standards for Criminal Justice*, for which IJA served as secretariat. Staff members first had considered annotating the twelve volumes of criminal justice standards to show how the juvenile law diverged, but they found the fundamental disparities more extensive than they had anticipated. The criminal justice standards did not address the issues presented by the separate courts and agencies established to handle problems affecting juveniles and their families. IJA began to plan a modest project to produce a single volume devoted to juvenile justice. Ten years and twenty-three volumes later, the *IJA-ABA Juvenile Justice Standards* were completed.

The project was an arduous task executed by about three hundred dedicated professionals throughout the nation, including prominent representatives of every discipline connected to the juvenile justice system: the law, the judiciary, medicine, social work, psychiatry, psychology, sociology, corrections, political science, law enforcement, education, and architecture. Scholars and practitioners joined task forces and working groups to perform research, analysis, drafting, reviewing, revising, and editing functions, supported by IJA professional and clerical staff.

The structure of the project was as intricate as the volumes of standards it produced. A planning committee chaired by the late Chief Judge Irving R. Kaufman of the United States Court of Appeals for the Second Circuit met in October 1971, followed by meetings of six planning subcommittees to identify the issues in the juvenile justice field and the areas to be covered. In February 1973, the ABA became cosponsor of the project and the IJA-ABA Joint Commission on *Juvenile Justice Standards* was established as its governing body, chaired by Chief Judge Kaufman. The Joint Commission consisted of twenty-nine members, of which half were lawyers and judges. A Minority Group Advisory Committee was created in 1973.

Four drafting committees supervised the work of the thirty scholars who were assigned as reporters to draft the individual volumes. The chairs of the drafting committees were members of the Joint Commission. Each volume and its reporter or reporters came within the jurisdiction of one of the drafting committees: Drafting Committee I: Intervention in the Lives of Children, Co-chairs William S. White and Margaret K. Rosenheim; II: Court Roles and Procedures, Chair Charles Z. Smith; III: Treatment and Corrections, Chair Allen F. Breed; and IV: Administration, Chair Daniel L. Skoler.

As the reporters met with their drafting committees or work groups within the committees, issues arose and were submitted to the Joint Commission for resolution at its periodic meetings. After the reporters' manuscripts were approved by the drafting committees, they were reviewed by the project staff and transmitted to the Joint Commission with pertinent comments on matters of cross-volume consistency. The members of the Joint Commission independently reviewed the contents of each volume on the agenda, followed by discussions of broad principles, as well as minute details of text and format. The volumes then were returned to the reporters with instructions for revisions.

In 1975 and 1976 all twenty-three volumes were published as tentative drafts and distributed widely to individuals and organizations concerned with juvenile justice for their comments and suggestions. The ABA assigned the volumes to the appropriate sections, committees, and other entities specializing in the areas covered by each volume, with the task of coordinating the resulting recommendations handled by the Committee on Juvenile Justice of the Section of Criminal Justice and its chair, Livingston Hall and the Juvenile Justice Standards Review Committee of the Section of Family Law, chaired by Marjorie Childs.

The reports, comments, and suggestions of the various individuals and groups, including the ABA entities, were submitted to the Executive Committee of the Joint Commission, which had been authorized to respond on behalf of the commission. It met in 1977 and 1978 to consider the proposed changes in the tentative drafts. Relatively minor changes were approved and the published tentative drafts were sent to the ABA House of Delegates, accompanied by minutes describing the Executive Committee's decisions with respect to the revisions to be made in the volumes. The ABA House of Delegates approved seventeen volumes in 1979 and three more in August 1980. Of the remaining three volumes, *The Standards Relating to Schools and Education* was withdrawn from consideration by the House of Delegates as too specialized, *The Standards Relating to Noncriminal Misbehavior* was tabled by the delegates as too controversial, and *The Standards Relating to Abuse and Neglect* was returned for revision. A revised volume on abuse and neglect was approved by the Joint Commission and published with the final revised drafts of all twenty-three IJA-ABA juvenile justice standards volumes in 1980, but the project ended in 1981 and no further submissions were made to the House of Delegates.

Basic Principles

Despite the complex and time-consuming path followed by the standards volumes from inception to final publication, it was straightforward for the underlying principles. As issue papers were analyzed and the subjects to be covered were identified, a pattern of interweaving concepts emerged and a value system that permeated all of the *Standards* became apparent.

The strongest influence was the 1967 Supreme Court decision in *In re Gault*. The Joint Commission adopted a due process model governed by equity and fairness, rejecting the more popular medical model premised on a need for treatment as the basis for the court's jurisdiction. From that choice, several principles flowed with logical precision, as follows:

1. Sanctions should be proportionate to the seriousness of the offense.

2. Sentences or dispositions should be fixed or determinate as declared by the court after a hearing, not indeterminate as determined by correctional authorities based on subsequent behavior or administrative convenience.

3. The least restrictive alternative to accomplish the purpose of the intervention should be the choice of decision makers at every stage, with written reasons for finding less drastic remedies inadequate required of every official decision maker.

Another feature of the juvenile justice system envisioned by the Joint Commission would require access to adequate and appropriate community-based services on a voluntary basis to the families and children who need them. This vision is set forth in full in the volume, *Standards Relating to Youth Service Agencies*. A network of social, educational, vocational, health, and other services would be made available to every juvenile and family, not imposed as official sanctions or dependent on welfare eligibility. Unfortunately, access to community-based services geared to the legitimate needs of the local residents is one of the unfulfilled goals of the standards. The principles that result from the assumption that communities would provide voluntary youth services and from the *Standards'* rejection of involuntary intervention without a finding of delinquency, child abuse, or neglect are:

4. Noncriminal misbehavior (status offenses or conduct that would not be a crime if committed by an adult) should be removed from juvenile court jurisdiction.

5. Limitations should be imposed on detention, treatment, or other intervention prior to adjudication and disposition.

A third element in the value system that distinguishes the *IJA-ABA Standards* is accountability in an open society in which the rights and responsibilities of individuals and agencies would be clearly delineated, protected, and enforced. The applicable principles are:

6. Visibility and accountability of decision making should replace closed proceedings and unrestrained official discretion.

7. Juveniles should have the right to decide on actions affecting their lives and freedom, unless they are found incapable of making reasoned decisions.

8. Parental roles in juvenile proceedings should be redefined with particular attention to possible conflicts between the interests of parent and child.

9. There should be a right to counsel for all affected interests at

all crucial stages of proceedings and an unwaivable right to counsel for juveniles.

Finally, the project relied on its idealized design of the family court as the centerpiece of its idealized juvenile justice system. Organized as a separate division of the court of original trial jurisdiction, with judges rotated at fixed intervals from the other trial courts and all of the personnel (judges, lawyers, police officers, corrections officials, social workers, and related service providers) trained to handle the special problems of families and children brought into contact with the judicial system, the family court would be uniquely equipped to implement the standards. It would be expected to deal effectively with all but the most egregious cases and even then to retain jurisdiction until every reasonable effort had failed and the criminal justice system could be shown to be more effective. The much-breached assumption that juvenile offenses would not be tried in criminal court except as a last resort is embodied in the tenth principle as follows:

> 10. Strict criteria should be established for waiver of juvenile court jurisdiction to regulate the transfer of juveniles to adult criminal court.

Conclusion

Even a casual reading of the IJA-ABA *Juvenile Justice Standards* in this book shows the extraordinary interconnection and logical consistency throughout the *Standards*. Unfortunately, a major barrier to implementation has been the unwillingness of any jurisdiction to adopt the *Standards* as a whole. In those states where some of the *Standards* have been incorporated into the juvenile codes, the absence of essential support from related standards has limited the effectiveness of those adopted.

For example, without voluntary community-based services, removal of status offenders from the court's jurisdiction creates many problems without solutions. Without a nonwaivable right to the assistance of counsel, a juvenile should not be expected to make an informed waiver of that or other rights. Standards for corrections administration depend upon standards for the size of facilities, for the permissible range of sanctions, and other conditions. The legislatures that have adopted the concept of fixed or determinate dispositions have not adopted the safeguards that go with the concept.

Nevertheless, the annotations to the black letter *Standards* that follow should suggest the degree to which the *Standards* have influenced our legal system. A reading of the original commentaries that accompanied the *Standards* would expand and enrich that understanding.

But those of us who worked so long on these *Standards* and who shared our pride in the final product have expected and continue to expect more. Publication of the annotated standards in such an accessible form is a significant step toward accomplishing the goals of the project. While many more steps still have to be taken, the ultimate destination of this long and remarkable journey remains clear. Increased familiarity with the contents of the standards and recognition of their potential for meaningful reform may transform the vision of full implementation of the IJA-ABA *Juvenile Justice Standards* into reality some day soon.

Barbara Flicker
Los Angeles, California

EDITOR'S INTRODUCTION

This volume is a dream come true for many who have been active in the Juvenile Justice Committee of the Criminal Justice Section of the American Bar Association. The idea of a single volume containing all the black letter *Juvenile Justice Standards* approved by the Association's House of Delegates was highly appealing, especially if the *Standards* could be accompanied by case annotations showing how the courts have used the twenty approved volumes in their opinions. As Barbara Flicker, the "mother" (or at least the midwife) of the *Standards* points out in her **Introduction**, there are three other volumes that were not approved by the House of Delegates, and this book includes the case citations to those three volumes as well—*The Standards Relating to Education, The Standards Relating to Abuse and Neglect,* and *The Standards Relating to Noncriminal Misbehavior.* In addition, the inclusion of the black letter *Standards* alone is not intended to diminish the importance or value of the commentary accompanying these statements in the individual volumes, and the reader is encouraged to consult that commentary in using the *Standards.*

The *Standards* have important roles to play in reforming juvenile justice, both in broad public policy decision-making and in individual case determinations. Alaire Bretz Reiffel, a former Project Director for the Juvenile Justice Standards Implementation Project, pointed to these roles in her helpful 1983 volume entitled the *Juvenile Justice Standards Handbook.* She identified those various actors in the juvenile justice system who could profit from the use of the *Standards*: **Trial Judges**, who can use them as guidelines in making individual case decisions, or in carrying out the significant number of administrative duties in the juvenile or family court; **Appellate Judges**, for whom the *Standards* may be an authoritative source for defining due process or delineating good practice; **Defense Attorneys** or **Public Defenders**, who can refer to the *Standards* for help in defining their roles, or in carrying out particular tasks in the representation of a juvenile or other private party in the court, or in arguing for a specific ruling on a contested point, or in drafting briefs on appeal; **Prosecutors**, largely absent during the first two-thirds of a century of the court's life, but who have achieved greater prominence in recent years, and who may need guidance in performing this new role or in equitably exercising their vast discretion; **Court** or **Correctional Agency Administrators**, individuals who can use guidance in carrying out difficult tasks and a variety of roles in a period when there are new and greater demands but less resources; **Teachers** and **Professors**, for whom the *Standards* may provide a general guide for teaching about the juvenile justice system based on a national model, instead of simply on a state or local basis; **Legislators and other Policymakers**, who can use the *Standards* as a caliper for judging legislative proposals or administrative directives, regulations or policies in an objective fashion; and the **News Media**, who should refer to the *Standards* as an authoritative reference source for understanding current issues.

Likewise, the *Standards* can play different roles in a variety of settings in influencing the juvenile justice system. First, they can be used in the **trial of cases**, where they can be used by counsel for the parties, guardians *ad litem*, judges, and court staff in providing models for the performance of their roles, and as authority for various courses of action. Particular volumes, such as those promulgating *Standards* for *Pretrial Court Proceedings, Adjudication, Dispositional Procedures, Prosecution, Counsel for Private Parties,* and *Appeals and Collateral Review*, give step-by-step guidance for the performance of function throughout the process. Second, the *Standards* can be useful in **drafting** pleadings, motions, trial memoranda, appellate briefs, and other documents in ongoing litigation. The *Standards* can be particularly used in **research**, where they and their commentary and annotations can speed up preparation for a case or brief. In **negotiations**, the *Standards* can represent the objective middle ground between two adversarial positions and facilitate the settlement of a case or the fashioning of a remedy in institutional litigation. The *Standards* also can be very fruitful in drafting **legislation** or implementing **policy reform**. Although the *Standards* are not written expressly in statutory or rule language, their provisions can be a good starting point for statutory revision or the development of rules or guidelines. For example, when Virginia revised its transfer statute in 1994, it eliminated the vague and troublesome phrase, "not . . . amenable to treatment or rehabilitation as a juvenile" and replaced it with more specific criteria for determining whether a youth is "not a proper person to remain within the jurisdiction of the juvenile court" drawn from Standard 2.2 of the *Standards on Transfer Between Courts.* Likewise, when the West Virginia Supreme Court of Appeals had to deal with overcrowded and deficient detention facilities across the state, the Court used the *Standards Relating to Interim Status* to draft guidelines for future detention decision-making in the state. (*Facilities Review Panel v. Coe*, 187 W.Va. 541, 420 S.E.2d 532, 537–41 (1992)) The 1994 *Final Report of the Governor's Advisory Council On Juvenile Justice* outlining proposals for systemic reform in New Jersey began with a quotation from the *Standards Relating to Juvenile Justice Planning*.

This is not the only set of standards relating to the juvenile justice system, but it tends to be the most authoritative across the entire system. However, the other sets of standards can be of great use to interested readers. Among the other resources are the general *Standards for the Administration of Juvenile Justice—Report of the National Advisory Committee for Juvenile Justice and Delinquency Prevention* and the volume entitled *Juvenile Justice and Delinquency Prevention—Report of the Task Force on Juvenile Justice and Delinquency Prevention*. More specialized standards include the *NDAA Prosecution Standard 19.2: Juvenile Delinquency*, issued by the National District Attorneys Association, the latest editions[1] of *Standards for Juvenile Community Residential Facilities, Standards for Juvenile Probation and Aftercare Services, Standards for Juvenile Detention Facilities,* and *Standards for Juvenile Training Schools,* promulgated by the Commission on Accreditation for Corrections and the American Correctional Association, and the most recent standards developed by the Interstate Consortium on Residential Child Care and the National Commission on Correctional Health Care. Many of these standards are based on or at least heavily cite the *IJA-ABA Juvenile Justice Standards*.

This volume is organized by setting forth each of the black letter *Standards* from the twenty approved volumes with an annotation following each individual standard that is cited in a court decision. After these twenty articulations of the approved *Standards* volumes, there are found annotations to those *Standards* in the two unapproved volumes that have been cited as well. Finally, there is an **Index** to the various *Standards* drawn from the 1983 *Handbook* published by the ABA's Juvenile Justice Standards Implementation Project which should be useful in locating particular standards.

> Robert E. Shepherd, Jr.
> University of Richmond Law School
> Richmond, Virginia

---

1. As of November, 1995, the Third Edition of the Standards is the latest, supplemented by an additional 1994 volume.

ABOUT THE AUTHORS

Barbara Flicker. Currently Director of the Inter-University Consortium on Child Welfare in Los Angeles, California, a project of California State University, Long Beach, UCLA and the University of Southern California, Barbara Flicker is a graduate of the New York University School of Law. During her law school career she took a year's leave of absence to work as a social investigator in the New York City Department of Social Services, an experience that kindled a continuing interest in the relationship between the justice and child welfare systems. After having three children and practicing law conventionally, she served as Associate Director of the Project on Welfare Law at NYU and as Public Affairs Counsel for the Community Service Society of New York. Ms. Flicker joined the Institute of Judicial Administration in 1973 and became Director of the IJA-ABA Juvenile Justice Standards Project two years later. She remained a consultant to the project until its conclusion, commuting between New York and California after July, 1976, as author of the *Summary Volume*, and as Executive Editor of the official revised edition of the *Standards* volumes published in 1980 and 1981. She was IJA Director from 1983 to 1986 and Consulting Director until 1991. A member of the New York and California bars, Ms. Flicker has served on the faculties of the NYU School of Law and its Graduate Schools of Social Work and Public Administration, and the University of Southern California Law Center and School of Public Administration.

Robert E. Shepherd, Jr. A graduate of Washington and Lee University and its school of law, Professor Shepherd is currently a Professor of Law at the University of Richmond School of Law in Richmond, Virginia. He served in the Army as a Captain in The Judge Advocate General's Corps after graduation from law school and engaged in the private practice of law in Richmond for seven years before becoming an Assistant Attorney General for Virginia. During that service he acted as counsel for the Division of Youth Services of the Virginia Department of Corrections, and as a member of the Juvenile Code Revision Committee. In 1975 he became an Associate Professor of Law at the University of Baltimore and directed the Juvenile Law Clinic there. In 1978 Professor Shepherd moved to the University of Richmond as an Associate Professor, Director of Clinical Programs, and Director of the Youth Advocacy Clinic. He is a former Chair of the Juvenile Justice Committee of the Criminal Justice Section of the American Bar Association, and has written the "Juvenile Justice" column in the Section's *Criminal Justice* magazine since 1987. He chairs the Commission on the Needs of Children for the Virginia Bar Association, serves as one of three citizen members on the Virginia Commission on Youth, is a member of the Board of Fellows for the National Center for Juvenile Justice, and is past Chair of the Government Relations Committee of the National Coalition for Juvenile Justice.

Patricia McGowan Wald. Judge Wald was appointed as a judge on the United States Court of Appeals for the District of Columbia Circuit in 1979 and she served as Chief Judge for that court from July 1986 to January 1991. She is a graduate of Connecticut College and Yale Law School and served as a law clerk to Judge Jerome N. Frank of the Second Circuit Court of Appeals after graduation from Yale. She was an attorney with the Neighborhood Legal Services Program, the Center for Law and Social Policy, and the Mental Health Law Project, serving as Litigation Director from 1975 to 1977. She was Assistant Attorney General for Legislative Affairs in the United States Department of Justice from 1977 to 1979. Judge Wald also was cochair of the Ford Foundation Drug Abuse Research Project, and is a Council Member and Second Vice-President of the American Law Institute and a Fellow of the American Academy of Arts and Sciences. She was a member of the IJA-ABA Joint Commission on Juvenile Justice Standards which promulgated the *Juvenile Justice Standards* during the 1970s.

STANDARDS RELATING TO ADJUDICATION
Robert O. Dawson, Reporter

PART I: REQUISITES FOR ADJUDICATION PROCEEDINGS TO BEGIN

1.1 Written petition.

   A. Each jurisdiction should provide by law that the filing of a written petition giving the respondent adequate notice of the charges is a requisite for adjudication proceedings to begin.

   B. If appropriate challenge is made to the legal sufficiency of the petition, the judge of the juvenile court should rule on that challenge before calling upon the respondent to plead.

1.2 Attorneys for respondent and the government.

The juvenile court should not begin adjudication proceedings unless the respondent is represented by an attorney who is present in court and the government is represented by an attorney who is present in court.

***State ex rel. J.M. v. Taylor*, 166 W.Va. 511, 276 S.E.2d 199, 203 (1981). The juvenile's right to counsel may be waived, but it should not be waived without the advice of counsel. (Citing Standard 1.2)**

1.3 Presence of respondent.

   A. The presence of the respondent should be required for adjudication proceedings to begin.

   B. The respondent should be afforded the right to be present throughout adjudication proceedings, although the juvenile court should be permitted to proceed without a respondent who is voluntarily absent after adjudication proceedings have begun.

1.4 Presence of parents of respondent and others.[1]

   A. Subject to subsection D of this standard, parents and other per-

---

1. Commissioner Justine Wise Polier objects to this standard as being so broadly drawn as to impair, rather than enlarge, due process rights of a child in requiring that juvenile courts shall make every reasonable effort to secure the presence of both parents. It does not require or even present consideration of past relationships between the child and both parents, including the prolonged absence of one parent or even the denial of paternity. It does not allow the court to consider the wishes of the custodial parent, of the child, or the best interests of the child.

sons required by law to be notified of adjudication proceedings should be entitled to be present throughout the proceedings.

B. The juvenile court should make every reasonable effort to secure the presence of both of respondent's parents at an adjudication proceeding.

C. If, after reasonable effort, only one of respondent's parents is present, the juvenile court should be empowered to proceed with adjudication proceedings. If, after reasonable effort, neither of the respondent's parents is present, or both have been excluded under subsection D of this standard, the juvenile court should be empowered to proceed with adjudication proceedings after appointing a guardian *ad litem* for the respondent.

D. Persons specified in subsection A should not be permitted to be present during adjudication proceedings if their presence would violate a rule on witnesses invoked by either the respondent or the government.

1.5 Opportunity to prepare for adjudication proceedings.

A. The juvenile court should determine whether the attorneys for the respondent and the government have had a reasonable opportunity to prepare for adjudication proceedings.

B. Attorneys for the respondent and the government have an obligation to exercise due diligence in preparation for adjudication proceedings and an obligation to make any motion for continuance at such time as to cause the least possible disruption of the work of the juvenile court.

PART II: STANDARDS APPLICABLE TO UNCONTESTED AND CONTESTED ADJUDICATION PROCEEDINGS

2.1 Recording adjudication proceedings.

A. A verbatim record should be made of all adjudication proceedings, whether or not the allegations in the petition are contested.

B. The record should be preserved and, with any exhibits, kept confidential.

C. The requirement of preservation should be subordinated to any order for expungement of the record, and the requirement of confidentiality should be subordinated to appropriate court orders on behalf of the respondent or the government for a verbatim transcript of the record for use in subsequent legal proceedings.

2.2 Amending the petition.

  A. Each jurisdiction should provide by law that the petition may be amended by the attorney for the government in the same manner and according to the same rules for amending the charging instrument as in a proceeding in criminal court.
  B. Each jurisdiction should provide by law that if the petition is amended, the respondent should be permitted a reasonable opportunity to prepare a defense to the amended allegations.

2.3 Double jeopardy protections.

Each jurisdiction should provide by law that the double jeopardy protections applicable to the trial of criminal cases should be applicable to delinquency adjudication proceedings.

2.4 Plea alternatives.

  A. Each jurisdiction should provide by law for oral pleading by a respondent to the allegations of the petition.
  B. The respondent should be permitted to admit or deny the allegations of the petition, and if the respondent refuses to plead, a plea of deny should be entered by the court.

2.5 Effect of admission.

An admission of an allegation of the petition should be regarded as consent by the respondent to an adjudication by the court of the admitted allegation without proof of it, subject to the requirement of Standard 3.5, relating to verifying the accuracy of the plea.

2.6 Effect of denial.

A denial of an allegation of the petition should be regarded as an assertion by the respondent of the right to require the government to prove its allegation and not as an assertion that the allegation denied is untrue.

2.7 Interpreters.

  A. When a witness is incapable of hearing or understanding the English language or is incapable of speaking or of speaking in the English language so as to be understood directly by counsel, court, and jury, an interpreter whom the witness can understand and who can understand the witness should be appointed by the judge of the juvenile court and compensated from public funds.
  B. When the respondent is incapable of hearing or understanding the English language, all of the proceedings should be interpreted

in a language that the respondent understands by an interpreter appointed by the judge of the juvenile court and compensated from public funds.

C. When the respondent is incapable of speaking or of speaking in a language understood by respondent's attorney, an interpreter who can understand the respondent should be appointed by the judge of the juvenile court and compensated from public funds to interpret communications from the respondent to respondent's attorney.

PART III: UNCONTESTED ADJUDICATION PROCEEDINGS

3.1 Capacity to plead.

A. The juvenile court should not accept a plea admitting an allegation of the petition without determining that the respondent has the mental capacity to understand his or her legal rights in the adjudication proceeding and the significance of such a plea.

B. In determining whether the respondent has the mental capacity to enter a plea admitting an allegation of the petition, the juvenile court should inquire into, among other factors:

1. the respondent's chronological age;
2. the respondent's present grade level in school or the highest grade level achieved while in school;
3. whether the respondent can read and write; and
4. whether the respondent has ever been diagnosed or treated for mental illness or mental retardation.

3.2 Admonitions before accepting a plea admitting an allegation of the petition.

The judge of the juvenile court should not accept a plea admitting an allegation of the petition without first addressing the respondent personally, in language calculated to communicate effectively with the respondent, and:

A. determining that the respondent understands the nature of the allegations;

B. informing the respondent of the right to a hearing at which the government must confront respondent with witnesses and prove the allegations beyond a reasonable doubt and at which respondent's attorney will be permitted to cross-examine the witnesses called by the government and to call witnesses on the respondent's behalf;

C. informing the respondent of the right to remain silent with respect to the allegations of the petition as well as of the right to testify if desired;

D. informing the respondent of the right to appeal from the decision reached in the trial;

E. informing the respondent of the right to a trial by jury;

F. informing the respondent that one gives up those rights by a plea admitting an allegation of the petition; and

G. informing the respondent that if the court accepts the plea, the court can place respondent on conditional freedom for (__) years or commit respondent to (the appropriate correctional agency) for (__) years.

In the Interest of S.K., 137 Ill. App. 3d 1065, 92 Ill. Dec. 767, 485 N.E.2d 578 (1985). The trial court must inform the juvenile of the dispositions that might result from a plea of guilty. (Citing Standard 3.2 G)

3.3 Responsibilities of the juvenile court judge with respect to plea agreements.

A. Subject to the qualification contained in subsection B. of this standard, the juvenile court judge should not participate in plea discussions.

B. If a plea agreement has been reached that contemplates entry of a plea admitting an allegation of the petition in the expectation that other allegations will be dismissed or not filed, or that dispositional concessions will be made, the juvenile court judge should require disclosure of the agreement and the reasons therefor in advance of the time for tender of the plea. Disclosure of the plea agreement should be on the record in the presence of the respondent. The court should then indicate whether it will concur in the proposed agreement. If the court concurs, but later decides not to grant the concessions contemplated by the plea agreement, it should so advise the respondent and then call upon the respondent either to affirm or withdraw the plea.

C. When a plea admitting an allegation of the petition is tendered as a result of a plea agreement, the juvenile court judge should give the agreement due consideration, but notwithstanding its existence, should reach an independent decision whether to grant the concessions contemplated in the agreement.

In re James B., 54 Md. App. 270, 458 A.2d 847, 851 (1983). When the trial judge decides not to accept the plea agreement he should advise the juvenile of that fact and afford him or her the opportunity to withdraw the plea. (Citing Standard 3.3 and quoting from 3.3 B)

3.4 Determining voluntariness of a plea admitting the allegations of the petition.

  A. The juvenile court should not **accept a plea** admitting an allegation of the petition without determining that the plea is voluntary.
  B. By inquiry of the attorneys for the respondent and for the government, the juvenile court should determine whether the tendered plea is the result of a plea agreement and, if so, what agreement has been reached.
  C. If the attorney for the government has agreed to seek concessions that must be approved by the court, the court should advise the respondent personally that those recommendations are not binding on the court and follow the procedures provided in Standard 3.3 B.
  D. The court should then address the respondent personally and determine whether any other promises or inducements or any force or threats were used to obtain the plea.

3.5 Determining accuracy of a plea admitting the allegations of the petition.

The juvenile court should not accept a plea admitting an allegation of the petition without making an inquiry and satisfying itself that the allegation admitted is true. The inquiry should be conducted:

  A. by requiring the attorney for the government to describe the proof that the government would expect to produce if the case were tried; or
  B. by personally questioning the respondent as to respondent's conduct in the case.

3.6 Inquiry concerning effectiveness of representation.

  A. The juvenile court should not accept a plea admitting an allegation of the petition unless it determines that the respondent was given the effective assistance of an attorney.
  B. The juvenile court should make that determination upon tender of a plea admitting an allegation of the petition and should do so by inquiring:

1. of the respondent and respondent's attorney concerning the number and length (but not the content) of conferences the attorney has had with respondent;
2. of the attorney for the respondent concerning the factual investigation, if any, that the attorney conducted in the case;
3. of the attorney for the respondent concerning the legal preparation, if any, that the attorney made on behalf of respondent;
4. of the respondent and respondent's attorney concerning what advice the attorney gave respondent concerning whether to admit or deny the allegations of the petition; and
5. of the respondent and respondent's attorney concerning whether there has been any conflict between them as to whether respondent should admit an allegation of the petition, and if there was, subject to the attorney-client privilege, the nature of that conflict.

3.7 Parental participation in uncontested cases.

A. Except when a parent is the complainant, the judge of the juvenile court should not accept a plea admitting an allegation of the petition without inquiring of the respondent's parent or parents who are present in court whether they concur in the course of action the respondent has chosen.

B. The judge of the juvenile court should consider the responses of the respondent's parents to the court's inquiry in exercising discretion on whether to reject the tendered plea.

3.8 Plea withdrawal.

A. The juvenile court should allow the respondent to withdraw a plea admitting an allegation of the petition whenever the respondent proves that withdrawal is necessary to correct a manifest injustice.

1. A motion for withdrawal is not barred because made subsequent to adjudication or disposition.
2. Withdrawal is necessary to correct a manifest injustice when the respondent proves:
    a. denial of the effective assistance of counsel guaranteed by constitution, statute, or rule;
    b. that the plea was not entered or ratified by the respondent;
    c. that the plea was involuntary, or was entered without knowledge of the allegations or that the disposition actually imposed could be imposed;

d. that respondent did not receive the concessions contemplated by the plea agreement and the attorney for the government failed to seek or not to oppose those concessions as promised in the plea agreement; or

e. that respondent did not receive the concessions contemplated by the plea agreement concurred in by the court, and did not affirm the plea after being advised that the court no longer concurred and after being called upon to either affirm or withdraw the plea.

3. The respondent should be permitted to move for withdrawal of the plea without alleging innocence of the allegations to which the plea has been entered.

B. Before the disposition of the case, the court should allow the respondent to withdraw the plea for any fair and just reason without proof of manifest injustice as defined in subsection 2 of this standard.

PART IV: CONTESTED ADJUDICATION PROCEDURES

4.1 Trial by jury.

A. Each jurisdiction should provide by law that the respondent may demand trial by jury in adjudication proceedings when the respondent has denied the allegations of the petition.

B. Each jurisdiction should provide by law that the jury may consist of as few as [six] persons and that the verdict of the jury must be unanimous.

State in the Interest of Dino, 359 So. 2d 586, 605 (La. 1978). Dissenting opinion cites Part IV of the Standards in support of the right to a jury trial.

In the Interest of N.E., 122 Wis. 2d 198, 361 N.W.2d 693, 698 (1985). Although Standards 4.1 and 6.1 indicate that a juvenile's right to a jury trial is a fundamental right, the court does not agree and a jury may be waived without complying with the stringent procedures for abandoning a fundamental right.

4.2 Rules of evidence.

The rules of evidence employed in the trial of criminal cases should be used in delinquency adjudication proceedings when the respondent has denied the allegations of the petition.

Burttram v. State, 448 So. 2d 497, 498 (Ala. Crim. App. 1984). The court

need not decide whether the rule requiring corroboration of an accomplice's testimony in adult criminal cases applies equally to juvenile delinquency proceedings as there was corroboration in this case. (Citing Standard 4.2 to support the proposition that criminal evidentiary rules apply in delinquency adjudications)

4.3 Burden of proof.

Each jurisdiction should provide by law that the government is required to adduce proof beyond a reasonable doubt that the respondent engaged in the conduct alleged when the respondent has denied the allegations of the petition.

4.4 Social information.

A. Except in preadjudication hearings in which social history information concerning the respondent is relevant and admissible, such as a detention hearing or a hearing to consider transfer to criminal court for prosecution as an adult, the judge of the juvenile court should not view a social history report or receive social history information concerning a respondent who has not been adjudicated delinquent.

B. Each jurisdiction should provide by law that when a jury is the trier of fact, it should not view a social history report or receive social history information concerning the respondent.

4.5 Role of parents in contested proceedings.

A respondent's parents or other persons required by law to be served with a copy of the petition should be permitted to make representations to the court either pro se or through counsel in a jury-waived contested adjudication proceeding.

PART V: THE ADJUDICATION DECISION

5.1 Adjudication required for juvenile court disposition.

A. Each jurisdiction should provide by law that a juvenile court adjudication that a respondent is delinquent, as alleged in a written petition, is a requisite for any juvenile court disposition of the respondent, except for voluntary participation in preadjudication programs.

B. The adjudication should be based upon respondent's plea admitting one or more of the allegations of the petition, or upon the government's proof that respondent violated the law as alleged in the petition.

5.2 Suspended adjudication.

A. A juvenile court ordinarily should not suspend or refrain from making an adjudication on condition that the respondent continue or engage in behavior specified by the court or probation personnel.

B. To the extent that such a suspension of adjudication is permitted, it should be used only when:

1. in an extraordinary case an adjudication would work a particularly onerous burden upon the respondent or respondent's family; and

2. the respondent requests or consents to a suspension of adjudication.

C. When a suspension of adjudication is permitted, each jurisdiction should provide by law that it constitutes a final judgment for purposes of appeal.

D. When a suspension of adjudication is permitted, it should not be used except when the evidence justifies a finding of delinquency and should never be used because of weaknesses in the government's proof.

***In the Matter of C.S. McP.*, 514 A.2d 446, 449 (D.C. 1986). Although the Standards do not appear to contemplate dismissal of charges at disposition, such action would be appropriate if the court found that the youth was not "in need of care or rehabilitation." (Citing Standard 5.2)**

5.3 Legal consequences of adjudication.

A. Each jurisdiction should provide by law that a juvenile court adjudication is not a conviction of crime and should not be viewed to indicate criminality for any purpose.

***Hu Yau-Leung v. Soscia*, 500 F.Supp. 1382, 1389 (E.D.N.Y. 1980). Since the offenses with which juvenile was charged in Hong Kong would be delinquency and not a crime in the United States, extradition would not be allowed because the acts were not a "felony." (Citing Standard 5.3 A)**

B. Each jurisdiction should provide by law that a juvenile court adjudication is not a proper subject for inquiry in applications for public or private employment and in applications for public or private educational or licensing programs.

C. Each jurisdiction should provide by law that a plea admitting the allegations of the petition, an adjudication by the juvenile court, or evidence adduced in a juvenile court adjudication proceeding is not admissible in any other judicial or administrative proceeding except subsequent juvenile proceedings concerning the same respondent to the extent otherwise admissible.

PART VI: PUBLIC ACCESS TO ADJUDICATION PROCEEDINGS

6.1 Right to a public trial.

Each jurisdiction should provide by law that a respondent in juvenile court adjudication proceeding has a right to a public trial.

State in the Interest of Dino, 359 So. 2d 586, 597 (La. 1978). Juvenile is entitled to a public trial as being one of "the essentials of due process and fair treatment" under the Louisiana Constitution. (Citing Standard 6.1)

In the Matter of Chase, 112 Misc. 2d 868, 446 N.Y.S.2d 1000, 1007 (Fam. Ct. N.Y. County 1982). There is a strong presumption in favor of a public trial in juvenile delinquency proceedings. (Citing Standard 6.1)

In the Interest of N.E., 122 Wis. 2d 198, 361 N.W.2d 693, 698 (1985). Although Standards 4.1 and 6.1 indicate that a juvenile's right to a jury trial is a fundamental right, the court does not agree and a jury may be waived without complying with the stringent procedures for abandoning a fundamental right.

6.2 Implementing the right to a public trial.
   A. Each jurisdiction should provide by law that the respondent, after consulting with counsel, may waive the right to a public trial.
   B. Each jurisdiction should provide by law that the judge of the juvenile court has discretion to permit members of the public who have a legitimate interest in the proceedings or in the work of the court, including representatives of the news media, to view adjudication proceedings when the respondent has waived the right to a public trial.

In the Matter of Chase, 112 Misc. 2d 868, 446 N.Y.S.2d 1000, 1007–8 (Fam. Ct. N.Y. County 1982). There is a strong presumption in favor of a public trial in juvenile delinquency proceedings. The juvenile's right to waive a public trial does not guarantee a closed trial and the court can still allow access to members of the public, including representatives of the media. (Citing Standard 6.2 B)

C. The judge of the juvenile court should honor any request by the respondent, respondent's attorney, or family that specified members of the public be permitted to observe the respondent's adjudication proceeding when the respondent has waived the right to a public trial.

D. The judge of the juvenile court should use judicial power to prevent distractions from and disruptions of adjudication proceedings and should use that power to order removed from the courtroom any member of the public causing a distraction or disruption.

People v. Williams, 97 Misc. 2d 24, 410 N.Y.S.2d 978, 985 (Dutchess County Court 1978). The legislature does not require that juvenile transfer hearings be conducted in private, and it is a matter within the court's discretion. (Citing Standards generally)

6.3 Prohibiting disclosure of respondent's identity.

A. Each jurisdiction should provide by law that members of the public permitted by the judge of the juvenile court to observe adjudication proceedings may not disclose to others the identity of the respondent when the respondent has waived the right to a public trial.

B. Each jurisdiction should provide by law that the judge of the juvenile court should announce to members of the public present to view an adjudication proceeding when the respondent has waived the right to a public trial that they may not disclose to others the identity of the respondent.

STANDARDS RELATING TO APPEALS AND COLLATERAL REVIEW

Michael Moran, Reporter

PART I: THE NATURE OF THE APPELLATE STRUCTURE

1.1 Appellate court structure.

  A. The structure of appellate courts should be consonant with the goals of appellate review:

    1. to correct errors in the application and interpretation of law and in the finding of facts;

    2. to insure substantial uniformity of treatment to persons in like situations;

    3. to provide for growth in keeping with the legislatively defined goals of the juvenile justice system as a whole.

  B. Appeals from juvenile court should be heard by that court of the state designated to hear and decide the initial appeal from the highest court of general trial jurisdiction.

1.2 The necessity of appellate review of juvenile court judgments.

  A. In order to recognize the goals of the entire juvenile justice system, it is essential that there be one appeal of right afforded to all parties materially affected by a juvenile court order, to review the facts found, the law applied, and the disposition ordered.

  B. Additional review by the initial court of appeals or by any higher appellate court may be had by leave of that court.

1.3 Facts found by a juvenile court judge or jury should be afforded the same weight as those found in the highest court of general trial jurisdiction.

1.4 No person who attains the age of eighteen years during the pendency of an appeal other than from a grant of waiver to adult criminal court, may thereafter be criminally prosecuted as an adult for any conduct arising from the same transaction that was the cause of juvenile court intervention.

PART II: REVIEWABILITY

2.1 Upon claim properly filed by any party, review should be had of any final order of the juvenile court. A final order should include:

A. any order finding absence of jurisdiction;
B. any order transferring jurisdiction from the juvenile court to another court;
C. any order finding a juvenile to be delinquent in which no disposition is made within [sixty] days or where disposition is to be extensively deferred, except when the juvenile requests that such order not become final;
D. any order of disposition after adjudication;
E. any order finding a juvenile to be neglected or abused;
F. any order terminating or modifying custodial rights.

State v. Gleason, 404 A.2d 573, 577 (Maine, 1979). Since the Maine Juvenile Code, 15 M.R.S.A. §§ 3401–3402 (Supp. 1978), tracks Standard 2.1 of the *Standards Relating to Appeals and Collateral Review*, the comment to that Standard is relevant to the interpretation of the relevant sections of the Code.

In re Juvenile Appeal (85-AB), 195 Conn. 303, 488 A.2d 778, 785 (1985). A juvenile court's transfer order is not a final judgment which appeal may be taken. Justice Healey, dissenting, cites Standard 2.1 B of the *Standards Relating to Appeals and Collateral Review*, along with Standard 2.4 of the *Standards Relating to Transfer Between Courts*, to support his position that a direct appeal should be permitted from a transfer order.

State v. Lafayette, 148 Vt. 288, 532 A.2d 560, 562 (1987). An order denying transfer of a criminal proceeding to a juvenile court was a final appealable order. (Citing Standard 2.1 B as authority, along with Standard 2.4 of the *Standards Relating to Transfer Between Courts*).

2.2 An appeal may be taken by any of the following parties:

A. the juvenile;
B. his or her parents, custodian, or guardian;
C. the state,
   1. of any final order in other than delinquency cases;
   2. of only the following orders in delinquency cases:
      a. an order adjudicating a state statute unconstitutional
      b. any order which by depriving the prosecution of evidence, by upholding the defense of double jeopardy, by holding that a cause of action is not stated under a statute, or by granting a motion to suppress, terminates a delinquency petition;

    c. an order which denies a petition to waive juvenile court jurisdiction in favor of adult criminal prosecution.

2.3 Review may be sought by leave of the court of appeals from interlocutory orders of the juvenile court, including a finding that juvenile court jurisdiction exists over the subject matter or juvenile in question.

PART III: THE RIGHT TO COUNSEL AND RECORDS

3.1 Any party entitled to an appeal under Standard 2.2 is entitled to be represented by counsel, and the appointment of counsel at public expense upon a determination of indigency.

3.2 Any party entitled to an appeal under Standard 2.2, or his or her counsel, is entitled to a copy of the verbatim transcript of the adjudication and dispositional hearings and any matter appearing in the court file.

3.3 Upon a determination of indigency, the above material should be provided the appellant at public expense.

PART IV: PROCEDURES

4.1 A system for expediting and granting preferences to appeals from the juvenile court should be provided.

4.2 It should be the duty of the juvenile court judge to inform the parties immediately after judgment and disposition orally and in writing of the right to appeal, the time limits and manner in which that appeal must be taken, and the right to court-appointed counsel and copies of any transcripts and records in the case of indigency.

4.3 The parties or their attorneys may agree to proceed upon a written, stipulated statement of the facts and procedural development without procuring a transcription of the stenographer's minutes of the testimony, and that statement, signed by the parties or their attorneys, should be transmitted to the appellate court as the record of testimony in the case.

PART V: STAYS OF ORDERS AND RELEASE PENDING APPEAL

5.1 The initiation of an appeal should not automatically operate to stay an order of the juvenile court.

State v. Doe, 103 N.M. 30, 702 P.2d 350, 352 (1984). A juvenile's appeal of a conviction of delinquency and commitment should not be stayed automatically pending appeal. (Citing Standard 5.1).

5.2 Any party, after the filing of a notice or claim of appeal or the entry of an order granting leave to appeal, may request the juvenile court to stay the effect of its order and/or release the juvenile pending appeal.

5.3 Upon the filing of an appeal of judgment and disposition, the release of the appellant, with or without conditions, should issue in every case unless the court orders otherwise. An order of interim detention should be permitted only where the disposition imposed, or most likely to be imposed, by the court includes some form of secure incarceration; and the court finds one or more of the following on the record:

A. that the juvenile would flee the jurisdiction or not appear before any court for further proceedings during the pendency of the appeal;
B. that there is substantial probability that the juvenile would engage in serious violence prior to the resolution of the appeal.

Juveniles should be given credit at disposition for any time spent in a secure facility pending appeal.

5.4 In neglect and abuse cases, the juvenile court may order the juvenile removed to a suitable place pending appeal if the court finds that the juvenile would be in imminent danger if left with or returned to his or her parents, guardian, or other person who is a party to the appeal.

5.5 In those cases in which a stay of judgment or disposition or release pending appeal is denied, the appellate court should afford the appeal the speediest treatment possible.

5.6 In those cases in which a stay of judgment or disposition or release pending appeal is denied by the juvenile court, the appellate court should be empowered to grant the relief requested upon application of a party.

PART VI: COLLATERAL AND SUPPLEMENTARY PROCEEDINGS

6.1 Orders of the juvenile court may be modified by that court at any time when it has jurisdiction over the matter after notice and opportunity for hearing to all parties, upon the petition of a party or by the juvenile court sua sponte.

In the Interest of B.L., **470 N.W.2d 343, 347 (Iowa, 1991). The jurisdiction of juvenile courts over matters not directly involved in or essential to an appeal is not suspended during that appeal. (Citing Standard 6.1)**

In the Matter of the Welfare of the C. Children, **470 N.W.2d 94, 99 (Minn. Ct. App. 1984). Juvenile courts retain jurisdiction over cases that are appeals, at least as to "matters not directly involved in or essential to the appeal." (Citing the commentary to Standard 6.1)**

6.2 Modification of the court's dispositional orders should be governed by the *Dispositions* volume, Standard 5.1 A., and the *Corrections Administration* volume, Standard 5.1 A.

6.3 Every order committing any juvenile into the custody of the state and every order adjudicating a juvenile to be neglected, regardless of custody, should be reviewed by the juvenile court without the request of any party not less than once in every six months.

6.4 The juvenile, his or her parents, custodian, or guardian may petition the juvenile court to inquire into the adequacy of the treatment being afforded the juvenile.

STANDARDS RELATING TO ARCHITECTURE OF FACILITIES

Allen M. Greenberg, Reporter

PART I: DEFINITIONS

1.1 Normalization.

Enabling juveniles within the juvenile justice system to project an image that does not mark them as deviant.

1.2 Community.

A limited territorial setting incorporating a network of relationships, and usually a cultural similarity, that provides most of the goods and services required by persons living within its boundaries.

1.3 Community setting.

The location and operation of a detention or corrections facility which depends upon interaction with a community for its educational, recreational, medical, and other resources.

1.4 Regional setting.

Locating a juvenile facility to serve a geographical area incorporating two or more communities.

1.5 Security measures.

Provisions to:

A. Limit or control the freedom of movement of residents of a juvenile facility; and
B. create a sense of security in residents by providing protection from abuse by others.

1.6 Management model.

A consistent pattern of attitudes and assumptions used by persons who exercise influence and authority as the basis of a system to organize and structure the behavior of others.

1.7 Architectural program.

A written document that describes and justifies space needs for a specific set of operations.

1.8 Operational program.

A plan of procedure under which action may be taken toward attaining a desired goal.

1.9 Soft architecture.

A design attitude that results in spaces and buildings that do not present an expectation of destructive behavior.

1.10 Orientation.

Process of conceptualizing the relative location and general organization of the various components in a building.

1.11 Detention.

Placement of an accused juvenile in a home or facility other than that of a parent, legal guardian, or relative, including facilities commonly called "detention," "shelter care," "training school," "group home," "foster care," and "temporary care."

1.12 Secure setting.

A setting characterized by physically restrictive construction and procedures which are intended to:

A. ensure that no persons enter or leave without staff permission; and
B. that all methods of entry and exit are under the exclusive control of staff

1.13 Nonsecure setting.

A nonsecure setting is characterized by close ties to the community and its resources, and a location in a community setting. It is intended to:

A. create permeable boundaries between facility and community;
B. provide an open setting with very limited controls, usually self-imposed, on residents' movements; and
C. promote normalization.

1.14 Youth corrections agency.

A state agency with responsibility for the administration of juvenile corrections (hereinafter referred to as "the agency").

1.15 Interim status agency.

A statewide agency with responsibility for all aspects of nonjudicial interim status decisions involving accused juvenile offenders.

PART II: VALUES AND PURPOSES

2.1 Normalization.

Facilities for the juvenile justice system should be designed with the objective of creating environments which will encourage normalization.

2.2 Small community-based facilities.

Existing large custodial facilities for juvenile detention and corrections should be phased out and replaced with a network of smaller, community-based facilities.

2.3 Flexible buildings.

The design of facilities for correction and detention should not impede administrative or policy changes.

2.4 Secure settings.

Secure settings should provide security measures which:
A. instill a sense of security and well-being in facility residents; and
B. rely on increased staff coverage rather than building plant.

2.5 Overcrowding.

Overcrowding is generally a symptom of an operational problem and does not imply the need for new construction.

2.6 Community norms.

Community norms should be considered and analyzed in planning and locating facilities for detention or corrections.

2.7 Personal space.

The stress of life in a secure setting requires recognition of the individual's need for some degree of personalization of space, privacy, and territoriality.

PART III: ARCHITECTURAL PROGRAM AND DESIGN

3.1 Architectural program.

An architectural program should be developed for each facility. The program should be a written document containing the following information:

A. statement of the general goals and purposes of the project;
B. description of the agency or organization to be served, including

its tasks, statutory authority, operating procedures, services provided, and administrative structure;

C. description of the management model (Standard 1.6) which is used as the basis of the current and future operations;

D. impact statement that:
   1. analyzes past and current workload and budget;
   2. projects future workload, staffing, programs, and operating and capital budgets; and
   3. assesses the impact of the proposed project on the overall operation of the agency;

E. justification of the project and its operating costs, exploring alternative management models and their impact on staffing, budget, and space requirements;

F. quantitative and qualitative description of space requirements for the proposed facility, including outdoor spaces, character, symbolism, and other descriptive factors;

G. outline of budget and time restrictions; and

H. study of alternate strategies to satisfy space requirements including leasing, renovation, and new construction.

3.2 Database

Establishment of an effective architectural program depends on developing a broad database which reflects the interests of all organizations, agencies, and persons concerned with the project.

3.3 Adaptive architecture.

Facilities should be programmed and planned to provide a variety of spatial configurations that can be adapted to the changing needs of programs and operations.

3.4 Buildings expectations.

Building design should not present an expectation of abusive behavior and vandalism and invite challenge by residents, nor should it be assumed that every juvenile behaves in a violent and destructive manner.

3.5 Conformity with codes.

All detention and corrections facilities should conform to the requirements of the latest editions of the National Fire Code, *Handbook of Fire Protection;* and the Building Officials' and Code Administrators' Basic Building Code, in addition to local fire safety, health, and building codes.

PART IV: GROUP HOMES

4.1 Group homes.

A group home is a community-based residential dwelling for housing juveniles, under the sponsorship of a public or private agency.

4.2 Capacity.

Group homes should have a capacity of between [four and twelve] juveniles, depending on program requirements.

4.3 Certification.

Group homes should be certified annually as conforming to public safety codes. In addition, they should be inspected at least twice a year by the agency[1] for quality of upkeep and suitability of facility for program.

4.4 Leasing or purchase of service.

The agency should favor leasing or purchase of service over investing capital funds in acquiring and renovating an existing structure or constructing a new one.

4.5 Standards for evaluating facilities.

The agency should develop standards for assessing the suitability of a building for use as a group home.

4.6 Governing body.

Private group homes should have a governing body constituted through the agency or through a private incorporated group. This governing body should include community representatives. When the agency operates a group home, the governing body should serve only an advisory purpose.

4.7 Location.

Group homes should be located in residential areas, near community resources and public transportation routes.

4.8 Physical appearance.

Group homes should be similar in appearance and in character to residential buildings in the neighborhoods in which they are located.

---

1. For this Part only, refers to interim status agency or youth corrections agency.

23

4.9 Sound construction.

A building under consideration for use as a group home should be sanitary and of sound construction, with modern, efficient utility systems.

4.10 Operating conditions.

Group home buildings should be fully operational before they are occupied by staff and juveniles.

4.11 Decoration of rooms.

Residents should be permitted to decorate their rooms.

4.12 No permanent staff living quarters.

Group homes should not ordinarily be the sole residence of staff.

4.13 Staff office.

Space for staff administration work should be provided.

4.14 Security of records.

A room for the secure storage of confidential records should be provided.

4.15 General physical requirements.

Group homes should provide a pleasant environment, sufficient space, and suitable equipment to meet program goals.

PART V: SECURE CORRECTIONS FACILITIES

5.1 Security.

Security in a secure corrections facility should recognize and balance the legitimate need for security and safety felt by staff and society with the residents' need for a setting that provides them with safety and a reasonable quality of life.

5.2 Appearance.

The exterior appearance of a secure facility should resemble residential buildings in the surrounding area.

5.3 Capacity.

Capacity of a secure corrections facility for adjudicated delinquents should be [twenty].

5.4 Location.

Secure corrections facilities should be located to facilitate the use of community-based services and continued contact between juvenile, family, and friends.

5.5 Internal organization.

A secure corrections facility should be planned like a large private house.

5.6 No control center.

A secure corrections facility should not have a control center, such as those which commonly provide centralized surveillance and control in a penal institution.

5.7 No permanent staff living quarters.

Secure corrections facilities should not be the sole residence of staff.

5.8 Security of records.

A room for the secure storage of confidential records should be provided.

5.9 Staff offices.

Space for staff administration work should be provided.

5.10 Isolation rooms.

An isolation room, if required, should be planned in conjunction with staff offices.

5.11 General physical requirements.

Secure corrections facilities should provide a pleasant environment, sufficient space, and suitable equipment to meet program goals.

5.12 Fixtures.

Built-in fixtures such as doors, locks, and windows should be domestic in character and encourage normalization.

PART VI: SECURE DETENTION FACILITIES

6.1 Secure detention facility.

A facility characterized by physically restrictive construction and procedures that are intended to prevent an accused juvenile from departing at will.

6.2 Supportive security.

In planning a detention facility, security should be supportive rather than deterrent.

6.3 Capacity.

Capacity of a secure detention facility should be [twelve to twenty] residents.

6.4 Location.

Location of secure detention facilities should take the following factors into account:

A. facilitation of the maintenance of ties between residents and their community, family, and friends;
B. accessibility to mass transit and highways to facilitate visits by family and friends;
C. accessibility to courts to avoid excessive time spent in transit to and from the court and waiting in court;
D. proximity to concentrations of law offices to facilitate attorney-client meetings; and
E. use of community settings.

6.5 Appearance.

The exterior appearance of the secure detention facility should resemble buildings in the surrounding area.

6.6 Certification.

Secure detention facilities should be certified annually in order to ensure conformity to all public safety codes. Unannounced inspections should be made at least four times per year to ascertain quality of maintenance and to ensure against overcrowding. Certification should include determination of the maximum number of residents the facility may hold at any time.

6.7 Internal organization.

The internal organization of a secure detention facility should be clear and unambiguous so as to minimize uncertainty due to lack of orientation. The facility should be planned like a large house.

6.8 Entrance spaces and waiting rooms.

Entrance spaces and waiting rooms in a secure detention facility should reflect a concern for normalization, the presumption of innocence, and the fact that appearance before an intake officer may not necessarily result in detention.

6.9 No control center.

A secure detention facility should not have a control center, such as those which commonly provide centralized surveillance and control in a penal institution.

6.10 No permanent staff living quarters.

Secure detention facilities should not be the sole residence of staff.

6.11 Security of records.

A room for the secure storage of confidential records should be provided.

6.12 Staff offices.

Space for staff administration work should be provided.

6.13 Isolation rooms.

An isolation room, if required, should be planned in conjunction with staff offices.

6.14 Interview rooms.

Secure detention facilities should have interview rooms for residents to meet privately with attorneys and family.

6.15 No vocational training or chapel.

No vocational training or chapel should be provided in a secure detention facility.

6.16 General physical requirements.

Secure detention facilities should provide a pleasant environment with good internal orientation, sufficient space, and suitable equipment to meet program goals.

6.17 Fixtures.

Built-in fixtures such as doors, locks, and windows should be domestic in character and encourage normalization.

STANDARDS RELATING TO CORRECTIONS ADMINISTRATION

Andrew Rutherford and Fred Cohen, Reporters

PART I: GENERAL PRINCIPLES

State ex rel. J.D.W. v. Harris, **173 W.Va. 690, 319 S.E.2d 815, 823 (1984). The *IJA-ABA Juvenile Justice Standards Relating to Corrections Administration* provide guidance, along with the standards of the American Correctional Association and the Commission on Accreditation for Corrections, for the operation of residential juvenile facilities.**

1.1 The administration of juvenile corrections: purposes.

The purpose of juvenile corrections is to carry out the court's dispositional order concerning adjudicated juveniles. The central purposes are the protection of the public, the provision of a safe, human, caring environment, and access to required services for juveniles.

1.2 Five general principles.

The administration of juvenile corrections should be guided by five general principles:

A. Control and care.

The administration of programs for adjudicated juveniles should provide for the degree of control required for public protection, as determined by the court, and a safe, human, caring environment that will provide for normal growth and development.

B. Least possible restriction of liberty.

The liberty of a juvenile should be restricted only to the degree necessary to carry out the purpose of the court's order.

C. Fairness and legal rights.

Programs for adjudicated juveniles should be characterized by fairness in all procedures, and by a careful adherence to legal rights.

D. Accountability.

The administration of juvenile corrections should be accountable on three levels: to the courts for the carrying out of the dispositional order; to the public, through the appropriate legislative or other public body, for the implementation of the statutory mandate and expenditure of public funds; and to the juvenile for the provision of a safe, human, caring environment and access to required services.

E. Minimization of the scope of juvenile corrections.

The administration of juvenile corrections should aim to provide services and programs that will allow the court to reduce the number of juveniles placed in restrictive settings.

PART II: JURISDICTION OF THE DEPARTMENT RESPONSIBLE FOR THE ADMINISTRATION OF JUVENILE CORRECTIONS

2.1 Statewide department.

A. Single statewide department.

There should be a preference for a single statewide department with responsibility for the administration of juvenile corrections rather than a proliferation of agencies at both the state and local level. The statewide department may be termed "the Department of Youth Services." In these standards it is referred to as "the department."

B. Location in executive branch of government.

The department should be located within the executive branch of the state government.

C. Exceptions to statewide jurisdiction.

When for political or geographic considerations, some programs are within the jurisdiction of local government and it is determined that they should remain subject to local control, the statewide department should be responsible for the setting and enforcement of standards and the provision of technical assistance, training, and fiscal subsidies.

2.2 Separate administration of juvenile and adult corrections.

A. Separation from adult corrections.

The department responsible for juvenile corrections should be operationally autonomous from the administration of adult corrections; the department should only have administrative responsibility for persons under eighteen years of age at the time of adjudication, or persons who are otherwise within the jurisdiction of the juvenile court.

B. Prohibition on transfers to adult corrections.

The department should not have authority to transfer a juvenile to the jurisdiction of the adult corrections agency, or to any institution or program administered by the adult corrections agency.

2.3 The department and mental health agencies.

A. Separation from mental health agencies.

The department should be administratively autonomous from the administration of mental health facilities.

B. Mental health services within correctional facilities.

The department should be responsible for providing either directly or by contract with a public or private mental health agency, necessary mental health care and services for juveniles within facilities operated by the department.

C. Transfers to mental health agencies.

When it is believed that a juvenile under the jurisdiction of the department is mentally ill or mentally retarded and in need of such intensive residential care, custody, and control as requires transfer to a facility operated by a mental health agency, the department should return the juvenile to juvenile court and require the initiation of proceedings in the court having jurisdiction for commitment of the mentally ill or mentally retarded to secure care. The law governing such admission or commitment for juveniles not adjudicated delinquent should apply in all respects. The provisions of this standard should never be used by the department for punitive purposes.

D. Court's power to compel agencies to accept juveniles for mental health services.

When any adjudicated juvenile is found by the court to be mentally ill or mentally retarded, the court should have the power to compel acceptance of such juvenile by the mental health agency best equipped to meet the juvenile's needs.

2.4 The responsibility of the federal government.

A. The role of the federal government.

The federal government should take an important leadership role in juvenile corrections through standard-setting and through funding of state and local programs. Federal activity should, as far as possible, be centralized within a single agency.

B. Juveniles adjudicated in federal courts.

Agencies of the federal government should not have program responsibility for adjudicated juveniles. Juveniles adjudicated in federal court should be placed under the jurisdiction of the appropriate state department.

2.5 The department and the private sector.

A. Alternative means of program provision.

The department may provide directly or may purchase from the private sector, programs required to carry out the court's dispositions. There should be a purchase of programs and services from the private sector when purchase avoids duplication and provides a wider range and greater flexibility and more adequately meets the needs of the individual juvenile than can be attained through direct provision by the department.

B.   Quality control for public and private programs.

Standards developed by the department for programs it administers should apply to programs purchased from the private sector. The department's monitoring activities should apply to both public and private programs.

PART III: ORGANIZATIONAL STRUCTURE AND PERSONNEL

3.1 Organization.

No one model of organization is appropriate for all jurisdictions. The following principles should be observed:

A.   Central administration should be responsible for overall departmental planning and policy development.

B.   The following functions can be either centralized or decentralized but are essential to effective administration:
  1. budget and fiscal control;
  2. personnel administration;
  3. program development and standard setting;
  4. program direction and control (supervision);
  5. program monitoring (see Standard 9.3 C);
  6. program evaluation;
  7. research;
  8. grievance mechanisms (see Standard 9.2).

C.   All of these administrative functions should serve to provide needed services to the juvenile near his or her home.

3.2 Departmental appointments.

A.   The director.

The department's director should be appointed by the governor of the state and should report directly to the governor.

B.   Director's appointing authority.

The director, within the context of a civil service merit system, should have appointing authority within the department. All appointments should be subject to an appropriate probationary period.

C. Short-term contracts.

The department's personnel policy should allow for short-term employment contracts, in addition to providing career opportunities.

D. Recruitment of youth counselors.

Youth counselor refers to personnel in direct or continual contact with juveniles. The department should recruit as youth counselors persons who demonstrate the potential for a high level of enthusiasm, sensitivity, and energy in working with adjudicated juveniles in program settings. This potential could be reflected in academic qualifications, personal experience, or in a combination of both.

E. Recruitment of specialists.

The department should ensure that the qualifications of specialists recruited to provide specific services should not be below the minimum established by relevant professional bodies.

F. Affirmative action.

The department's recruitment policy and procedure should clearly demonstrate a preference for affirmative action, and in light of this preference, the department should closely examine the recruitment practices of the private agencies with which it contracts. Affirmative action policies should include but not be limited to:

1. a preference for matching the ethnic and racial groups represented by the juveniles in the department's care with staff appointments and promotions;
2. the appointment, training, and promotion of women and men on an equivalent basis, based on job qualifications and needs;
3. career appointments for ex-offenders. Recognition should be given to their personal experience, which may be more relevant to the correctional process than formal academic qualifications. Educational training should be made available to augment such experience.

3.3 Personnel training.

A. The importance of personnel training.

The department should ensure that resources are made available for a high level of personnel training. Each program director should be responsible for making staff time available for training requirements.

B. Preservice and probationary training.

All personnel with direct supervisory responsibility for juveniles should receive a minimum of eighty hours of preservice training, and a further forty-eight hours during the first six months of employment. The training should consist of a comprehensive orientation in the tasks to be undertaken. The components of such training should include:

1. departmental policies, with special attention to the personnel code of conduct;
2. the background, needs, and rights of adjudicated and non-adjudicated juveniles, community resources, and individual and cultural differences;
3. supervision and security requirements as determined by the type of disposition; and
4. on-going problems faced by probationary personnel.

C. In-service training.

All personnel with direct supervisory responsibility for juveniles should receive a minimum of eighty hours of in-service training each year. The components of such training should include:

1. departmental policies, with attention given to modifications and to legal developments affecting the administration of juvenile corrections;
2. on-going problems faced by personnel;
3. preparation for new tasks and program settings.

D. Training and the private sector.

The department should review the training programs of the private agencies with which it contracts. When adequate training is not provided by the private agency, the contract between the department and the private agency should include an agreement that the department extend its training resources to the private agency.

E. Job rotation.

The department should provide opportunities for employees to broaden their knowledge and skills through a variety of job assignments, job enrichment, and job rotation.

3.4 Code of conduct for personnel.

A. Department's responsibility to develop code of conduct.

The department should develop a code of conduct for all personnel.

B. Code of conduct and contract of employment.

The code of conduct for employees should be a part of the employment contract entered into by the department and each employee.

C. Minimum requirements for the code of conduct.

The minimum requirements for the code of conduct should include:

1. conformance with personnel requirements for public employees;
2. an emphasis on the essential role played by staff in ensuring the integrity of all aspects of the department's policy;
3. stress on the staff's responsibility to provide a safe, human, caring environment for the juvenile and to respect all rights of juveniles set forth in these standards;
4. a prohibition of any form of physical or verbal abuse of juveniles by staff members or by other juveniles with the tacit approval of the staff;
5. an affirmative obligation on the part of staff to report violations by personnel of the code of conduct.

D. Disciplinary policies and procedures.

The department should develop disciplinary policies and procedures for personnel, in accordance with rules established for other public employees.

E. Departmental code of conduct and private agencies.

The department should ensure that the code of conduct for personnel is made known to all staff working in private agencies from which the department purchases programs and services. When private agency staff are not able to meet the standards laid down in the code, the department should terminate its contract with the agency.

F. Judicial remedies for juveniles and their parents.

There should be judicial remedies for juveniles and their parents or guardians, including the waiver of sovereign immunity and the award of counsel's fees to successful litigants, for violations of the code of conduct for personnel provided in these standards. Costs may be awarded against the plaintiff in suits found to be frivolous.

3.5 Management-employee relations.

Where adequate procedures are not provided for under civil service arrangements, the department should:

A. establish formal procedures for the determination of salaries and working conditions;
B. respect the union and bargaining rights of staff, within the context of civil service employment.

3.6 Volunteers.

A. Purposes.

The department should actively involve volunteers in programs, not to replace regular staff, but to enrich and supplement on-going programs.

B. Selection and recruitment of volunteers.

The department should recruit volunteers whose interests and capabilities are related to the identified needs of the juvenile.

C. Training and supervision of volunteers.

Volunteers should be provided with preservice orientation training and be supervised in their work by an experienced employee of the department or the private agency with which the department has contracted.

D. Use of volunteers in advocacy, program-planning, and monitoring activities.

Volunteers should be provided opportunities to participate in the planning and monitoring of juvenile corrections programs. They should also be involved in organizations that advocate change and reform in the area of juvenile corrections. Additionally, volunteers should play a critical role in the independent monitoring of juvenile corrections programs by private groups. See Standard 9.4 A.2.

PART IV: REQUIRED FEATURES OF ALL PROGRAMS

4.1 Definition of program.

A program for adjudicated juveniles is defined as any setting or activity directly administered or purchased by the department for the purpose of implementing the court's disposition.

4.2 Program directors and advisory committees.

A. Program director.

Each program should have a designated director, in whose absence an acting director should be designated. The program director should be accountable to the department for all aspects of the management of the program. In the case of a program purchased from the private sector, accountability to the department should be provided for in the contract between the department and the private agency.

B. Program advisory committees.

The department should encourage program directors to set up advisory committees of local persons to advise on aspects of program management and to facilitate the development of links with the community.

4.3 Legal status.

A juvenile who is adjudicated delinquent should suffer no loss in civil rights, except those rights that are suspended or modified by the nature of the disposition imposed, and by any special conditions allowed by law and made applicable by the court.

4.4 General considerations in determining rights and responsibilities.

Distinctions in the objectives of the juvenile justice system and in the level of development of juveniles require that the determination of the rights and responsibilities of juveniles under correctional supervision should not be based solely on their adult counterparts. In some situations, juveniles should be afforded more of the same rights extended to adults (e.g., medical and dental care attuned to rapidly developing bodies and the need for preventive care). In other situations, a similar right should be recognized, but the legally acceptable adult solution viewed as inadequate (e.g., a right of access to the courts, which may be satisfied for adults by providing an adequate law library and allowing legal assistance by fellow inmates but satisfied for juveniles only by providing legal services). There are other situations in which juveniles will be under a set of obligations not similarly required for adults (e.g., compulsory school attendance, compulsory vaccinations, etc.).

4.5 Due process applicable.

Basic concepts of due process of law should apply to a juvenile under correctional supervision. Alterations in the status or placement of a juvenile that result in more security, additional obligations, or less personal freedom should be subject to regularized proceedings designed to allow for challenge through the presentation of evidence to an impartial tribunal. The relative formality of such proceedings should be based on the importance of the juvenile's interest at stake, the permissible sanction, and the nature of the setting in which the decision is to be made. The more restrictive the setting, or the greater the permissible restriction or sanction, the greater the degree of formality required.

4.6 Program regulations.

The department, using these standards as a basis, should develop regulations for all programs that it administers or purchases.

4.7 Annual statement.

A. Program director's obligation to submit annual statement to the department.

Each program director should submit an annual statement to the department that sets forth, within the framework established by the department's regulations, the program's purpose, methods, and central features. At a minimum this statement should include:
1. elements of the safe, human, caring environment that are provided;
2. program regulations;
3. services available through the program;
4. the nature and extent of links between the program and the community;
5. staff duties, qualifications, and experience.

The statement should also include a summary of the data assembled by the program in accordance with Standard 9.3 C.1.

B. Review by the department of program director's statement.

A preliminary statement in conformance with subsection A should be reviewed and approved by the department before any program is given authority by the department to operate or, in the case of private agencies, authorized to receive funds from the department. In the case of a program purchased from the private sector, the statement should form an integral part of the contract between the department and the private agency. The annual review of the program director's statement should be a major consideration in the department's decision as to whether to renew the authority to operate or receive public funds.

4.8 Prohibition on all forms of corporal punishment; limitations on the use of physical force by personnel.

A. Prohibition on all forms of corporal punishment.

No corporal punishment of any adjudicated juvenile within the jurisdiction of the department should be permitted. This prohibition allows no exceptions and applies equally to public and private programs.

B. Limitations on the use of physical force by personnel in relation to juveniles.

Personnel should be prohibited from the direct use or tacit approval of juveniles' use of physical force against other juveniles except:
1. as necessary in self-defense or to prevent imminent injury to the juvenile, another person, or substantial property injury;
2. to prevent escape; or
3. when a juvenile's refusal to obey an order seriously disrupts

the functioning of the facility. No more force should be used than is necessary to achieve the legitimate purpose for which it is used.

C. Any personnel using physical force against any juvenile should immediately file a written report with the department setting forth the circumstances of the act, the degree of force used, and the reasons for the use of force.

D. The provisions of this standard should be made a part of the code of conduct for personnel set forth in Standard 3.4.

4.9 Safe, human, caring environment.

A. Department's obligation to ensure a safe, human, caring environment.

A safe, human, caring environment is required by all juveniles in order to achieve normal growth and development. The department should have an affirmative obligation to ensure that all programs provide, and in no way inhibit, this safe, human, caring environment.

B. Components of a safe, human, caring environment.

A safe, human, caring environment includes the provision of opportunities for juveniles to:

1. enhance individuality and self-respect;
2. enjoy privacy;
3. develop intellectual and vocational abilities;
4. retain family and other personal ties;
5. express cultural identity;
6. relate and socialize with peers of both sexes;
7. practice religious beliefs;
8. explore political, social, and philosophical ideas;
9. enjoy a nutritious and varied diet;
10. receive dental and medical care, including birth control advice and services;
11. have a choice of recreational activities;
12. be safe from physical and psychological attack and abuse.

4.10 The provision of services.

A. The department's obligation to provide access to required services.

Over and above the provision of a safe, human, caring environment, the department should ensure that adjudicated juveniles have access to those services that are required for their individual needs.

B. Services that all juveniles have an obligation to receive.

The department should ensure that adjudicated juveniles obtain those services that nonadjudicated juveniles have an obligation to receive. Such services should be of no less quality than those provided to juveniles not under correctional supervision.

C. Services necessary to prevent clear harm to physical health.

The department should ensure that adjudicated juveniles obtain any services necessary to prevent clear harm to their physical health.

D. Services mandated by the court as a condition to nonresidential disposition.

The department should ensure that adjudicated juveniles obtain services determined by the court as a condition of a nonresidential disposition. As required by the *Dispositions* volume, such services should not be mandated by the court if they may have harmful effects.

E. Requirement of the juvenile's informed consent to all other services.

The department should ensure that the informed written consent of the juvenile is obtained by the program director for any services other than those described in subsections A, B, C, and D, above. Any such consent may be withdrawn at any time.

F. Limitations on the use of drugs.

Stimulant, tranquilizing, and psychotropic drugs should only be used when:

1. in addition to the consent of the juvenile, the consent of the parents or guardian of any juvenile under the age of sixteen is obtained;
2. such drugs are prescribed and administered by a licensed physician;
3. the program has a procedure, approved by the department, for recording all administrations of such drugs to juveniles, and for monitoring the short- and long-term effects of such drugs by a licensed physician who is independent of the department (the record maintained by the program should include the type and quantity of the drug administered, together with the date and time of day; the physician's reason for the prescription; the physician's observations of the effects of the drug, together with the written observations of other personnel and those of the juvenile);
4. personnel who directly administer drugs to juveniles have received specialized training.

Under no circumstances should stimulant, tranquilizing, or psychotropic drugs be used for purposes of program management or control, or for purposes of experimentation and research. In emergency situations and when the consent of the juvenile cannot be obtained, drugs may be administered subject to the seventy-two-hour emergency treatment provisions contained in the *Noncriminal Misbehavior* volume.

G. Limitations on techniques that manipulate the environment of the juvenile.

The department should limit the use of techniques that manipulate the environment of the juvenile or are of an intrusive nature. Such methods, which include behavior modification techniques, should only be used when:

1. in addition to the consent of the juvenile, the consent of the parents or guardian of any juvenile under the age of sixteen, or if parental consent is denied or unavailable, the approval of the court, is obtained;
2. none of the rights set forth in these standards is infringed;
3. there is no reduction in the safe, human, caring environment required by Standard 4.9.

Such techniques should be clearly explained to the juvenile. Under no circumstances should such techniques be used for purposes of program management or control.

H. Prohibition on the use of organic therapies.

Under no circumstances should the department permit the use of highly intrusive techniques such as psychosurgery or electrical stimulation of the brain.

4.11 Procedures to determine programs and services.

A. Responsibility of the department.

The department should develop procedures for the selection of appropriate programs and services in accordance with the principle of informed consent and other limitations set forth in Standard 4.10.

B. Organization and location.

1. It should be the responsibility of the local office of the statewide corrections department to administer procedures for program selection. This may be undertaken by field office staff working in close collaboration with personnel at settings for preadjudicated juveniles and with court personnel.
2. Location of the juvenile during the program placement decision.

In the case of nonresidential dispositions, the juvenile should continue to reside at home during the transitional period when the decision as to program placement is made. In the case of residential dispositions the department may:

    a. make the program placement decision while the juvenile is within a setting administered by the agency responsible for interim status;

    b. place the juvenile in the residential program nearest to his or her home during the decision-making period;

    c. establish transitional residential centers (secure and non-secure in accordance with the court's disposition) that provide a setting for placement decisions. Residence in such centers should be brief in duration and should not exceed [one week].

C. Criteria for program placement.

The department should establish criteria for program placement decisions. Such criteria should include:

1. Location of the juvenile's home. In accordance with Standard 7.3, there should be a presumption in favor of placing the juvenile in the program nearest to his or her home. In the case of residential dispositions, the wishes of the juvenile should be solicited and taken into account.

2. Age and sex of the juvenile. The placement decision should take into account the age and sex of the juvenile, and the age and sex distributions of each program and of any program criteria relating to age and sex agreed to by the department and the program director.

3. Needs of the juvenile for services. In accordance with the requirements of Standard 4.10, an assessment should be made of the juvenile's need for services and a determination made as to which program setting will best provide access to such services.

D. Information.

1. Preference for use of existing relevant information. There should be a preference for the use of existing relevant information, rather than the generation of new information, unless additional information is needed for the placement decision.

2. Limitations on testing. The department should ensure that psychological tests and other means of obtaining information relevant to the placement decision are undertaken only with the juvenile's informed consent when nonadjudicated

juveniles would not be legally obligated to undergo such tests or to provide such information.

E. Decisions about placement and services as an on-going process.

The placement decision and the determination of appropriate services should be reviewed regularly by local staff and program personnel.

4.12 Mixing of adjudicated and nonadjudicated juveniles.

In terms of access to programs and services, there should be no automatic prohibition on the mixing of adjudicated and nonadjudicated juveniles, in other than secure facilities.

4.13 The duration of services.

If a juvenile wishes to continue to receive services beyond the period of the disposition, the department should make these services available, if possible. Such services should, whenever possible, be funded from sources outside the juvenile justice system. When funded by the department, the duration of such voluntary aftercare should not exceed six months beyond the period of the disposition. Such services should not be provided unless the informed consent of the juvenile is obtained.

4.14 Work performed by adjudicated juveniles.

A. Limitations on coerced work.

Juveniles under correctional supervision should have a right not to participate in coerced work assignments unless:
  1. the work is performed in the community as a part of a conditional disposition; or
  2. the work is reasonably related to the juvenile's housekeeping or personal hygienic needs; or
  3. the work is part of an approved vocationally oriented program for the juvenile.

B. Compensation.
  1. When the juvenile is required to work as part of a program under subsection A.3, and to the extent that such work benefits the facility or program, the juvenile should be compensated for such work. The state should not make any set-off claim for care, custody, or services against such compensation. Such compensation should be guided by the appropriate minimum wage statutes with consideration given to the age and capability of the juvenile.
  2. Juveniles who volunteer for work assignments not connected

with personal housekeeping or hygienic needs should also be fairly compensated for such work and not be subject to set-off claims against such compensation.

3. Juveniles injured while performing work as described in this standard should be entitled to workmen's compensation benefits.

C. Juvenile's access to earnings.

A special account, in the nature of a trust fund, should be established for the juvenile's earnings, and reasonable rules established for periodic withdrawal, expenditure, and release of the entire fund when correctional supervision is terminated.

4.15 Records and confidentiality.

A. The department should develop procedures to ensure the confidentiality of all information pertaining to juveniles within its jurisdiction.

B. The department should ensure that links with computer systems do not infringe on the preservation of confidentiality.

C. The juvenile's access to his or her own records should be governed by the *Juvenile Records and Information Systems* volume.

PART V: MODIFICATION OF DISPOSITIONS

5.1 Procedure for reduction of a disposition.

A. A petition for reduction of a disposition may be filed with the dispositional court any time after the imposition of the order of disposition. The proper parties and the requisite grounds for such petition are set out in Part V of the *Dispositions* volume.

B. The court may reduce the disposition on the basis of the petition and any supportive documents that have been filed initially or subsequently at the request of the court.

C. If the court does not order the reduction of the disposition within [fifteen] days of the filing of the petition, then the petitioner should be entitled to a full dispositional hearing to be held within [thirty] days of the filing of the petition. Such hearings should be conducted in accordance with the relevant provisions of Part VI of the *Dispositional Procedures* volume.

D. Courts should develop rules which impose reasonable limits on the frequency with which such petitions may be filed by the juvenile or the juvenile's parents or guardian. Special provision should be made for additional filings when any subsequent petition raises a matter that was not previously brought to the attention of the court.

5.2 Procedure for willful noncompliance with order of disposition.

A. The department may petition the dispositional court charging the juvenile with a willful violation of the order of disposition.

B. Unless the petition is dismissed, the court should conduct a hearing on the petition in which the petitioner should have the burden of proving willful noncompliance by clear and convincing evidence. The juvenile and counsel for the juvenile should be given prior notice of the charges; should be present at all stages of such proceedings; and should have an opportunity to be heard, to be confronted with adverse witnesses, to cross-examine, and to offer evidence.

C. If the petition is sustained, the judge should make specific, written findings that are sufficient to provide effective appellate review.

D. Upon a finding of willful noncompliance, the court should determine the appropriate means to achieve compliance. If the court preliminarily determines that a disposition of the next most severe category may be imposed, the hearing should be conducted in accordance with Part VI of the *Dispositional Procedures* volume. If the court determines that only a warning or the modification of any previously imposed conditions may be imposed, the juvenile and his or her counsel should be present, have an opportunity to address the court, and be granted disclosure of any information in the court's possession bearing on disposition. No additional formality need be observed except as justice may require in appropriate cases.

PART VI: NONRESIDENTIAL PROGRAMS

6.1 General requirements.

A. Range of programs.
The department should make special efforts to develop and sustain a wide variety of nonresidential programs.

B. Purposes.
Such programs should be administered so as to enhance the juvenile's education, regular employment, or other activities necessary for normal growth and development.

C. The department should ensure that the cultural and geographic roots of the juvenile are respected.

6.2 Community supervision.

A. Purpose and definition.

Community supervision refers to the supervision of an adjudicated juvenile by a designated field worker under varying levels of intensity and in compliance with any other conditions included in the court's dispositional order. Community supervision involves the field worker in the combination of surveillance and service provision or brokerage tasks.

B. Administration.

1. The department should normally perform community supervision functions through its local offices. Administrative arrangements should be determined according to local considerations and may include the purchase of services by the department from the private sector.
2. Field offices should be established and located in the area served. In rural outlying areas, the department may use mobile offices.

C. Conditions.

The court may specify a limited number of conditions designed to carry out a community supervision order. The court should determine conditions that fit the circumstances of the juvenile as indicated by the offense for which he or she has been adjudicated. Such conditions should:

1. be least restrictive of the liberty or privacy of the juvenile and should respect the privacy of others;
2. ensure a safe, human, caring environment as defined by these standards;
3. provide for the juvenile's education, regular employment, or other activities necessary for normal growth and development.

Conditions may also include:

1. curfew stipulations or prohibitions from specified places;
2. determination of the intensity of the level of supervision (the court may, for example, in conjunction with the department, establish high, medium, and low levels of community supervision);
3. the payment of any fines or restitution orders as ordered by the court.

D. Discretion by the department to modify conditions.

Unless the court specifies to the contrary, the department should have the discretion to remove any conditions included in the community supervision order or to reduce the level of intensity. The court and the juvenile should be provided with written notification of any such modification.

E. Supervision practice.

The department should ensure that:

1. a field worker is assigned to each juvenile who is subject to a community supervision order;

2. the field worker, at the earliest opportunity, explains to the juvenile and the juvenile's parents or guardian the purposes of the supervision, any conditions specified by the court, and the range of services available;

3. the workloads of field workers should be determined according to the level of supervision intensity, using the following ratios as guides: high level: one field worker to fifteen juveniles; medium level: one field worker to thirty-five juveniles; low level: one field worker to fifty juveniles.

6.3 Day custody and community service programs.

A. Day custody programs.

The court may order the juvenile to a program of day custody, requiring him or her to be present at a specified place for all or part of every day or for certain days. The court may attach conditions to the order, subject to the limitations on community supervision orders set forth in Standard 6.2 C.

B. Community service programs.

1. Nature of the order. The court may order the juvenile to participate in a community service program. The court should specify the number of work hours required and the nature of the work to be undertaken. Work assignments should be for the general welfare of the community, within the ability of the juvenile and, where possible, related to the nature of the juvenile's offense. They should not expose the juvenile to public ridicule. The court should specify whether any earnings should be withheld from the juvenile. Any juvenile subject to a community service order should be covered by workmen's compensation benefits.

2. Administration. It should be the responsibility of the local office to identify suitable work locations. Community service

programs may be administered by the nearest field office with responsibility for community supervision.

PART VII: RESIDENTIAL PROGRAMS

7.1 Secure and nonsecure facilities: definition and certification.

A secure facility is one that is used exclusively for juveniles who have been adjudicated delinquent and is characterized by exclusive staff control over the rights of its residents to enter or leave the premises on a twenty-four-hour basis.

A nonsecure facility refers to such residential programs as foster homes, group homes, and halfway houses, characterized by a small number of residents who have the freedom to enter or leave the premises under staff supervision.

The department should certify each residential program as secure or nonsecure, and such certification, unless overturned in a court proceeding brought for that purpose, should determine any distinction in rights and responsibilities made in these standards.

7.2 Limitation on the size of residential facilities: maximum size of [twelve to twenty].

No residential facility should house more than [twelve to twenty] adjudicated juveniles. The department should discontinue the use of any residential setting that contains more than twenty adjudicated juveniles.

7.3 Links between juveniles and their homes.

In the determination of program placement, there should be a strong presumption in favor of retaining the juvenile within his or her own home community and against disrupting the juvenile's cultural and geographical roots. The department should ensure that links between the juvenile and his or her home and community are facilitated and preserved.

7.4 Limitations on the use of out-of-state programs.

  A. Out-of-state programs should be utilized only when the department:

    1. provides the court with written reasons showing that the program is not available within the state, why the department has not provided the program within the state, and why in-state programs are not sufficient to meet the juvenile's needs;

2. ensures that juveniles are placed in out-of-state programs only when such programs conform to these standards; and
3. monitors such programs in accordance with Standard 9.3 C.

7.5 Presumption in favor of coeducational programs.

There should be a presumption in favor of coeducational programs. When programs are not coeducational, there should be opportunities for frequent social contact between juveniles of both sexes.

7.6 General requirements of all residential programs.

A. The facility should conform in all respects to applicable health, fire, housing, and sanitation codes.
B. The juvenile should have reasonable access to a telephone to speak with counsel, the court, or any office of the department. Calls to family and friends should be allowed, subject to reasonable hours restrictions, and, when long distance calls are made, to prior approval. The department should provide for a reasonable number of free telephone calls.
C. The juvenile should be able to send unopened letters and should not be required to disclose the contents of correspondence. Incoming parcels and letters may be inspected, but only in the presence of the juvenile to determine whether they contain such contraband as drugs or weapons.
D. Visits by the juvenile's family and friends should be liberally permitted, subject to the juvenile's schedule of activities and reasonable time limitations. At a minimum, visits should be allowed twice weekly.

   Nonintrusive routine searches, such as metal detectors and baggage checks, are permissible; intrusive searches require consent or probable cause to believe the visitor may possess contraband; and other searches, such as patdowns, are permissible if there is a reasonable expectation that contraband is present.
E. Unless the juvenile is in a secure facility under restrictions that prohibit leaving the facility, reasonable access to social, athletic, or cultural events in the community should be provided.
F. The juvenile should be permitted, but never required, to attend religious services of his or her choice. The religious preference of the parents may be solicited or received by someone in authority, and such preference should be made known to the juvenile. However, the parents' religious preference should not be used to co-

erce belief or attendance at religious services, or to alter a different preference held by the juvenile.

G. No censorship should be exercised over what the juvenile may listen to on the radio or watch on television. Reasonable regulation may be imposed on the amount, frequency, and time of day for such activities. There should be no censorship of reading materials, except that regulations may be developed for juveniles under the age of [twelve] concerning access to obscene material.

H. The juvenile should be offered a varied and tastefully prepared diet that conforms to accepted nutritional standards. A special diet should be provided for a juvenile with particular medical needs, or when necessary to comply with the requirements of a juvenile's religious or cultural heritage.

I. The juvenile should be permitted to wear his or her own clothing. If the juvenile does not have adequate clothing, the program should make funds available for its purchase, and such clothing should be sufficiently varied as to avoid any institutional appearance among the juveniles. The department's budgetary guidelines should allow for the purchase of clothing, when required, at the time of discharge from the program.

Rules relating to the length or style of hair, facial hair, cosmetics, clothing, and the like should be based only on safety and health objectives and not the personal preferences of those in authority.

J. The sleeping and privacy arrangements for juveniles should be sufficiently varied so that individual and small group arrangements are available according to the needs and desires of the juvenile. There should be a prohibition against the predominant use of dormitory arrangements in which the opportunity for privacy and solitude are minimal and the need to provide surveillance-type security is mandated by the close proximity of the juveniles to one another.

K. Searches of the juvenile, the juvenile's room, sleeping area, or property should not be routinely undertaken. When there are reasonable grounds to believe that a search may uncover violations of the penal law or the regulations of the facility, including a belief that a weapon may be found, then a search may be authorized by the administrative head of the facility.

A record should be kept of the grounds for the search, when it was conducted, and what, if anything, was discovered and seized. The juvenile should generally be afforded the right to be present during any search of his or her room or property.

L. Comprehensive medical and dental care should be provided for each juvenile. No surgery should be permitted—except in the case of a grave emergency—without the informed consent of the juvenile and the parents or guardian.

M. Regulations necessary for the smooth functioning of the facility should be in writing and be provided and explained to the juvenile as soon as possible upon the juvenile's arrival at the facility.

N. Access to legal counsel should be readily available in order to preserve the juvenile's right to contest the adjudication or disposition, to provide access to the courts on issues related to the governance or maintenance of the facility after all administrative remedies provided in these standards have been exhausted, and to preserve or perfect any legal claims the juvenile may have that are unrelated to the adjudication, the disposition, or the facility.

7.7 Transfers between programs.

The department should have discretion to transfer juveniles between programs within the category of disposition determined by the court. Transfers should adhere to the following substantive and procedural requirements:

A. A request for a transfer may be initiated by the juvenile or by the program director. The request should be in writing and directed to a designated official within the department. When the request is received, it should be the responsibility of the department to notify the parents or guardian of the juvenile and to solicit their views on the request. When the request is initiated by the program director, the department should ascertain the views of the juvenile concerning the proposed transfer.

B. Unless the department finds that there is no reasonable basis for the transfer, that there are no vacancies, or that there are sufficient grounds to reject the request, the request from either party should ordinarily be granted.

C. Unless the transfer involves an emergency relating to the health and safety of the juvenile or others, the department should provide notice at least seven days in advance to the juvenile and the juvenile's parents or guardian. Any objections should be expeditiously reviewed by the department. If, after review, the department decides against allowing the transfer, the reasons for rejecting the request should be placed in the juvenile's file, and the juvenile may thereafter utilize the grievance mechanisms to pursue any continuing objection.

D. When a proposed nonemergency transfer will result in a reduction of services, such transfer should be delayed until the resolution of any grievance that may be filed by the juvenile.

E. A major consideration in transfer decisions should be the proximity of the programs involved to the juvenile's home and community. If the proposed transfer results in placing the juvenile farther from home and the juvenile objects to the transfer, the department should show in writing that the court-ordered disposition cannot be provided nearer to the juvenile's home. A similar obligation resides with the department when the juvenile has requested a transfer to a program nearer home and the request has been denied. Considerations of proximity to the juvenile's home should be given priority in transfers to a program for which there is a waiting list.

7.8 Limitations on restraints and weapons.

A. Mechanical restraints.

Given the small size of programs, it should not be necessary to use mechanical restraints within the facility. The program director may authorize the use of mechanical restraints during transportation only.

B. Chemical restraints.

In extreme situations, chemical restraints may be used under strict controls. The department should develop regulations governing their use.

C. Weapons.

Under no circumstances should personnel take any weapons into the facility.

7.9 Provision of good-time credit.

The department may credit [5] percent good-time against the length of those dispositions subject to the disciplinary process set out in Part VIII. Good-time credits once earned should be forfeited only as a sanction of the disciplinary process.

7.10 Nonsecure programs.

A. Intermittent custody.
   1. Defined. Intermittent custody may be ordered by the court, requiring that the juvenile be resident on an overnight or weekend basis in a nonsecure facility.

2. Program. The program should meet the basic requirements for residential programs as determined in these standards with modifications that allow for noncontinuous residence. The department may use part of the capacity of group homes for the purpose of intermittent custody.

B. Foster homes.

1. Defined. A foster home is the home of one or more persons who, in addition to any children of their own, take in juveniles as temporary family members.

2. The foster home. The department should only use foster homes that are in compliance with state requirements. It should also ensure that the home has sufficient space to provide personal comfort and privacy for all persons living there.

3. Foster parents and family members. Members of the foster family should be in good physical health and should supply the department with a report of a physical examination on an annual basis. Foster parents should receive in-service training and support services from the department or the private agency involved.

4. Placement of juveniles. The department should ensure that the preferences of the juvenile are closely adhered to in the placement of a juvenile in a foster home.

5. The department's supervisory responsibility. The department should retain ultimate supervisory responsibility for any juvenile placed in a foster home.

C. Group homes.

1. Defined. A group home is a community-based residential dwelling for housing juveniles under the sponsorship of a public or private agency.

2. Maximum size. Group homes may have a capacity of between [four and twelve] juveniles depending on program requirements.

3. Use of community resources. Juveniles in the group home should whenever possible attend schools within the local school district. The group home should make full use of, and not duplicate, other community resources and services.

4. Program characteristics. The department should make use of a wide range of group home types. In accordance with Standard 4.10 E, it should ensure that the juvenile's informed consent is obtained prior to participation in any services. When a group home has adopted a "treatment" program approach that re-

quires participation of all residents in the services provided, the juvenile should be allowed a preplacement stay. Any juvenile not willing to take part in such a program should be granted a transfer.

5. Staffing. Staffing requirements should be determined according to the type of group home program. As a general rule, there should be at least [one] staff person on duty with full-time supervisory responsibility for every [five] juveniles, during those times when juveniles are in the facility. At least one staff person should sleep at the facility. There should be twenty-four-hour staff coverage. Other staffing patterns should be based on the program objectives and components and the characteristics of the juveniles in residence.

D. Other nonsecure settings.

Within the category of "group home," the department may use other nonsecure settings. Alternative nonsecure settings may include:

1. Rural programs. The department may use programs such as forestry camps, ranches, and farms that provide specific work or recreational activities in a rural setting. These programs may be most appropriately provided on a contract basis rather than being directly administered by the department.

2. Boarding schools. The department may purchase placements in boarding schools or other residential settings which primarily provide for nonadjudicated juveniles.

3. Apartment settings. For juveniles of working age, the department should experiment with the use of apartment complexes and other residential settings with or without resident staff.

7.11 Secure programs.

A. Limitations.

1. Maximum size. As set forth in Standard 7.2, the maximum size of a secure facility should not exceed [twelve to twenty] juveniles.

2. Strategies to reduce the number of secure beds. The department should develop strategies to reduce the number of secure beds within its jurisdiction.

B. Physical characteristics.

1. Living arrangements. The living arrangements should conform as nearly as possible to those provided for nonsecure facilities. As to items such as heat, ventilation, lighting, and sleeping

areas, there should be no difference between secure and non-secure facilities.

2. Security. Security refers to the provision of staff and resident safety, and to the prevention of escapes from the facility. Means to ensure security should consist of both physical features of the building and staffing arrangements. Given the facility's small size, there should be no surveillance of residents by closed-circuit television, listening systems, or other such devices.

C. Security classification.

1. Purpose. The department should develop a security classification scheme for the residents of secure facilities. The purpose of the scheme should be to allow juveniles placed in the lower security category opportunities to participate in activities outside the facility.

2. Criteria. The department's classification scheme should be based on the nature of current and previous offenses and on any history of violence and escape from secure facilities. The criteria should also include any findings of disciplinary proceedings concerning a juvenile while in the program. The extent to which a juvenile participates in services should not be a classification criterion.

3. Determination of security category. The determination of the security category should be made by the program director, subject to the approval of the local office. The juvenile should be notified of the security category and given an opportunity to challenge the determination through the grievance mechanism set forth in Standard 9.2.

D. Activities in the local community.

There should be a presumption in favor of juveniles within the lower security category taking full part in educational, work release, and recreational activities in the local community.

E. Program activities in the facility.

When it is not possible for juveniles to leave the facility, educational, recreational, and other activities should be provided within the secure facility.

1. Education. The department should ensure that educational services provided within the secure setting are at least equal in quality to those available in the community and that they meet the individual needs of the juvenile. Given the size of the facility, educational services should be either on an individual or

small group basis. The department should experiment with different methods in the deployment of educational personnel, including the use of a team of teachers to serve a number of facilities. The department may contract with public or private agencies for its teaching requirements or directly employ such personnel.

2. Vocational training. Similar considerations should apply to the provision of vocational training opportunities as apply to education. When possible, vocational training should be linked to work release programs.

3. Recreational activities. Juveniles should have access to a choice of individual and group recreational activities for at least two hours each day. Such activities should provide opportunities for strenuous physical exercise.

F. Staffing.

Staffing arrangements should aim to provide a safe, human, caring environment. Workloads developed by the department should provide for at least one staff person with full-time supervisory responsibility on duty for every [four] juveniles. Given the small size of the facility, all staff persons should be in direct interaction with juveniles. At least one staff person should be on duty and awake at night. Night duty may be performed by regular staff persons on a rotating basis, or by a special classification of personnel trained to handle emergencies.

G. Furloughs.

Juveniles in the lower security category should be permitted a weekend furlough at least every [two] months. All juveniles, regardless of security category, should be permitted a furlough of at least five days duration during the month prior to discharge.

H. Isolation.

1. Isolation of juveniles should be utilized only in accordance with the standards on discipline in Part VIII or as a temporary emergency measure when the juvenile is engaging in conduct that creates an imminent danger of physical harm to the juvenile or others.

2. Emergency isolation. When a juvenile is isolated because of conduct that creates a danger to self or others, the incident should be reported immediately to the program director and, when necessary, to the appropriate medical personnel. The case should be immediately reviewed, any required medical attention immediately undertaken, and a plan devised for the ear-

liest release of the juvenile from isolation or for the provision of care in a more appropriate setting. Eight hours during the daytime should constitute the maximum duration for such confinement.

3. Protective custody. A juvenile may be isolated at his or her own request when such request arises out of a legitimate fear for his or her personal safety. When such protective custody is granted, the program director should immediately identify and resolve the underlying problem giving rise to the juvenile's request. Eight hours during the daytime should constitute the maximum duration for such confinement.

4. When possible, isolation should be accomplished in the juvenile's own room. The program director should determine whether any items should be removed from the room during the period of isolation. Such decision should be based on whether or not such items may be used as instruments of self-injury and not as a punitive measure.

5. If the facility does not utilize individual rooms, a room may be specially designated. Such room should resemble, as nearly as possible, the ordinary rooms of the facility.

6. If a room specially designated as an isolation room is required, such room should be planned and located in the staff office area and not in the bedroom section of the facility.

7. No special diet or extraordinary sensory or physical deprivations should be imposed in addition to the room confinement. Reading materials and regular periods of indoor and outdoor exercise should be available.

8. All juveniles in isolation should be visited at least hourly by a specially designated and trained staff person and should be provided one hour of recreation in every twenty-four-hour period of isolation.

   When the isolation is an emergency measure growing out of violent behavior, a staff member should remain with the juvenile. If considerations of safety make it impossible for the staff member to remain, the staff member should maintain constant observation of the juvenile.

   When the juvenile is in isolation at his or her own request, the regular staff visits should be designed to clearly identify and quickly resolve the problem that led to the request for isolation.

9. Each incident during the period of isolation, along with the

reasons for and the resolution of the matter, should be recorded and subject to at least monthly review by the program director and an individual or individuals assigned such a review function in the department.

PART VIII: THE DISCIPLINARY SYSTEM

8.1 Scope and application.

These standards apply to juveniles who as a result of an adjudication and an order of disposition have been removed from their homes and placed in a secure or nonsecure facility, with the exception of juveniles placed in foster homes. Disciplinary matters in the foster home setting, whether it be a long-term or short-term placement, should be governed by the law that regulates the parent-child relationship and any particular laws of the jurisdiction applicable to foster home [or group home] placements.

8.2 Objectives.

The objectives of these standards are:
A. to allow those charged with the custody and control of juveniles to reasonably regulate the behavior of those in their charge and to impose disciplinary measures congruent with the willful violation of the applicable regulations;
B. to promote fairness and regularity in the disciplinary system;
C. to separate major infractions from minor infractions and to prohibit the imposition of disciplinary measures in certain cases;
D. to promote the use of written regulations and to ensure that the juvenile know as precisely as possible what conduct is expected of him or her and what sanctions may be imposed;
E. to provide a procedural format for the imposition of disciplinary measures; and
F. to prohibit cruel and unusual punishment within juvenile correctional facilities.

8.3 Major infractions.

A. When a juvenile in a correctional facility is believed to have committed an offense that is a felony under the law of the jurisdiction, such offense should be processed in the same manner as an offense charged against a juvenile who is not in a correctional facility. If the charge is not otherwise pursued, the matter should be treated within the correctional facility as a major infraction.

B. If the appropriate authority elects to prosecute or refer the matter to juvenile court, some change may be required in the status of the accused juvenile within the facility for his or her own protection, for the protection of other residents, or for purposes of institutional integrity. The disciplinary board (see Standard 8.8) should determine whether probable cause exists to believe that the named juvenile is guilty of the alleged offense. If such cause is found to exist, the program director should determine whether restrictive measures are necessary for the protection of the juvenile, the protection of other residents, or for purposes of institutional integrity. If it is determined that restrictive measures are required, the least restrictive measures should always be used.

C. Representative of offenses that should be considered as major infractions are: murder; kidnapping; manslaughter; armed robbery; burglary; assault causing serious physical injury; rape; physical restraint of another with the threat of serious harm; arson; tampering with a witness; bribery; escape by use of force; possession of a proscribed narcotic drug;[1] inciting a riot; theft or destruction of property valued at $500 or more; and sexual abuse.

8.4 Minor infractions.

A. A minor infraction that is an offense under the penal law may or may not be officially reported, according to the discretion of the person in charge of the facility. If it is reported and the appropriate authority elects to take action, then the procedures set out in Standard 8.3 should apply.

B. Representative of offenses that should be considered as minor infractions are: assault with no serious bodily injury; escape without use of force; threatening the physical safety of others; theft or destruction of property valued at under $500; creating a disturbance; engaging in a riot; lying to a person in authority; willful and repeated disobedience of valid orders; reporting a false alarm; being in possession of or under the influence of alcohol or marijuana; and refusal to perform work assignments.

8.5 Petty infractions.

Representative of offenses that should be considered as petty infractions are: theft of property valued at $5.00 or less; unauthorized use of

---

1. "Narcotic drug" is not intended to include marijuana or any of its derivatives.

property belonging to another; possession of contraband other than that treated in other categories; creating a fire, health, or safety hazard; unauthorized leaving of the facility for less than twenty-four hours; attempted escape; refusal to attend school or classes when mandated by the compulsory school attendance law; and violation of any of the valid regulations of the facility not otherwise covered in the above standards.

8.6 Conduct that may not be subject to disciplinary action.

Juveniles should not be subject to disciplinary action for any of the following behavior:

A. sexual behavior that is not forbidden by statute or reasonable institutional regulations;
B. refusal to attend religious services;
C. refusal to conform in matters of personal appearance or dress to any institutional rule that is not related to health or safety;
D. refusal to permit a search of the person or of personal effects that is not authorized by these standards;
E. refusal to continue participation in any counseling, treatment, rehabilitation, or training program, with the exception of school or class attendance mandated by the compulsory school attendance law;
F. refusal to address staff in any particular manner or displaying what is viewed as a negative, hostile, or any other supposed attitude deemed undesirable;
G. possession of any printed or otherwise recorded material unless such possession is specifically forbidden by these standards;
H. refusal to eat a particular type of food;
I. refusal to behave in violation of the juvenile's religious beliefs;
J. refusal to participate in any study, research, or experiment;
K. refusal to take drugs designed to modify behavior or to submit to nonemergency, surgical interventions without consent.

8.7 Sanctions.

A. The sanctions available for less serious infractions may also be used for more serious infractions.
B. Major infractions—up to [ten] days room confinement, the loss of or prohibition from accrual of any or all good-time credits, a suspension of the privilege of earning good-time credits for a period not to exceed [thirty] days, and the suspension of designated privileges for a period not to exceed [thirty] days.

C. Minor infractions—up to [five] days room confinement, the loss of or prohibition from accrual of good-time credits not to exceed one-half of that currently earned, and the suspension of designated privileges for a period not to exceed [fifteen] days.
D. Petty infractions—reprimand and warning, and the suspension of designated privileges for a period not to exceed [seven] days. A second petty infraction may be treated as a minor infraction but only if the juvenile is given advance written notice of such decision.
E. Designated privileges described—the type of privileges subject to suspension should include access to movies, radio, television, and the like; participation in recreational or athletic activities; participation in outside activities; off-ground privileges; and access to the telephone, except for calls to the juvenile's family or attorney.
F. Punishments proscribed—no corporal punishment should be inflicted, nor should a juvenile be required to wear special clothing or insignia, eat a restricted diet, alter the regular sleeping pattern, engage in arduous physical labor, or be under a rule of silence, or any other punishment designed to cause contempt, ridicule, or physical pain.

8.8 Disciplinary board: composition, when required.

A petty infraction need not be heard in a formal hearing. Discipline should be invoked on the basis of a written report submitted to the program director. The juvenile should be informed of the charge and be given an opportunity to be heard before the program director, or his or her designee.

Major and minor infractions should be subject to a hearing before an impartial disciplinary board, composed of five members. Two members of the board should be employees of the facility, and two members should be selected from a rotating group of citizens who have volunteered to serve on the board and who are appointed in a manner that will ensure their independence. The fifth member should be a nonvoting chairperson. A majority vote should be required for any decision by the board. The board should meet when there are cases to be heard.

8.9 Disciplinary procedure.

No sanctions should be imposed nor any record of the charge maintained for a major or a minor infraction unless the following procedural requirements are met:

A. Notice—verbal notice of the intent to prefer a charge should be given immediately after discovery of the alleged infraction, with written notice required within twenty-four hours thereafter. Such written notice should specify the rule violated; contain a brief description of the alleged conduct; and give the date, time, and place of the alleged conduct.
B. Time of hearing—the hearing should be held not later than seven days after service of the written notice. The juvenile should be notified in writing of the time and place for the hearing as soon as that decision has been made.
C. Representation—the juvenile may select as a representative at the hearing an employee of the facility, an employee of the department, another resident, his or her own counsel, or any person who is a regular volunteer for that purpose.
D. Hearing—the chairperson of the disciplinary board should read the charge and ask the juvenile either to admit or deny it. If the charge is denied, the chairperson should call and question the person making the charge, the juvenile, and any other persons deemed material witnesses. The juvenile or the juvenile's representative should have the opportunity to cross-examine any witness, subject to the discretion of officials of the correctional facility, to inspect and challenge any documentary or physical evidence, and to introduce evidence and call witnesses only when permitting the juvenile to do so would not be unduly hazardous to institutional safety or correctional goals.
E. Decision—the board should render a written decision based on clear and convincing evidence and should notify the juvenile and the juvenile's representative of such decision within twenty-four hours. The decision should include:
   1. a finding either of guilty or not guilty;
   2. the reasons for the decision;
   3. a summary of the evidence relied upon;
   4. the sanction to be imposed, along with reasons for the sanction.
F. Record—the decision, when final, should become a part of the juvenile's record.
G. Finality and review—a petty infraction should not be subject to further review. A minor infraction may be reviewed by the program director, at the request of the juvenile. A major infraction should be automatically reviewed by the program director. Such review should include the decision and the sanction imposed.

The reviewer may reverse the board's finding of guilt or reduce the severity of the sanction. Appeals from the program director's decision should be made to the independent review body described in Standard 9.2 C.11.

PART IX: ACCOUNTABILITY

9.1 Basic requirements.

A. Additional mechanisms.

In addition to the accountability mechanisms that appear throughout these standards, five additional mechanisms are set forth in this Part. These are: information systems; grievance procedures; monitoring procedures; evaluation activities; and a planning process open to public scrutiny.

B. General principles.

Full accountability depends upon a combination of mechanisms within the department and independent of the department, upon similar application to privately and publicly administered programs, and upon access by the public to information concerning such mechanisms.

9.2 Grievance mechanism.

A. Defined.

A grievance mechanism is an administrative procedure through which the complaints of individuals about residential programs or department policies, personnel, conditions, or procedures can be expressed and resolved.

B. No single model is preferred.

While the establishment of some grievance mechanism is highly desirable, no single model or procedure exists that could be implemented in all residential programs for juveniles in the country. One of the essential elements for success should be resident and staff collaboration on details, and implementation should be guided by certain fundamental principles.

C. Principles to govern individualized grievance mechanisms.

1. Every resident assigned to any program unit should have the means to file a grievance and make use of any grievance procedure that is developed.
2. Each facility should design a mechanism appropriate to its physical set-up, the age and size of its population, and the

focus of its program. The mechanism should be subject to review and approval by the department.

3. There should be available to any resident with an emergency grievance or problem, a course of action that can provide for immediate redress.

4. Elected residents and designated staff should participate in the development of procedures and in the operation of the grievance mechanism.

5. The mechanism employed should be simple and the levels of review kept to a minimum.

6. Residents should be entitled to representation and other assistance at all levels, including informal resolution within the established procedure.

7. There should be brief time limits for the receipt of all responses to a grievance as well as for action that is required to relieve the grievance.

8. A course of action should be open to all parties to a grievance, staff and residents alike, for appealing a decision.

9. A juvenile should be guaranteed a speedy, written response to his or her grievance with reasons for the action taken. In the absence of such a response, there should be further recourse available to the juvenile.

10. Monitoring and evaluation of the entire operation by persons not connected with the facility should be required.

11. The procedure should include, as a final review, some form of independent review by a party or parties outside the department. Such review may be in the form of binding or nonbinding arbitration.

12. No reprisals should be permitted against anyone using the grievance mechanism.

13. The grievance mechanism should include an impartial method for determining whether a complaint falls within its jurisdiction.

14. Implementation of the grievance mechanism is a vital factor in its potential for success. This calls for administrative leadership and commitment, resident and staff involvement, a strong orientation and explanation program for new residents, and outside monitoring.

9.3 Organization of research and planning within the department.

A. Research and planning division.

The department should establish a research and planning division within its central office with organizational status similar to that of other divisions within the department. The division should have responsibility for:

1. the assembly and processing of data concerning all department activities;
2. continuous monitoring of all programs;
3. ensuring program effectiveness;
4. short- and long-term planning for the department;
5. coordination with appropriate state agencies.

B. Information system.

The research and planning division should develop an information system designed to serve the department's data needs for administration, research, and planning. The data assembled should include:

1. basic characteristics of juveniles within the department's jurisdiction;
2. program descriptions and features;
3. departmental organizational arrangements such as local offices, field offices, and other units of administration;
4. characteristics of department personnel; and
5. fiscal data.

C. Monitoring activities.

The division should ensure program quality through the monitoring of all programs. Monitoring should include the compilation of basic data on all programs and regular visits to programs by monitoring teams. Monitoring should be designed to ensure compliance with the department's standards and the program's statement of purpose.

1. Basic program data. The division should establish guidelines for basic program data that should be recorded and provided to the division at least annually. At a minimum such data should include:
   a. standardized information on juveniles in the program;
   b. details concerning personnel and volunteers;
   c. narrative history of the program from inception;
   d. line item accounts of the program's allocation of funds and expenditures;
   e. description of the links between the program and the community within which it is located;
   f. description of regulations and standardized data on disciplinary hearings;

g. description and data on the provision of a safe, human, caring environment;

h. description and data on services provided;

i. details concerning the relationship between the program and other public and private agencies.

2. Visits to programs by monitoring team. The division should send a monitoring team to visit each program at least twice annually. Depending on the nature of the program, the monitoring team should usually consist of two or three persons, and the visit should be for a period of up to one week. When appropriate, unannounced follow-up visits should be made. At a minimum, the monitoring team should:

a. systematically interview all juveniles and staff involved in the program;

b. observe every aspect of the program; and

c. review the program's procedures for recording information.

3. Use of monitoring results. The monitoring results should be used as the basis for decisions concerning required program changes or the termination of particular programs.

D. Evaluation of programs: process and outcome.

Evaluation refers to the measurement of program processes and outcomes. Depending on the level of independent evaluation, the division should carry out its own evaluation activities. Program evaluation should be of two types:

1. Process evaluation. Process evaluation determines whether the program is being implemented in accordance with its stated purposes and methods. The criteria for measurement should include the level of humaneness and fairness of the program's day-to-day operations, and the extent and quality of its community links.

2. Outcome evaluation. Outcome evaluation measures the program's effectiveness in terms of producing change in the direction of stated goals. Outcome evaluation should also endeavor to locate and measure unanticipated consequences of particular activities. The measurement criteria should include rates of recidivism, the personal development of juveniles under correctional supervision, and fiscal costs.

E. Planning.

The division should ensure that the department's short- and long-term planning includes:

1. full use of research findings;
2. close coordination with the planning activities of other criminal justice and children's service agencies;
3. providing public access to the department's planning documents, at least annually, and allowing public participation in the planning process; and
4. continuous review and modification based upon results of departmental monitoring and evaluation activities.

F. The department's annual report.

The division should have primary responsibility for the preparation of the department's annual report. The report should be published and widely disseminated. The report should include:

1. a summary of the department's program activities;
2. information on the operation of disciplinary and grievance mechanisms;
3. data concerning juveniles and department personnel;
4. the department's fiscal accounts; and
5. the department's planning for the future.

9.4 Independent monitoring and evaluation activities.

A. Independent monitoring of programs.

Monitoring activities, similar to those set forth in Standard 9.3 C., should also be performed independently of the department. Such activities should include:

1. Monitoring by a public agency. Jurisdictions should provide for the independent monitoring of juvenile corrections programs by a public agency. No single organizational model for such monitoring is preferred. The central considerations in the establishment of such an agency are its independence from the department with responsibility for juvenile corrections, and complete access to all programs and information.
2. Monitoring by private groups. Private groups should also monitor department programs. The department should recognize that such groups, which may focus either on all aspects of a program or on particular aspects of care and services, play an important role in maintaining a high level of program quality.

B. Independent evaluation.

Most evaluation activity should be undertaken independently of the department. There should be a diversification of evaluation functions among public and private agencies and universities. Evaluation should include the program process and outcome evaluation set forth in Standard 9.3 D. Additionally, there should be system-wide evaluation that addresses several or all programs within a given jurisdiction. Such evaluation should measure the impact of programs and other departmental activity on the juvenile justice process as a whole. The measurement criteria for the system-wide evaluation should include crime rates, fiscal costs, and movement of juveniles through the system.

STANDARDS RELATING TO COUNSEL FOR PRIVATE PARTIES

Lee Teitelbaum, Reporter

PART I. GENERAL STANDARDS

1.1 Counsel in juvenile proceedings, generally.

The participation of counsel on behalf of all parties subject to juvenile and family court proceedings is essential to the administration of justice and to the fair and accurate resolution of issues at all stages of those proceedings.

***State ex rel. Juvenile Dept. of Multnomah Co. v. Geist,* 310 Ore. 176, 796 P.2d 1193, 1201 (1990). The standard for the determination of the effectiveness of counsel in an action for the termination of parental rights is whether the proceeding was "fundamentally fair." (Citing *Standards Relating to Counsel for Private Parties* generally)**

1.2 Standards in juvenile proceedings, generally.

    (a) As a member of the bar, a lawyer involved in juvenile court matters is bound to know and is subject to standards of professional conduct set forth in statutes, rules, decisions of courts, and codes, canons or other standards of professional conduct. Counsel has no duty to execute any directive of the client that is inconsistent with law or these standards. Counsel may, however, challenge standards that he or she believes limit unconstitutionally or otherwise improperly representation of clients subject to juvenile court proceedings.

    (b) As used in these standards, the term "unprofessional conduct" denotes conduct which is now or should be subject to disciplinary sanction. Where other terms are used, the standard is intended as a guide to honorable and competent professional conduct or as a model for institutional organization.

1.3 Misrepresentation of factual propositions or legal authority.

It is unprofessional conduct for counsel intentionally to misrepresent factual propositions or legal authority to the court or to opposing counsel and probation personnel in the course of discussions concerning entrance of a plea, early disposition or any other matter related to the juvenile court proceeding. Entrance of a plea concerning the client's responsibility in law for alleged misconduct or concerning the existence in law of an alleged status offense is a statement of the party's posture with respect to the proceeding and is not a representation of fact or of legal authority.

1.4 Relations with probation and social work personnel.

A lawyer engaged in juvenile court practice typically deals with social work and probation department personnel throughout the course of handling a case. In general, the lawyer should cooperate with these agencies and should instruct the client to do so, except to the extent such cooperation is or will likely become inconsistent with protection of the client's legitimate interests in the proceeding or of any other rights of the client under the law.

1.5 Punctuality.

A lawyer should be prompt in all dealings with the court, including attendance, submission of motions, briefs and other papers, and in dealings with clients and other interested persons. It is unprofessional conduct for counsel intentionally to use procedural devices for which there is no legitimate basis, to misrepresent facts to the court or to accept conflicting responsibilities for the purpose of delaying court proceedings. The lawyer should also emphasize the importance of punctuality in attendance in court to the client and to witnesses to be called, and, to the extent feasible, facilitate their prompt attendance.

1.6 Public statements.
  (a) The lawyer representing a client before the juvenile court should avoid personal publicity connected with the case, both during trial and thereafter.
  (b) Counsel should comply with statutory and court rules governing dissemination of information concerning juvenile and family court matters and, to the extent consistent with those rules, with the ABA *Standards Relating to Fair Trial and Free Press.*

1.7 Improvement in the juvenile justice system.

In each jurisdiction, lawyers practicing before the juvenile court should actively seek improvement in the administration of juvenile justice and the provision of resources for the treatment of persons subject to the jurisdiction of the juvenile court.

PART II. PROVISION AND ORGANIZATION OF LEGAL SERVICES

2.1 General principles.
  (a) Responsibility for provision of legal services.

Provision of satisfactory legal representation in juvenile and family court cases is the proper concern of all segments of the legal community. It is, accordingly, the responsibility of courts, defender agencies, legal professional groups, individual practitioners and educational institutions to ensure that competent counsel and adequate supporting services are available for representation of all persons with business before juvenile and family courts.

    (i) Lawyers active in practice should be encouraged to qualify themselves for participation in juvenile and family court cases through formal training, association with experienced juvenile counsel or by other means. To this end, law firms should encourage members to represent parties involved in such matters.

    (ii) Suitable undergraduate and postgraduate educational curricula concerning legal and nonlegal subjects relevant to representation in juvenile and family courts should regularly be available.

    (iii) Careful and candid evaluation of representation in cases involving children should be undertaken by judicial and professional groups, including the organized bar, particularly but not solely where assigned counsel—whether public or private—appears.

(b) Compensation for services.

    (i) Lawyers participating in juvenile court matters, whether retained or appointed, are entitled to reasonable compensation for time and services performed according to prevailing professional standards. In determining fees for their services, lawyers should take into account the time and labor actually required, the skill required to perform the legal service properly, the likelihood that acceptance of the case will preclude other employment for the lawyer, the fee customarily charged in the locality for similar legal services, the possible consequences of the proceedings, and the experience, reputation and ability of the lawyer or lawyers performing the services. In setting fees lawyers should also consider the performance of services incident to full representation in cases involving children, including counseling and activities related to locating or evaluating appropriate community services for a client or a client's family.

    (ii) Lawyers should also take into account in determining fees the capacity of a client to pay the fee. The resources of parents who agree to pay for representation of their children in juvenile court proceedings may be considered if there is no adversity of interest as defined in Standard 3.2, *infra*, and if the parents understand that a lawyer's entire loyalty is to the child and that the parents have no control over the case. Where adversity of interests or desires between parent and child becomes apparent during the course of representation, a lawyer should be ready to reconsider the fee taking into account the child's resources alone.

(iii) As in all other cases of representation, it is unprofessional conduct for a lawyer to overreach the client or the client's parents in setting a fee, to imply that compensation is for anything other than professional services rendered by the lawyer or by others for him or her, to divide the fee with a layman, or to undertake representation in cases where no financial award may result on the understanding that payment of the fee is contingent in any way on the outcome of the case.

(iv) Lawyers employed in a legal and/or public defender office should be compensated on a basis equivalent to that paid other government attorneys of similar qualification, experience and responsibility.

(c) Supporting services.

Competent representation cannot be assured unless adequate supporting services are available. Representation in cases involving juveniles typically requires investigatory, expert and other nonlegal services. These should be available to lawyers and to their clients at all stages of juvenile and family court proceedings.

(i) Where lawyers are assigned, they should have regular access to all reasonably necessary supporting services.

(ii) Where a defender system is involved, adequate supporting services should be available within the organization itself.

(d) Independence.

Any plan for providing counsel to private parties in juvenile court proceedings must be designed to guarantee the professional independence of counsel and the integrity of the lawyer-client relationship.

2.2 Organization of services.

(a) In general.

Counsel should be provided in a systematic manner and in accordance with a widely publicized plan. Where possible, a coordinated plan for representation which combines defender and assigned counsel systems should be adopted.

(b) Defender systems.

(i) Application of general defender standards.

A defender system responsible for representation in some or all juvenile court proceedings generally should apply to staff and offices engaged in juvenile court matters its usual standards for selection, supervision, assignment and tenure of lawyers, restrictions on private practice, provision of facilities and other organizational procedures.

(ii) Facilities.

If local circumstances require, the defender system should maintain a separate office for juvenile court legal and supporting staff, located in a place convenient to the courts and equipped with adequate library, interviewing and other facilities. A supervising attorney experienced in juvenile court representation should be assigned to and responsible for the operation of that office.

(iii) Specialization.

While rotation of defender staff from one duty to another is an appropriate training device, there should be opportunity for staff to specialize in juvenile court representation to the extent local circumstances permit.

(iv) Caseload.

It is the responsibility of every defender office to ensure that its personnel can offer prompt, full and effective counseling and representation to each client. A defender office should not accept more assignments than its staff can adequately discharge.

(c) Assigned counsel systems.

(i) An assigned counsel plan should have available to it an adequate pool of competent attorneys experienced in juvenile court matters and an adequate plan for all necessary legal and supporting services.

(ii) Appointments through an assigned counsel system should be made, as nearly as possible, according to some rational and systematic sequence. Where the nature of the action or other circumstances require, a lawyer may be selected because of his or her other special qualifications to serve in the case, without regard to the established sequence.

2.3 Types of proceedings.

  (a) Delinquency and in need of supervision proceedings.

   (i) Counsel should be provided for any juvenile subject to delinquency or in need of supervision proceedings.

   (ii) Legal representation should also be provided the juvenile in all proceedings arising from or related to a delinquency or in need of supervision action, including mental competency, transfer, post-disposition, probation revocation, and classification, institutional transfer, disciplinary or other administrative proceedings related to the treatment process which may substantially affect the juvenile's custody, status or course of treatment. The nature of the forum and the formal classification of the proceedings is irrelevant for this purpose.

  (b) Child protective, custody and adoption proceedings.

  Counsel should be available to the respondent parents, including the father of an illegitimate child, or other guardian or legal custodian in a neglect or dependency proceeding. Independent counsel should also be provided for the juvenile who is the subject of proceedings affecting his or her status or custody. Counsel should be available at all stages of such proceedings and in all proceedings collateral to neglect and dependency matters, except where temporary emergency action is involved and immediate participation of counsel is not practicable.

French v. French, **452 So.2d 647, 651 (Fla. Dist. Ct. App. 1984). Concurring and dissenting judge urges that an independent advocate for the child be considered in domestic relations proceedings where the custody or interests of the child are involved. (Citing and quoting Standard 2.3)**

Department of Public Welfare v. J.K.B., **379 Mass. 1, 393 N.E.2d 406, 409 (1979). The interests of the state agency and of the parents may not necessarily coincide with those of the child. (Citing Standard 2.3(b))**

2.4 Stages of proceedings.

  (a) Initial provision of counsel.

   (i) When a juvenile is taken into custody, placed in detention or made subject to an intake process, the authorities taking such action have the responsibility promptly to notify the juvenile's lawyer, if there is one, or advise the juvenile with respect to the availability of legal counsel.

(ii) In administrative or judicial postdispositional proceedings which may affect the juvenile's custody, status or course of treatment, counsel should be available at the earliest stage of the decisional process, whether the respondent is present or not. Notification of counsel and, where necessary, provision of counsel in such proceedings is the responsibility of the judicial or administrative agency.

(b) Duration of representation and withdrawal of counsel.

(i) Lawyers initially retained or appointed should continue their representation through all stages of the proceedings, unless geographical or other compelling factors make continued participation impracticable.

(ii) Once appointed or retained, counsel should not request leave to withdraw unless compelled by serious illness or other incapacity, or unless contemporaneous or announced future conduct of the client is such as seriously to compromise the lawyer's professional integrity. Counsel should not seek to withdraw on the belief that the contentions of the client lack merit, but should present for consideration such points as the client desires to be raised provided counsel can do so without violating standards of professional ethics.

(iii) If leave to withdraw is granted, or if the client justifiably asks that counsel be replaced, successor counsel should be available.

PART III. THE LAWYER-CLIENT RELATIONSHIP

3.1 The nature of the relationship.

(a) Client's interests paramount.

However engaged, the lawyer's principal duty is the representation of the client's legitimate interests. Considerations of personal and professional advantage or convenience should not influence counsel's advice or performance.

(b) Determination of client's interests.

(i) Generally.

In general, determination of the client's interests in the proceedings, and hence the plea to be entered, is ultimately the responsibility of the client after full consultation with the attorney.

(ii) Counsel for the juvenile.

[a] Counsel for the respondent in a delinquency or in need of supervision proceeding should ordinarily be bound by the client's definition of his or her interests with respect to admission or denial of the facts or conditions alleged. It is appropriate and desirable for counsel to advise the client concerning the probable success and consequences of adopting any posture with respect to those proceedings.

[b] Where counsel is appointed to represent a juvenile subject to child protective proceedings, and the juvenile is capable of considered judgment on his or her own behalf, determination of the client's interest in the proceeding should ultimately remain the client's responsibility, after full consultation with counsel.

In re Lisa G., 127 N.H. 585, 504 A.2d 1, 4 (1986). The role of appointed counsel for a child in children in need of services (CHINS) cases is to advocate for the child and the child's position. (Citing Standard 3.1(b))

Marquez v. Presbyterian Hospital, 159 Misc. 2d, 608 N.Y.S.2d 1012, 1015 (S. Ct. Bronx Co. 1994). The adversarial role for the law guardian has predominated in child protection proceedings in New York, and in the routine case the client's decisions are binding on the lawyer. (Citing Standard 3.1(b)(ii)[b])

[c] In delinquency and in need of supervision proceedings where it is locally permissible to so adjudicate very young persons, and in child protective proceedings, the respondent may be incapable of considered judgment in his or her own behalf.

[1] Where a guardian ad litem has been appointed, primary responsibility for determination of the posture of the case rests with the guardian and the juvenile.

[2] Where a guardian ad litem has not been appointed, the attorney should ask that one be appointed.

[3] Where a guardian ad litem has not been appointed and, for some reason, it appears that independent advice to the juvenile will not otherwise be available, counsel should inquire thoroughly into all circumstances that a careful and competent person in the juvenile's position should consider in determining the juvenile's interests with respect to the proceeding. After consultation with the juvenile, the parents (where their interests do not

appear to conflict with the juvenile's) and any other family members or interested persons, the attorney may remain neutral concerning the proceeding, limiting participation to presentation and examination of material evidence or, if necessary, the attorney may adopt the position requiring the least intrusive intervention justified by the juvenile's circumstances.

(iii) Counsel for the parent.

It is appropriate and desirable for an attorney to consider all circumstances, including the apparent interests of the juvenile, when counseling and advising a parent who is charged in a child protective proceeding or who is seeking representation during a delinquency or in need of supervision proceeding. The posture to be adopted with respect to the facts and conditions alleged in the proceeding, however, remains ultimately the responsibility of the client.

In the Matter of Apel, **96 Misc. 2d 839, 409 N.Y.S.2d 928, 929 (Fam. Ct. Ulster Co. 1978). Although the role of the Law Guardian in delinquency proceedings is regarded generally as adversarial, the role is not so clear in child protective matters. (Citing Standards generally)**

3.2 Adversity of interests.

(a) Adversity of interests defined.

For purposes of these standards, adversity of interests exists when a lawyer or lawyers associated in practice:

   (i)   Formally represent more than one client in a proceeding and have a duty to contend in behalf of one client that which their duty to another requires them to oppose.

   (ii) Formally represent more than one client and it is their duty to contend in behalf of one client that which may prejudice the other client's interests at any point in the proceeding.

   (iii) Formally represent one client but are required by some third person or institution, including their employer, to accommodate their representation of that client to factors unrelated to the client's legitimate interests.

(b) Resolution of adversity.

At the earliest feasible opportunity, counsel should disclose to the client any interest in or connection with the case or any other matter that might be relevant to the client's selection of a lawyer. Counsel should at the same time seek to determine whether adversity of interests potentially exists and, if so, should immediately seek to withdraw from representation of the client who will be least prejudiced by such withdrawal.

3.3 Confidentiality.

(a) Establishment of confidential relationship.

Counsel should seek from the outset to establish a relationship of trust and confidence with the client. The lawyer should explain that full disclosure to counsel of all facts known to the client is necessary for effective representation and at the same time explain that the lawyer's obligation of confidentiality makes privileged the client's disclosures relating to the case.

(b) Preservation of client's confidences and secrets.

    (i)   Except as permitted by 3.3(d), below, an attorney should not knowingly reveal a confidence or secret of a client to another, including the parent of a juvenile client.

    (ii) Except as permitted by 3.3(d), below, an attorney should not knowingly use a confidence or secret of a client to the disadvantage of the client or, unless the attorney has secured the consent of the client after full disclosure, for the attorney's own advantage or that of a third person.

(c) Preservation of secrets of a juvenile client's parent or guardian.

The attorney should not reveal information gained from or concerning the parent or guardian of a juvenile client in the course of representation with respect to a delinquency or in need of supervision proceeding against the client, where (1) the parent or guardian has requested the information be held inviolate, or (2) disclosure of the information would likely be embarrassing or detrimental to the parent or guardian and (3) preservation would not conflict with the attorney's primary responsibility to the interests of the client.

    (i)   The attorney should not encourage secret communications when it is apparent that the parent or guardian believes those communications to be confidential or privileged and disclosure may become necessary to full and effective representation of the client.

    (ii) Except as permitted by 3.3(d), below, an attorney should not knowingly reveal the parent's secret communication to others or use a secret communication to the parent's disadvantage or to the advantage of the attorney or of a third person, unless (1) the parent competently consents to such revelation or use after full disclosure or (2) such disclosure or use is necessary to the discharge of the attorney's primary responsibility to the client.

(d) Disclosure of confidential communications.

In addition to circumstances specifically mentioned above, a lawyer may reveal:

(i) Confidences or secrets with the informed and competent consent of the client or clients affected, but only after full disclosure of all relevant circumstances to them. If the client is a juvenile incapable of considered judgment with respect to disclosure of a secret or confidence, a lawyer may reveal such communications if such disclosure (1) will not disadvantage the juvenile and (2) will further rendition of counseling, advice or other service to the client.

(ii) Confidences or secrets when permitted under disciplinary rules of the ABA *Code of Professional Responsibility* or as required by law or court order.

(iii) The intention of a client to commit a crime or an act which if done by an adult would constitute a crime, or acts that constitute neglect or abuse of a child, together with any information necessary to prevent such conduct. A lawyer must reveal such intention if the conduct would seriously endanger the life or safety of any person or corrupt the processes of the courts and the lawyer believes disclosure is necessary to prevent the harm. If feasible, the lawyer should first inform the client of the duty to make such revelation and seek to persuade the client to abandon the plan.

(iv) Confidences or secrets material to an action to collect a fee or to defend himself or herself or any employees or associates against an accusation of wrongful conduct.

3.4 Advice and service with respect to anticipated unlawful conduct.

It is unprofessional conduct for a lawyer to assist a client to engage in conduct the lawyer believes to be illegal or fraudulent, except as part of a bona fide effort to determine the validity, scope, meaning or application of a law.

3.5 Duty to keep client informed.

The lawyer has a duty to keep the client informed of the developments in the case, and of the lawyer's efforts and progress with respect to all phases of representation. This duty may extend, in the case of a juvenile client, to a parent or guardian whose interests are not adverse to the juvenile's, subject to the requirements of confidentiality set forth in 3.3, above.

PART IV. INITIAL STAGES OF REPRESENTATION

4.1 Prompt action to protect the client.

Many important rights of clients involved in juvenile court proceedings can be protected only by prompt advice and action. Lawyers should immediately inform clients of their rights and pursue any investigatory or procedural steps necessary to protection of their clients' interests.

4.2 Interviewing the client.

  (a) The lawyer should confer with a client without delay and as often as necessary to ascertain all relevant facts and matters of defense known to the client.
  (b) In interviewing a client, it is proper for the lawyer to question the credibility of the client's statements or those of any other witness. The lawyer may not, however, suggest expressly or by implication that the client or any other witness prepare or give, on oath or to the lawyer, a version of the facts which is in any respect untruthful, nor may the lawyer intimate that the client should be less than candid in revealing material facts to the attorney.

4.3 Investigation and preparation.

  (a) It is the duty of the lawyer to conduct a prompt investigation of the circumstances of the case and to explore all avenues leading to facts concerning responsibility for the acts or conditions alleged and social or legal dispositional alternatives. The investigation should always include efforts to secure information in the possession of prosecution, law enforcement, education, probation and social welfare authorities. The duty to investigate exists regardless of the client's admissions or statements of facts establishing responsibility for the alleged facts and conditions or of any stated desire by the client to admit responsibility for those acts and conditions.
  (b) Where circumstances appear to warrant it, the lawyer should also investigate resources and services available in the community and, if appropriate, recommend them to the client and the client's family. The lawyer's responsibility in this regard is independent

of the posture taken with respect to any proceeding in which the client is involved.

(c) It is unprofessional conduct for a lawyer to use illegal means to obtain evidence or information or to employ, instruct or encourage others to do so.

4.4 Relations with prospective witnesses.

The ethical and legal rules concerning counsel's relations with lay and expert witnesses generally govern lawyers engaged in juvenile court representation.

PART V. ADVISING AND COUNSELING THE CLIENT

5.1 Advising the client concerning the case.

(a) After counsel is fully informed on the facts and the law, he or she should with complete candor advise the client involved in juvenile court proceedings concerning all aspects of the case, including counsel's frank estimate of the probable outcome. It is unprofessional conduct for a lawyer intentionally to understate or overstate the risks, hazards or prospects of the case in order unduly or improperly to influence the client's determination of his or her posture in the matter.

(b) The lawyer should caution the client to avoid communication about the case with witnesses where such communication would constitute, apparently or in reality, improper activity. Where the right to jury trial exists and has been exercised, the lawyer should further caution the client with regard to communication with prospective or selected jurors.

5.2 Control and direction of the case.

(a) Certain decisions relating to the conduct of the case are in most cases ultimately for the client and others are ultimately for the lawyer. The client, after full consultation with counsel, is ordinarily responsible for determining:
   (i)   the plea to be entered at adjudication;
   (ii) whether to cooperate in consent judgment or early disposition plans;
   (iii) whether to be tried as a juvenile or an adult, where the client has that choice;
   (iv) whether to waive jury trial;
   (v)   whether to testify on his own behalf.

(b) Decisions concerning what witnesses to call, whether and how to conduct cross-examination, what jurors to accept and strike, what trial motions should be made, and any other strategic and tactical decisions not inconsistent with determinations ultimately the responsibility of and made by the client, are the exclusive province of the lawyer after full consultation with the client.

(c) If a disagreement on significant matters of tactics or strategy arises between the lawyer and the client, the lawyer should make a record of the circumstances, his or her advice and reasons, and the conclusion reached. This record should be made in a manner which protects the confidentiality of the lawyer-client relationship.

5.3 Counseling.

A lawyer engaged in juvenile court representation often has occasion to counsel the client and, in some cases, the client's family with respect to nonlegal matters. This responsibility is generally appropriate to the lawyer's role and should be discharged, as any other, to the best of the lawyer's training and ability.

PART VI. INTAKE, EARLY DISPOSITION AND DETENTION

6.1 Intake and early disposition, generally.

Whenever the nature and circumstances of the case permit, counsel should explore the possibility of an early diversion from the formal juvenile court process through subjudicial agencies and other community resources. Participation in pre- or nonjudicial stages of the juvenile court process may well be critical to such diversion, as well as to protection of the client's rights.

6.2 Intake hearings.

(a) In jurisdictions where intake hearings are held prior to reference of a juvenile court matter for judicial proceedings, the lawyer should be familiar with and explain to the client and, if the client is a minor, to the client's parents, the nature of the hearing, the procedures to be followed, the several dispositions available, and their probable consequences. The lawyer should further advise the client of his or her rights at the intake hearing, including the privilege against self-incrimination where appropriate, and of the use that may later be made of the client's statements.

(b) The lawyer should be prepared to make to the intake hearing officer arguments concerning the jurisdictional sufficiency of the allegations made and to present facts and circumstances relating to the occurrence of and the client's responsibility for the acts or conditions charged or to the necessity for official treatment of the matter.

6.3 Early disposition.

(a) When the client admits the acts or conditions alleged in the juvenile court proceeding and after investigation the lawyer is satisfied that the admission is factually supported and that the court would have jurisdiction to act, the lawyer should, with the client's consent, consider developing or cooperating in the development of a plan for informal or voluntary adjustment of the case.

(b) A lawyer should not participate in an admission of responsibility by the client for purposes of securing informal or early disposition when the client denies responsibility for the acts or conditions alleged.

6.4 Detention.

(a) If the client is detained or the client's child is held in shelter care, the lawyer should immediately consider all steps that may in good faith be taken to secure the child's release from custody.

(b) Where the intake department has initial responsibility for custodial decisions, the lawyer should promptly seek to discover the grounds for removal from the home and may present facts and arguments for release at the intake hearing or earlier. If a judicial detention hearing will be held, the attorney should be prepared, where circumstances warrant, to present facts and arguments relating to the jurisdictional sufficiency of the allegations, the appropriateness of the place of and criteria used for detention, and any noncompliance with procedures for referral to court or for detention. The attorney should also be prepared to present evidence with regard to the necessity for detention and a plan for pretrial release of the juvenile.

(c) The lawyer should not personally guarantee the attendance or behavior of the client or any other person, whether as surety on a bail bond or otherwise.

PART VII. ADJUDICATION

7.1 Adjudication without trial.

(a) Counsel may conclude, after full investigation and preparation, that under the evidence and the law, the charges involving the client will probably be sustained. Counsel should so advise the client and, if negotiated pleas are allowed under prevailing law, may seek the client's consent to engage in plea discussions with the prosecuting agency. Where the client denies guilt, the lawyer cannot properly participate in submitting a plea of involvement where the prevailing law requires that such a plea be supported by an admission of responsibility in fact.

(b) The lawyer should keep the client advised of all developments during plea discussions with the prosecuting agency and should communicate to the client all proposals made by the prosecuting agency. Where it appears that the client's participation in a psychiatric, medical, social, or other diagnostic or treatment regime would be significant in obtaining a desired result, the lawyer should so advise the client and, when circumstances warrant, seek the client's consent to participation in such a program.

7.2 Formality, in general.

While the traditional formality and procedure of criminal trials may not in every respect be necessary to the proper conduct of juvenile court proceedings, it is the lawyer's duty to make all motions, objections, or requests necessary to protection of the client's rights in such form and at such time as will best serve the client's legitimate interests at trial or on appeal.

7.3 Discovery and motion practice.

(a) Discovery.

(i) Counsel should promptly seek disclosure of any documents, exhibits, or other information potentially material to representation of clients in juvenile court proceedings. If such disclosure is not readily available through informal processes, counsel should diligently pursue formal methods of discovery including, where appropriate, the filing of motions for bills of particulars, for discovery and inspection of exhibits, documents and photographs, for production of statements by and evidence favorable to the respondent, for production of a list of witnesses, and for the taking of depositions.

    (ii) In seeking discovery, the lawyer may find that rules specifically applicable to juvenile court proceedings do not exist in a particular jurisdiction or that they improperly or unconstitutionally limit disclosure. In order to make possible adequate representation of the client, counsel should in such cases investigate the appropriateness and feasibility of employing discovery techniques available in criminal or civil proceedings in the jurisdiction.

(b) Other motions.

  Where the circumstances warrant, counsel should promptly make any motions material to the protection and vindication of the client's rights, such as motions to dismiss the petition, to suppress evidence, for mental examination, or appointment of an investigator or expert witness, for severance, or to disqualify a judge. Such motions should ordinarily be made in writing when that would be required for similar motions in civil or criminal proceedings in the jurisdiction. If a hearing on the motion is required, it should be scheduled at some time prior to the adjudication hearing if there is any likelihood that consolidation will work to the client's disadvantage.

7.4 Compliance with orders.

(a) Control of proceedings is principally the responsibility of the court, and the lawyer should comply promptly with all rules, orders, and decisions of the judge. Counsel has the right to make respectful requests for reconsideration of adverse rulings and has the duty to set forth on the record adverse rulings or judicial conduct which counsel considers prejudicial to the client's legitimate interests.

(b) The lawyer should be prepared to object to the introduction of any evidence damaging to the client's interests if counsel has any legitimate doubt concerning its admissibility under constitutional or local rules of evidence.

7.5 Relations with court and participants.

(a) The lawyer should at all times support the authority of the court by preserving professional decorum and by manifesting an attitude of professional respect toward the judge, opposing counsel, witnesses and jurors.

    (i) When court is in session, the lawyer should address the court and not the prosecutor directly on any matter relating to the case unless the person acting as prosecutor is giving evidence in the proceeding.

(ii) It is unprofessional conduct for a lawyer to engage in behavior or tactics purposely calculated to irritate or annoy the court, the prosecutor or probation department personnel.

(b) When in the company of clients or clients' parents, the attorney should maintain a professional demeanor in all associations with opposing counsel and with court or probation personnel.

7.6 Selection of and relations with jurors.

Where the right to jury trial is available and exercised in juvenile court proceedings, the standards set forth in sections 7.2 and 7.3 of the ABA *Standards Relating to the Defense Function* should generally be followed.

7.7 Presentation of evidence.

It is unprofessional conduct for a lawyer knowingly to offer false evidence or to bring inadmissible evidence to the attention of the trier of fact, to ask questions or display demonstrative evidence known to be improper or inadmissible, or intentionally to make impermissible comments or arguments in the presence of the trier of fact. When a jury is empaneled, if the lawyer has substantial doubt concerning the admissibility of evidence, he or she should tender it by an offer of proof and obtain a ruling on its admissibility prior to presentation.

7.8 Examination of witnesses.

(a) The lawyer in juvenile court proceedings should be prepared to examine fully any witness whose testimony is damaging to the client's interests. It is unprofessional conduct for counsel knowingly to forego or limit examination of a witness when it is obvious that failure to examine fully will prejudice the client's legitimate interests.

(b) The lawyer's knowledge that a witness is telling the truth does not preclude cross-examination in all circumstances but may affect the method and scope of cross-examination. Counsel should not misuse the power of cross-examination or impeachment by employing it to discredit the honesty or general character of a witness known to be testifying truthfully.

(c) The examination of all witnesses should be conducted fairly and with due regard for the dignity and, to the extent allowed by the circumstances of the case, the privacy of the witness. In general, and particularly when a youthful witness is testifying, the lawyer should avoid unnecessary intimidation or humiliation of the witness.

(d) A lawyer should not knowingly call as a witness one who will claim a valid privilege not to testify for the sole purpose of impressing that claim on the fact-finder. In some instances, as defined in the ABA *Code of Professional Responsibility*, doing so will constitute unprofessional conduct.

(e) It is unprofessional conduct to ask a question that implies the existence of a factual predicate which the examiner knows cannot be supported by evidence.

7.9 Testimony by the respondent.

(a) It is the lawyer's duty to protect the client's privilege against self-incrimination in juvenile court proceedings. When the client has elected not to testify, the lawyer should be alert to invoke the privilege and should insist on its recognition unless the client competently decides that invocation should not be continued.

(b) If the respondent has admitted to counsel facts which establish his or her responsibility for the acts or conditions alleged, and if the lawyer, after independent investigation, is satisfied that those admissions are true, and the respondent insists on exercising the right to testify at the adjudication hearing, the lawyer must advise the client against taking the stand to testify falsely and, if necessary, take appropriate steps to avoid lending aid to perjury.

  (i) If, before adjudication, the respondent insists on taking the stand to testify falsely, the lawyer must withdraw from the case if that is feasible and should seek the leave of the court to do so if necessary.

  (ii) If withdrawal from the case is not feasible or is not permitted by the court, or if the situation arises during adjudication without notice, it is unprofessional conduct for the lawyer to lend aid to perjury or use the perjured testimony. Before the respondent takes the stand in these circumstances, the lawyer should, if possible, make a record of the fact that respondent is taking the stand against the advice of counsel without revealing that fact to the court. Counsel's examination should be confined to identifying the witness as the respondent and permitting the witness to make his or her statement to the trier of fact. Counsel may not engage in direct examination of the respondent in the conventional manner and may not recite or rely on the false testimony in argument.

7.10 Argument.

The lawyer in juvenile court representation should comply with the rules generally governing argument in civil and criminal proceedings.

PART VIII. TRANSFER PROCEEDINGS

8.1 In general.

A proceeding to transfer a respondent from the jurisdiction of the juvenile court to a criminal court is a critical stage in both juvenile and criminal justice processes. Competent representation by counsel is essential to the protection of the juvenile's rights in such a proceeding.

8.2 Investigation and preparation.

(a) In any case where transfer is likely, counsel should seek to discover at the earliest opportunity whether transfer will be sought and, if so, the procedure and criteria according to which that determination will be made.

(b) The lawyer should promptly investigate all circumstances of the case bearing on the appropriateness of transfer and should seek disclosure of any reports or other evidence that will be submitted to or may be considered by the court in the course of transfer proceedings. Where circumstances warrant, counsel should promptly move for appointment of an investigator or expert witness to aid in the preparation of the defense and for any other order necessary to protection of the client's rights.

8.3 Advising and counseling the client concerning transfer.

Upon learning that transfer will be sought or may be elected, counsel should fully explain the nature of the proceeding and the consequences of transfer to the client and the client's parents. In so doing, counsel may further advise the client concerning participation in diagnostic and treatment programs which may provide information material to the transfer decision.

8.4 Transfer hearings.

If a transfer hearing is held, the rules set forth in Part VII of these standards shall generally apply to counsel's conduct of that hearing.

8.5 Posthearing remedies.

If transfer for criminal prosecution is ordered, the lawyer should act promptly to preserve an appeal from that order and should be prepared to make any appropriate motions for post-transfer relief.

PART IX. DISPOSITION

9.1 In general.

The active participation of counsel at disposition is often essential to protection of clients' rights and to furtherance of their legitimate interests. In many cases, the lawyer's most valuable service to clients will be rendered at this stage of the proceeding.

In re Manuel R., **207 Conn. 725, 543 A.2d 719, 727 (1988). Counsel for a juvenile "can perform a variety of useful functions during the dispositional phase of a delinquency proceeding. In particular, the child might be informed that a primary obligation of defense counsel is to augment and investigate the placement recommendations of the state so that the ultimate disposition is tailored to the child's individual needs." (citing Standards 9.1–9.5)**

State ex rel. D.D.H. v. Dostert, **165 W.Va. 448, 269 S.E.2d 401, 413 (1980). The defense counsel has an important role in the development of an appropriate disposition for a juvenile in a delinquency case. (Citing the** *Standards Relating to Juvenile [sic] Counsel for Private Parties* **generally)**

9.2 Investigation and preparation.

    (a) Counsel should be familiar with the dispositional alternatives available to the court, with its procedures and practices at the disposition stage, and with community services that might be useful in the formation of a dispositional plan appropriate to the client's circumstances.

    (b) The lawyer should promptly investigate all sources of evidence, including any reports or other information that will be brought to the court's attention, and interview all witnesses material to the disposition decision.

        (i) If access to social investigation, psychological, psychiatric or other reports or information is not provided voluntarily or promptly, counsel should be prepared to seek their disclosure and time to study them through formal measures.

        (ii) Whether or not social and other reports are readily available, the lawyer has a duty independently to investigate the client's circumstances, including such factors as previous history, family relations, economic condition, and any other information relevant to disposition.

(c) The lawyer should seek to secure the assistance of psychiatric, psychological, medical or other expert personnel needed for purposes of evaluation, consultation, or testimony with respect to formation of a dispositional plan.

9.3 Counseling prior to disposition.

(a) The lawyer should explain to the client the nature of the disposition hearing, the issues involved, and the alternatives open to the court. The lawyer should also explain fully and candidly the nature, obligations, and consequences of any proposed dispositional plan, including the meaning of conditions of probation, the characteristics of any institution to which commitment is possible, and the probable duration of the client's responsibilities under the proposed dispositional plan. Ordinarily, the lawyer should not make or agree to a specific dispositional recommendation without the client's consent.

(b) When psychological or psychiatric evaluations are ordered by the court or arranged by counsel prior to disposition, the lawyer should explain the nature of the procedure to the client and encourage the client's cooperation with the person or persons administering the diagnostic procedure.

(c) The lawyer must exercise discretion in revealing or discussing the contents of psychiatric, psychological, medical and social reports, tests or evaluations bearing on the client's history or condition or, if the client is a juvenile, the history or condition of the client's parents. In general, the lawyer should not disclose data or conclusions contained in such reports to the extent that, in the lawyer's judgment based on knowledge of the client and the client's family, revelation would be likely to affect adversely the client's well-being or relationships within the family and disclosure is not necessary to protect the client's interests in the proceeding.

9.4 Disposition hearing.

(a) It is the lawyer's duty to insist that proper procedure be followed throughout the disposition stage and that orders rendered be based on adequate reliable evidence.

   (i)   Where the dispositional hearing is not separate from adjudication or where the court does not have before it all evidence required by statute, rules of court or the circumstances of the case, the lawyer should seek a continuance until such evidence can be presented if to do so would serve the client's interests.

(ii) The lawyer at disposition should be free to examine fully and to impeach any witness whose evidence is damaging to the client's interests and to challenge the accuracy, credibility, and weight of any reports, written statements, or other evidence before the court. The lawyer should not knowingly limit or forego examination or contradiction by proof of any witness, including a social worker or probation department officer, when failure to examine fully will prejudice the client's interests. Counsel may seek to compel the presence of witnesses whose statements of fact or opinion are before the court or the production of other evidence on which conclusions of fact presented at disposition are based.

(b) The lawyer may, during disposition, ask that the client be excused during presentation of evidence when, in counsel's judgment, exposure to a particular item of evidence would adversely affect the well-being of the client or the client's relationship with his or her family, and the client's presence is not necessary to protecting his or her interests in the proceeding.

9.5 Counseling after disposition.

When a dispositional decision has been reached, it is the lawyer's duty to explain the nature, obligations, and consequences of the disposition to the client and his or her family, and to urge upon the client the need for accepting and cooperating with the dispositional order. If appeal from either the adjudicative or dispositional decree is contemplated, the client should be advised of that possibility, but the attorney must counsel compliance with the court's decision during the interim.

PART X. REPRESENTATION AFTER DISPOSITION

10.1 Relations with the client after disposition.

(a) The lawyer's responsibility to the client does not necessarily end with dismissal of the charges or entry of a final dispositional order. The attorney should be prepared to counsel and render or assist in securing appropriate legal services for the client in matters arising from the original proceeding.

    (i) If the client has been found to be within the juvenile court's jurisdiction, the lawyer should maintain contact with both the client and the agency or institution involved in the disposition plan in order to ensure that the client's rights are respected and, where necessary, to counsel the client and the client's family concerning the dispositional plan.

    (ii) Whether or not charges against the client have been dismissed, where the lawyer is aware that the client or the client's family needs and desires community or other medical, psychiatric, psychological, social or legal services, he or she should render all possible assistance in arranging for such services.

(b) The decision to pursue an available claim for postdispositional relief from judicial and correctional or other administrative determinations related to juvenile court proceedings, including appeal, habeas corpus, or an action to protect the client's right to treatment, is ordinarily the client's responsibility after full consultation with counsel.

10.2 Postdispositional hearings before the juvenile court.

(a) The lawyer who represents a client during initial juvenile court proceedings should ordinarily be prepared to represent the client with respect to proceedings to review or modify adjudicative or dispositional orders made during earlier hearings or to pursue any affirmative remedies that may be available to the client under local juvenile court law.

(b) The lawyer should advise the client of the pendency or availability of a postdispositional hearing or proceeding and of its nature, issues, and potential consequences. Counsel should urge and, if necessary, seek to facilitate the prompt attendance at any such hearing of the client and of any material witnesses who may be called.

10.3 Counsel on appeal.

(a) Trial counsel, whether retained or appointed by the court, should conduct the appeal unless new counsel is substituted by the client or by the appropriate court. Where there exists an adequate pool of competent counsel available for assignment to appeals from juvenile court orders and substitution will not work substantial disadvantage to the client's interests, new counsel may be appointed in place of trial counsel.

(b) Whether or not trial counsel expects to conduct the appeal, he or she should promptly inform the client, and where the client is a minor and the parents' interests are not adverse, the client's parents of the right to appeal and take all steps necessary to protect that right until appellate counsel is substituted or the client decides not to exercise this privilege.

(c) Counsel on appeal, after reviewing the record below and undertaking any other appropriate investigation, should candidly inform the client as to whether there are meritorious grounds for appeal and the probable results of any such appeal and should further explain the potential advantages and disadvantages associated with appeal. However, appellate counsel should not seek to withdraw from a case solely because his or her own analysis indicates that the appeal lacks merit.

10.4 Conduct of the appeal.

The rules generally governing conduct of appeals in criminal and civil cases govern conduct of appeals in juvenile court matters.

10.5 Postdispositional remedies: protection of the client's right to treatment.

(a) A lawyer who has represented a client through trial and/or appellate proceedings should be prepared to continue representation when postdispositional action, whether affirmative or defensive, is sought, unless new counsel is appointed at the request of the client or continued representation would, because of geographical considerations or other factors, work unreasonable hardship.

(b) Counsel representing a client in postdispositional matters should promptly undertake any factual or legal investigation in order to determine whether grounds exist for relief from juvenile court or administrative action. If there is reasonable prospect of a favorable result, the lawyer should advise the client, and if their interests are not adverse, the client's parents of the nature, consequences, probable outcome, and advantages or disadvantages associated with such proceedings.

(c) The lawyer engaged in postdispositional representation should conduct those proceedings according to the principles generally governing representation in juvenile court matters.

10.6 Probation revocation; parole revocation.

(a) Trial counsel should be prepared to continue representation if revocation of the client's probation or parole is sought, unless new counsel is appointed or continued representation would, because of geographical or other factors, work unreasonable hardship.

(b) Where proceedings to revoke conditional liberty are conducted in substantially the same manner as original petitions alleging delinquency or need for supervision, the standards governing representation in juvenile court generally apply. Where special procedures are used in such matters, counsel should advise the client concerning those procedures and be prepared actively to participate in the revocation proceedings at the earliest stage.

10.7 Challenges to the effectiveness of counsel.

(a) A lawyer appointed or retained to represent a client previously represented by other counsel has a good faith duty to examine prior counsel's actions and strategy. If, after investigation, the new attorney is satisfied that prior counsel did not provide effective assistance, the client should be so advised and any appropriate relief for the client on that ground should be vigorously pursued.

(b) A lawyer whose conduct of a juvenile court case is drawn into question may testify in judicial, administrative, or investigatory proceedings concerning the matters charged, even though in so doing the lawyer must reveal information which was given by the client in confidence.

STANDARDS RELATING TO COURT ORGANIZATION AND ADMINISTRATION

Ted Rubin, Reporter

PART I: ORGANIZATIONAL STRUCTURE OF COURTS OF JUVENILE JURISDICTION

1.1 Organizational structure: general principles.

The traditional juvenile court jurisdiction should be included in a family court division of the highest court of general trial jurisdiction.

A. The exclusive original jurisdiction of this division should encompass: juvenile law violations; cases of abuse and neglect; cases involving the need for emergency medical treatment; voluntary and involuntary termination of parental rights proceedings; adoption proceedings; appointment of legal guardians for juveniles; proceedings under interstate compacts on juveniles and on the placement of juveniles; intrafamily criminal offenses; proceedings in regard to divorce, separation, annulment, alimony, custody, and support of juveniles; proceedings to establish paternity and to enforce support; and proceedings under the Uniform Reciprocal Enforcement of Support Act. Mental illness and retardation commitment proceedings concerning juveniles and adults should be governed by the law of the jurisdiction applicable to such proceedings for nonadjudicated persons.

B. Calendaring methods should follow the general principle that the same judge should consider the different legal issues that relate to all members of the same family. Further, the judge who presides at an adjudicatory hearing should conduct the disposition hearing of the case.

C. General intake procedures to determine the need for formal judicial consideration of juvenile delinquency referrals should be adapted and applied to the different types of cases within the jurisdiction of the family court division.

D. The court should encourage probation and social service agencies working with court clientele to maximize single staff member responsibility for an entire family.

1.2 Juvenile intake, probation, and detention services.

The [juvenile intake function, juvenile probation services,] and juvenile detention programs should be administered by the executive branch of government.

PART II: JUDICIAL AND CHIEF ADMINISTRATIVE PERSONNEL PERFORMING COURT FUNCTIONS

2.1 Judges.

Judges of the family court division should be assigned from among the judges of the highest court of general trial jurisdiction. Their assignment to the family court division should be:

A. by appointment of the presiding judge of the highest court of general trial jurisdiction;

B. with special consideration given to the aptitude, demonstrated interest, and experience of each judge;

C. [on a modified rotation system], with indefinite tenure discouraged;

D. if at all practical, on a full-time basis; and

E. accompanied by the supporting personnel, equipment, and facilities necessary for effective functioning.

2.2 Referees; judicial officers.

Only judges should perform judicial case decision-making functions.

2.3 Court administrator.

A. Each family court division with [four] or more judges (and, where justified by caseload, in divisions with fewer judges) should have a full-time court administrator. This official should be an assistant to the general trial court administrator. The division administrator should be appointed by the general trial court administrator with the concurrence of the presiding judge of the general trial court but should function under the supervision of the presiding judge of the family court division.

B. In less populous jurisdictions, the general trial court administrator should direct the staff members of the family court division.

PART III: COURT FUNCTIONS

3.1 Rule making.

The family court division should operate under formally adopted:

A. rules of procedure;

B. rules of administration; and

C. guidelines.

3.2 Case decision making.

A judge should render all judicial decisions on cases before the court. No judicial proceedings should be heard by nonjudicial personnel. Adjudicatory proceedings should be conducted in a formal manner. The monitoring of its orders is an essential function of the family court division. Provision should be made for party-initiated and agency-initiated review of court orders.

In the Interest of J.A., 138 Wis. 2d 483, 406 N.W.2d 372, 379 (1987). The juvenile or family court judge should play a role in urging the improvement of agency services to children within the court's jurisdiction, although the use of administrative channels may be preferable to the use of *sua sponte* orders.

3.3 Case processing time standards.

Time standards for judicial hearing of juvenile cases should be promulgated and monitored. These should include:
  A. detention and shelter hearings: not more than twenty-four hours following admission to any detention or shelter facility;
  B. adjudicatory or transfer (waiver) hearings:
    1. concerning a juvenile in a detention or shelter facility: not later than fifteen days following admission to such facility;
    2. concerning a juvenile who is not in a detention or shelter facility: not later than thirty days following the filing of the petition;
  C. disposition hearings: not later than fifteen days following the adjudicatory hearing.

The court may grant additional time in exceptional cases that require more complex evaluation.

3.4 Management responsibilities.

Under the supervision of the presiding judge of the family court division, the court administrator should administer or perform the following functions:
  A. case flow management;
  B. budget and fiscal control;
  C. records management;
  D. implementing legal procedures;
  E. personnel systems management;
  F. space facilities, equipment, and library materials;

G. management information system;
H. training program coordination;
I. planning and development;
J. jury management;
K. procurement of supplies and services;
L. monitoring and liaison responsibility with probation, detention, and social service agencies;

In the Interest of J.A., 138 Wis. 2d 483, 406 N.W.2d 372, 379 (1987). See discussion in Standard 3.2 above.

M. public information; and
N. secretariat for meetings of division judges.

3.5 Community relations function.

A. The family court division should develop and implement a program of community relations and public information to include:
   1. regular written and oral public presentations of data and experience concerning the functions, progress, and problems of the court and the juvenile justice system;
   2. advocacy for law reform and improved agency services and facilities;

In the Interest of J.A., 138 Wis. 2d 372, 406 N.W.2d 372 (1987). See the discussion in Standard 3.2 above.

   3. development of close working relationships with community agencies serving court clientele;
   4. leadership in effectuating a juvenile justice council composed of representatives of key juvenile justice agencies.
B. A representative family court division citizens' advisory committee should be appointed by the presiding judge of the general trial court. The advisory committee should advise, critique, and assist the division in achieving a more effective family court.

PART IV: RESPONSIBILITY OF THE FAMILY COURT DIVISION TO EFFECTUATE ITS DUTIES AND ORDERS

4.1 General principles.

The family court division should have available those personnel, facilities, and services necessary for the effective discharge of its responsibilities. The doctrine of inherent powers should be employed only when the court can show all of the following:

A. all possible approaches to obtain the necessary resource have been tried and have failed;

B. the expense in question is a necessary as opposed to a desirable expense; and

C. failure to obtain this resource would render the court unable to fulfill its legal duties.

STANDARDS RELATING TO DISPOSITIONAL PROCEDURES

Fred Cohen, Reporter

PART I: DISPOSITIONAL AUTHORITY

1.1 Authority vested in judge.

Authority to determine and impose the appropriate disposition should be vested in the juvenile court judge.

PART II: DISPOSITIONAL INFORMATION

2.1 General principles.

  A. Information that is relevant and material to disposition may be obtained by persons acting on behalf of the juvenile court only after an adjudication, with the exceptions noted hereafter.
  B. The sources for dispositional information and the techniques for gathering such information are subject to legal standards, as provided in Standards 2.2 and 2.3.
  C. The information required for the imposition of an appropriate disposition should be directly related to the stated objectives for the selection and imposition of available dispositional alternatives and the nature and quantum of discretion vested in the judge.
  D. It should not be assumed that more information is also better information, or that the accumulation of dispositional information, particularly of the subjective and evaluative type, is necessarily an aid to decision making.
  E. Dispositional information should be subject to rules governing admissibility and burdens of persuasion as provided in Standard 2.5.
  F. Information relating to disposition should be broadly shared among the parties to the proceeding and any individual or agency officially designated as appropriate for the custody or care of the juvenile, as provided in Standard 2.4.
  G. Any such information should not be considered a public record.

2.2 Obtaining information.

  A. No investigation for dispositional purposes should be undertaken by representatives of the state, nor any additional information of record gathered, until it has been determined that the juvenile has engaged in the conduct alleged in the charging instrument, unless the juvenile and the juvenile's attorney consent in writing to an earlier undertaking.

B. Information in the form of oral or written statements relevant to disposition may be obtained from the juvenile, subject to the following limitations:

1. The statement should be voluntary as determined by the totality of circumstances surrounding the questioning, and the juvenile should have full knowledge of the possible adverse dispositional consequences that may ensue.

2. In determining voluntariness, special consideration should be given to the susceptibility of the juvenile to any coercion, exhortations, or inducements which may have been used.

3. The juvenile should be afforded the right to consult with and be advised by counsel prior to any questioning by a representative of the state when such questioning is designed to elicit dispositional information.

4. It should clearly appear of record that the juvenile was advised that the information solicited may be used in a dispositional proceeding and that it may result in adverse dispositional consequences.

2.3 Information base.

A. The information essential to a disposition should consist of the juvenile's age; the nature and circumstances of the offense or offenses upon which the underlying adjudication is based, such information not being limited to that which was or may be introduced at the adjudication; and any prior record of adjudicated delinquency and disposition thereof.

B. Information concerning the social situation or the personal characteristics of the juvenile, including the results of psychological testing, psychiatric evaluations, and intelligence testing, may be considered as relevant to a disposition.

C. The social history may include information concerning the family and home situation; school records, in accordance with the *Juvenile Records and Information Systems* volume; any prior contacts with social agencies; and other similar items. The social history report should be in writing and should indicate clearly the sources of the information, the number of contacts made with such sources, and the total time expended on investigation and preparation.

D. When the state seeks to obtain and utilize information concerning the personal characteristics of the juvenile, such information should first be sought without resort to any form of confinement or institutionalization.

   1. In the unusual case, where some form of confinement or institutionalization is represented by the state as being a necessary condition for obtaining this information, and the juvenile or his or her attorney objects, the court should conduct a hearing on the issue and determine whether the proposed confinement is necessary.

   2. At such hearing the juvenile prosecutor should set forth the reasons for considering the information relevant to the dispositional decision. The juvenile prosecutor should also indicate what nonconfining alternatives were explored and demonstrate their inefficacy or unavailability. An order for examination and confinement under this standard should be limited to a maximum of thirty days, and should specify the nature and objectives of the examinations to be undertaken, as well as the place where such examinations are to be conducted.

In the Matter of Vinson, **298 N.C. 640, 260 S.E.2d 591, 607–08 (1979). Juvenile courts in dispositional hearings should consider a "broad spectrum of information" helpful to making an appropriate disposition. (Citing Standard 2.3)**

2.4 Sharing information.

A. No dispositional decision should be made on the basis of a fact or opinion that is not disclosed to the attorney for the juvenile. Should there be a compelling reason for nondisclosure to the juvenile, as for example when the names of prospective adoptive parents appear, the court may advise the attorney for the juvenile not to disclose.

B. The information that may be developed in accordance with Part II should be shared sufficiently prior to any predisposition conference which may be held, and sufficiently prior to the disposition hearing to allow for independent investigation, verification, and the development of rebuttal information.

C. The right of access to dispositional information creates a professional obligation that counsel for the juvenile avail himself or herself of the opportunity.

D. The juvenile prosecutor has a right to disclosure of dispositional information coextensive with that of the attorney for the juvenile.

2.5 Rules of evidence.

A. Dispositional information should be relevant and material.

State v. Wright, 456 N.W.2d 661, 663 (Iowa 1991). A waiver or transfer hearing is comparable to a dispositional hearing and evidence need only be relevant and material. (Citing Standard 2.5)

People v. Williams, 111 Mich. App. 818, 314 N.W.2d 769 (1982). Waiver proceedings are like dispositional hearings with respect to evidentiary questions and evidence need only be relevant and material. (Citing Standard 2.5 A)

In the Matter of the Welfare of T.D.S., 289 N.W.2d 137, 140 (Minn. 1980). Reliable hearsay testimony is admissible at a reference to adult court proceeding because it is like a dispositional hearing and the evidence need only be relevant and material. (Citing Standard 2.5)

B. When a more severe dispositional alternative is selected in preference to a less severe one, the selection of such alternative should be supported by a preponderance of the evidence.

In the Matter of J.H., 758 P.2d 1287 (Alaska 1988). A party seeking a restrictive disposition must establish by a preponderance of the evidence that it is "the least restrictive alternative appropriate to the needs of the juvenile and the protection of the community" pursuant to Alaska delinquency Rule 11(e). (Citing Standard 2.5 B, and the commentary thereto)

PART III: PARTIES PRESENT

3.1 Necessary and allowable parties.

The juvenile, the attorney for the juvenile, the juvenile's parents or guardian or their attorney, and the juvenile prosecutor should be present at all stages of the disposition proceeding. Other parties with a bona fide interest in the proceedings may be present at the discretion of the court.

3.2 Summons.

The parents or guardian may be summoned to appear. Should the parents or guardian fail to appear after notice, or if reasonable efforts to locate and produce them fail, then the proceedings may be conducted but the court should determine whether or not the interests of the child require the appointment of a guardian *ad litem.*

PART IV: CUSTODY AWAITING DISPOSITION

4.1 Custody or release.

Decisions concerning the custody or release of juvenile offenders after adjudication and prior to final disposition should be governed by the standards in the *Interim Status* volume.

PART V: PREDISPOSITION CONFERENCE AND DISPOSITION AGREEMENTS: EXPERIMENTATION SUGGESTED

5.1 Predisposition conferences.

Jurisdictions concerned with the administration of juvenile justice are encouraged to experiment with various forms of predisposition conferences. Such conferences should follow the formal adjudication and precede any formal dispositional hearing.

5.2 Objectives.

Such conferences may be designed to achieve all or some of the following objectives:
  A. The identification of dispositional facts that may be at issue;
  B. The determination of whether any controversy on dispositional facts will require the production of evidence;
  C. The determination of whether any person who has prepared a written report or provided significant information to one who has prepared such a report will be called to testify at the disposition hearing; and
  D. To present and discuss dispositional alternatives and, wherever possible, to arrive at an agreed upon disposition.

5.3 Written agreements and judicial approval.

If the parties arrive at a disposition agreement, such agreement should be reduced to writing and provide for review and final approval by the judge who has ultimate dispositional authority.

5.4 Adoption of rules; evaluation.
  A. Jurisdictions that experiment with such conferences should provide administrative rules to govern such details as place, time,

who shall be present, who shall conduct the conference, whether a record should be kept, and any limitations or guidelines that should apply concerning the agreed upon disposition.

B. A jurisdiction that adopts a comprehensive program for predisposition conferences should consider the incorporation of an evaluation component designed to test such matters as costs, efficiency, patterns of agreement and disagreement, the juvenile's sense of justice concerning such proceedings, and similar items.

PART VI: FORMAL DISPOSITION HEARING

6.1 Prerequisites.

A. If a predisposition conference results in a dispositional agreement, the agreement should be introduced in writing in open court and approved by the judge, as required in Standard 5.3.
B. If a predisposition conference held in accordance with Part V does not result in an agreed upon disposition, or if the judge disagrees with such disposition in any material respect, a formal dispositional hearing should be conducted, with a full record made and preserved.
C. The court should provide written notice to the parties concerning the date, time, and place for such hearing, sufficiently in advance of the hearing to allow adequate time for preparation.

In the Matter of Vinson, 298 N.C. 640, 260 S.E.2d 591, 607–08 (1979). Juveniles should be afforded a formal disposition hearing with written notice and adequate time for preparation. (Citing Standard 6.1)

6.2 Compulsory process.

The parties should be entitled to compulsory process for the appearance of any persons, including character witnesses and persons who have prepared any report to be utilized at the hearing, to testify at the hearing.

6.3 Conduct of the hearing.

As soon as practicable after the adjudication and any predisposition conference that may be held, a full disposition hearing should be conducted at which the judge should:

A. be advised as to any stipulations or disagreements concerning dispositional facts;
B. allow the juvenile prosecutor and the attorney for the juvenile to

present evidence, in the form of written presentations or by witnesses, concerning the appropriate disposition;

C. afford the juvenile and the juvenile's parents or legal guardian an opportunity to address the court:

State v. Ricky G., **110 N.M. 596, 798 P.2d 596, 598–99 (1990). The child should be given the opportunity to address the court during the disposition hearing as the youth's views may be relevant and material and such participation may have rehabilitative value. (Citing Standard 6.3 C)**

D. hear argument by the attorney for the juvenile and the juvenile prosecutor concerning the appropriate disposition;

E. allow both attorneys to question any documents and cross-examine any witnesses;

F. allow both attorneys to examine any person who prepares any report concerning the juvenile, unless the attorney expressly waives that right.

PART VII: IMPOSITION AND CORRECTION OF DISPOSITION

7.1 Findings and formal requisites.

A. The judge should determine the appropriate disposition as expeditiously as possible after the dispositional hearing, and when the disposition is imposed;

State v. Cody R., **113 N.M. 140, 823 P.2d 940, 942 (1991). The determination of an appropriate disposition is vested in the sound discretion of the children's court judge. (Citing Standard 7.1)**

1. make specific findings on all controverted issues of fact and on the weight attached to all significant dispositional facts in arriving at the disposition decision;

2. state for the record, in the presence of the juvenile, the reasons for selecting the particular disposition and the objective or objectives desired to be achieved thereby;

In re John H., **21 Cal. 3d 18, 145 Cal. Rptr. 357, 577 P.2d 177, 182 (1978). A judge should indicate for the record the reasons for removing a juvenile from his home and committing him to the California Youth Authority. Concurring justices opinions. (Citing Standard 7.1)**

Glenda Kay S. v. State, **103 Nev. 53, 732 P.2d 1356, 1360 (1987). In all cases where the disposition includes commitment to a training center** or comparable institution, "the judge of the juvenile division must state on the record, in the presence of the juvenile, the reasons for selecting such a disposition and must state in particular why the disposition serves the welfare of the child or the interests of the state, or both." (Citing Standard 7.1 A).

    3. when the disposition involves any deprivation of liberty or any form of coercion, indicate for the record those alternative dispositions, including particular places and programs, that were explored and the reason for their rejection;

In the Matter of J.H., 758 P.2d 1287 (Alaska 1988). A party seeking a restrictive disposition must establish by a preponderance of the evidence that it is "the least restrictive alternative appropriate to the needs of the juvenile and the protection of the community" pursuant to Alaska delinquency Rule 11(e). (Citing Standard 7.1 A.3.)

In the Matter of Vinson, 298 N.C. 640, 260 S.E.2d 591, 607–08 (1979). Although more formal fact-finding by judges in juvenile commitments would be helpful for appellate review, the fact-finding order need not be as detailed as advocated in Standard 7.1.

    4. state with particularity the precise terms of the disposition that is imposed, including credit for any time previously spent in custody; and,

    5. advise the juvenile and the juvenile's attorney of the right to appeal and of the procedure to be followed if the appellant is unable to pay the cost of an appeal.

  B. The court may correct an illegal disposition at any time and may correct a disposition imposed in an illegal manner within [120 days] of the imposition of the disposition.[1]

---

1. Commission member Justine Wise Polier regards this provision for correcting dispositions as too narrow. She does not believe it should be limited to illegal dispositions but should embrace the requirement to review dispositions when the child, the parents, or the agency having custody of the child requests review by reason of a change of circumstance or evidence that the child is ready for a less restrictive placement.

STANDARDS RELATING TO DISPOSITIONS

Linda R. Singer, Reporter

PART I: GENERAL PURPOSES AND LIMITATIONS

1.1 Purpose.

The purpose of the juvenile correctional system is to reduce juvenile crime by maintaining the integrity of the substantive law proscribing certain behavior and by developing individual responsibility for lawful behavior. This purpose should be pursued through means that are fair and just, that recognize the unique characteristics and needs of juveniles, and that give juveniles access to opportunities for personal and social growth.

Glenda Kay S. v. State, 103 Nev. 53, 732 P.2d 1356, 1359 (1987). "The state's interest and purpose in enacting laws relating to juvenile delinquency is well put" in Standard 1.1 of the *Standards Relating to Dispositions.*

1.2 Coercive dispositions: definition and requirements.

A disposition is coercive when it limits the freedom of action of the adjudicated juvenile in any way that is distinguishable from that of a nonadjudicated juvenile and when the failure or refusal to comply with the disposition may result in further enforcement action.

The imposition of any coercive disposition by the state imposes the obligation to act with fairness and to avoid arbitrariness. This obligation includes the following requirements:

A. Adjudicated violation of substantive law.

No coercive disposition may be imposed unless there has been an adjudicated violation of the substantive law.

B. Specification of disposition by statute.

No coercive disposition may be imposed unless pursuant to a statute that prescribes the particular disposition with reasonable specificity.

C. Procedural regularity and fairness.

The imposition and implementation of all coercive dispositions should conform to standards governing procedural regularity and fairness.

D. Information concerning obligations.

Juveniles should be given adequate information concerning the obligations imposed on them by all coercive dispositions and the consequences of failure to meet such obligations. Such information should be given in the language primarily spoken by the juvenile.

E. Legislatively determined maximum dispositions.

The maximum severity and duration of all coercive dispositions should be determined by the legislature, which should limit them according to the seriousness of the offense for which the juvenile has been adjudicated.

F. Judicially determined dispositions.

The nature and duration of all coercive dispositions should be determined by the court at the time of sentencing, within the limitations established by the legislature.

G. Availability of resources.

No coercive disposition should be imposed unless the resources necessary to carry out the disposition are shown to exist. If services required as part of a disposition are not available, an alternative disposition no more severe should be employed.

H. Physical safety.

No coercive disposition should subject the juvenile to unreasonable risk of physical harm.

I.   Prohibition of collateral disabilities.

No collateral disabilities extending beyond the term of the disposition should be imposed by the court, by operation of law, or by any person or agency exercising authority over the juvenile.

PART II: DISPOSITIONAL CRITERIA

2.1 Least restrictive alternative.

In choosing among statutorily permissible dispositions, the court should employ the least restrictive category and duration of disposition that is appropriate to the seriousness of the offense, as modified by the degree of culpability indicated by the circumstances of the particular case, and by the age and prior record of the juvenile. The imposition of a particular disposition should be accompanied by a statement of the facts relied on in support of the disposition and the reasons for selecting the disposition and rejecting less restrictive alternatives.

In the Matter of J.H., **758 P.2d 1287, 1291 (Alaska App. 1988). Since the statute setting forth the various alternative dispositions gives no guidance among the options, the court has articulated the "least restrictive alternative" endorsed by Standard 2.1.**

R.P. v. State, 718 P.2d 168, 169–70 (Alaska App. 1988). The juvenile court "must consider and reject less restrictive alternatives *prior* to imposition of more restrictive alternatives." Also, the state has the burden of proving that less restrictive options are inappropriate. The court must enter specific written findings why the less restrictive alternatives were rejected. (Citing Standard 2.1)

State v. DeLong, 456 A.2d 877, 886 (1983). The court should have imposed a less restrictive disposition than sentencing this fifteen-year-old sexual abuse victim to seven days in jail for refusing to testify in her adoptive father's criminal trial according to the dissenting justice. (Citing Standard 2.1)

In the Matter of the Welfare of L.K.W., 372 N.W.2d 392, 398 (Minn. Ct. App. 1985). There is "a preference for the least restrictive action consistent with the child's problem" in making a delinquency disposition. (Citing Standard 2.1)

2.2 Needs and desires of the juvenile.

Once the category and duration of the disposition have been determined, the choice of a particular program within the category should include consideration of the needs and desires of the juvenile.

PART III: DISPOSITIONS

3.1 Nominal: reprimand and release.

The court may reprimand the juvenile for the unlawful conduct, warn against future offenses, and release him or her unconditionally.

In the Matter of C.S. McP., 514 A.2d 446, 449 (D.C. Ct. App. 1986). The most lenient, specific nominal disposition in the Standards "does not explicitly authorize dismissal." (Citing Standard 3.1 among others)

3.2 Conditional.

The court may sentence the juvenile to comply with one or more conditions, which are specified below, none of which involves removal from the juvenile's home. Such conditions should not interfere with the juvenile's schooling, regular employment, or other activities necessary for normal growth and development.

A. Suspended sentence.

The court may suspend imposition or execution of a more severe, statutorily permissible sentence with the provision that the juvenile meet certain conditions agreed to by him or her and specified in the sentencing order. Such conditions should not exceed, in severity or duration, the maximum sanction permissible for the offense.

B. Financial.
1. Restitution.
   a. Restitution should be directly related to the juvenile's offense, the actual harm caused, and the juvenile's ability to pay.
   b. The means to carry out a restitution order should be available.
   c. Either full or partial restitution may be ordered.
   d. Repayment may be required in a lump sum or in installments.
   e. Consultation with victims may be encouraged but not required. Payments may be made directly to victims, or indirectly, through the court.
   f. The juvenile's duty of repayment should be limited in duration; in no event should the time necessary for repayment exceed the maximum term permissible for the offense.
2.. Fine.
   a. Imposition of a fine is most appropriate in cases where the juvenile has derived monetary gain from the offense.
   b. The amount of the fine should be directly related to the seriousness of the juvenile's offense and the juvenile's ability to pay.
   c. Payment of a fine may be required in a lump sum or installments.
   d. Imposition of a restitution order is preferable to imposition of a fine.
   e. The juvenile's duty of payment should be limited in duration; in no event should the time necessary for payment exceed the maximum term permissible for the offense.
3. Community service.
   a. In sentencing a juvenile to perform community service, the judge should specify the nature of the work and the number of hours required.
   b. The amount of work required should be related to the seriousness of the juvenile's offense.
   c. The juvenile's duty to perform community service should be limited in duration; in no event should the duty to work exceed the maximum term permissible for the offense.

C. Supervisory.

1. Community supervision.

The court may sentence the juvenile to a program of community supervision, requiring him or her to report at specified intervals to a probation officer or other designated individual and to comply with any other reasonable conditions that are designed to facilitate supervision and are specified in the sentencing order.

2. Day custody.

The court may sentence the juvenile to a program of day custody, requiring him or her to be present at a specified place for all or part of every day or of certain days. The court also may require the juvenile to comply with any other reasonable conditions that are designed to facilitate supervision and are specified in the sentencing order.

D. Remedial.

1. Remedial programs.

The court may sentence the juvenile to a community program of academic or vocational education or counseling, requiring him or her to attend sessions designed to afford access to opportunities for normal growth and development. The duration of such programs should not exceed the maximum term permissible for the offense.

2. Prohibition of coercive imposition of certain programs.

This standard does not permit the coercive imposition of any program that may have harmful effects. Any such program should comply with the requirements of Standard 4.3 concerning informed consent.

3.3 Custodial.

A. Custodial disposition defined.

A custodial disposition is one in which a juvenile is removed coercively from his or her home.

B. Presumption against custodial dispositions.

There should be a presumption against coercively removing a juvenile from his or her home, and this category of sanction should be reserved for the most serious or repetitive offenses. It should not be used as a substitute for a judicial finding of neglect, which should conform to the standards in the *Abuse and Neglect* volume.

R.P. v. State, **718 P.2d 168, 169–70 (Alaska App. 1986). The juvenile court must consider more than the seriousness of the offense in making a dispositional decision, and there is "a presumption against co-**

ercively removing a child from his or her home in all but extreme cases." (Citing Standard 3.3)

   C. Exclusiveness of custodial dispositions.

    A custodial disposition is an exclusive sanction and should not be used simultaneously with other sanctions. However, this does not prevent the imposition of a custodial disposition for a specified period of time to be followed by a conditional disposition for a specified period of time, provided that the total duration of the disposition does not exceed the maximum term of a custodial disposition permissible for the offense.

   D. Continuous and intermittent confinement.

    Custodial confinement may be imposed on a continuous or an intermittent basis, not to exceed the maximum term permissible for the offense. Intermittent confinement includes:

    1. night custody;

    2. weekend custody.

   E. Levels of custody.

    Levels of custody include nonsecure residences and secure facilities.

    1. Nonsecure residences.

      No court should sentence a juvenile to reside in a nonsecure residence unless the juvenile is at least ten years old and unless the court finds that any less severe disposition would be grossly inadequate to the needs of the juvenile and that such needs can be met by placing the juvenile in a particular nonsecure residence.

    2. Secure facilities.

      a. A juvenile may be sentenced to a period of confinement in a secure facility; such a disposition, however, should be a last resort, reserved only for the most serious or repetitive offenses.

      b. No court should sentence a juvenile to confinement in a secure facility unless the juvenile is at least twelve years old and unless the court finds that such confinement is necessary to prevent the juvenile from causing injury to the personal or substantial property interests of another.

      c. Secure facilities should be coeducational, located near population centers as close as possible to the juvenile's home, and limited in population.

PART IV: PROVISION OF SERVICES

4.1 Right to services.

All publicly funded services to which nonadjudicated juveniles have access should be made available to adjudicated delinquents. In addition, juveniles adjudicated delinquent should have access to all services necessary for their normal growth and development.

A. Obligations of correctional agencies.

Correctional agencies have an affirmative obligation to ensure that juveniles under their supervision obtain all services to which they are entitled.

B. Purchase of services.

Services may be provided directly by correctional agencies or obtained, by purchase or otherwise, from other public or private agencies. Whichever method is employed, agencies providing services should set standards governing the provision of services and establish monitoring procedures to ensure compliance with such standards.

C. Prohibition against increased dispositions.

Neither the severity nor the duration of a disposition should be increased in order to ensure access to services.

D. Obligation of correctional agency and sentencing court.

If access to all required services is not being provided to a juvenile under the supervision of a correctional agency, the agency has the obligation to so inform the sentencing court. In addition, the juvenile, his or her parents, or any other interested party may inform the court of the failure to provide services. The court also may act on its own initiative. If the court determines that access to all required services in fact is not being provided, it should employ the following:

    1. Reduction of disposition or discharge.

    Unless the court can ensure that the required services are provided forthwith, it should reduce the nature of the juvenile's disposition to a less severe disposition that will ensure the juvenile access to the required services, or discharge the juvenile.

    2. Affirmative orders.

    In addition, the sentencing court, or any other court with the requisite jurisdiction, may order the correctional agency or other public agencies to make the required services available in the future.

4.2 Right to refuse services; exceptions.

Juveniles who have been adjudicated delinquent have the right to refuse all services, subject to the following exceptions:

A. Participation legally required of all juveniles.

Juveniles who have been adjudicated delinquent may be required to participate in all types of programs in which participation is legally required of juveniles who have not been adjudicated delinquent.

B. Prevention of clear harm to physical health.

Juveniles may be required to participate in certain programs in order to prevent clear harm to their physical health.

C. Remedial dispositions.

Juveniles subject to a conditional disposition may be required to participate in any program specified in the sentencing order, pursuant to Standard 3.2 D.

4.3 Requirement of informed consent to participate in certain programs.

Informed, written consent should be obtained before a juvenile may be required to participate in any program designed to alter or modify his or her behavior if that program may have harmful effects.

A. Juveniles below the age of sixteen.

If the juvenile is under the age of sixteen, his or her consent and the consent of his or her parent or guardian should be obtained.

B. Juveniles above the age of sixteen.

If the juvenile is sixteen or older, only the juvenile's consent need be obtained.

C. Withdrawal of consent.

Any such consent may be withdrawn at any time.

PART V: MODIFICATION AND ENFORCEMENT OF DISPOSITIONAL ORDERS

Dispositional orders may be modified as follows.

5.1 Reduction because disposition inequitable.

A juvenile, his or her parents, the correctional agency with responsibility for the juvenile, or the sentencing court on its own motion may petition the sentencing court (or an appellate court) at any time during the course of the disposition to reduce the nature or the duration of the disposition on the basis that it exceeds the statutory maximum; was imposed in an illegal manner; is unduly severe with reference to the seriousness of the offense, the culpability of the juvenile, or the dispositions given by the same or other courts to juveniles convicted of similar offenses; or if it appears at the time of the application that by doing so it can prevent an unduly harsh or inequitable result.

5.2 Reduction because services not provided.

The sentencing court should reduce a disposition or discharge the juvenile when it appears that access to required services is not being provided, pursuant to Standard 4.1 D.

5.3 Reduction for good behavior.

The correctional agency with responsibility for a juvenile may reduce the duration of the juvenile's disposition by an amount not to exceed [5] percent of the original disposition if the juvenile has refrained from major infractions of the dispositional order or of the reasonable regulations governing any facility to which the juvenile is assigned.

5.4 Enforcement when juvenile fails to comply.

The correctional agency with responsibility for a juvenile may petition the sentencing court if it appears that the juvenile has willfully failed to comply with any part of the dispositional order. In the case of a remedial sanction, compliance is defined in terms of attendance at the specified program, and not in terms of performance.

If, after a hearing, it is determined that the juvenile in fact has not complied with the order and that there is no excuse for the noncompliance, the court may do one of the following:

A. Warning and order to comply.

The court may warn the juvenile of the consequences of failure to comply and order him or her to make up any missed time, in the case of supervisory, remedial, or custodial sanctions or community work; or missed payment, in the case of restitution or fines.

B. Modification of conditions and/or imposition of additional conditions.

If it appears that a warning will be insufficient to induce compliance, the court may modify existing conditions or impose additional conditions calculated to induce compliance, provided that the conditions do not exceed the maximum sanction permissible for the offense. The duration of the disposition should remain the same, with the addition of any missed time or payments ordered to be made up.

C. Imposition of more severe disposition.

If it appears that there are no permissible conditions reasonably calculated to induce compliance, the court may sentence the juvenile to the next most severe category of sanctions for the remaining du-

ration of the disposition. The duration of the disposition should remain the same, except that the court may add some or all of the
missed time to the remainder of the disposition.

D. Commission of a new offense.

Where conduct is alleged that constitutes a willful failure to comply with the dispositional order and also constitutes a separate offense, prosecution for the new offense is preferable to modification
of the original order. The preference for separate prosecution in no
way precludes the imposition of concurrent dispositions.

STANDARDS RELATING TO INTERIM STATUS: THE RELEASE, CONTROL AND DETENTION OF ACCUSED JUVENILE OFFENDERS BETWEEN ARREST AND DISPOSITION

Daniel J. Freed and Timothy P. Terrell, Reporters

PART I: INTRODUCTION

1.1 Scope and overview.

The standards in this volume set out in detail the decision-making process that functions between arrest of a juvenile on criminal charges and final disposition of the case. By limiting the discretion of officials involved in that process, and by imposing affirmative duties on them to release juveniles or bear the burden of justification for not having done so, the standards seek to reduce the volume, duration, and severity of detention, and of other curtailment of liberty during the interim period.

1.2 Separate standards for different decision makers.

Separate rules should define the interim period authority and responsibility of police officers, intake officials, attorneys for the juvenile and the state, judges, and detention officials, to reflect differences in:

A. their respective roles in the interim decision-making process;
B. the extent to which the discretion exercised by each is subject to control and review by others; and
C. the time, information, and resources available to each at the time of decision.

1.3 Guidelines for measuring progress.

To the extent that these standards require time-consuming or costly modifications in the law, practice, and facilities of a jurisdiction, they should be viewed as guidelines by which to measure the progress of the jurisdiction toward compliance with the stated goals. Detailed specifications are presented wherever possible, so that departures from them will be visible, and officials can be called to account for them.

PART II: DEFINITIONS

2.1 Interim period.

The interval between the arrest or summons of an accused juvenile charged with a criminal offense and the implementation of a final judicial disposition. The term "interim" is used as an adjective referring to this interval, e.g., "interim status," "interim liberty," and "interim detention."

2.2 Arrest.

The taking of an accused juvenile into custody in conformity with the law governing the arrest of persons believed to have committed a crime.

2.3 Custody.

Any interval during which an accused juvenile is held by the arresting police authorities.

2.4 Status decision.

A decision made by an official that results in the interim release, control, or detention of an arrested juvenile. In the adult criminal process, it is often referred to as the bail decision.

2.5 Release.

The unconditional and unrestricted interim liberty of a juvenile, limited only by the juvenile's promise, appear at judicial proceedings as required. It is sometimes referred to as "release on own recognizance."

2.6 Control.

A restricted or regulated nondetention interim status, including release on conditions or under supervision.

2.7 Release on conditions.

The release of an accused juvenile under written requirements that specify the terms of interim liberty, such as living at home, reporting periodically to a court officer, or refraining from contact with named witnesses.

2.8 Release under supervision.

The release of an accused juvenile to an individual or organization that agrees in writing to assume the responsibility for directing, managing, or overseeing the activities of the juvenile during the interim period.

2.9 Detention.

Placement during the interim period of an accused juvenile in a home or facility other than that of a parent, legal guardian, or relative, including facilities commonly called "detention," "shelter care," "training school," "receiving home," "group home," "foster care," and "temporary care."

2.10 Secure detention facility.

A facility characterized by physically restrictive construction and procedures that are intended to prevent an accused juvenile who is placed there from departing at will.

2.11 Nonsecure detention facility.

A detention facility that is open in nature and designed to allow maximum participation by the accused juvenile in the community and its resources. It is intended primarily to minimize psychological hardships on an accused juvenile offender who is held out-of-home, rather than to restrict the freedom of the juvenile. These facilities include, but are not limited to:

A. single family foster homes or temporary boarding homes;
B. group homes with a resident staff, which may or may not specialize in a particular problem area, such as drug abuse, alcohol abuse, etc.; and
C. facilities used for the housing of neglected or abused juveniles.

2.12 Regional detention facility.

A detention facility that serves a geographic area of sufficient population to require a maximum daily capacity for that facility of twelve juveniles.

2.13 Citation.

A written order issued by a law enforcement officer requiring a juvenile accused of violating the criminal law to appear in a designated court at a specified date and time. The form requires the signature either of the juvenile to whom it is issued, or of the parent to whom the juvenile is released.

2.14 Summons.

An order issued by a court requiring a juvenile against whom a charge of criminal conduct has been filed to appear in a designated court at a specific date and time.

2.15 Treatment.

Any medical or psychiatric response to a diagnosis of a need for such response, including the systematic use of drugs, rules, programs, or other measures, for the purpose of either improving the juvenile's physical health or modifying on a long-range basis the accused juvenile's behavior or state of mind. "Treatment" includes, among other things, programs commonly described as "behavior modification," "group therapy," and "milieu therapy. "

2.16 Testing.

The use of measures administered to the accused juvenile for the purpose of:

A. identifying medical or personal characteristics, the latter including such things as knowledge, abilities, aptitudes, qualifications, or emotional traits; and
B. determining the need for some form of treatment.

2.17 Parent.

Any of the following:

A. the juvenile's natural parents, stepparents, or adopted parents, unless their parental rights have been terminated;
B. if the juvenile is a ward of any person other than his or her parent, the guardian of the juvenile;
C. if the juvenile is in the custody of some person other than his or her parent whose knowledge of or participation in the proceedings would be appropriate, the juvenile's custodian; and
D. separated and divorced parents, even if deprived by judicial decree of the respondent juvenile's custody.

2.18 Final disposition.

The implementation of a court order of

A. release based upon a finding that the juvenile is not guilty of committing the offense charged; or
B. supervision, punishment, treatment, or correction based upon a finding that the juvenile is guilty of committing the offense charged.

2.19 Diversion.

The unconditional release of an accused juvenile, without adjudication of criminal charges, to a youth service agency or other program outside the juvenile justice system, accompanied by a formal termination of all legal proceedings against the juvenile and erasure of all records concerning the case.

PART III: BASIC PRINCIPLES

Facilities Review Panel v. Coe, **187 W.Va. 541, 420 S.E.2d 532, 535–41 (1992). The West Virginia Supreme Court of Appeals promulgated standardized juvenile detention guidelines to govern decisions in that state based on the American Bar Association *Juvenile Justice Standards Relating to Interim Status* as modified "to fit the specialized needs" of the West Virginia juvenile justice system.**

L.O.W. v. District Court, **623 P.2d 1253, 1259–60 (Colo. 1981). The American Bar Association's *Juvenile Justice Standards Relating to Interim Status* concerning detention are more precise than the Colorado Children's Code. (Citing Standards 3.1-3.3)**

3.1 Policy favoring release.

Restraints on the freedom of accused juveniles pending trial and disposition are generally contrary to public policy. The preferred course in each case should be unconditional release.

3.2 Permissible control or detention.

The imposition of interim control or detention on an accused juvenile may be considered for the purposes of:
   A. protecting the jurisdiction and process of the court;
   B. reducing the likelihood that the juvenile may inflict serious bodily harm on others during the interim period; or
   C. protecting the accused juvenile from imminent bodily harm upon his or her request.

However, these purposes should be exercised only under the circumstances and to the extent authorized by the procedures, requirements, and limitations detailed in Parts IV through X of these standards.

3.3 Prohibited control or detention.

Interim control or detention should not be imposed on an accused juvenile:
   A. to punish, treat, or rehabilitate the juvenile;
   B. to allow parents to avoid their legal responsibilities;
   C. to satisfy demands by a victim, the police, or the community;
   D. to permit more convenient administrative access to the juvenile;
   E. to facilitate further interrogation or investigation; or
   F. due to a lack of a more appropriate facility or status alternative.

3.4 Least intrusive alternative.

When an accused juvenile cannot be unconditionally released, conditional or supervised release that results in the least necessary interference with the liberty of the juvenile should be favored over more intrusive alternatives.

3.5 Values.

Whenever the interim curtailment of an accused juvenile's freedom is permitted under these standards, the exercise of authority should reflect the following values:

A. respect for the privacy, dignity, and individuality of the accused juvenile and his or her family;
B. protection of the psychological and physical health of the juvenile;
C. tolerance of the diverse values and preferences among different groups and individuals;
D. insurance of equality of treatment by race, class, ethnicity, and sex;
E. avoidance of regimentation and depersonalization of the juvenile;
F. avoidance of stigmatization of the juvenile; and
G. insurance that the juvenile receives adequate legal assistance.

3.6 Availability of adequate resources.

The attainment of a fair and effective system of juvenile justice requires that every jurisdiction should, by legislation, court decision, appropriations, and methods of administration, provide services and facilities adequate to carry out the principles underlying these standards. Accordingly, the absence of funds cannot be a justification for resources or procedures that fall below the standards or unnecessarily infringe on individual liberty. Accused juveniles should be released or placed under less restrictive control whenever a form of detention or control otherwise appropriate is unavailable to the decision maker.

PART IV: GENERAL PROCEDURAL STANDARDS

Facilities Review Panel v. Coe, 187 W.Va. 541, 420 S.E.2d 532, 535–41 (1992). The West Virginia Supreme Court of Appeals promulgated standardized juvenile detention guidelines to govern decisions in that state based on the American Bar Association *Juvenile Justice Standards Relating to Interim Status* as modified "to fit the specialized needs" of the West Virginia juvenile justice system.

L.O.W. v. District Court, 623 P.2d 1253, 1259–60 (Colo. 1981). The American Bar Association *Juvenile Justice Standards Relating to In-*

terim Status concerning detention are more precise than the Colorado Children's Code. (Citing Standards 4.2-4.3)

4.1 Scope.

As an introduction to the standards in Parts V through IX, which create separate guidelines for each participant in the interim process, the procedures and prohibitions in Part IV are standards applicable to all interim decision makers.

4.2 Burden of proof.

The state should bear the burden at every stage of the proceedings of persuading the relevant decision maker with clear and convincing evidence that restraints on an accused juvenile's liberty are necessary, and that no less intrusive alternative will suffice.

4.3 Written reasons and review.

Whenever a decision is made at any stage of the proceedings to adopt an interim measure other than unconditional release, the decision maker should concurrently state in writing or on the record with specificity the evidence relied upon for that conclusion, and the authorized purpose or purposes that justify that action. A decision or order to hold an accused juvenile in detention should be invalid if the reasons for it are not attached to it. The statement of reasons should become an integral part of the record, and should be subject to and available for review at each succeeding stage of the process.

4.4 Use of social history information.

Prior to adjudication, information gathered about the background of an accused juvenile for purposes of determining an interim status should be limited to that which is essential to a decision concerning unconditional release or the least intrusive alternative. Information so gathered should be disclosed only to the persons and to the extent necessary to reach, carry out, and review that decision, and should be available for no other purpose. If the juvenile is convicted, the information gathered in the preadjudication stage may be used in determining an appropriate disposition.

4.5 Limitations on treatment or testing.

    A. Involuntary.

        1. Prior to adjudication, an accused juvenile should not be involuntarily subjected to treatment or testing of any kind by the

state or any private organization associated with the interim process except:

    a. to test for the presence of a contagious or communicable disease that would present an unreasonable risk of infection to others in the same facility;

    b. to provide emergency medical aid; or

    c. to administer tests required by the court for determining competency to stand trial.

2. After adjudication, an accused juvenile may be subjected to involuntary, nonemergency testing only to the extent found necessary by a court, after a hearing, to aid in the determination of an appropriate final disposition.

B. Voluntary.

1. While in detention, an accused juvenile should be entitled to a prompt medical examination and to provision of appropriate nonemergency medical care, with the informed consent of the juvenile and a parent in accordance with subsection 2 below. Requirements of consent should be governed by the Rights of Minors volume.

2. Informed, written consent should be obtained before a juvenile may be required to participate in any program, designed to alter or modify behavior, that may have potentially harmful effects.

    a. If the juvenile is under the age of sixteen, his or her consent and the consent of his or her parents both should be obtained.

    b. If the juvenile is sixteen or older, only the juvenile's consent should be obtained.

    c. Any such consent may be withdrawn at any time.

4.6 Violation of release conditions.

A willful violation by an accused juvenile of the conditions of release, or a willful failure to appear in court in response to a citation or summons, should be grounds for the issuance by the court of a summons based on that violation or failure to appear. A violation of conditions or a failure to appear should not constitute a criminal offense for which dispositional sanctions may be imposed, but should authorize the court to review, modify, or terminate the release conditions.

4.7 Prohibition against money bail.

The use of bail bonds in any form as an alternative interim status should be prohibited.

L.O.W. v. District Court, 632 P.2d 1253, 1258 (Colo. 1981). The trial court did not abuse its discretion in refusing to grant bail to a juvenile as the juvenile code safeguards obviate the need for bail in pre-adjudication proceedings. The court cited Standard 4.7 as recognizing and cautioning that bail could become a substitute for more appropriate forms of release.

PART V: STANDARDS FOR THE POLICE

5.1 Policy favoring release.

Each police department should adopt policies and issue written rules and regulations requiring release of all accused juveniles at the arrest stage pursuant to Standard 5.6 A, and adherence to the guidelines specified in Standard 5.6 B in discretionary situations. Citations should be employed to the greatest degree consistent with the policies of public safety and insuring appearance in court to release a juvenile on his or her own recognizance, or to a parent.

5.2 Special juvenile unit.

Each police department should establish a unit or have an officer specially trained in the handling of juvenile cases to effect arrests of juveniles when arrest is necessary, to make release decisions concerning juveniles, and to review immediately every case in which an arrest has been made by another member of the department who declines to release the juvenile. All arrest warrants, summonses, and possible citations involving accused juveniles should be handled by this unit.

5.3 Duties.

The arresting officer should have the following duties in regard to the interim status of an accused juvenile:
A. Inform juvenile of rights. The officer should explain in clearly understandable language the warnings required by the constitution regarding the right to silence, the making of statements, and the right to the presence of an attorney. The officer should also inform every arrested juvenile who is not promptly released from custody of the right to have his or her parent contacted by the department. In any situation in which the accused does not understand English, or in which the accused is bilingual and English is not his or her principal language, the officer should provide the necessary information in the accused's native language,

or provide an interpreter who will assure that the juvenile is informed of his or her rights.

B. Notification of parent. The arresting officer should make all reasonable efforts to contact a parent of the accused juvenile during the period between arrest and the presentation of the juvenile to any detention facility. The officer should inform the parent of the juvenile's right to the presence of counsel, appointed if necessary, and of the juvenile's right to remain silent.

C. Presence of attorney. The right to have an attorney present should be subject to knowing, intelligent waiver by the juvenile following consultation with counsel. If the police question any arrested juvenile concerning an alleged offense in the absence of an attorney for the juvenile, no information obtained thereby or as a result of the questioning should be admissible in any proceeding.

D. Recording of initial status decision. If the arresting officer does not release the juvenile within two hours, the reasons for the decision should be recorded in the arrest report and disclosed to the juvenile, counsel, and parent.

E. Notification of facility. Whenever an accused juvenile is taken into custody and not promptly released, the arresting officer should promptly inform the juvenile facility intake official of all relevant factors concerning the juvenile and the arrest, so that the official can explore interim status alternatives.

F. Transportation to facility. The police should, within [two to four hours] of the arrest, either release the juvenile or, upon notice to and concurrence by the intake official, take the juvenile without delay to the juvenile facility designated by the intake official. If the intake official does not concur, that official should order the police to release the juvenile.

5.4 Holding in police detention facility prohibited.

The holding of an arrested juvenile in any police detention facility prior to release or transportation to a juvenile facility should be prohibited.

5.5 Interim status decision not made by police.

The observations and recommendations of the police concerning the appropriate interim status for the arrested juvenile should be solicited by the intake official, but should not be determinative of the juvenile's interim status.

5.6 Guidelines for status decision.

A. Mandatory release. Whenever the juvenile has been arrested for a crime which in the case of an adult would be punishable by a sentence of [less than one year], the arresting officer should, if charges are to be pressed, release the juvenile with a citation or to a parent, unless the juvenile is in need of emergency medical treatment (Standard 4.5 A.1 b), requests protective custody (Standard 5.7), or is known to be in a fugitive status.

B. Discretionary release. In all other situations, the arresting officer should release the juvenile unless the evidence as defined below demonstrates that continued custody is necessary. The seriousness of the alleged offense should not, except in cases of a class one juvenile offense involving a crime of violence, be sufficient grounds for continued custody. Such evidence should only consist of one or more of the following factors as to which reliable information is available to the arresting officer:

1. that the arrest was made while the juvenile was in a fugitive status;
2. that the juvenile has a recent record of willful failure to appear at juvenile proceedings.

5.7 Protective custody.

A. Notwithstanding the issuance of a citation, the arresting officer may take an accused juvenile to an appropriate facility designated by the intake official if the juvenile would be in immediate danger of serious bodily harm if released, and the juvenile requests such custody.

B. A decision to continue or relinquish protective custody shall be made by the intake official in accordance with Standard 6.7.

PART VI: STANDARDS FOR THE JUVENILE FACILITY INTAKE OFFICIAL

Facilities Review Panel v. Coe, **187 W.Va. 541, 420 S.E.2d 532, 535–41 (1992). The West Virginia Supreme Court of Appeals promulgated standardized juvenile detention guidelines to govern decisions in that state based on the American Bar Association *Juvenile Justice Standards Relating to Interim Status* as modified "to fit the specialized needs" of the West Virginia juvenile justice system.**

6.1 Under authority of statewide agency.

The juvenile facility intake official should be an employee of or subject to the authority of the statewide agency charged with responsibility for all aspects of nonjudicial interim status decisions, as that agency is described in Standards 11.1 and 11.2.

When, for political or geographic considerations, some agencies are within the jurisdiction of local government, the statewide department should be responsible for the setting and enforcement of standards and the provision of technical assistance, training, and fiscal subsidies.

6.2 Twenty-four-hour duty.

An intake official should be available twenty-four hours a day, seven days a week, to be responsible for juvenile custody referrals.

6.3 Location of official.

In order to facilitate prompt and effective interim decisions, and to reduce the unnecessary transportation and detention of arrested juveniles, the intake official should be located at the most accessible office and position in the interim process. This central office need not be a place of juvenile detention.

6.4 Responsibility for status decision.

Once an arrested juvenile has been brought to a juvenile facility, the responsibility for maintaining or changing interim status rests entirely with the intake official, subject to review by the juvenile court. Release by the facility should be mandatory in any situation in which the arresting officer was required to release the juvenile but failed to do so.

6.5 Procedural requirements.

A. Provide information. The intake official should:
   1. inform the accused juvenile of his or her rights, as in Standard 5.3 A;
   2. inform the accused juvenile that his or her parent will be contacted immediately to aid in effecting release; and
   3. explain the basis for detention, the interim status alternatives that are available, and the right to a prompt release hearing.
B. Notify parent. If the arresting officer has been unable to contact a parent, the intake official should make every effort to effect such contact. If the official decides that the juvenile should be released, he or she may request a parent to come to the facility and accept release.
C. Notify attorney. Unless the accused juvenile already has a public or private attorney, the intake official should promptly call a public defender to represent the juvenile.

D. Reach status decision.
  1. The intake official should determine whether the accused juvenile is to be released with or without conditions, or be held in detention.
  2. If the juvenile is not released, the intake official should prepare a petition for a release hearing before a judge or referee, which should be filed with the court no later than the next court session, or within [twenty-four hours] after the juvenile's arrival at the intake facility, whichever is sooner. The petition should specify the charges on which the accused juvenile is to be prosecuted, the reasons why the accused was placed in detention, the reasons why release has not been accomplished, the alternatives to detention that have been explored, and the recommendations of the intake official concerning interim status.
  3. If the court is not in session within the [twenty-four-hour] period, the intake official should contact the judge, by telephone or otherwise, and give notice of the contents of the petition.
E. Continue release investigation. If an accused juvenile remains in detention after the initial court hearing, the intake official should review in detail the circumstances of the arrest and the alternatives to continued detention. A report on these investigations, including any information that the juvenile's attorney may wish to have added, should be presented to the court at the status review hearing within seven days after the initial hearing.
F. Maintain records. A written record should be kept of the incidence, duration, and reasons for interim detention of juveniles. Such records should be retained by the intake official and staff, and should be available for inspection by the police, the prosecutor, the court, and defense counsel. The official should continuously monitor these records to ascertain the emergence of patterns that may reflect misuse of release standards and guidelines, the inadequacy of release alternatives, or the need to revise standards.

6.6 Guidelines for status decision.

A. Mandatory release. The intake official should release the accused juvenile unless the juvenile:
  1. is charged with a crime of violence which in the case of an adult would be punishable by a sentence of one year or more, and which if proven is likely to result in commitment to a

security institution, and one or more of the following additional factors is present:

    a. the crime charged is a class one juvenile offense;

    b. the juvenile is an escapee from an institution or other placement facility to which he or she was sentenced under a previous adjudication of criminal conduct;

    c. the juvenile has a demonstrable recent record of willful failure to appear at juvenile proceedings, on the basis of which the official finds that no measure short of detention can be imposed to reasonably ensure appearance; or

  2. has been verified to be a fugitive from another jurisdiction, an official of which has formally requested that the juvenile be placed in detention.

B. Mandatory detention. A juvenile who is excluded from mandatory release under subsection A should not, pro tanto, be automatically detained. No category of alleged conduct or background in and of itself should justify a failure to exercise discretion to release.

C. Discretionary situations.

  1. Release vs. detention. In every situation in which the release of an arrested juvenile is not mandatory, the intake official should first consider and determine whether the juvenile qualifies for an available diversion program, or whether any form of control short of detention is available to reasonably reduce the risk of flight or misconduct. If no such measure will suffice, the official should explicitly state in writing the reasons for rejecting each of these forms of release.

  2. Unconditional vs. conditional or supervised release. In order to minimize the imposition of release conditions on persons who would appear in court without them, and present no substantial risk in the interim, each jurisdiction should develop guidelines for the use of various forms of release based upon the resources and programs available, and analysis of the effectiveness of each form of release.

  3. Secure vs. nonsecure detention. Whenever an intake official determines that detention is the appropriate interim status, secure detention may be selected only if clear and convincing evidence indicates the probability, of serious physical injury to others, or serious probability of flight to avoid appearance in court. Absent such evidence, the accused should be placed in

an appropriate form of nonsecure detention, with a foster home to be preferred over other alternatives.

K.L.F. v. State, 790 P.2d 708, 709–712 (Alaska App. 1990). Predisposition detention of the juvenile was appropriate pursuant to Alaska Delinquency Rule 12(b), and it was not necessary to look to the IJA-ABA Standards for guidance. The court has relied on the Standards for guidance in other cases because the relevant statutes or rules there were not sufficiently specific. The specific rule here was adopted after the promulgation of the Standards and there is therefore reason to believe that the drafters of the Rules were fully aware of the Standards provisions.

6.7 Protective detention.

   A. Placement in a nonsecure detention facility solely for the protection of an accused juvenile should be permitted only upon the voluntary written request of the juvenile in circumstances that present an immediate threat of serious bodily harm to the juvenile if released.
   B. In reaching this decision, or in reviewing a protective custody decision made by the arresting officer, the intake official should first consider all less restrictive alternatives and all reasonably ascertainable factors relevant to the likelihood and immediacy of serious bodily harm resulting from interim release or control.

PART VII: STANDARDS FOR THE JUVENILE COURT

7.1 Authority to issue summons in lieu of arrest warrant.

Judges should be authorized to issue a summons (which may be served by certified mail or in person) rather than an arrest warrant in every case in which a complaint, information, indictment, or petition is filed or returned against an accused juvenile not already in custody.

7.2 Policy favoring summons over warrant.

In the absence of reasonable grounds indicating that, if an accused juvenile is not promptly taken into custody, he or she will flee to avoid prosecution, the court should prefer the issuance of a summons over the issuance of an arrest warrant.

7.3 Application for summons or warrant.

Whenever an application for a summons or warrant is presented, the court should require all available information relevant to an interim status decision, the reasons why a summons or warrant should be issued, and information concerning the juvenile's schooling or employment that might be affected by service of a summons or warrant at particular times of the day.

7.4 Arrest warrant to specify initial interim status.

A. Every warrant issued by a court for the arrest of a juvenile should specify an interim status for the juvenile. The court may order the arresting officer to release the juvenile with a citation, or to place the juvenile in any other interim status permissible under these standards.

B. The warrant should indicate on its face the interim status designated. If any form of detention is ordered, the warrant should indicate the place to which the accused juvenile should be taken, if other than directly to court. In each such case, the court should simultaneously file a written statement indicating the reasons why no measure short of detention would suffice.

7.5 Service of summons or warrant.

In the absence of compelling circumstances that prompt the issuing court to specify to the contrary, a summons or warrant should not be served on an accused juvenile while in school or at a place of employment.

7.6 Release hearing.

A. Timing. An accused juvenile taken into custody should, unless sooner released, be accorded a hearing in court within [twenty-four hours] of the filing of the petition for a release hearing required by Standard 6.5 D.2.

B. Notice. Actual notice of the detention review hearing should be given to the accused juvenile, the parents, and their attorneys, immediately upon an intake official's decision that the juvenile will not be released prior to the hearing.

C. Rights. An attorney for the accused juvenile should be present at the hearing in addition to the juvenile's parents, if they attend. There should be a strong presumption against the validity of a waiver of any constitutional or statutory right of the juvenile, and no waiver should be valid unless made in writing by the juvenile and his or her counsel.

D. Information. At the review hearing, information relevant to the interim status of an accused juvenile, other than information bearing on the nature and circumstances of the offense charged and the weight of the evidence against the accused juvenile, need not conform to the rules pertaining to the admissibility of evidence in a court of law.

E. Disclosure. The juvenile and the attorney should have full access to all information and records upon which a judge relies in refusing to release the juvenile from detention, or in imposing conditions of supervision.

F. Probable cause. At the time of the initial detention hearing, the burden should be on the state to demonstrate that there is probable cause to believe that the juvenile committed the offense charged.

G. Notice of right to appeal. Whenever a court orders detention, or denies release upon review of an order of detention, it should simultaneously inform the juvenile, orally and in writing, of his or her rights to an automatic seven-day review under Standard 7.9 and to immediate appellate review under Standard 7.12.

7.7. Guidelines for status decisions.

A. Release alternatives. The court may release the juvenile on his or her own recognizance, on conditions, under supervision, including release on a temporary, nonovernight basis to the attorney if so requested for the purpose of preparing the case, or into a diversion program.

B. Mandatory release. Release by the court should be mandatory when the state fails to establish probable cause to believe the juvenile committed the offense charged or in any situation in which the arresting officer or intake official was required to release the juvenile but failed to do so, unless the court is in possession of additional information which justifies detention under these standards.

C. Discretionary situations. In all other cases, the court should review all factors that officials earlier in the process were required by these standards to have considered. The court should review with particularity the adequacy of the reasons for detention recorded by the police and the intake official.

D. Written reasons. A written statement of the findings of facts and reasons why no measure short of detention would suffice should be made part of the order and filed immediately after the hearing by any judge who declines to release an accused juvenile from detention. An order continuing the juvenile in detention should be construed as authorizing nonsecure detention only, unless it contains an express direction to the contrary, supported by reasons. If the court orders release under a form of control to which the juvenile objects, the court should upon request by the attorney for the juvenile, record the facts and reasons why unconditional release was denied.

7.8 Judicial participation.

A. Every juvenile court judge should visit each secure facility under the jurisdiction of that court at least once every [sixty days].
B. Whenever feasible, a judge other than the one who presided at the detention hearing should preside at the trial.

7.9 Continuing detention review.

A. The court should hold a detention review hearing at or before the end of each seven-day period in which a juvenile remains in interim detention. At the first detention review hearing after the expiration of the time prescribed for execution of the dispositional order, the judge must execute such order forthwith, or fully explain on the record the reasons for the delay, or release the juvenile.
B. A list of all juveniles held in any form of interim detention, together with the length of such detention and the reasons for detention, should be prepared by the intake official and presented weekly to the presiding judge. Such reports, with names deleted, should simultaneously be made public to describe the number, duration, and reasons for interim detention of juveniles.

7.10. Speedy trial.

To curtail detention and reduce the risks of release and control, all juvenile offense cases should be governed by the following timetable:

A. Each case should proceed to trial:
  1. within [fifteen days] of arrest or the filing of charges, whichever occurs first, if the accused juvenile has been held in detention by order of a court for more than [twenty-four hours]; or
  2. within [thirty days] in all other cases.
B. In any case in which the juvenile is convicted of a criminal offense, a disposition should be carried out:
  1. within [fifteen days] of conviction if the juvenile is held in detention by order of a court following conviction; or

2. within [thirty days] of conviction in all other cases.

The time prescribed for carrying out the disposition may be extended at the request of the juvenile, if necessary in order to secure a better placement.

C. The limits stated in A and B may be extended not more than [sixty days] if the juvenile is released, and not more than [thirty days] if the juvenile is in detention, when:

1. the prosecution certifies that a witness or other evidence necessary to the state's case will not be available, despite the prosecution's best efforts, during the original time limits;
2. any proceeding concerning waiver of the juvenile court's jurisdiction is pending;
3. a motion for change of venue made by either the prosecution or the juvenile is pending; or
4. a request for extradition is pending.

D. The limits stated in A and B may also be extended for specified periods authorized by the court when:

1. the juvenile is a fugitive from court proceedings; or
2. deferred adjudication or disposition for a specific period has been agreed to in writing by the juvenile and his or her attorney.

E. The limits in A and B may be phased in during a period not to exceed [twelve months] from the effective date of adoption of these standards, in order to enable a court to obtain the necessary resources to adjudicate cases on the merits. During such period, the maximum limit for detention cases should be [thirty days] from arrest to trial and [thirty days] from trial to final disposition.

F. In any case in which trial or disposition fails to meet these standards, the charges should be dismissed with prejudice.

7.11 Relaxation of interim status.

An intake official may at any time relax the conditions of a juvenile's interim status if, under rules prescribed by the court or under a specific court order, circumstances no longer justify continuing the restrictions initially imposed. Written notice of any such modification should be filed with the appropriate court. More stringent measures may not be imposed without prior notice to the court and counsel for the juvenile.

7.12 Appellate review of detention decision.

The attorney for the juvenile may at any time, upon notice to the prosecutor, appeal and be entitled to an immediate hearing within [twenty-four hours] on notice or motion from a court order imposing detention or denying release from detention. A copy of the order and written statement of reasons should accompany such appeal, and decisions on appeal should be filed at the conclusion of the hearing.

7.13 Status during appeal.

Upon the filing of an appeal of judgment and disposition, the release of the appellant, with or without conditions, should issue in every case unless the court orders otherwise. An order of interim detention should be permitted only where the disposition imposed, or most likely to be imposed, includes some form of secure incarceration *and* the court finds one or more of the following on the record:
  A. that the juvenile would flee the jurisdiction or not appear before any court for further proceedings during the pendency of the appeal; or
  B. that there is a substantial probability that the juvenile would engage in serious violence prior to the resolution of his or her appeal.

7.14 Speedy appeal.

  A. The appeal of judgment and disposition filed by a juvenile held in interim detention for more than ten days pursuant to an order under Standard 7.13 should be resolved within ninety days of the date of such order, unless deferred consideration and resolution of the appeal has been agreed to in writing by the juvenile and his or her attorney.
  B. Failure to meet this time limitation should result in release of the juvenile.

PART VIII: STANDARDS FOR THE DEFENSE ATTORNEY

8.1 Conflicts of interest.

The potential for conflict of interest between an accused juvenile and his or her parents should be clearly recognized and acknowledged. In every case, doubt as to a conflict should be resolved by the appointment of separate counsel for the child and by advising parents of their right to counsel and, if they are unable to afford counsel, of their right to have the court appoint such counsel. All parties should be informed by the initial attorney that he or she is counsel for the juvenile, and that in the event of disagreement between a parent or guardian and the juvenile, the attorney is required to serve exclusively the interests of the accused juvenile.

8.2 Duties.

It should be the duty of counsel for an accused juvenile to explore promptly the least restrictive form of release, the alternatives to detention, and the opportunities for detention review, at every stage of the proceedings where such an inquiry would be relevant.

8.3 Visit detention facility.

Whenever an accused juvenile is held in some form of detention, the attorney should periodically visit the juvenile, at no less than seven day intervals, and review personally his or her well-being, the conditions of the facility, and opportunities to relax the conditions of detention or to secure release. A report on each such visit should be retained in the attorney's permanent file of the case.

PART IX: STANDARDS FOR THE PROSECUTOR

9.1 Duties.

The prosecutor should review the charges, evidence, and the background of the juvenile prior to the initial court hearing in every case in which an accused juvenile is held in detention. On the basis of such review, the prosecutor should move at the initial hearing to dismiss the charges if prosecution is not warranted, to reduce charges to the extent excessive, and to eliminate detention or unduly restrictive control to the extent necessary to bring the juvenile's interim status into compliance with these standards.

9.2 Policy of encouraging release.

It should be the policy of prosecutors to encourage the police and other interim decision makers to release accused juveniles with a citation or without forms of control. Special efforts should be made to enter into stipulations to this effect in order to avoid unnecessary detention inquiries and to promote efficiency in the administration of justice.

9.3 Visit detention facilities.

Each prosecutor should, in the same manner required of judges under Standard 7.8 and defense counsel under Standard 8.3, visit at least once every [sixty days] each secure detention facility in which accused juveniles prosecuted by his or her office are lodged.

PART X: STANDARDS FOR JUVENILE DETENTION FACILITIES

10.1 Applicability to waiver of juvenile court jurisdiction.

When jurisdiction of the juvenile court is waived, and the juvenile is detained pursuant to adult pretrial procedures, the juvenile should be detained in a juvenile facility and in accordance with the standards in this part.

10.2 Use of adult jails prohibited.

The interim detention of accused juveniles in any facility or part thereof also used to detain adults is prohibited.

***State ex re. R.C.F. v. Wilt*, 162 W.Va. 424, 252 S.E.2d 168, 171 (1979). It is unlawful under West Virginia law to incarcerate a juvenile in a county jail prior to an adjudication of delinquency. This statute is consistent with the IJA-ABA Juvenile Justice Standards and recognizes that "the exposure of juveniles to adult offenders even for a short time can do but ill for the child."**

10.3 Policy favoring nonsecure alternatives.

A sufficiently wide range of nonsecure detention and nondetention alternatives should be available to decision makers so that the least restrictive interim status appropriate to an accused juvenile may be selected. The range of facilities available should be reviewed by all concerned agencies annually to ensure that juveniles are not being held in more restrictive facilities because less restrictive facilities are unavailable. A policy should be adopted in each state favoring the abandonment or reduction in size of secure facilities as less restrictive alternatives become available.

10.4 Mixing accused juvenile offenders with other juveniles.

  A. In nonsecure facilities. The simultaneous housing in a nonsecure detention facility of juveniles charged with criminal offenses and juveniles held for other reasons should not be prohibited.
  B. In secure facilities. Juveniles not charged with crime should not be held in any secure detention facility for accused juvenile offenders.

10.5 Population limits.

  A. Individual facilities. The population of an interim detention facility during any twenty-four-hour period should not exceed [twelve to twenty] juveniles. This maximum may be exceeded only in unusual, emergency circumstances, with a written report presented immediately to each juvenile court judge and to the statewide agency described in Part XI.

B. Statewide. A primary goal of each assessment effort should be to establish, within one year, a quota of beds available in all facilities within the state for the holding of accused juveniles in secure detention. The quota should be reduced annually thereafter, as alternative forms of control are developed. The quota should be binding on the statewide agency as a mandatory ceiling on the number of accused juveniles who may be held in detention at any one time; provided that it may be exceeded temporarily for a period not to exceed sixty days in any calendar year if the agency certifies to the governor of the state and to the legislature, and makes available to the public, in a written report, that unusual emergency circumstances exist that require a specific new quota to be set for a limited period. The certification should state the cause of the temporary increase in the quota and the steps to be taken to reduce the population to the original quota.

10.6 Education.

All accused juveniles held in interim detention should be afforded access to the educational institution they normally attend, or to equivalent tutorial or other programs adequate to their needs, including an educational program for "exceptional children."

10.7 Rights of juveniles in detention.

Each juvenile held in interim detention should have the following rights, among others:

A. Privacy. A right to individual privacy should be honored in each institution. Because different children will desire different settings and will often change their minds, substantial allowance should be made for individual choice, and for private as well as community areas, with due regard for the safety of others.

B. Attorneys. A private area within each facility should be available for conferences between the juvenile and his or her attorney at any time between 9 A.M. and 9 P.M. daily.

C. Visitors. Private areas within each facility should be available as contact visiting areas. The period for visiting, although subject to reasonable regulation by the facility staff, should cover at least eight hours every day of the week and should conform to school regulations when the juvenile is attending school outside the facility. All regulations concerning visitors and visiting hours should be subject to review by the juvenile court.

D. Telephone. Each juvenile in detention should have ready access to a telephone between 9 A.M. and 9 P.M. daily. Calls may be limited in duration, but not in content nor as to parties who may be contacted, except as otherwise specifically directed by the court. Local calls should be permitted at the expense of the institution, but should under no circumstances be monitored. Long distance calls in reasonable number may be made to a parent or attorney at the expense of the institution, and to others, collect.

E. Restrictions on force. Reasonable force should only be used to restrain a juvenile who demonstrates by observed behavior that he or she is a danger to himself or herself or to others, or who attempts to escape. All circumstances concerning any use of force or unusual restrictions, including the circumstances that gave rise to such use, should be reported immediately to the juvenile facility administrator and the juvenile's attorney and parent.

F. Mail. Mail from or to an accused juvenile should not be opened by authorities. If reasonable grounds exist to believe that mail may contain contraband, it should be examined only in the presence of the juvenile.

10.8 Detention inventory.

The statewide interim agency should during its first year and annually thereafter, conduct an inventory of secure detention facilities to ascertain the extent of, reasons for, and alternatives to the secure detention of accused juveniles. The inventory should include:

A. the places of secure detention;
B. the daily population and turnover;
C. annual admissions;
D. range of duration of secure detention;
E. annual juvenile days of secure detention;
F. costs of secure detention;
G. trial status of those in secure detention;
H. reasons for termination of secure detention;
I. disposition of secure detention cases;
J. correlation of secure detention to postadjudication disposition;
K. qualifications and training of staff;
L. staffing patterns and deployment of staff resources.

The results of the inventory should be published annually. The agency should conduct a similar inventory of nonsecure detention facilities, beginning in the agency's second year. The inventory should draw attention to the differences in the use of detention by locality and by characteristics of the detention population.

PART XI: GENERAL ADMINISTRATIVE STANDARDS

11.1 Centralized interim status administration in a statewide agency.

A. To facilitate the creation of an adequate interim decision-making process, with the resources necessary to implement it and an information system to monitor it, the responsibility for all aspects of nonjudicial interim status decisions involving accused juvenile offenders should be centralized in a single statewide agency. This centralization should include both personnel and facility administration. The agency should be part of the [executive] branch of the state government, although contracting with private nonprofit organizations should be permitted initially. All detention facility personnel, and all public employees involved in release, control, and supervision programs for accused juveniles should be employed by or otherwise responsible to this agency. The statewide agency should have responsibility for the coordination and review of all release and control of, and detention programs for, accused juveniles.

B. Each juvenile court and local police department should have available to it representatives of the agency and facilities developed by the agency.

C. The juvenile facility intake officials described in Part VI of these standards should be the local representatives of the statewide agency. They should be empowered to make or recommend the pretrial release, control, and detention decisions authorized by these standards, and to relax the restrictions imposed on a juvenile in accordance with Standard 7.11.

11.2 General administrative standards: planning, funding, and inspection.

A. The statewide agency in each state, in consultation with the court and representatives of law enforcement and attorneys for the defense should develop a statewide plan for the governance of local and regional facilities for accused juveniles, and for the necessary transportation between courts and facilities.

B. The agency, in cooperation with the administrators of other youth services and public welfare, should develop a statewide program for the provision of nonsecure detention facilities for accused juveniles, in accordance with the Architecture of Facilities volume.

C. To ensure that the standards are being met, representatives of the statewide agency should periodically and at least semiannually conduct unannounced inspections of all juvenile facilities in the state and file with the agency written reports within thirty days of each such inspection. Such reports should be periodically compiled and submitted to the legislature and the public. Current reports on any particular institution should be available on reasonable request. Whenever, on the basis of such reports, the agency or any court finds that a facility fails to meet promulgated standards, further detention of juveniles therein should be the subject of a warning. Copies of such warnings should be served upon the person in charge of the detention facility. Unless corrected and approved within sixty days after notification and publication of the warning, a facility that has been warned should thereafter be prohibited from housing any juvenile until such time as the warning is removed.

11.3 Construction moratorium.

An indefinite moratorium should be imposed on the construction or expansion of any facility for the detention of accused juveniles. No funds for any such purpose should be considered until an inventory of existing facilities has been completed and assessed, and until all reasonable release and control alternatives have been implemented and evaluated. Because a moratorium may have the effect of continuing substandard conditions in existing facilities, and of increasing the cost of eventual construction, its imposition should be accompanied by:

A. establishment of a timetable for completing the required inventory, program development, and evaluations;

B. public acknowledgment by all organizations in the juvenile justice system that alleviation of the volume, duration, and conditions of juvenile detention is their joint responsibility; and

C. specification, in periodic reports to the courts, governor, legislature, bar, and public of the plans and progress of the reassessment and reform effort.

11.4 Policy favoring experimentation.

The standards for each type of interim status, particularly including secure and nonsecure detention facilities, should not remain static. As experience develops, the statewide agency's standards governing the nature and use of these alternatives and facilities should be elevated. Experimentation under published criteria should be encouraged, and innovative techniques from other jurisdictions continuously examined.

STANDARDS RELATING TO JUVENILE DELINQUENCY AND SANCTIONS

John M. Junker, Reporter

PART I: PRELIMINARY PRINCIPLES

1.1 Purposes.

The purposes of a juvenile delinquency code should be:

A. to forbid conduct that unjustifiably and without excuse inflicts or risks substantial harm to individual or public interests;
B. to safeguard conduct that is without fault or culpability from condemnation as delinquent;
C. to give fair warning of what conduct is prohibited and of the consequences of violation;
D. to recognize the unique physical, psychological, and social features of young persons in the definition and application of delinquency standards.

1.2 Burden of proof.

When there is some evidence supporting an affirmative defense to juvenile delinquency liability, the prosecution should be required to disprove such defense beyond a reasonable doubt.

1.3 Discretionary dismissal.

The juvenile court should have the discretion to dismiss a delinquency proceeding if, having regard to the nature of the conduct charged to constitute an offense and the nature of the attendant circumstances, it finds that:

A. the person or persons whose personal or property interests were threatened or harmed by the conduct charged to constitute the offense were members of the juvenile's family, and the juvenile's conduct may be more appropriately dealt with by parental authority than by resort to delinquency sanctions; or
B. the conduct charged to constitute the offense
    1. did not actually cause or threaten the harm or evil sought to be prevented by the law defining the offense or did so only to a trivial extent, or
    2. presents such other extenuations that it cannot reasonably be regarded as within the contemplation of the legislature in forbidding the conduct.

In the Matter of C.S. McP., 514 A.2d 446, 449 (D.C. Ct. App. 1986). The Standards do not seem to contemplate outright dismissal of a delinquency charge at disposition, but such action would be justified where the evidence does not show that the juvenile is in need of rehabilitation. (Citing Standard 1.3)

PART II: JURISDICTION

2.1 Age.

The juvenile court should have exclusive original jurisdiction in all cases in which conduct constituting an offense within the court's delinquency jurisdiction is alleged to have been committed by a person

> A. not less than ten and not more than seventeen years of age at the time the offense is alleged to have been committed; and

In the Matter of Andrew M., 91 Misc. 2d 813, 398 N.Y.S.2d 824, 826 (Kings Co. Fam. Ct. 1977). The common law defense of lack of capacity due to immaturity is available to an eight-year-old child if proven factually. (Citing Standard 2.1)

In the Matter of Robert M., 110 Misc. 2d 113, 441 N.Y.S.2d 860, 862 (N.Y. Co. Fam. Ct. 1981). The presumption of infancy is inapplicable in delinquency cases. In any event, the Standards minimum age of ten represents a departure from most existing laws and other model acts. (Citing Standards generally)

State ex rel. M.C.H. v. Kinder, 173 W.Va. 387, 317 S.E.2d 150 (1984). Juveniles aged seven and nine should not be placed in secure detention absent extraordinary circumstances. This is especially true in light of the common law presumptions against criminal culpability and the Standard limitation on delinquency liability at age ten. (Citing Standard 2.1 A.)

> B. not more than twenty years of age at the time juvenile court delinquency proceedings are initiated with respect to such conduct; and
> C. for whom the period of limitations for such offense has not expired.

2.2 Offense.

> A. The delinquency jurisdiction of the juvenile court should include only those offenses which are:

1. punishable by incarceration in a prison, jail, or other place of detention, and
2. except as qualified by these standards, in violation of an applicable federal, state, or local criminal statute or ordinance, or
3. in violation of an applicable state or local statute or ordinance defining a major traffic offense.[1]

B. For purposes of this standard, major traffic offense should include:
   1. any driving offense by a juvenile less than thirteen years of age at the time the offense is alleged to have been committed, and

   2. any traffic offense involving reckless driving; driving while under the influence of alcohol, narcotics, or dangerous drugs; leaving the scene of an accident; and such other offenses as the enacting jurisdiction may deem sufficiently serious to warrant the attention of the juvenile court.

C. Any offense excluded by this standard from juvenile court jurisdiction should be cognizable in the court having jurisdiction over adults for such offenses, notwithstanding that the alleged offender's age is within the limits prescribed by Standard 2.1 *supra*.

2.3 Elimination of uniquely juvenile offenses.

Juvenile delinquency liability should include only such conduct as would be designated a crime if committed by an adult.

PART III: GENERAL PRINCIPLES OF LIABILITY

3.1 *Mens rea*—lack of *mens rea* an affirmative defense.

Where an applicable criminal statute or ordinance does not require proof of some culpable mental state, it should be an affirmative defense to delinquency liability that the juvenile:

A. was neither negligent nor reckless with respect to any material element of an offense penalizing the unintended consequence of risk-creating conduct; or

---

1. Commission member Wald noted her disagreement with the limitation of juvenile court jurisdiction stated in Standard 2.2 A.2 and A.3. She feels that any offense that might result in detention, jail, or prison for a child should be included in juvenile court jurisdiction.

B. acted without knowledge or intention with respect to any material element of an offense penalizing conduct or the circumstances or consequences of such conduct.

3.2 *Mens rea*—reasonableness defense.

Where an applicable criminal statute or ordinance penalizes risk creating conduct, it should be a defense to juvenile delinquency liability that the juvenile's conduct conformed to the standard of care that a reasonable person of the juvenile's age, maturity, and mental capacity would observe in the juvenile's situation.

3.3 Consent.

A. Where delinquency liability is defeated or diminished by consent to the conduct charged to constitute the offense, such consent should not be deemed ineffective solely on the ground that it was given by a person who, by reason of youth, was legally incompetent to authorize the conduct.
B. Effective consent by a juvenile should be a defense to juvenile delinquency liability based on conduct that causes or threatens bodily harm where:
    1. the bodily harm caused or threatened by the conduct consented to is not serious; or
    2. the conduct and the harm are reasonably foreseeable hazards of participation in a contest, sport, game, or play.
C. Consent by the person whose interest was infringed by conduct charged to constitute an offense should be implied in juvenile delinquency proceedings when such conduct was, within a customary license or tolerance, neither expressly forbidden by such person nor inconsistent with the purpose of the law defining the offense.

3.4 Parental authority.

A. A juvenile should not be adjudicated delinquent for complicity in an offense committed by another if he or she terminated his or her involvement in such offense prior to its commission and
    1. gave timely warning to law enforcement authorities or to a parent, legal guardian, or custodian, or to an adult otherwise entrusted with the care or supervision of the juvenile; or
    2. otherwise made a reasonable effort to prevent the commission of the offense.
B. It should be a defense to delinquency liability that a juvenile en-

gaged in conduct charged to constitute an offense because a parent, legal guardian, or custodian, or an adult otherwise entrusted with the care or supervision of the juvenile, used or threatened to use force or disciplinary measures against him or her or another which a person of reasonable firmness in the juvenile's situation would have been unable to resist.

3.5 Responsibility.

Juvenile delinquency liability should not be imposed if, at the time of the conduct charged to constitute the offense, as a result of mental disease or defect, the juvenile lacked substantial capacity to appreciate the criminality of his or her conduct or to conform his or her conduct to the requirements of the law.

PART IV: SANCTIONS

4.1 Types of sanctions.

The sanctions that a juvenile court may impose upon a juvenile adjudged to have committed a juvenile offense should be of three types, from most to least severe, as follows.

A. Custodial, where the juvenile is ordered
  1. to be confined in a secure facility as defined in these standards; or
  2. to be placed in a nonsecure facility, including a foster home or residence as defined in these standards.
B. Conditional, where the juvenile is ordered
  1. periodically to report to probation or other authorities; or
  2. to perform or refrain from performing certain acts; or
  3. to make restitution to persons harmed by his or her offense or to pay a fine; or
  4. to undergo any similar sanction not involving a change in the juvenile's residence or legal custody.
C. Nominal, where the juvenile is reprimanded, warned, or otherwise reproved and unconditionally released.
D. For purposes of this standard,
  1. the following institutions or designated portions thereof are secure facilities: . . . . [to be designated by the enacting jurisdiction]
  2. the following types of facilities or designated portions thereof

are nonsecure facilities: . . . . [to be designated by the enacting jurisdiction]

In the Matter of C.S. McP., 514 A.2d 446, 449 (D.C. Ct. App. 1986). The Standards do not seem to contemplate outright dismissal of a delinquency charge at disposition, but such action would be justified where the evidence does not show that the juvenile is in need of rehabilitation. (Citing Standard 1.3)

4.2 Classes of juvenile offenses.

    A. Offenses within the criminal jurisdiction of the juvenile court should be classified as class one through class five juvenile offenses.

    B. Where, under a criminal statute or ordinance made applicable to juveniles pursuant to Standard 2.2, the maximum sentence authorized upon conviction for such offense is:

       1. death or imprisonment for life or for a term in excess of [twenty] years, it is a class one juvenile offense;

In the Matter of the Interest of Wolf, 99 Idaho 476, 583 P.2d 1011, 1026 (1978). A class one juvenile offense for the purpose of the *Standards Relating to Transfer Between Courts* is defined in the *Standards Relating to Juvenile Delinquency and Sanctions.*

       2. imprisonment for a term in excess of [five] but not more than [twenty] years, it is a class two juvenile offense;

       3. imprisonment for a term in excess of [one] year but not more than [five] years, it is a class three juvenile offense;

       4. imprisonment for a term in excess of [six] months but not more than [one] year, it is a class four juvenile offense;

       5. imprisonment for a term of [six] months or less, it is a class five juvenile offense;

       6. not prescribed, it is a class five juvenile offense.

PART V: LIMITS ON TYPE AND DURATION OF DELINQUENCY SANCTIONS

5.1 Orders imposing sanctions.

Juvenile court orders imposing sanctions should specify:

    A. the nature of the sanction; and

    B. the duration of such sanction; and,

    C. where such order affects the residence or legal custody of the juvenile, the place of residence or confinement ordered and the person or agency in whom custody is vested;[2] and

D. the juvenile court judge's reasons for the sanction imposed, pursuant to Dispositions Standard 2.1.

5.2 Limitations on type and duration of sanctions.

A. The juvenile court should not impose a sanction more severe than,

1. where the juvenile is found to have committed a class one juvenile offense,
    a. confinement in a secure facility or placement in a nonsecure facility or residence for a period of [thirty-six] months or
    b. conditional freedom for a period of [thirty-six] months;
2. where the juvenile is found to have committed a class two juvenile offense,
    a. confinement in a secure facility or placement in a nonsecure facility or residence for a period of [eighteen] months, or
    b. conditional freedom for a period of [twenty-four] months;
3. where the juvenile is found to have committed a class three juvenile offense,
    a. confinement in a secure facility or placement in a nonsecure facility or residence for a period of [six] months, or
    b. conditional freedom for a period of [eighteen] months;
4. where the juvenile is found to have committed a class four juvenile offense,
    a. confinement in a secure facility for a period of [three] months if the juvenile has a prior record, or
    b. placement in a nonsecure facility or residence for a period of [three] months, or
    c. conditional freedom for a period of [twelve] months;
5. where the juvenile is found to have committed a class five juvenile offense,
    a. placement in a nonsecure facility or residence for a period of [two months] if the juvenile has a prior record, or
    b. conditional freedom for a period of [six] months.

B. For purposes of this standard, a juvenile has a "prior record" only

---

2. Commission member Wald would not require that the disposition order specify the "place of residence" but only the level of secure or nonsecure confinement and would leave the precise placement to the discretion of corrections officials. Commission member Polier concurs with this opinion.

when he or she has been formally adjudged previously to have committed:

1. an offense that would amount to a class one, two, or three juvenile offense, as defined in Standard 4.2, within the twenty-four months preceding the commission of the offense subject to sanctioning; or
2. three offenses that would amount to class four or five juvenile offenses, as defined in Standard 4.2, at least one of which was committed within the twelve months preceding the commission of the offense subject to sanctioning.

C. The juvenile court may impose a sanction consisting of confinement or placement for a specified period of time followed by conditional freedom for a specified period of time, provided that the total duration does not exceed the maximum term permissible as a custodial sanction for the offense.

5.3 Multiple juvenile offenses.

A. When a juvenile is found to have committed two or more juvenile offenses during the same transaction or episode, the juvenile court should not impose a sanction more severe than the maximum sanction authorized by Standard 5.2 for the most serious such offense.

B. When, in the same proceeding, a juvenile is found to have committed two or more offenses during separate transactions or episodes, the juvenile court should not impose a sanction:
1. more severe in nature than the sanction authorized by Standard 5.2 for the most serious such offense; or
2. longer in duration than a period equal to one and a half times the period authorized by Standard 5.2 for the most serious such offense.

C. When, at the time a juvenile is charged with an offense, the charging authority or its agents have evidence sufficient to warrant charging such juvenile with another juvenile offense falling within the court's jurisdiction, the failure jointly to charge such offense should thereafter bar the initiation of juvenile court delinquency proceedings based on such offense.

5.4 Termination of orders imposing sanctions.

A juvenile court order imposing sanctions should terminate no later than the [twenty-first] birthday of the juvenile subject to such order.

STANDARDS RELATING TO THE JUVENILE PROBATION FUNCTION: INTAKE AND PREDISPOSITION INVESTIGATIVE SERVICES

Josephine Gittler, Reporter

PART I: DEFINITIONS

1.1 Definitions as used herein:

A. "Juvenile probation" is an organizational entity that furnishes intake, investigative, and probation supervision services to juvenile courts.

B. "Juvenile probation services" consist of intake, investigative, and probation supervision services.

C. A "juvenile probation officer" is an individual who provides intake, investigative, or probation supervision services.

D. A "complaint" is a report made to a juvenile court that alleges that a juvenile is delinquent and that initiates the intake process.

E. A "petition" is a formal legal pleading that initiates formal judicial proceedings against a juvenile who is the subject of a complaint to determine whether the court has and should exercise jurisdiction over the juvenile.

F. "Intake services" consist of the intake screening and disposition of complaints.

G. "Intake" is a preliminary screening process initiated by the receipt of a complaint, the purpose of which is to determine what action, if any, should be taken upon the complaint.

H. An "intake officer" is an individual who screens complaints and makes intake dispositional decisions with respect to complaints.

I. "Investigative services" consist of the conducting of predisposition investigations and the preparation of predisposition reports.

J. A "predisposition investigation" is the collection of information relevant and necessary to the court's fashioning of an appropriate dispositional order after a juvenile has been adjudicated delinquent.

K. A "predisposition report" is a report based upon a predisposition investigation furnished to the court prior to the court's issuance of a dispositional order.

L. An "investigation officer" is an individual who conducts predisposition investigations and prepares predisposition reports.

155

M. "Probation supervision services" consist of the supervision of juveniles who have been placed on judicial probation.

N. "Judicial probation" refers to the supervision of a juvenile who has been adjudicated delinquent and who remains in his or her own home, by a designated individual or agency for a designated period of time during which he or she may be required to comply with certain restrictive conditions with respect to his or her conduct and activities pursuant to a dispositional order of the court.

O. "Parent" means the juvenile's natural parent, guardian, or custodian.

PART II: JUVENILE COURT INTAKE

SECTION I: GENERAL STANDARDS

2.1 Availability and utilization of intake services.

Intake services should be available to and utilized by all juvenile courts.

SECTION II: DISPOSITIONAL ALTERNATIVE AT INTAKE

2.2 Judicial disposition of a complaint.

"Judicial disposition of a complaint" is the initiation of formal judicial proceedings against the juvenile who is the subject of a complaint through the filing of a petition. After intake screening, judicial disposition of a complaint may be made.

2.3 Unconditional dismissal of a complaint.

The "unconditional dismissal of a complaint" is the termination of all proceedings against a juvenile. Unconditional dismissal of a complaint is a permissible intake dispositional alternative.

2.4 Nonjudicial disposition of a complaint.

A. "Nonjudicial disposition of a complaint" is the taking of some action on a complaint without the initiation of formal judicial proceedings through the filing of a petition or the issuance of a court order.

B. The existing types of nonjudicial dispositions are as follows:

1. "Nonjudicial probation" is a nonjudicial disposition involving the supervision by juvenile intake or probation personnel of a juvenile who is the subject of a complaint, for a period of time during which the juvenile may be required to comply with

certain restrictive conditions with respect to his or her conduct and activities.

2. The "provision of intake services" is the direct provision of services by juvenile intake and probation personnel on a continuing basis to a juvenile who is the subject of a complaint.

3. A "conditional dismissal of a complaint" is the termination of all proceedings against a juvenile subject to certain conditions not involving the acceptance of nonjudicial supervision or intake services. It includes a "community agency referral," which is the referral of a juvenile who is the subject of a complaint to a community agency or agencies for services.

C. A "community agency referral" is the only permissible nonjudicial disposition, subject to the conditions set forth in Standard 2.4 E. Intake personnel should refer juveniles in need of services whenever possible to youth service bureaus and other public and private community agencies. Juvenile probation agencies and other agencies responsible for the administration and provision of intake services and intake personnel should actively promote and encourage the establishment and the development of a wide range of community-based services and programs for delinquent and nondelinquent juveniles.

D. Nonjudicial probation, provision of intake services, and conditional dismissal other than community agency referral are not permissible intake dispositions.

E. A nonjudicial disposition should be utilized only under the following conditions:

1. A nonjudicial disposition should take the form of an agreement of a contractual nature under which the intake officer promises not to file a petition in exchange for certain commitments by the juvenile and his or her parents or legal guardian or both with respect to their future conduct and activities.

2. The juvenile and his or her parents or legal guardian should voluntarily and intelligently enter into the agreement.

3. The intake officer should advise the juvenile and his or her parents or legal guardian that they have the right to refuse to enter into an agreement for a nonjudicial disposition and to request a formal adjudication.

4. A nonjudicial disposition agreement should be limited in duration.

5. The juvenile and his or her parents or legal guardian should

be able to terminate the agreement at any time and to request formal adjudication.

6. The terms of the nonjudicial agreement should be clearly stated in writing. This written agreement should contain a statement of the requirements set forth in subsections 2–5. It should be signed by all the parties to the agreement, and a copy should be given to the juvenile and his or her parents or legal guardian.

7. Once a nonjudicial disposition of a complaint has been made, the subsequent filing of a petition based upon the events out of which the original complaint arose should be permitted for a period of [three (3)] months from the date the nonjudicial disposition agreement was entered into. If no petition is filed within that period, its subsequent filing should be prohibited. The juvenile's compliance with all proper and reasonable terms of the agreement should be an affirmative defense to a petition filed within the [three-month] period.

2.5 Consent decree.

A. A consent decree is a court order authorizing supervision of a juvenile for a specified period of time during which the juvenile may be required to fulfill certain conditions or some other disposition of the complaint without the filing of a petition and a formal adjudicatory proceeding.

A consent decree should be permissible under the following conditions:

1. The juvenile and his or her parents or legal guardian should voluntarily and intelligently consent to the decree.

2. The intake officer and the judge should advise the juvenile and his or her parents or legal guardian that they have the right to refuse to consent to the decree and to request a formal adjudication.

3. The juvenile should have an unwaivable right to the assistance of counsel in connection with an application for a consent decree. The intake officer should advise the juvenile of this right.

4. The terms of the decree should be clearly stated in the decree, and a copy should be given to all the parties to the decree.

5. The decree should not remain in force for a period in excess of six (6) months. Upon application of any of the parties to the decree, made before expiration of the decree, the decree, after

notice and hearing, may be extended for not more than an additional three (3) months by the court.

6. The juvenile and his or her parents or legal guardian should be able to terminate the agreement at any time and to request the filing of a petition and formal adjudication.

7. Once a consent decree has been entered, the subsequent filing of a petition based upon the events out of which the original complaint arose should be permitted for a period of [three (3)] months from the date the decree was entered. If no petition is filed within that period, its subsequent filing should be prohibited. The juvenile's compliance with all proper and reasonable terms of the decree should be an affirmative defense to a petition filed within the [three-month] period.

SECTION III: CRITERIA FOR INTAKE DISPOSITIONAL DECISIONS

2.6 Necessity for and desirability of written guidelines and rules.

A. Juvenile probation agencies and other agencies responsible for intake services should issue written guidelines and rules with respect to criteria for intake dispositional decisions. The objective of such administrative guidelines and rules is to confine and control the exercise of discretion by intake officers in the making of intake dispositional decisions so as to promote fairness, consistency, and effective dispositional decisions.

B. These guidelines and rules should be reviewed and evaluated by interested juvenile justice system officials and community-based delinquency control and prevention agencies.

C. Legislatures and courts should encourage or require rule making by these agencies with respect to criteria for intake dispositional decisions.

2.7 Legal sufficiency of complaint.

A. Upon receipt of a complaint, the intake officer should make an initial determination of whether the complaint is legally sufficient for the filing of a petition on the basis of the contents of the complaint and an intake investigation. In this regard the officer should determine:

1. whether the facts as alleged are sufficient to establish the court's jurisdiction over the juvenile; and

2. whether the competent and credible evidence available is sufficient to support the charges against the juvenile.

B. If the officer determines that the facts as alleged are not sufficient to establish the court's jurisdiction, the officer should dismiss the complaint. If the officer finds that the court has jurisdiction but determines that the competent and credible evidence available is not sufficient to support the charges against the juvenile, the officer should dismiss the complaint.

C. If the legal sufficiency of the complaint is unclear, the officer should ask the appropriate prosecuting official for a determination of its legal sufficiency.

2.8 Disposition in best interests of juvenile and community.

A. If the intake officer determines that the complaint is legally sufficient, the officer should determine what disposition of the complaint is most appropriate and desirable from the standpoint of the best interests of the juvenile and the community. This involves a determination as to whether a judicial disposition of the complaint would cause undue harm to the juvenile or exacerbate the problems that led to his or her delinquent acts, whether the juvenile presents a substantial danger to others, and whether the referral of the juvenile to the court has already served as a desired deterrent.

B. The officer should determine what disposition is in the best interests of the juvenile and the community in light of the following:

1. The seriousness of the offense that the alleged delinquent conduct constitutes should be considered in making an intake dispositional decision. A petition should ordinarily be filed against a juvenile who has allegedly engaged in delinquent conduct constituting a serious offense, which should be determined on the basis of the nature and extent of harm to others produced by the conduct.

2. The nature and number of the juvenile's prior contacts with the juvenile court should be considered in making an intake dispositional decision.

3. The circumstances surrounding the alleged delinquent conduct, including whether the juvenile was alone or in the company of other juveniles who also participated in the alleged delinquent conduct, should be considered in making an intake dispositional decision. If a petition is filed against one of the juveniles, a petition should ordinarily be filed against the other juveniles for substantially similar conduct.

4. The age and maturity of the juvenile may be relevant to an intake dispositional decision.
5. The juvenile's school attendance and behavior, the juvenile's family situation and relationships, and the juvenile's home environment may be relevant to an intake dispositional decision.
6. The attitude of the juvenile to the alleged delinquent conduct and to law enforcement and juvenile court authorities may be relevant to an intake dispositional decision, but a nonjudicial disposition of the complaint or the unconditional dismissal of the complaint should not be precluded for the sole reason that the juvenile denies the allegations of the complaint.
7. A nonjudicial disposition of the complaint or the unconditional dismissal of the complaint should not be precluded for the sole reason that the complainant opposes dismissal.
8. The availability of services to meet the juvenile's needs both within and outside the juvenile justice system should be considered in making an intake dispositional decision.
9. The factors that are not relevant to an intake dispositional decision include but are not necessarily limited to the juvenile's race, ethnic background, religion, sex, and economic status.

State v. Doe, 97 N.M. 792, 643 P.2d 1244, 1246–47 (1982). In judging what factors are to be considered in assessing a best interests determination for the filing of a delinquency petition, a court should consider the various criteria delineated in Standard 2.8. The seriousness of the offense may be determinative of such an assessment.

SECTION IV: INTAKE PROCEDURES

2.9 Necessity for and desirability of written guidelines and rules.

Juvenile probation agencies and other agencies responsible for intake services should develop and publish written guidelines and rules with respect to intake procedures.

2.10 Initiation of intake proceedings and receipt of complaint by intake officer.

A. An intake officer should initiate proceedings upon receipt of a complaint.
B. Any complaint that serves as the basis for the filing of a petition should be sworn to and signed by a person who has personal knowledge of the facts or is informed of them and believes that they are true.

2.11 Intake investigation.

A. Prior to making a dispositional decision, the intake officer should be authorized to conduct a preliminary investigation in order to obtain information essential to the making of the decision.

B. In the course of the investigation the intake officer may:
   1. interview or otherwise seek information from the complainant, a victim of, witness to, or coparticipant in the delinquent conduct allegedly engaged in by the juvenile;
   2. check existing court records, the records of law enforcement agencies, and other public records of a nonprivate nature;
   3. conduct interviews with the juvenile and his or her parents or legal guardian in accordance with the requirements set forth in Standard 2.14.

C. If the officer wishes to make any additional inquiries, he or she should do so only with the consent of the juvenile and his or her parents or legal guardian.

D. It is the responsibility of the complainant to furnish the intake officer with information sufficient to establish the jurisdiction of the court over the juvenile and to support the charges against the juvenile. If the officer believes the information to be deficient in this respect, he or she may notify the complainant of the need for additional information.

2.12 Juvenile's privilege against self-incrimination at intake.

A. A juvenile should have a privilege against self-incrimination in connection with questioning by intake personnel during the intake process.

B. Any statement made by a juvenile to an intake officer or other information derived directly or indirectly from such a statement is inadmissible in evidence in any judicial proceeding prior to a formal finding of delinquency unless the statement was made after consultation with and in the presence of counsel.

2.13 Juvenile's right to assistance of counsel at intake.

A juvenile should have an unwaivable right to the assistance of counsel at intake:

A. in connection with any questioning by intake personnel at an intake interview involving questioning in accordance with Standard 2.14 or other questioning by intake personnel; and

B. in connection with any discussions or negotiations regarding a nonjudicial disposition, including discussions and negotiations in the course of a dispositional conference in accordance with Standard 2.14.

2.14 Intake interviews and dispositional conferences.

A. If the intake officer deems it advisable, the officer may request and arrange an interview with the juvenile and his or her parents or legal guardian.

B. Participation in an intake interview by the juvenile and his or her parents or legal guardian should be voluntary. They should have the right to refuse to participate in an interview, and the officer should have no authority to compel their attendance.

C. At the time the request to attend the interview is made, the intake officer should inform the juvenile and his or her parents or legal guardian either in writing or orally that attendance is voluntary and that the juvenile has the right to be represented by counsel.

D. At the commencement of the interview, the intake officer should:
   1. explain to the juvenile and his or her parents or legal guardian that a complaint has been made and explain the allegations of the complaint;
   2. explain the function of the intake process, the dispositional powers of the intake officer, and intake procedures;
   3. explain that participation in the intake interview is voluntary and that they may refuse to participate; and
   4. notify them of the right of the juvenile to remain silent and the right to counsel as heretofore defined in Standard 2.13.

E. Subsequent to the intake interview, the intake officer may schedule one or more dispositional conferences with the juvenile and his or her parents or legal guardian in order to effect a nonjudicial disposition.

F. Participation in a dispositional conference by a juvenile and his or her parents or legal guardian should be voluntary. They should have the right to refuse to participate, and the intake officer should have no authority to compel their attendance.

G. The intake officer may conduct dispositional conferences in accordance with the procedures for intake interviews set forth in subsections D and E.

2.15 Length of intake process.

A decision at the intake level as to the disposition of a complaint should be made as expeditiously as possible. The period within which the decision is made should not exceed thirty (30) days from the date the complaint is filed in cases in which the juvenile who is the subject of a complaint has not been placed in detention or shelter care facilities.

SECTION V: SCOPE OF INTAKE OFFICER'S DISPOSITIONAL POWERS

2.16 Role of intake officer and prosecutor in filing of petition: right of complainant to file a petition.

  A. If the intake officer determines that a petition should be filed, the officer should submit a written report to the appropriate prosecuting official requesting that a petition should be filed. The officer should also submit a written statement of his or her decision and of the reasons for the decision to the juvenile and his or her parents or legal guardian. All petitions should be countersigned and filed by the appropriate prosecuting official. The prosecutor may refuse the request of the intake officer to file a petition. Any determination by the prosecutor that a petition should not be filed should be final.
  B. If the intake officer determines that a petition should not be filed, the officer should notify the complainant of his or her decision and of the reasons for the decision and should advise the complainant that he or she may submit the complaint to the appropriate prosecuting official for review. Upon receiving a request for review, the prosecutor should consider the facts presented by the complainant, consult with the intake officer who made the initial decision, and then make the final determination as to whether a petition should be filed.
  C. In the absence of a complainant's request for a review of the intake officer's determination that a petition should not be filed, the intake officer should notify the appropriate prosecuting official of the officer's decision not to request the filing of a petition in those cases in which the conduct charged would constitute a crime if committed by an adult. The prosecutor should have the right in all such cases, after consultation with the intake officer, to file a petition.

PART III: PREDISPOSITION INVESTIGATIONS AND REPORTS

3.1 Availability and utilization of investigative services.

Investigative services should be made available to and utilized by all juvenile courts.

3.2 Necessity for and desirability of written guidelines and rules.

Juvenile probation agencies and other agencies performing investigative services should establish written guidelines and rules for the conduct of predisposition investigations and the preparation and submission of predisposition reports.

3.3 Scope of investigation; formulation of postdisposition plan; format, contents, length, and disclosure of report.

A. The scope of a predisposition investigation that the investigating officer conducts should be carefully tailored to the needs of the individual case and should vary depending upon the type of case and the issues involved. The officer should only collect evidence relevant to the court's dispositional decision.

B. When it is appropriate for the investigating officer to conduct a comprehensive investigation, the officer may secure information from existing records of the juvenile court, law enforcement agencies, schools, and other agencies with which the juvenile has come in contact and from interviews and conferences with the juvenile, the juvenile's family, school personnel, and individuals having knowledge of the juvenile.

C. An officer conducting a predisposition investigation may refer a juvenile for a physical or mental examination to a physician, psychiatrist, or psychologist only if a court order authorizing an examination is obtained. Such a court order should be issued only after a hearing on the need for such an examination.

D. The officer conducting the predisposition investigation should explore community resources as well as other resources that might be available to assist the juvenile. The officer should then formulate a postdisposition plan for the care and, where appropriate, for the treatment of the juvenile.

E. A written predisposition report summarizing the significant findings of the investigation should be prepared. The format, contents, and length of the report should be flexible. A comprehensive report should ordinarily include the following:
   1. a summary of the facts with respect to the conduct of the juvenile that led to the adjudication;
   2. a summary of the juvenile's prior contacts with the juvenile

court and law enforcement agencies, including the disposition following each contact and the reasons therefor;

3. a summary of the juvenile's home environment, family relationships and background;
4. a summary of the juvenile's school and employment status and background;
5. a summary of the juvenile's interests and activities;
6. a summary of any significant physical problems of the juvenile and description of any behavior problems of the juvenile that the officer learns of or observes in the course of the investigation, provided the officer is careful not to represent these observations as qualified professional evaluations;
7. a summary of the results and recommendations of any significant physical and mental examinations; and
8. an evaluation of the foregoing information, a recommendation as to disposition, and a suggested postdisposition plan of care and treatment.

F. The predisposition report should contain only information that is relevant to the court's dispositional decision, and all information should be presented in a concise, factual, and unbiased manner. The report should indicate how much time and effort was expended upon the investigation and the sources of information in the report.

G. The predisposition report should not be open to public inspection, but the juvenile's counsel and the attorney representing the state in connection with dispositional proceedings should be given access to the report.

3.4 Investigation; when conducted. Report; when submitted.

A. An investigating officer should not conduct a predisposition investigation until a juvenile has been adjudicated delinquent, unless the juvenile with the advice of counsel consents to an earlier investigation.

B. An investigating officer should submit the predisposition report to the court subsequent to adjudication and prior to disposition. In no event should the court consider the report in advance of adjudication.

PART IV: ORGANIZATION AND ADMINISTRATION OF JUVENILE INTAKE AND PREDISPOSITION INVESTIGATIVE SERVICES

4.1 Specialization of the intake, investigative, and probation supervision functions.

A. Whenever possible, intake screening, predisposition investigations, and supervision of juveniles should be treated as specialized functions.
B. Juvenile probation agencies or other agencies responsible for performing these three functions should not ordinarily simultaneously assign probation supervision duties as well as intake screening and predisposition investigative duties to the same individual. Such agencies should either establish separate units for each of these three functions or establish one unit with the responsibility for intake screening and predisposition investigation and another unit with the responsibility for supervision of juvenile probationers.

4.2 Executive agency administration vs. judicial administration.

Intake and predisposition investigative services should be administered by an [executive] agency rather than by the judiciary.

4.3 State vs. local organization and administration.

Intake and predisposition investigative services should be organized and administered either at the state level on a statewide basis or partly at the state level and partly at the local level.

4.4 Financing of intake and predisposition investigative services.

State funds should be made available to subsidize intake and predisposition investigative services in jurisdictions where local juvenile probation agencies or other local agencies provide these services and these services are presently financed primarily out of local funds.

PART V: INTAKE AND INVESTIGATIVE PERSONNEL

5.1 Qualifications and selection of officers.

A. Statewide mandatory minimum standards should be established for the selection procedures and for the qualifications of individuals to be employed as juvenile intake and investigating officers in professional staff positions.
B. The qualifications required for professional staff positions may include formal education or training of a certain type and duration, previous work experience of a certain type and duration, previous job performance of a certain quality, and personal characteristics and skills that are related to successful performance of intake and investigating duties.
C. The minimum educational requirements for entry level profes-

sional staff positions should be a bachelor's degree supplemented by a year of graduate study in social work or the behavioral sciences, a year of full-time employment under professional supervision for a correctional or social services agency, or equivalent experience.

D. Agencies should select individuals for professional staff positions upon a merit basis.

E. Agencies should recruit and employ as juvenile intake and investigating officers individuals, including minority group members and women, from a wide variety of backgrounds.

5.2 Tenure and promotion.

A. Intake and investigating officers should not be subject to arbitrary discharge during or after a probationary period.

B. Juvenile probation agencies and other agencies responsible for intake and investigative services should establish career ladders, and juvenile intake and investigating officers should be promoted in accordance with such career ladders on a merit basis. Career ladders should be structured so that officers have the choice of promotion along two different tracks. One promotion track should be available for officers who wish to do intake screening and conduct predisposition investigations. Another promotion track should be available for officers who wish to perform supervisory or administrative duties.

5.3 Education and training.

A. The appropriate state agency should establish statewide mandatory minimum standards for preservice and inservice education and training programs for intake and investigating officers.

B. State and local agencies responsible for providing predisposition investigative services should jointly plan and develop preservice and inservice training programs for officers at every level.

C. Colleges and universities should be encouraged to establish and maintain both undergraduate and graduate degree programs that will prepare individuals who wish to perform intake and investigative services.

5.4 Salary scales.

A. Salary scales of intake and investigative personnel at every level should be commensurate with their education, training, and experience and comparable to those in related fields.

B. Salary scales should be structured so that promotion to a supervisory position is not the only means of obtaining a salary increase. Merit salary increases should be available for outstanding job performance and for completion of advanced education or training.

5.5 Workloads and staff ratios.

A. Juvenile probation agencies and other agencies responsible for intake and predisposition investigative services should establish standards for workloads and staff ratios.
B. Workloads of intake and investigating officers should vary depending upon such factors as the specific functions performed by an officer, the complexity and seriousness of the cases that the officer handles, the education and training of the officer, the availability of clerical and other support services, and the availability of community resources that can be utilized by the officer in performing his or her duties.

5.6 Employment of paraprofessionals and use of volunteers.

A. Juvenile probation agencies and other agencies responsible for intake and predisposition investigative services should recruit, employ, and train individuals who do not possess the qualifications necessary for employment as intake and investigating officers as paraprofessional aides to assist intake and investigating officers. Paraprofessionals should be given an opportunity to participate in career development programs that can lead to advancement on the career ladder to professional staff positions.
B. Agencies should recruit and employ as paraprofessionals individuals from a wide variety of backgrounds, including minority group members and women.
C. Juvenile intake and investigating officers should establish and maintain programs utilizing citizen volunteers.
D. Citizen volunteers may successfully perform a wide variety of functions ranging from the direct provision of services to juveniles to office work of an administrative or clerical nature.
E. Volunteers may be recruited from a wide variety of backgrounds and sources depending upon the functions they are to perform. Juvenile intake and investigating officers should carefully screen volunteers in order to insure that they have the qualifications necessary for the work to which they will be assigned.

F. Agencies should establish preservice and inservice orientation and training programs for volunteers.

STANDARDS RELATING TO JUVENILE RECORDS AND INFORMATION SERVICES

Michael L. Altman, Reporter

SECTION I: GENERAL STANDARDS

PART I: DEFINITIONS

1.1 Juvenile agency.

A juvenile agency is:

A. any court, other than a divorce court or a court determining adoptions, that has the legal authority to issue orders pertaining to the custody or liberty of a juvenile;
B. any publicly funded agency that has the legal authority to confer or deny clinical, evaluative, counseling, medical, educational, or residential services to a juvenile;
C. any private agency that is licensed to provide such services to a juvenile;
D. any private agency that has a contract with a public agency to provide such services to a juvenile; and
E. any private agency that regularly provides such services to juveniles as a result of referrals to the private agency by a public agency.

1.2 Juvenile.

A juvenile is any person under the age of eighteen or any person who, as a result of a delinquency or neglect petition, is subject either to an order of commitment or to conditions of probation or release that in any way restrict the liberty of the person.

1.3 Juvenile record.

A juvenile record is any record of or in the custody of a juvenile agency pertaining to a juvenile and maintained in a manner so that the juvenile is identified or may be identified. A juvenile record includes records maintained in any manner, automated or manual, and retrievable in any form: handwritten files, tape recordings, computer tapes, microfilm, or any other form.

1.4 Parent.

A parent is a person with whom a juvenile regularly lives and who is the natural, adoptive, or surrogate parent of a juvenile.

1.5 Surrogate parent.

A surrogate parent is an adult person who has been appointed by a court as legal guardian of the juvenile, or an adult person who has voluntarily assumed the role of parent with respect to the juvenile. A surrogate parent does not include an agency or institution, or a person employed by an agency or institution, to which the juvenile has been committed or referred by order of the court.

1.6 Direct access.

Direct access is the right to enter the record room, file cabinet, or other place where juvenile records are stored, for the purpose of withdrawing a record so that it may be observed by an authorized person for an authorized purpose.

1.7 Access.

Access is the right to view and photocopy a juvenile record but not the right to enter the place where the juvenile records are physically stored.

1.8 Indirect access.

Indirect access is the right to receive information from a juvenile record but not the right to view or photocopy the actual record.

1.9 Dissemination.

Dissemination is the provision of direct access, access, or indirect access to a juvenile record.

1.10 Third person.

A third person is any agency or person other than:
A. the juvenile who is the subject of a juvenile record;
B. a parent or attorney of the juvenile; or
C. an employee of the juvenile agency that has custody of the juvenile's record.

1.11 Centralized information system.

A centralized information system is an information system, whether automated or manual, in which two or more juvenile agencies participate for the purpose of gathering, storing, processing, or disseminating information pertaining to identified or identifiable juveniles.

PART II: GENERAL POLICIES PERTAINING TO INFORMATION

2.1 Juveniles' privacy committee.
A. Each jurisdiction should establish by statute at least one juveniles'

privacy committee. The members of the committee should include persons who have knowledge and expertise in juvenile advocacy, delivery of services to juveniles, information systems, and criminal justice agency activities affecting juveniles.

B. The committee should have the authority to examine and evaluate juvenile records and information issues pertaining to juveniles and the right to conduct such inquiries and investigations as it deems necessary.

C. The committee should periodically make recommendations concerning privacy, juvenile records, and information practices and policies pertaining to juveniles.

D. The committee should have the authority to receive automation statements submitted by juvenile agencies pursuant to Standard 4.6, in order to computerize juvenile records.

E. The committee should have the authority to receive proposals submitted by juvenile agencies to establish a centralized information system.

F. The committee should have the authority to commence civil actions against juvenile agencies for declaratory judgments, cease and desist orders, and other appropriate injunctive relief in cases involving the failure to promulgate written rules and regulations pursuant to Standard 2.2 or the improper collection, retention, or dissemination of a juvenile record or identifiable information pertaining to juveniles.

2.2 Rules and regulations.

A juvenile agency should develop written rules and regulations, consistent with these standards, governing the agency's collection, retention, and dissemination of information pertaining to juveniles. Copies of the rules and regulations should be filed with the juveniles' privacy committee and made available to the public.

2.3 Civil remedy.

The legislature of each jurisdiction should promulgate a statute making it a tort to improperly collect, retain, or disseminate information pertaining to juveniles. Improper collection, retention, or dissemination should be presumed if such acts are committed in violation of an applicable federal, state, or local law or in violation of a juvenile agency's duly promulgated rules or regulations. In such cases, a juvenile should be entitled to monetary compensation, if actual damages are incurred as a result of the improper collection, retention, or dissemination of information; to an appropriate equitable remedy, if the improper act has not been corrected or there is a reasonable possibility that the improper act may be repeated; to punitive damages if it is established that the improper act was willful; and to attorneys' fees and other reasonably incurred litigation costs if the juvenile establishes that the collection, retention, or dissemination of information was improper.

2.4 Criminal penalty.

The legislature of each jurisdiction should promulgate a statute making it a misdemeanor for any person to unlawfully and willfully obtain or attempt to obtain a juvenile record, or information from such a record; to unlawfully and willfully provide access, disclose, or attempt to communicate information from a juvenile record; or to unlawfully and willfully destroy or falsify information in or to be included in a juvenile record.

2.5 Administrative sanctions.

The rules and regulations promulgated by a juvenile agency should provide for disciplinary sanctions to be imposed, including dismissal, where appropriate, for violation of any law or rule of the juvenile agency pertaining to the collection, retention, or dissemination of information and should further provide procedures for filing disciplinary complaints and for according a hearing to personnel who are the subject of a complaint.

2.6 Correction of records; periodic audits.

A. The rules and regulations promulgated by each juvenile agency should establish a procedure by which a juvenile, or his or her representative, may challenge the correctness of a record and which further provides for notice to be given to each juvenile over the age of ten who is the subject of a juvenile record of the availability of such a procedure. Such notice should also be given to a parent of the juvenile if the parent has a right of access to the record pursuant to Standard 5.2.

B. The procedure established to provide an opportunity to challenge the correctness of a record should include the right to a hearing before an official of the juvenile agency who has the authority to make any corrections that may be necessary as a result of a challenge and should also include procedures by which a juvenile or his or her parents may file a statement of disagreement and ex-

planation which will become a part of the record if the challenge is rejected.
C. Each juvenile agency should periodically conduct an audit to verify that adequate controls have been established to ensure the accuracy and completeness of its juvenile records.

2.7 Training programs.

Each juvenile agency should provide training programs for its personnel and should develop operations manuals describing the laws, policies, and practices concerning the collection, retention, and dissemination of information pertaining to juveniles.

2.8 Researcher's privilege.

Statutes should be promulgated providing that information collected or retained by an approved researcher or evaluator is privileged.

PART III: COLLECTION OF INFORMATION

3.1 Relationship of information and decision making.

The rules and regulations promulgated by a juvenile agency governing the collection of information pertaining to juveniles should take into account that:
A. too much as well as too little information can inhibit the process of decision;
B. the need for information increases as the options available to the decision maker increase and decreases as the available options decrease; and
C. information that is collected is often misused, misinterpreted, or not used.

3.2 Purposes of information collection.

A juvenile agency should only collect information with respect to juveniles if the information is being collected for proper purposes. Those purposes are limited to:
A. making lawful decisions pertaining to juveniles;
B. managing the agency effectively and efficiently;
C. evaluating the agency; and
D. approved research.

3.3 Standards for the collection of information.

A juvenile agency should only collect information pertaining to an identifiable juvenile if:

A. reasonable safeguards have been established to protect against the misuse, misinterpretation, and improper dissemination of the information:

B. the information is both relevant and necessary to a proper purpose for collecting the information;

C. the information will be utilized within a reasonable period of time for a proper purpose;

D. an evaluation (conducted pursuant to Standard 3.4) indicates that it would be reasonable to rely upon the type of information for the purposes for which it is collected;

E. the cost of collecting the information, considered in relation to the significance of the purpose for collecting the information, does not appear to be excessive;

F. the collection of the information does not involve an invasion of privacy; and

G. it is reasonable to expect that the information collected will be accurate.

3.4 Periodic evaluation of information collection practices and policies.

A juvenile agency should periodically prepare or cause to be prepared a written evaluation of its policies and practices with respect to the collection of information pertaining to juveniles. Each such evaluation should include consideration of the following:

A. the specific information that is being collected;

B. the cost of collecting the information;

C. the reliability of the information that is being collected;

D. the purpose of collecting the information;

E. the extent to which the information collected is used for the purposes for which it is collected;

F. the validity of relying upon the information for the purposes for which it is collected;

G. the extent to which or the risk that the information is or may be misused or misinterpreted;

H. the extent to which the information is regarded as private or the means of collecting the information may be regarded as an invasion of privacy;

I. the extent to which the information is necessary for making a particular decision;

J. the effect of making decisions in individual cases without the information.

The written evaluation should be a public record and available to the public and consumers of the agency's services.

3.5 Information collected for research or evaluation.

A. A juvenile agency should permit the collection of information for purposes of research or evaluation.
B. Any person who, for purposes of research or evaluation, seeks to collect information from or concerning an identifiable juvenile should file a formal written application, pursuant to Standard 5.6, with the juvenile agency that will provide access to the juvenile or to information concerning the juvenile.
C. Any person who seeks to collect information from or concerning an identifiable juvenile, pursuant to this standard, should obtain the written consent of the juvenile, if the juvenile is emancipated or over the age of fifteen, and his or her parents after informing them of the purposes for which the information is to be collected, the safeguards that have been established to ensure the security of the information, and the right of the juvenile or his or her parents to refuse their consent to the collection of such information.
D. A juvenile and his or her parents need not be informed and their consent need not be obtained if the information is collected in a manner so that it cannot be linked with an identifiable juvenile or the information is not of a personal nature.

3.6 Collection of personal information.

A juvenile agency should not collect information of a personal nature from a juvenile without first informing the juvenile, if over the age of ten, of the agencies or persons who have a right of access to the information that may be collected. If information of a personal nature is to be collected from a juvenile not over the age of ten, a parent of the juvenile should be so informed.

PART IV: RETENTION OF INFORMATION

4.1 Information retention as a separate decision.

The decision of a juvenile agency to retain information in written form or in a form so that it may be retrieved by third persons is a separate decision which should be made in addition to the initial decision to collect the information.

4.2 Standards for the retention of information.

The decision of a juvenile agency to retain information pertaining to an identifiable juvenile, in written form or in any other retrievable form, should be based upon a determination that:

A. the information is collectible, as set forth in Standard 3.3;
B. the information is accurate;
C. it is reasonable to expect that the information will be utilized at a later time;
D. reasonable safeguards have been established to protect against the misuse, misinterpretation, and improper dissemination of the information; and
E. it is likely that retaining the information in written or other retrievable form will ensure that the information will be recalled more accurately; or
F. the information has been collected as a part of a formal judicial or administrative proceeding.

4.3 Duty of disclosure of record retention.

A juvenile agency should not retain a juvenile record without making a reasonable effort to notify in writing the juvenile who is the subject of the record and a parent of the juvenile, if a parent has a right of access to the record pursuant to Standard 5.2, that:

A. the record has been retained;
B. there is a right of access to the record; and
C. there is a right to challenge the accuracy of the record as well as the agency's right to retain the record.

4.4 Retention of administrative data.

Information collected by a juvenile agency for the purpose of making internal administrative decisions or for the purpose of internal evaluation should not be retained in a form so that individual juveniles may be identified unless such identification is necessary for internal purposes during the period of evaluation.

4.5 Limited use of labels.

A juvenile record should not include summary conclusions or labels describing an identified juvenile's behavioral, social, medical, or psychological history or predicting an identified juvenile's future behavior, capacity, or attitudes unless the underlying factual basis, meaning, and implications are explained in terms that are understandable to a non-professional person, and their use is necessary.

4.6 Retention of information in computers.

A. The decision by a juvenile agency to use a computerized system to store information pertaining to identifiable juveniles should be subject to evaluation and comment by a juveniles' privacy committee.

B. Before a juvenile agency utilizes a computerized information system pertaining to identifiable juveniles, it should submit an "automation statement" to a juveniles' privacy committee for evaluation and comment.

C. The "automation statement" should include a detailed description of the system to be utilized, the data to be stored in the system, the purposes of the system, the quality controls to be provided, access and dissemination provisions, methods for protecting privacy and ensuring system and personnel security, provision for an independent audit, and estimated costs of establishing and maintaining the system.

D. The data included in a computerized system pertaining to identifiable juveniles should be objective and factual and should not include data of a subjective or predictive nature.

E. A proposed computerized system should satisfy the following criteria:

1. the ability of the juvenile agency to deliver services to juveniles will be substantially enhanced by the proposed computerized system;

2. the proposed system includes only the minimum objective data necessary to accomplish the purposes of automation;

3. the proposed system is designed to ensure the accuracy, confidentiality, and security of the data to be included in the system;

4. the proposed system is programmed to ensure compliance with Standard 3.3 (pertaining to the collection of information), Standard 4.2 (pertaining to the retention of information), and Part V (pertaining to the dissemination of information);

5. the juveniles whose records are to be computerized are identified by an arbitrary nonduplicating number instead of by name; and

6. the economic and privacy costs of automation are less than the benefits to be obtained by automation.

F. A juveniles' privacy committee should publicize the fact that an "automation statement" has been filed, make the statement available to interested citizens, groups, and agencies, and provide an opportunity for the receipt of comments and evidence with respect to the statement and the juvenile agency that has proposed the system.

G. After evaluating a proposed computerized system, the juveniles' privacy committee should issue a written evaluation and that evaluation should be a public record.

4.7 Centralized record keeping limited.

A. The legislature of each jurisdiction should promulgate a statute prohibiting juvenile agencies from utilizing centralized information systems in which information pertaining to identified juveniles is or may be shared, or through which individual information systems are or may be linked, except as provided in Standard 4.7 B.

B. The only data that should be stored in a centralized information system are the minimum data necessary to identify the juvenile, the names of those agencies that have provided or will provide services to the juvenile or his or her family, and the dates that those services were or will be provided.

C. Before any centralized information system is utilized that contains the minimum data authorized by subsection B and before any information system is designed to provide for the sharing or linking of juvenile record information, a proposal for the information system should be submitted to a juveniles' privacy committee for evaluation and comment.

PART V: DISSEMINATION OF INFORMATION

5.1 Direct access limited to designated personnel.

Direct access to a juvenile record should be limited to those clerical and professional persons specifically designated by the chief administrator of each juvenile agency. The number of persons so designated should be kept to a minimum based upon a criterion of necessity.

5.2 Access by the juvenile and his or her representatives.

A juvenile, his or her parents, and the juvenile's attorney should, upon request, be given access to all records and information collected or retained by a juvenile agency which pertain to the juvenile except:

A. if the information is likely to cause harm, the provisions of Standard 5.5 should be applied; and

B. if the information or record has been obtained by a juvenile agency (other than a juvenile court) in connection with the provision of counseling, psychological, psychiatric, or medical services to the juvenile, and the juvenile has a legal right to receive those services without the consent of his or her parents, then the information or record should not in any way be disclosed or disseminated to the juvenile's parents unless the written consent of the juvenile is obtained and the juvenile has been fully informed of his or her right not to have the information or record disclosed to his or her parents.

5.3 Access by agency personnel.

The personnel of a juvenile agency should not be given access or indirect access to a juvenile record possessed by the agency except for the purpose of providing services to the juvenile or for other proper agency purposes.

5.4 Access by third persons.

Except as permitted by Standards 5.3, 5.6, and 5.7, access or indirect access to a juvenile record should only be accorded to a third person under the following circumstances:

A. the juvenile, if over the age of ten, is informed of the specific information to be disclosed, the purposes of disclosure, and the possible consequences of disclosure; and

B. a parent of the juvenile is informed of the specific information to be disclosed, the purposes of disclosure, and the possible consequences of disclosure, except, a parent should not be so informed if the parent does not have a right of access to the information pursuant to Standard 5.2; and

C. the juvenile, if emancipated or over the age of fifteen, or, if his or her parent is not informed of the proposed disclosure in accordance with subsection B, has consented to the proposed disclosure of the information; and

D. a parent of the juvenile has consented to the proposed disclosure in those instances in which consent of the juvenile is not required by subsection C; and

E. the juvenile agency that has possession of the information has reevaluated the information within the past ninety days and has determined that, to the best of its knowledge, the information is accurate, or the record contains a clear and conspicuous statement of the last date the record was reviewed for accuracy and completeness, and also a warning that conditions may have changed since that date; and

F. the juvenile agency that has possession of the information has determined that disclosure of the information to the third person is appropriate; and

G. the third person to whom access or indirect access is to be accorded executes a written nondisclosure agreement or promises to execute such an agreement within forty-eight hours; or

H. a compelling health or safety need exists, consent is not reasonably obtainable pursuant to subsection C above, and disclosure is made to a court for the purpose of obtaining consent.

5.5 Special obligation when information may be harmful.

If it is determined by a professional person who has been assigned responsibility for a juvenile or his or her case that disclosure of certain information is likely to cause severe psychological or physical harm to the juvenile or his or her parents, the professional person should either:

A. arrange to provide professional counseling for the juvenile and his or her parents so that, upon disclosure of the potentially harmful information, the family will have one appropriate professional support; or

B. withhold the potentially harmful information from the juvenile and his or her parents until that information has been disclosed to an independent representative of the juvenile, selected by the juvenile, so that the representative may make an independent judgment of whether the information is accurate and disclosure of the information to the juvenile or his or her parents is necessary; or

C. delete the potentially harmful information from all records of the juvenile agency and ensure that the information will not be used in any way against the juvenile.

5.6 Access for research or evaluation.

A. Any person who seeks access to or information from juvenile records for purposes of research or evaluation should file a formal written application with the juvenile agency that has custody of the records. A copy of the application should also be sent to the juveniles' privacy committee.

B. The juvenile agency should approve the application if, after considering the views of the juveniles' privacy committee, and after examining the application, the applicant, and such other information that may be available, the juvenile agency is satisfied that:

1. the applicant has adequate training and qualifications to undertake the proposed research or evaluation project;
2. the proposed project is to be undertaken for valid educational, scientific, or other public purposes;
3. the application includes an acceptable and detailed description of the proposed project including a specific statement of the information required and the purpose for which the project requires the information;
4. the proposed project is designed to preserve the anonymity of the juveniles who are the subject of records or information to which access is sought;
5. the applicant has agreed in a sworn statement not to reproduce any information from a juvenile record, except for internal purposes, and has agreed not to disclose any information from a juvenile record to an unauthorized person; and
6. the applicant has agreed to provide a list of the names and addresses of each person who will be a member of the staff of the proposed project and to provide a sworn statement, signed by each of them, not to disclose any information from a juvenile record to an unauthorized person.

C. Before approving or disapproving an application for research or evaluation, the juvenile agency should make written findings with respect to the criteria set forth in subsection B.

D. Upon approving or disapproving an application, the written findings and conclusion with respect to the application should be filed with the juveniles' privacy committee.

E. Any final reports, findings, or conclusions of the research or evaluation project should be a public record and should be presented so that individual juveniles cannot be identified either directly or indirectly.

F. A juvenile agency that approves a research or evaluation project and the juveniles' privacy committee should have the right to inspect any approved project. If at any time the juvenile agency has reason to believe that the project is not being carried forward as agreed or is being conducted in a manner contrary to the research application, it should terminate the project's access to records or impose such other restrictions as may be necessary and proper.

G. If an application filed pursuant to this standard is disapproved, the applicant should be given the right to appeal the disapproval to a court of general jurisdiction.

5.7 Access to juvenile records for law enforcement or judicial purposes limited.

A. Access to juvenile records should not be provided to a law enforcement agency by a juvenile agency unless:
1. the consent of the juvenile who is the subject of the record or his or her parents is obtained in accordance with Standard 5.4; or
2. a judge determines, after *in camera* examination of the record of a designated juvenile, that such access is relevant and necessary.
B. Juvenile records should only be produced for a legal proceeding pursuant to a subpoena.
C. Juvenile records, other than records retained by or for a juvenile court, and the information contained therein, should not be admissible in any proceeding unless:
1. the juvenile who is the subject of the record or his or her parents consent to the disclosure of the record or information in accordance with Standard 5.4 and the record or information is otherwise admissible; or
2. a judge determines, after examining the record or information *in camera*, that the record or information is not all or a part of a social or psychological history (prepared by or for a juvenile agency other than a juvenile court), that it is relevant and necessary for the purpose of the proceeding, and that the admission of the record or information is warranted, notwithstanding that its admission may be inconsistent with the juvenile's expectation of privacy.
D. In cases in which a juvenile's record is admitted pursuant to subsection C.2, the reasons for its admission should be set forth in writing and made a part of the record.

5.8 Destruction of records.

A. The rules and regulations of a juvenile agency should provide for the periodic destruction of its juvenile records based upon appropriate criteria such as: the death of the subject of the record, the age of the record, the likelihood that the record will not be useful to the agency or the juvenile in the future and the benefits to be derived from retaining the record are outweighed by the risk that its further retention may cause harm to the juvenile if it is improperly disseminated.

B. Whenever possible, a juvenile agency should provide an opportunity to the juvenile who is the subject of a record to obtain a copy of the record before it is destroyed if further retention of the record by the juvenile might be useful.

SECTION II: SPECIFIC STANDARDS FOR JUVENILES' SOCIAL AND PSYCHOLOGICAL HISTORIES

PART VI: DEFINITION

6.1 Social or psychological histories.

A social or psychological history is information retained in any retrievable form by a juvenile agency, pertaining to an identifiable juvenile's family, social, or psychological background, for the purposes of:

A. providing counseling to the juvenile;
B. making a decision whether to confer or deny a service, a placement, or other benefit to the juvenile;
C. predicting whether the juvenile will engage in future antisocial conduct; and
D. determining the disposition of a juvenile case either before or after the juvenile has been adjudicated, neglected, or delinquent.

PART VII: PREPARATION OF SOCIAL HISTORIES

7.1 Duty to inform of history preparation.

A. Before information is collected for the purpose of preparing a social or psychological history of a juvenile, the juvenile, if over the age of ten, and, if required by subsection B, a parent of the juvenile should be informed of:
1. the purposes of the history;
2. the persons and agencies that are likely to be provided access to the history;
3. the persons and agencies that are likely to be contacted to provide information for the history;
4. the persons and qualifications of the persons who will prepare the history; and
5. the right of the juvenile, his or her parents, or representative

to deny consent to the preparation of the history when such consent is required by Standard 7.2.

B. A parent of the juvenile who is to be the subject of the history should be given the information required by Standard 7.1 A unless the juvenile agency which is preparing the history or causing it to be prepared is an agency other than a juvenile court or other than an agency acting for a juvenile court and the history is to be prepared in connection with the provision of counseling, psychological, psychiatric, or medical services to the juvenile which the juvenile has a legal right to receive without parental consent.

7.2 Consent to prepare history; when required.

Before information is selected for the purpose of preparing a social or psychological history of a juvenile by or for a juvenile agency, other than a juvenile court, consent should be obtained from:

A. the juvenile;
   1. if the history is to be prepared in connection with the provision of counseling, psychological, psychiatric, or medical services to the juvenile which the juvenile has a legal right to receive without parental consent, or
   2. if the juvenile is emancipated or over the age of fifteen;
B. a parent of the juvenile if the history is to be prepared in connection with the provision of services to the juvenile, which services may only be provided upon obtaining parental consent.

PART VIII: RETENTION OF SOCIAL HISTORIES

8.1 Duty to account for and ensure the security of social histories.

A juvenile agency that prepares or has received a copy of a social or psychological history of a juvenile should:

A. ensure that the history is stored in a secure place to which only authorized personnel have access and which is separate from legal records, administrative records, and records pertaining to adults; and
B. retain a log of all requests for information from or copies of the history, the identity of each person making a request, the dates of the request, the reasons for the request, and the disposition of the request.

PART IX: DISSEMINATION OF SOCIAL HISTORIES

9.1 Providing access to social histories.

    A. A juvenile agency that has prepared or that has received a copy of a social or psychological history should provide access to the history to the juvenile, his or her parents, and the juvenile's attorney, in accordance with Standards 5.2 and 5.5. If the native language of the juvenile or his or her parents is not English, the history should be appropriately translated. If the history contains professional language or other information that may not be understood by the juvenile or his or her parents, the history should be explained to them by the appropriate professional.

    B. A social or psychological history of a juvenile, and the contents of such a history, are confidential and should not be disseminated by a juvenile agency to any person, except as provided in subsection A, unless the consent of a parent and/or juvenile is obtained pursuant to Standard 5.4.

    C. A juvenile agency that has prepared a social or psychological history for another agency or that releases a copy of the history to a third person should not release the history in summary form. A detailed factual explanation of any diagnosis or conclusion should be set forth and labels should only be included in accordance with Standard 4.5. A statement, e.g., that a juvenile is mentally retarded or schizophrenic, without a detailed description of the symptoms, the instruments and methods utilized in evaluation, and the extent of evaluation should not be released.

PART X: DESTRUCTION OF SOCIAL HISTORIES

10.1 Duty to destroy history.

    A. If a juvenile agency, other than an institution or court that has custody or control of the juvenile, possesses a social or psychological history of a juvenile, and the juvenile thereafter becomes eighteen years of age, the juvenile agency should send a written notice to the juvenile at his or her last known address informing him or her that the history will be destroyed within thirty days unless the juvenile files a written objection to the destruction.

    B. Such juvenile agency that possesses a social or psychological history of a juvenile should destroy that history and all references to it, if the juvenile does not object, within thirty days after notice is sent, pursuant to subsection A, except that in the case of a juvenile who is subject to the custody or control of a court or institution beyond the age of eighteen, the history and all references to it should be destroyed within 180 days after the juvenile has been released from such custody or control.

C. If a juvenile agency has "closed" the case of a juvenile who is the subject of a history, it may destroy that history and all references to it prior to the juvenile's eighteenth birthday.

D. Before destroying a history pursuant to this standard, the juvenile agency should provide a copy of that history to the juvenile if the juvenile can be located and if he or she so requests.

E. Upon destruction of a history, the juvenile agency should notify all other agencies to which it has sent copies of the history and they should immediately destroy all notations or references in their files that a history has been prepared.

SECTION III: SPECIFIC STANDARDS FOR THE RECORDS OF JUVENILE COURTS

PART XI: LEGISLATION

11.1 Need for comprehensive legislation.

The legislature of each jurisdiction should promulgate a comprehensive statute regulating the practices and policies of juvenile courts with respect to the collection, retention, dissemination, and use of information and records pertaining to juveniles.

11.2 Purposes of comprehensive legislation.

The purposes of comprehensive legislation pertaining to juvenile court records should be to:

A. establish a system of organizing and controlling the collection and retention of juvenile records and information pertaining to juveniles;

B. protect juveniles from the adverse consequences of disclosure of juvenile records;

C. establish safeguards to protect against the misuse, misinterpretation, and improper dissemination of juvenile records;

D. limit the collection and retention of juvenile records so that unnecessary and improper information is not collected or retained;

E. limit the information and juvenile records that may be disseminated to and used by third persons;

F. provide juveniles and their parents with maximum access to juvenile records pertaining to them;
G. regulate and provide for access to juvenile records by researchers and monitors; and
H. provide for the timely destruction of juvenile records.

PART XII: RECORDS OF JUVENILE COURTS

12.1 Duty to keep records.

A. Each juvenile court should maintain or cause to be maintained accurate, complete, and up-to-date records of all proceedings involving juveniles.
B. Records of legal proceedings involving juveniles should be kept separate from probation records.
C. Records of legal proceedings should at least include summary records, case indexes, case files, and statistical reports as set forth in Part XIII.

PART XIII: RECORDS OF LEGAL PROCEEDINGS

13.1 Summary records.

A. Each juvenile court should maintain or cause to be maintained a "summary record" of all proceedings of the court in which a juvenile is the subject of the proceedings and should designate a person to be responsible for such records.
B. The "summary record" should be limited to objective data and should include such information as the nature of the complaint, a summary of all formal proceedings, and the result of all proceedings.
C. The "summary record" should not include:
    1. records maintained by probation officers;
    2. information of a subjective or evaluative nature; or
    3. the name and address of the juvenile and his or her parents or other data of a similar identifying nature.
D. The "summary record" of each juvenile should be assigned a number when the matter is first referred to the court and that number should thereafter appear on all documents, records, and files of the court pertaining to the juvenile.
E. The "summary records" of active and closed cases should be

maintained separately in a secure place that is separate from the place where similar records are maintained for adults.

13.2 Case indexes.

A. Each juvenile court should maintain indexes to its active and closed cases and should designate a person to be responsible for such indexes.

B. The indexes should be maintained alphabetically, by the name of the juvenile, and should include only the following information: the name, address, and age of the juvenile, the name and address of the juvenile's parents, and the number assigned to the matter pursuant to Standard 13.1 D.

C. The personnel of each juvenile court who are provided direct access to the case indexes should be designated in writing by the court and the number of such persons should be limited to ensure that access to records may be meaningfully regulated and carefully controlled.

D. The personnel of each juvenile court should not maintain or develop any system, other than the official indexes, for indexing court files and records.

E. The indexes of active and closed cases should be maintained separately in a secure place that is separate from the place where similar indexes are maintained for adults.

13.3 Case files.

A. Each juvenile court should maintain a "case file" on each case in which a juvenile is the subject of a complaint or petition and should designate a person to be responsible for such files.

B. The "case file" on each case should include such formal documents as the complaint or petition, summonses, warrants, motions, legal memoranda, judicial orders or decrees, but not social histories.

C. The case files of active and closed cases should be maintained separately in a secure place that is separate from the place where similar files are maintained for adults.

13.4 Statistical reports.

A. Each juvenile court should prepare a monthly and annual statistical report of all proceedings of the court involving juveniles. The statistical report should include a maximum amount of aggregate data so that all of the proceedings of the court will be fully reported.

B. The chief justice of the highest court of each jurisdiction or his or her designee should develop standardized forms for collecting and reporting the data to ensure uniformity.

PART XIV: PROBATION RECORDS

14.1 Responsibility for and manner of retention.

A. All documents, reports, memoranda, and other information pertaining to a juvenile received or prepared by probation officers should be placed in either a "temporary probation file" or a "permanent probation file."

B. Each juvenile court or agency should designate a person to be responsible for all probation files, the collection of information by or for probation officers, and the dissemination of information from probation files.

C. The probation files of active and closed cases should be maintained separately in a secure place that is separate from the place where the probation files of adults are maintained.

14.2 Temporary probation files.

A. A "temporary probation file" should contain all unverified or unevaluated information which is being collected for an active case and all working papers and notes of the probation officer to whom the case has been assigned.

B. Upon meeting the criteria set forth in Standard 14.3, information included in a temporary probation file may be placed in the "permanent probation file." In any case, all information collected and retained in the "temporary probation file" should be destroyed within three months after it is collected or within ten days after the case has been closed, whichever is sooner.

14.3 Permanent probation files.

A. Before any information may be included in a "permanent probation file" a probation officer should determine that the information is verified and accurate.

B. A "permanent probation file," and the information included therein, should be the only file or information that is provided to a judge by a probation officer for purposes of the disposition of a case.

14.4 Duty to inform of probation investigation.

Before commencing an investigation of a juvenile, a probation officer should provide a parent of the juvenile and/or the juvenile with information pertaining to the investigation in accordance with Standard 7.1.

14.5 Duty to review and explain contents of report.

A. Before providing his or her report or recommendations or any information from the "permanent probation file" to a court, a probation officer responsible for the case should review and explain the contents of the report and file with the juvenile, his or her parents, and the juvenile's attorney (if the juvenile has an attorney) except, if disclosure of certain information is likely to cause harm, disclosure should be governed by Standard 5.5.
B. If the native language of the juvenile or his or her parents is not English, the report and contents of the file should be translated or reviewed and explained to them in their native language.
C. The juvenile and his or her parents should be informed that they have a right, and they should be given an opportunity to exercise their right, to make additions or corrections to the report and, if they do so, those additions or corrections should either be incorporated into the report or noted in an appendix to the report.

14.6 Duty to regulate information practices of outside agencies.

A juvenile court should ensure that every agency, organization, or department to which a juvenile is referred for care, treatment, or services has established and implemented written rules and regulations that protect the confidentiality and security of the records of the juveniles who have been referred by the court and that are consistent with the principles of these standards.

PART XV: ACCESS TO JUVENILE RECORDS

15.1 General policy on access.

A. Juvenile records should not be public records.
B. Access to and the use of juvenile records should be strictly controlled to limit the risk that disclosure will result in the misuse or misinterpretation of information, the unnecessary denial of opportunities and benefits to juveniles, or an interference with the purposes of official intervention.

Jeffery v. McHugh, 273 S.E.2d 837, 838 (W.Va. 1981). The court records of a juvenile who apparently hanged himself in an adult jail should be kept confidential in light of the general policy on anonymity, in spite of the youth's death. (Citing Standards 15.1 and 15.6)

The Ogden Newspapers, Inc. v. City of Williamstown, 453 S.E.2d 631, (W.Va. 1994). In weighing the public's "right to know with the strong public policy in favor of the confidentiality of juvenile court records, police incident reports should be redacted to preserve the identity of the youths before releasing them to news media. Even though the incident reports are public records, the goal of protecting juvenile anonymity is sufficiently strong to require this action prior to release. (Citing *Jeffery v. McHugh* and Standard 15.1)

15.2 Access to case files.

    A. Each juvenile court should provide access to a "case file" to the following persons;

        1. the juvenile who is the subject of the file, his or her parents, and his or her attorney;

        2. the prosecutor who has entered his or her appearance in the case;

        3. a party, and if he or she has an attorney who has entered an appearance on his or her behalf, the attorney;

        4. a judge, probation officer, or other professional person to whom the case has been assigned or before whom a proceeding with respect to the juvenile is pending or scheduled; and

        5. a person who is granted access for research purposes in accordance with Standard 5.6.

    B. A person who is a member of the clerical or administrative staff of a juvenile court, who has been previously designated in writing by the court, may be given direct access to a "case file" if such access is needed for authorized internal administrative purposes.

    C. A juvenile court should not provide access to nor permit the disclosure of information from a "case file" except in accordance with this standard.

15.3 Access to summary records.

    A. Each juvenile court should provide access to "summary records" to the following persons:

        1. those persons enumerated in Standard 15.2 A;

        2. the state juvenile correctional agency, if the juvenile is detained by or is otherwise subject to the custody or control of the agency;

3. the state department of motor vehicles, provided that the information given to the department is limited to information relating to traffic offenses that is specifically required by statute to be given to the department for the purpose of regulating automobile licensing;

4. a law enforcement agency for the purpose of executing an arrest warrant or other compulsory process or for the purpose of a current investigation.

B. A juvenile court should notify the law enforcement agency that arrested the juvenile or that initiated the filing of the complaint or petition of the final disposition of the case after such information is entered in the "summary record."

C. A juvenile court may provide direct access to a "summary record" to those persons enumerated in Standard 15.2 B.

D. A juvenile court should not provide access to nor permit the disclosure of information from a "summary record" except in accordance with subsections A and B of this standard.

E. A probation officer or other professional person may provide indirect access to a "summary record" with the written consent of the juvenile and his or her parents if the disclosure of summary information pertaining to the juvenile's record is necessary for the purpose of securing services or a benefit for the juvenile.

15.4 Access to probation records.

A. Each juvenile court should provide access to a "temporary probation file," in accordance with Standard 9.1, to the juvenile who is the subject of the file, his or her parents, and his or her attorney and may permit the disclosure of information from a "temporary probation file" to other persons but only if such disclosure is necessary and for the sole purpose of verifying the information.

B. Each juvenile court should provide access to a "permanent probation file," in accordance with Standard 9.1, to the juvenile who is the subject of the file, his or her parents, and his or her attorney.

C. Each juvenile court should provide access to a "permanent probation file" to those persons enumerated in Standard 15.2 A, subsections 2, 4, and 5, and Standard 15.3 A.2.

D. A person who is a member of the clerical, administrative, or professional staff of the probation office of a juvenile court, who has been previously designated in writing by the court, may be given direct access to a probation file if such access is needed for authorized internal administrative purposes.

  E. A juvenile court may permit the disclosure of information from
      a "permanent probation file" to:
      1. a person, agency, or department, with respect to a juvenile who
          has been committed to the care of the person, agency, or de-
          partment;
      2. a person, agency, or department that is providing or may pro-
          vide services to the juvenile, upon obtaining the written con-
          sent of the juvenile or his or her parents after informing the
          juvenile and his or her parents of the information to be dis-
          closed and the purposes of disclosure and provided further
          that the information that is disclosed is limited to the infor-
          mation necessary to provide or secure the services involved.
  F. A juvenile court should not provide access to nor permit the dis-
      closure of information from a probation file except in accordance
      with this standard.

15.5 Access for research and evaluation.

Each juvenile court should accord access to its juvenile records for
the purpose of research and monitoring in accordance with Standard
5.6.

15.6 Secondary disclosure limited.

A person, other than the juvenile, his or her parents, and his or her
attorney, who is accorded access to information, pursuant to Section III
of these standards, should not disclose that information to any other
person unless that person is also authorized to receive that information
pursuant to this Section.

**Jeffery v. McHugh, 273 S.E.2d 837, 838 (W.Va. 1981). See the discussion
of this case following Standard 15.1.**

15.7 Waiver prohibited.

The consent of a juvenile, his or her parents, or his or her attorney
should not be sufficient to authorize the dissemination of a juvenile
record to a person who is not specifically accorded the right to receive
such information, pursuant to this Part, except as provided in Standard
15.4 E.2.

15.8 Nondisclosure agreement.

Any person, other than the juvenile who is the subject of a juvenile
record, his or her parents, and his or her attorney, to whom a juvenile
record or information from a juvenile record is to be disclosed, should

be required to execute a nondisclosure agreement in which the person should certify that he or she is familiar with the applicable disclosure provisions and promise not to disclose any information to an unauthorized person.

PART XVI: CORRECTION OF JUVENILE RECORDS

16.1 Rules providing for the correction of juvenile records.

Rules and regulations should be promulgated which provide a procedure by which a juvenile, or his or her representative, may challenge the correctness of a record and which further provide for notice of the availability of such a procedure to be given to each juvenile who is the subject of a record.

PART XVII: DESTRUCTION OF JUVENILE RECORDS

17.1 General policy.

It should be the policy of juvenile courts to destroy all unnecessary information contained in records that identify the juvenile who is the subject of a juvenile record so that a juvenile is protected from the possible adverse consequences that may result from disclosure of his or her record to third persons.

17.2 Cases terminating prior to adjudication of delinquency.

In cases involving a delinquency complaint, all identifying records pertaining to the matter should be destroyed when:
   A. the application for the complaint is denied;
   B. the complaint or petition is dismissed; or
   C. the juvenile is adjudicated not delinquent.

17.3 Cases involving an adjudication of delinquency.

In cases in which a juvenile is adjudicated delinquent, all identifying records pertaining to the matter should be destroyed when:
   A. no subsequent proceeding is pending as a result of the filing of a delinquency or criminal complaint against the juvenile;
   B. the juvenile has been discharged from the supervision of the court or the state juvenile correctional agency;
   C. two years have elapsed from the date of such discharge; and
   D. the juvenile has not been adjudicated delinquent as a result of a charge that would constitute a felony for an adult.

17.4 Cases involving a neglect petition.

In cases involving a neglect petition, all identifying records pertaining to the matter should be destroyed when:

    A. no subsequent proceeding is pending as a result of the filing of a neglect petition or delinquency complaint against the juvenile;

    B. the juvenile is no longer subject to a disposition order of the court; and

    C. the youngest sibling is older than sixteen years of age.

17.5 Providing notification of destruction to other agencies.

    A. Whenever a juvenile's record is destroyed pursuant to this Part, the juvenile court should notify:

        1. the chief of police of the department that arrested the juvenile or made application for the petition or complaint that was filed;

        2. the commissioner of the state correctional agency if the juvenile was committed to the agency;

        3. the commissioner of the state probation department; and

        4. any other agency or department that the juvenile court has reason to believe may have either received a copy of any portion of the juvenile's record or included a notation regarding the juvenile's record in its own records.

    B. Upon receipt of notification pursuant to subsection A, the person, agency, or department should search its records and files and destroy any copies or notations of the juvenile's record that have been destroyed by the juvenile court.

17.6 Providing notice of destruction to the juvenile.

    A. Before destroying a juvenile's record, the juvenile court should offer to provide a copy of that record to the juvenile if he or she can be located.

    B. Upon destroying a juvenile's record, the juvenile court should send a written notice to the juvenile at his or her last known address informing him or her that the juvenile court record has been destroyed and that the juvenile may inform any person that, with respect to the matter involved, he or she has no record and, if the matter involved is a delinquency complaint, the juvenile may inform any person that he or she was not arrested or adjudicated delinquent except that, if he or she is not the defendant and is called as a witness in a criminal or delinquency case, the juvenile may be required by a judge to disclose that he or she was adjudicated delinquent.

17.7 Effect of destruction of a juvenile record.

  A. Whenever a juvenile's record is destroyed by a juvenile court, the proceeding should be deemed to have never occurred and the juvenile who is the subject of the record and his or her parents may inform any person or organization, including employers, banks, credit companies, insurance companies, and schools that, with respect to the matter in which the record was destroyed, he or she was not arrested, he or she did not appear before a juvenile court, and he or she was not adjudicated delinquent or neglected.

  B. Notwithstanding subsection A, in any criminal or delinquency case, if the juvenile is not the defendant and is called as a witness, the juvenile may be ordered to testify with respect to whether he or she was adjudicated delinquent and matters relating thereto.

PART XVIII: USE OF JUVENILE RECORDS

18.1 Use of juvenile records by third persons.

Public and private employers, licensing authorities, credit companies, insurance companies, banks, and educational institutions should be prohibited from inquiring, directly or indirectly, and from seeking any information relating to whether a person has been arrested as a juvenile, charged with committing a delinquent act, adjudicated delinquent, or sentenced to a juvenile institution, except the state agency or department responsible for juvenile justice may be authorized to inquire and seek such information pertaining to persons being considered for positions requiring ex-offenders.

18.2 Application forms.

All applications for licenses, employment, credit, insurance, or schooling, used by a licensing authority, employer, credit company, insurance company, bank, or educational institution, which seek information concerning the arrests or convictions or criminal history of the applicant should include the following statement: "It is unlawful for a licensing authority, employer, credit company, insurance company, bank, or educational institution to ask you, directly or indirectly, whether you have been arrested as a juvenile, charged with committing a delinquent act, adjudicated a delinquent, or sentenced to a juvenile institution. If you have been asked to disclose such information, you should report that fact to the state attorney general. If you have a juvenile record, you may answer that you have never been arrested, charged, or adjudicated delinquent for committing a delinquent act or sentenced to a juvenile institution."

18.3 Response to juvenile record inquiries.

If a person who is not authorized to receive record information pertaining to a juvenile seeks such information, the person to whom the request for information is made should inform the person who seeks the information that no record exists. If the information is sought on behalf of an employer, credit company, insurance company, bank, licensing authority, or educational institution, the person to whom the request for information was made should report the matter to the state attorney general.

18.4 Admissibility of juvenile records.

An adjudication of any juvenile as a delinquent, or the disposition ordered upon such an adjudication, or any information or record obtained in any case involving such a proceeding, should not be lawful or proper evidence against such juvenile for any purpose in any proceeding except:

A. in subsequent proceedings against the same juvenile for purposes of disposition or sentencing, if the record of the prior proceeding has not been destroyed;

B. in an appeal of the same case, information or records obtained for or utilized in the initial trial of the matter should be admissible upon appeal, if the information or record is otherwise lawful and proper evidence; and

C. in a criminal trial involving the same matter after waiver of juvenile court jurisdiction. Evidence not otherwise admissible in a criminal trial is not made admissible by its being introduced at the waiver hearing.

SECTION IV: STANDARDS FOR POLICE RECORDS

PART XIX: GENERAL

19.1 Rules and regulations.

A. Each law enforcement agency should promulgate rules and regulations pertaining to the collection, retention, and dissemination of law enforcement records pertaining to juveniles.

B. Such rules and regulations should take into account the need of law enforcement agencies for detailed and accurate information concerning crimes committed by juveniles and police contacts with juveniles, the risk that information collected on juveniles may be misused and misinterpreted, and the need of juveniles to mature into adulthood without the unnecessary stigma of a police record.

19.2 Duty to keep complete and accurate records.

A. All information pertaining to the arrest, detention, and disposition of a case involving a juvenile should be complete, accurate, and up-to-date.

19.3 Allocation of responsibility for record keeping.

Each law enforcement agency should designate a specific person or persons to be responsible for the collection, retention, and dissemination of law enforcement records pertaining to juveniles.

19.4 Retention of records in a secure and separate place.

Each law enforcement agency should maintain law enforcement records and files concerning juveniles in a secure place separate from adult records and files.

19.5 Duty to account for release of law enforcement records.

Law enforcement agencies should keep a record of all persons and organizations to whom information in the law enforcement records pertaining to juveniles has been released, the dates of the request, the reasons for the request, and the disposition of the request for information.

19.6 Juveniles' fingerprints; photographs.

A. Law enforcement officers investigating the commission of a felony may take the fingerprints of a juvenile who is referred to court. If the court does not adjudicate the juvenile delinquent for the alleged felony, the fingerprint card and all copies of the fingerprints should be destroyed.
B. If latent fingerprints are found during the investigation of an offense and a law enforcement officer has reason to believe that they are those of the juvenile in custody, he or she may fingerprint the juvenile regardless of age or offense for purposes of immediate comparison with the latent fingerprints. If the comparison is negative, the fingerprint card and other copies of the fingerprints taken should be immediately destroyed. If the comparison is positive and the juvenile is referred to court, the fingerprint card and other copies of the fingerprints should be delivered to

the court for disposition. If the juvenile is not referred to court, the prints should be immediately destroyed.

C. If the court finds that a juvenile has committed an offense that would be a felony for an adult, the prints may be retained by the local law enforcement agency or sent to the [state depository] provided that they be kept separate from those of adults under special security measures limited to inspection for comparison purposes by law enforcement officers or by staff of the [state depository] only in the investigation of a crime.

D. A juvenile in custody should be photographed for criminal identification purposes only if necessary for a pending investigation unless the case is transferred for criminal prosecution.

E. Any photographs of juveniles, authorized under subsection D, that are retained by a law enforcement agency should be destroyed:

1. immediately, if it is concluded that the juvenile did not commit the offense which is the subject of investigation; or

2. upon a judicial determination that the juvenile is not delinquent; or

3. when the juvenile's police record is destroyed pursuant to Standard 22.1.

F. Any fingerprints of juveniles that are retained by a law enforcement agency should be destroyed when the juvenile's police record is destroyed pursuant to Standard 22.1.

G. Willful violation of this standard should be a misdemeanor.

19.7 Statistical reports.

A. Each law enforcement agency should prepare a monthly and annual statistical report of crimes committed by juveniles and of the activities of the agency with respect to juveniles.

B. The statistical report should include a maximum amount of aggregate data so that there can be meaningful analysis of juvenile crime and the activities of the agency with respect to juveniles.

C. The principal state law enforcement agency of each state should develop standardized forms for collecting and reporting data to insure uniformity.

19.8 Juveniles' privacy committee.

A juveniles' privacy committee should have authority with respect to law enforcement records pertaining to the arrest, detention, and dis-

position of cases involving juveniles that is commensurate with the
authority of the committee set forth in Standard 2.1.

PART XX: ACCESS TO POLICE RECORDS

20.1 Police records not to be public records.

Records and files maintained by a law enforcement agency pertaining to the arrest, detention, adjudication, or disposition of a juvenile's case should not be a public record.

20.2 Access by the juvenile and his or her representatives.

A juvenile, his or her parents, and the juvenile's attorney should, upon request, be given access to all records and files collected or retained by a law enforcement agency which pertain to the arrest, detention, adjudication, or disposition of a case involving the juvenile.

20.3 Disclosure to third persons.

A. Information contained in law enforcement records and files pertaining to juveniles may be disclosed to:
   1. law enforcement officers of any jurisdiction for law enforcement purposes;
   2. a probation officer, judge, or prosecutor for purposes of executing the responsibilities of his or her position in a matter relating to the juvenile who is the subject of the record;
   3. the state juvenile correctional agency if the juvenile is currently committed to the agency;
   4. a person to whom it is necessary to disclose information for the limited purposes of investigating a crime, apprehending a juvenile, or determining whether to detain a juvenile;
   5. a person who meets the criteria of Standards 5.6 and 5.7.
B. Information contained in law enforcement records and files pertaining to a juvenile should not be released to law enforcement officers of another jurisdiction unless the juvenile was adjudicated delinquent or convicted of a crime or unless there is an outstanding arrest warrant for the juvenile.
C. Information that is released pertaining to a juvenile should include the disposition or current status of the case.

20.4 Warnings and nondisclosure agreements.

Prior to disclosure of information concerning a juvenile to a law enforcement agency outside of the jurisdiction, that agency should be informed that the information should only be disclosed to law enforcement personnel, probation officers, judges, and prosecutors who are currently concerned with the juvenile. The outside agency should also be informed that the information will not be disclosed unless the agency is willing to execute a nondisclosure agreement.

20.5 Response to police record inquiries.

The response and procedure for answering inquiries regarding the police record of a juvenile should be in accordance with Standard 18.3.

PART XXI: CORRECTION OF POLICE RECORDS

21.1 Rules providing for the correction of police records.

Each law enforcement agency should promulgate rules and regulations permitting a juvenile or his or her representative to challenge the correctness of a police record pertaining to the juvenile.

PART XXII: DESTRUCTION OF POLICE RECORDS

22.1 Procedure and timing of destruction of police records.

Upon receipt of notice from a juvenile court that a juvenile record has been destroyed or if a juvenile is arrested or detained and has not been referred to a court, a law enforcement agency should destroy all information pertaining to the matter in all records and files, except that if the chief law enforcement officer of the agency, or his or her designee, certifies in writing that certain information is needed for a pending investigation involving the commission of a felony, that information, and information identifying the juvenile, may be retained in an intelligence file until the investigation is terminated or for one additional year, whichever is sooner.

STANDARDS RELATING TO MONITORING

Stephen R. Bing and J. Larry Brown, Reporters

PART I: GENERAL STANDARDS

1.1 Definitions.

A. Monitoring process.

Monitoring, for the purposes of these standards, represents the process of overseeing and examining the operations of the various components of the juvenile justice system. This process involves such considerations as:

1. the determination of data and information needs and the generation or collection of needed data and information;
2. the identification of existing norms or standards for, and objectives of, the operations of various components of the system;
3. the evaluation of whether these operations are in compliance with the applicable standards and meet the stated objectives;
4. the assurance of compliance with standards;
5. the provision of data and evaluations for any necessary alteration of standards or modification of objectives; and
6. the dissemination of findings and conclusions resulting from the activities performed in 1 through 5 above.

B. Monitoring mechanism.

A monitoring mechanism is any agency, component of an agency, committee, or other group or individual designated to oversee or examine the operations of a component or components of the juvenile justice system.

1.2 Goals of the monitoring process and monitoring mechanisms.

The general goals of the monitoring process and monitoring mechanisms should be:

A. to ensure that all juveniles' substantive and procedural rights are protected and that all pertinent laws, administrative rules and regulations, and executive or judicial policies pertaining to juveniles are continuously complied with in any executive or judicial process, program, or facility under state or other public or private aegis, within the juvenile justice system;
B. to evaluate the fairness, humaneness, availability, and effectiveness of any such executive or judicial process, program, or facility;

C. to identify and evaluate alternatives to all forms of coercive intervention in juveniles' lives, including but not limited to coercive intervention at the arrest, pretrial, trial, and disposition stages, and all forms of incarceration or institutionalization; and to conduct or cause to be conducted research on the efficacy of such alternatives;

D. to gather, evaluate, and disseminate information to components of the juvenile justice system and to the general public that provides the basis for remedies for illegal, unsound, unfair, or inhumane policies and practices, and that increases public awareness of policies and practices concerning juveniles; and to evaluate the speed, efficacy, and consequences of reform;

E. to evaluate the adequacy and effectiveness of existing standards and criteria that apply to decisions made in any executive or judicial process, program, or facility within the juvenile justice system; to identify and evaluate the needs for additional or more comprehensive standards and criteria; and to ensure the uniform application of standards;

F. to identify and evaluate the existing documentary, informational, and databases for monitoring the juvenile justice system, and, if necessary, to develop and implement additional provisions to ensure that information gathering, data collection, written records, and record maintenance are adequate for monitoring purposes.

G. to prevent discrimination in the juvenile justice system on the basis of race, sex, age, language, or family background.

1.3 Monitoring mechanisms.

The monitoring mechanisms employed should include but are not limited to:

A. independent, external mechanisms including private attorneys, educators, statewide executive commissions, local and regional citizen advisory councils, ombudsmen systems, and legislative committees;

B. court-based mechanisms including the juvenile court, the appellate court, and the courts with general or limited jurisdiction empowered to hear matters concerning any aspect of the juvenile justice system;

C. juvenile justice agency-based mechanisms performing a self-monitoring role for the functions of such agencies, including but not limited to police, prosecutor, probation and intake, and juvenile correction and detention functions.

1.4 General principles for monitoring systems.

A. Each jurisdiction should develop a structure of monitoring mechanisms that will provide optimal scrutiny of all agencies, processes, programs, and facilities of the juvenile justice system and will ensure systematic, accurate, and effective monitoring on both an individual case and a general systemic basis.

B. The monitoring system developed should constitute a multi-tiered mix of local, regional, and statewide monitoring mechanisms. This multitiered mix should consist of a combination of appropriate internal self-monitoring and court-based monitoring mechanisms in addition to independent monitoring mechanisms external to the components of the juvenile justice system.

C. Internal self-monitoring should be made a basic requirement for all agencies, processes, programs, or facilities.

1.5 Criteria for selection of monitoring mechanisms.

The selection of the appropriate type of mechanism or mechanisms to be assigned the monitoring of any specific executive or judicial agency, process, program, or facility, under state or other public or private aegis within the juvenile justice system should be based on the following factors:

A. The degree of visibility of the decision makers, the decision-making process, and the decisions made affecting juveniles and their families;

B. The amount of discretion inherent in the decision-making function or activity;

C. The degree of coercion or intervention in the lives of juveniles and their families;

D. The importance of the rights or interests of juveniles and their families to be protected;

E. The adequacy and effectiveness of self-monitoring; and

F. The possibility, frequency, and reliability of review by some other agency of the juvenile justice system.

1.6 Access to and use of information.

A. Each jurisdiction should adopt laws and institute practices that will ensure that each monitoring mechanism:

1. is afforded the broadest possible access, relevant to its particular function and consistent with notions of privacy, to all appropriate information, records, data, and staff of the judicial or

executive process, agency, program, or facility that is being monitored;

2. has necessary powers to conduct investigations, secure testimony and production of documents, and perform on-site inspections of agencies, facilities, and institutions. Such powers, however, should be no broader than is reasonably sufficient for, commensurate with, and essential to the given monitoring mechanism's performance of its functions.

B. Monitoring mechanisms should employ any and all appropriate methods relevant to their particular functions to obtain and document information concerning the activities of executive and judicial processes, agencies, programs, and facilities in the juvenile justice system.

1. Methods of information gathering and documentation should include but not necessarily be limited to:
   a. the collection of all pertinent reports, data, records, and the like;
   b. on-site visits, inspections, and observations, including the use of film or videotape to record and document conditions and activities;
   c. interviews of agency, program, and facility staff and juveniles subject to their jurisdiction and authority; and
   d. executive and public investigative hearings.

2. When monitoring activities involve the use of records that include identifying information:
   a. that fact alone should not be a basis for denying access to the records;
   b. all necessary steps should first be taken by the agency to prevent disclosure of the identities of juveniles who are the subjects of the records;
   c. if it is not possible to expunge identifying characteristics, access to the records should be denied the monitor;
   d. under all circumstances monitors and agencies should be subject to the provisions of the *Juvenile Records and Information Systems* volume with respect to disclosure of the identities of the juveniles who are the subjects of the records, including any applicable civil and criminal penalties for improper collection, retention, or dissemination of information pertaining to juveniles.

C. Each jurisdiction should adopt laws and institute practices that give monitoring mechanisms broad authority to publish and disseminate findings, reports, and recommendations for reform.

D. Monitoring mechanisms should regularly and periodically publish and disseminate reports of activities, findings, and recommendations to the legislature, to judicial or executive agencies, programs, or facilities, to other monitoring mechanisms, and to the public. Concepts of confidentiality and individual privacy should, however, be observed. Any and all appropriate media should be used to accomplish the greatest possible dissemination of reports. The term media includes: newspapers, academic journals, and any other publications in general; radio; public and private seminars and conferences; television, documentary and educational films, and other visual media.

1.7 Remedial and compliance enforcement powers.

A. Each jurisdiction should adopt laws and institute practices that will ensure that monitoring mechanisms have appropriate authority to propose reforms and improvements based on information gathered pursuant to monitoring activities and to enforce compliance with existing laws, rules, regulations, standards, and proposed reforms and improvements.

B. The nature and extent of both remedial and compliance enforcement powers granted to specific monitoring mechanisms should be relevant to and commensurate with the type of monitoring mechanism and the scope of its functions.

C. Remedial and enforcement powers should include but not necessarily be limited to the authority:

1. to draft and disseminate proposals for changes in legislation, administrative rules and regulations, executive or judicial policies, practices, and the like relating to any process, program, or facility for juveniles, based on information gathered pursuant to monitoring activities;

2. to require agencies responsible for any process, program, or facility for juveniles to produce plans or procedures to correct problems or improve policies and practices;

3. to appoint masters or ombudsmen to agencies or facilities, when necessary, to oversee the implementation of reforms or improvements in accordance with the plans developed;

4. to bring suit when remedies are not implemented or are implemented improperly.

PART II: MONITORING FOCAL POINTS

2.1 Discretionary decisions.

A. Monitoring mechanisms should focus their activities on the de-

cisions of the agency, process, program, or facility being monitored wherein the exercise of discretion is permitted or occurs.
  B. The determination of the need for and the frequency and intensity
of monitoring such decisions should be based on a consideration
of the factors listed in Standard 1.5.
  C. The identification of the discretionary decisions made, the decision makers, and the extent of discretion permitted should be a
primary concern of the monitoring process. In performing this
task each monitoring mechanism should:
    1. identify the standards or criteria, if any, that should be applied
by the decision maker to the decision-making process;
    2. determine that such standards or criteria are being properly
applied in all cases in a uniform manner; and
    3. evaluate the adequacy and effectiveness of such standards or
criteria in promoting fundamental fairness and consistency.

2.2 Guaranteed rights.

Monitoring mechanisms should identify the nature and extent of the
rights of persons under the jurisdiction of any agency, process, program, or facility that is monitored, the manner in which notification of
these rights should be given, and the manner in which waiver of these
rights should be made. Two primary tasks of the monitoring process
should be:
  A. to determine whether substantive and procedural rights are complied with, notification of such rights is properly and timely
given, and any waivers of these rights are properly obtained; and
  B. to evaluate the effectiveness of the rights granted, the manner of
giving notice of these rights, and the procedures for obtaining
waivers in protecting individuals from unjust, unfair, or improper interventions and coercive actions.

2.3 Mandated provisions, duties, and obligations.

Monitoring mechanisms should identify the mandatory provisions,
duties, and obligations of any agency, process, program, or facility being monitored. Two primary tasks of the monitoring process should be:
  A. to determine that each provision is observed and each duty and
obligation is properly performed and executed; and
  B. to evaluate the effectiveness of such provisions, duties, and
obligations in promoting, among other considerations, a just,
fair, and efficient means of processing and serving juveniles who

are under the jurisdiction of the agency, process, program, or facility.

2.4 Organizational and operational functions.

Monitoring mechanisms should identify the organizational aspects and operational functions of any agency, process, program, or facility being monitored. A primary focus of the monitoring process should be to examine these areas and evaluate the organizational structure and operational performance in terms of efficiency in cost and time, internal and external accountability, achievement of objectives, and other similar considerations.

2.5 Records and informational bases for the monitoring process.

A. Monitoring mechanisms should determine whether the discretionary decisions of the agency, process, program, or facility being monitored are recorded in writing and indicate the standards or criteria that were applied, the manner in which they were applied, and the results that were obtained. When decisions are not recorded pursuant to this standard, each appropriate monitoring mechanism should undertake the implementation of such procedures as are necessary to provide the information specified herein.

B. Monitoring mechanisms should determine whether the agency, process, program, or facility being monitored records in writing the manner in which notification of rights has been given, and waiver of rights has been obtained; the manner in which mandatory provisions have been observed and duties and obligations have been performed; and whether this manner conforms with the procedures established for these activities. When such records are not made, or when established procedures are not followed, the appropriate monitoring mechanism should undertake the implementation of such remedies as are necessary to ensure that records are kept and procedures followed.

2.6 User participation.

Monitoring mechanisms should determine the nature and extent, and evaluate the impact of, the participation of the receivers of services and programs and the users of facilities for juveniles and their families, both in the determination of the types, objectives, and priorities for development of, and in the evaluation of, such services, programs, and facilities.

SPECIFIC MONITORING MECHANISMS

PART III: DEFENSE COUNSEL OR COUNSEL FOR PRIVATE PARTIES

3.1 Monitoring individual cases.

A. The primary responsibility for monitoring individual cases rests with counsel for the juvenile.

B. Counsel should be provided for the entire period during which the juvenile is under the jurisdiction of the court.

C. Priority should be given by the legislature to adequate funding of programs that provide counsel for juveniles. Adequate funding includes funding for capable support services, e.g, investigatory, expert, social, and psychological, as well as for sufficient numbers of attorneys to handle the caseload.

D. Counsel should be cognizant of his or her monitoring capability in individual cases, and perform a monitoring function in accordance with these standards insofar as applicable in order to facilitate coordination and cooperation with systemic monitoring activities. When necessary, counsel should commence legal action, including filing of appropriate motions in juvenile court, seeking appellate review, initiating civil suits, and applying for writs, to compel the adoption of or compliance with standards and practices that provide a basis for monitoring.

3.2 Establishment of lawyers' committee.

Whether counsel is provided by public defender or legal aid organization, arrangement with the private bar, or by some other means, a specific lawyers' committee of the bar association comprised of counsel representing juveniles in the juvenile justice system should be established on a local or regional basis, to systematically monitor the activities and performance of the juvenile justice agencies in accordance with the applicable provisions of these standards and the *Counsel for Private Parties* volume.

3.3 Role of lawyers' committee.

In performing this monitoring function, the lawyers' committee should:

A. advise, assist, criticize, and evaluate local or regional juvenile justice agencies;

B. publish regular, periodic reports on its findings in all appropriate media;

C. draft and disseminate comments on proposals for changes in legislation, rules, regulations, policies, and practices relating to activities of the juvenile justice system;

D. ensure that the bases for monitoring provided for under these standards and the other volumes of the Juvenile Justice Standards Project or similar bases under the laws, rules, and regulations of the jurisdiction, are established and maintained;

E. assist and cooperate with the monitoring activities conducted by any other monitoring mechanism to the fullest extent possible while preserving client confidentialities.

PART IV: STATE COMMISSION ON JUVENILE ADVOCACY

4.1 Creation and staffing of commission.

Each state through appropriate legislation, should provide for the appointment by the governor of a commission on juvenile advocacy. Appointments should be for staggered terms of similar duration and should be renewable for an additional similar period. Members of any one political party should constitute no more than a bare majority of the commission.

A. The appointments should be made subject to legislative approval and the positions should be full-time at a salary and rank of a state agency director or commissioner, but not subject to state civil service requirements.

B. Recommendations for appointments should be sought from all agencies and organizations that have established records as vigorous advocates for equal rights and opportunities for all juveniles. The commission members, in turn, should also have such records. Minority groups and women should be represented on the commission.

C. The commission should have an adequate supportive staff of full-time investigators, lawyers, budget examiners, planners, and other professionals as required to perform its responsibilities who, in addition to their professional qualifications, also have established records as vigorous advocates for equal rights and opportunities for juveniles.

4.2 Activities of the commission.

The commission should perform the following activities:

A. monitor (including the evaluation function) all aspects of the juvenile justice system within the state on an ongoing basis in accordance with the applicable provisions of these standards;
B. draft and disseminate proposals for changes in legislation, rules, regulations, policies, and practices relating to any aspect of the juvenile justice system, based on information gathered pursuant to such monitoring activities, and hold public hearings on any such proposed changes;
C. publish regular and periodic reports on its findings in all appropriate media;
D. report its findings directly to the governor and chief administrative judge responsible for the juvenile court system in the state and locality;
E. appoint consultants to an agency or a facility to oversee the implementation of remedies affecting juveniles in accordance with plans, standards, or procedures adopted by the agency;
F. staff, on a temporary basis, legislative or judicial study or investigation commissions, committees, or other bodies probing juveniles' problems or issues.

4.3 Powers.

The commission should have the power and authority to:

A. gain access to all appropriate information, records, staff, and persons subject to the jurisdiction of any agency involved in the juvenile justice system;
B. investigate any aspect of the juvenile justice system, hold executive and public hearings, perform on-site inspection of facilities, and attend executive, judicial, and legislative meetings pertinent to the operation of the juvenile justice system, and, with the additional authority from the appropriate court, subpoena records and witnesses;
C. require agencies responsible for any aspect of the juvenile justice system to produce plans or procedures to remedy problems;
D. bring suit against an agency when proposed remedies are not being implemented or are implemented improperly.

4.4 Review of commission orders.

Any agency subject to any order of the commission, having good and reasonable cause to believe that the order is in excess of the commission's authority or otherwise improper, should be authorized to seek a judicial opinion from the highest court of general trial jurisdiction in the state as to the agency's duty and obligation to comply with such order.

PART V: COMMUNITY ADVISORY COUNCILS

5.1 Establishment and role.

All agencies involved in the juvenile justice system, including juvenile courts, probation, police, youth corrections, juvenile protective services departments, and school districts should promote, encourage, assist, and cooperate in the formulation of community advisory councils to advise, assist, criticize, and monitor the functions performed and services rendered by the agencies.

- A. The monitoring activities of the community advisory councils should be performed in accordance with these standards as applicable.
- B. The community advisory councils should be granted access to persons, agencies, institutions, records, data, and information necessary to perform their monitoring functions in accordance with these standards.
- C. The community advisory councils should periodically report their findings to the respective agencies, the community, and the commission on juvenile advocacy.

PART VI: LEGISLATURE-BASED MONITORING

6.1 Creation of legislative committee.

Each state's legislature should establish a permanent standing committee or subcommittee on juveniles and juveniles' services.

6.2 Functions of committee.

- A. Such committee or subcommittee should meet periodically to review the state of juvenile justice and juveniles' services systems within the state and report its findings to the legislative body as a whole and to the public through any appropriate media.
- B. The committee on juveniles and juveniles' services should perform the following functions:
   1. monitor, including evaluation of, all aspects of the juvenile justice system within the state in accordance with the applicable provisions of these standards;

2. draft and disseminate or review and evaluate all proposals for changes or additions to state laws pertaining to the juvenile justice system;
3. review, evaluate, and comment upon all proposed appropriations of funds pertaining to any aspect of the juvenile justice system.

6.3 Powers of committee.

The committee on juveniles and juveniles' services should have the same powers as other legislative committees to hold hearings, conduct investigations, subpoena witnesses or records, impose sanctions for failure to comply with committee directives, and publicize reports and findings.

PART VII: OMBUDSMAN-BASED MONITORING

7.1 Definition.

These standards define ombudsman as a government official who hears and investigates complaints by private citizens against government agencies—specifically juvenile justice agencies and community agencies servicing juvenile court clientele.

7.2 Criteria for placement of ombudsmen.

A. The appointment of ombudsmen in the juvenile justice system should be promoted and encouraged, whenever appropriate under these standards, by all agencies and monitoring mechanisms.
B. The determination of the need for an ombudsman in an agency should be based on, but not necessarily be limited to, the following criteria:
   1. the degree of visibility of the decision makers, decisions, and activities of the agency to other mechanisms;
   2. the frequency and adequacy of the monitoring of the decision makers, decisions, and activities of the agency by other mechanisms;
   3. the availability, promptness, and adequacy of review for any person aggrieved by a decision or activity of the agency;
   4. the degree of harm that might occur to an aggrieved person resulting from a decision or activity not subject to prompt and immediate investigation and review;
   5. the existence and adequacy of remedies available to a person aggrieved by a decision or activity of the agency; and

6. the responsiveness of the agency in the past in correcting and eliminating discovered abuses of discretion or improper actions.

C. An ombudsman may be appointed on a permanent or temporary basis depending on the nature of the function to be monitored and in accordance with the criteria in subsection B. The activities of an ombudsman should be governed in accordance with the applicable provisions of these standards.

7.3 Powers of ombudsmen.

Whenever an ombudsman is appointed, whether on a temporary or permanent basis, he or she should:

A. be independent of the agency he or she investigates;
B. have full powers of investigation;
C. be authorized to recommend action and publicize recommendations but should not be authorized to take direct action to correct situations.

7.4 Appointment and supervision of ombudsmen.

A. Whenever a commission on juvenile advocacy is established pursuant to these standards, it should exercise the authority to appoint ombudsmen, supervise their activities, receive their reports, and act on their recommendations.
B. In any jurisdiction where there is an ombudsman's office already established either by legislation or by executive order, such office should exercise the authority specified in subsection A.
C. In all other jurisdictions where neither A nor B applies, an ombudsman's office should be established to exercise the specified authority.

PART VIII: PRIVATE-SECTOR ACTIVITIES

8.1 Independent research.

Independent, impartial research and evaluation activities conducted by federal contract research centers, private foundations, university-based research centers, academics working as individuals, and private corporations engaged in juvenile justice research should be promoted, encouraged, and assisted by all agencies and monitoring mechanisms in the juvenile justice system. All primary research data should be made available to bona fide researchers, subject to provisions for the protection of the rights of privacy of individuals.

8.2 Advocacy groups.

Independent juveniles' rights advocacy organizations should be included in the monitoring process and should be encouraged, assisted, and cooperated with by all monitoring mechanisms in efforts to enforce or prevent the violation of juveniles' rights.

PART IX: COURT-BASED MONITORING

9.1 The courts as monitoring resources.

Appellate courts, juvenile courts, and civil courts having jurisdiction over matters concerning the activities of the juvenile justice system should be cognizant of their role in monitoring other judicial or executive agencies in individual cases, and should, when appropriate, perform such monitoring in accordance with these monitoring standards, insofar as applicable, in order to facilitate coordination and cooperation with systemic monitoring activities.

9.2 Implementation in the juvenile court.

A. In order to facilitate its monitoring activities, the juvenile court should ensure that the bases for monitoring provided for under these standards or similar bases under the laws, rules, and regulations of the jurisdiction are implemented and maintained. When necessary, the court should invoke its inherent powers, including its rule-making powers, to require individuals and agencies within the scope of its jurisdiction to adopt and comply with practices designed to provide a basis for monitoring.

B. Juvenile court judges should further continuously monitor the facilities to which they assign juveniles, including making periodic on-site inspections, to determine that proper care and treatment are being provided. Judges should not only keep informed of the conditions in the facilities but also should make reports to effect change when needed.

C. Pursuant to the *Court Organization and Administration* volume:

1. the juvenile court should appoint an officer of the court full-time to direct, coordinate, supervise, and report on the performance, results, and findings of the juvenile court's monitoring activities;

2. a citizens' advisory committee should assist the court in performing its monitoring activities; and

3. appropriations for juvenile court operations should include

sufficient resources to permit the court to properly perform its monitoring activities.

D. The highest court in the state, or other designated court or agency responsible for the overall administration of the court system in the state, should establish a department to receive, compile in a systematic manner, and disseminate the results of monitoring activities and findings prepared by the juvenile courts within the state. The widest possible access to juvenile court monitoring reports by citizen groups, individuals, juvenile justice agencies, and other public and private agencies serving court clientele should be permitted and encouraged.

9.3 The appellate process as a monitoring resource.

In order to promote the monitoring function currently performed at the appellate level:

A. it is essential that applicable court rules permit at least one appeal, as of right, to all parties materially affected by a juvenile court's "final" order as defined by Standard 2.1 of the *Appeals and Collateral Review* volume;

B. appeal should be permitted by leave of the court from all orders of the juvenile court other than the "final" orders referred to in subsection A. Leave to appeal such interlocutory orders should be liberally granted; and

C. all decisions relating to appeal from or collateral review of juvenile court proceedings, including decisions to grant or deny leave to appeal, and decisions to grant or deny stays of orders and release pending appeal should be published in writing, specifying the reasons for the court's decisions and the facts supporting them.

9.4 Implementation in civil courts.

A. The applicable provisions of the monitoring standards should be applied in the litigation of all civil complaints, whether denominated test-case litigation or not, brought on behalf of a class of plaintiffs or on behalf of an individual plaintiff, in the juvenile court or in any other judicial forum where such complaints are based upon the application or implementation of any laws, rules, regulations, or practices of the juvenile court or other agencies affiliated with the juvenile justice system.

B. For monitoring purposes, one objective of all the parties involved in such litigation, and the court wherein the matter is being tried, should be to provide the broadest information base possible for the court to render a proper decision. This should include full use of court authority and rules relating to discovery, appointment of experts, designation of special masters, etc.

C. To facilitate full discovery, the trial court should, when appropriate, appoint its own experts to assist the court in determining the nature and extent of the data and information required and in obtaining the necessary data and information.

D. At any point in the proceedings, when the trial court deems it appropriate under these standards or otherwise, the court should appoint a master in accordance with the appropriate rules of procedure for the forum to assist the court in making findings, determining relief, monitoring the implementation of court orders, or performing any other function permitted under the rules of procedure for the forum.

PART X: SELF-MONITORING BY JUVENILE JUSTICE AGENCIES

10.1 General principles.

A. Self-monitoring activities conducted by juvenile justice agencies should be performed in accordance with the applicable provisions of these standards.

B. Each agency should monitor its activities on a continuous basis to ensure that it is discharging its duties and obligations and observing mandatory provisions in accordance with the standards applicable to its functions.

C. Each agency should:
  1. identify the key decisions it makes with respect to the processing of juveniles and their parents under its authority;
  2. develop criteria and guidelines to be applied by agency personnel to the decision-making process, when the exercise of discretion is permitted; and
  3. closely scrutinize the decisions made by its personnel to ensure that guidelines and criteria are being properly applied.

D. Each agency should ensure that rules or regulations requiring documentation of discretionary decisions, sufficient for monitoring requirements, are developed and complied with in order to facilitate both the agency's self-monitoring activities and the monitoring activities conducted by other mechanisms. Such documentation should be specific and should include:

1. the reasons and supporting facts relied upon for the decision;
2. the options considered; and
3. the reasons for rejecting any and all less intrusive and less coercive options.

E. Each agency should prepare frequent, periodic reports summarizing the activities of and the actions taken by the agency, and evaluating these and the agency's organizational and administrative functions in terms of efficiency in cost and time involved, results obtained, objectives achieved, compliance with rules, regulations, criteria, or standards, and other similar considerations. These reports should be distributed to the appropriate supervising authority, if any, to the appropriate external, independent monitoring mechanisms, and to the public through publication by any appropriate media.

F. Each agency should assist and cooperate fully with mechanisms assigned to monitor the agency. Each agency should promptly implement the recommendations of such monitoring mechanisms.

STANDARDS RELATING TO PLANNING
FOR JUVENILE JUSTICE
Suzanne and Leonard Buckle, Reporters

PART I: GENERAL PRINCIPLES FOR JUVENILE JUSTICE AGENCIES

1.1 Definition of planning.

Planning should be employed within the juvenile justice agencies and among interest groups concerned with juvenile justice to mean the process of applying systematic thought to the future in such a way that a desired future state is conceived and a process for attaining that state is defined and initiated.

   A. Planning, as defined above, is necessarily both an intellectual process and a political process; because it is future-oriented, it is also necessarily experimental, both in its intellectual methods and its political processes.
   B. Planning should be a flexible process in which the plan and its implementation are constantly being modified to reflect changes in the purposes of the planners and the environment of planning.

1.2 Coordination of services.

   A. Coordination of services within juvenile justice systems should be defined as the process of bringing services into harmony without reducing the authority of component agencies.
   B. Coordination of services on a planned basis should be attempted only under the following conditions:
      1. that it can be shown that greater economies of scale will more than compensate for the costs of coordination efforts;
      2. that lack of coordination can be demonstrated to result in inequitable distribution of services or resources to juveniles; or
      3. that clear understanding exists among the agencies to be coordinated concerning the function to be coordinated, the means by which coordination is to take place, and the specific benefit to be realized by each agency and by the client group.

1.3 Purposive duplication.

   A. Purposive duplication of services should be defined as planned duplication of any or all services available in an existing system.

B. Purposive duplication should be attempted under the following conditions:
   1. when greater diversity of services is required in a juvenile justice system;
   2. when specialized conditions require provision of services on a modified basis for a minority of the juveniles served by the juvenile justice system;
   3. when a particular problem is regarded as meriting special attention but a successful model of service is absent.
C. Neither coordination by plan nor purposive duplication of services should generally be attempted with respect to administrative services, including planning, information gathering and analysis, monitoring, and decision making.

PART II: ORGANIZATION OF THE JUVENILE JUSTICE PLANNING NETWORK

2.1 Juveniles' services agencies.

A. State legislatures should mandate the creation of juveniles' services agencies as line departments at the highest level of the executive branch of the state government.
B. Juveniles' services agencies should perform the following administrative functions: planning for services to juveniles; monitoring and evaluating the quality of services provided throughout the state; allocating state revenues dedicated to juveniles' services; setting standards for personnel practices and service quality; and conducting or administering experimental or demonstration programs and programs for the most difficult juveniles and those with special needs.
C. Juveniles' services agencies should address the needs of all juvenile delinquents and neglected or abused juveniles. They may also have responsibility for all orphaned juveniles and all juveniles who by reason of physical, psychological, or emotional problems are regarded as being in need of direct care, custody, or supervision by the state.
D. State legislatures should permit the geographically centralized provision of services to juveniles only under the following conditions:
   1. regional juvenile justice service agencies responsible for the ju-

venile have attempted and failed to provide services within close geographical proximity to the juvenile's home; or

2. the juvenile is a member of a small group whose special needs are provided for through centrally operated programs which could not be provided in each region of the state and which can be demonstrated to be more effective than those programs administered locally.

2.2 Regional juvenile justice service agencies.

A. State legislatures should mandate the creation of regional juvenile justice service agencies as subdivisions of the juveniles' services agency. They should be organized at as great a level of geographic decentralization as is consistent with provision of an adequate range and quality of services.

B. Regional juvenile justice service agencies should perform the following functions: direct provision of services or treatment, acquisition of services from a purchase of services system, superintendency of community-based services, and coordination with any county or local planning or operating agency in its geographical area. They may perform diversion, intake, or probation services.

C. Regional juvenile justice service agencies should be mandated to provide services or treatment to address the needs or behavior of all juvenile delinquents, juveniles who would have been regarded as status offenders, and neglected or abused juveniles. They may also have responsibility for providing services for all orphaned juveniles and all juveniles who, by reason of physical, psychological, or emotional problems are deemed as being in need of direct care, custody, or supervision by the state.

D. Regional juvenile justice service agencies should be advised by a board composed of people concerned with and affected by the juvenile justice agencies, but not employed by them.

2.3 Purchase of services system.

A. The purchase of services system should be defined as any arrangement whereby public agencies pay for services rendered to juveniles by nonpublic agencies.

B. Regional juvenile justice service agencies should maintain a presumption against private, profitmaking agencies in obtaining services through the purchase of services system.

C. No services should be provided through the purchase of services system or otherwise which would cause any juvenile to be removed from the territorial limits of the state.

D. Regional juvenile justice service agencies (or the agency authorized by the juvenile justice service agency) should make services available through the purchase of services system under the following conditions:

1. that the purchasing agency would otherwise have to build new facilities in order to provide services required for correction or treatment of juveniles;

2. that a large number of specialized services are needed to meet individual needs of juveniles;

3. that a new program is best conducted as a demonstration or an experiment and does not fit a category unsuitable for purchase of services.

E. Facilities for secure detention or incarceration or intensive treatment should not generally be provided through the purchase of services system.

F. The regional juvenile justice service agency (or other agency authorized to provide services) should conduct regular formal and in formal evaluations of the quality of services being provided by nonpublic agencies.

G. Standards for the purchase of services system should be developed by the juveniles' services agency and should be drawn from prior evaluation so as to control only those aspects of service provision found to be directly related to the success of the service offered.

H. Providers of services through the purchase of services system should be reimbursed in a timely manner at a fair rate of compensation as determined by negotiation with the juveniles' services agency.

I. At least 25 percent of purchase of services funding should be allocated to provide capital for formation of new agencies or new facilities created by existing agencies.

2.4 Local juvenile justice boards.

A. State legislatures should provide for local juvenile justice boards in all cities and counties of each state.

B. Local juvenile justice boards should perform three functions:

1. monitoring agencies of the purchase of services network located in their geographical areas;

2. supervising or operating juvenile justice services provided at the subregional level;

3. initiating and reviewing proposals for revision of the system of service provision in their areas.

C. Local juvenile justice boards should be composed of persons located within the geographical areas of the boards and who are concerned with or affected by the juvenile justice system but not employed by agencies involved in the provision of juvenile justice services. Guidelines established by the juveniles' services agency should ensure adequate representation of those communities and groups most directly affected, and an open and equitable process for selecting members.

D. Local juvenile justice boards should be provided an executive director and adequate budget for the accomplishment of their responsibilities. Funds for these purposes should be allocated by the state legislature as a portion of the planning budget of the juvenile justice system.

PART III: FUNCTIONS OF THE JUVENILE JUSTICE PLANNER

3.1 Definitions of planning modes.

A. Agency planning should be defined as the process of planning the allocation of resources within an agency and the monitoring of its performance to aid innovation of methods of accomplishing the mandate of the agency. It is the overall planning process primarily concerned with maintaining the continued organizational effectiveness of the agency and the process by which the agency alters its mode of operation to adapt to changes in its environment.

B. Advocacy planning should be defined as the process of building a constituency for juvenile justice and promoting the shared interests of that constituency in funding, programmatic, and other decisions affecting juvenile justice. As such, it is largely directed outward, focusing on the process of consciously pursuing the interests of juveniles with regard to services.

C. Program planning should be defined as the application of the planning process to innovation of approaches to juvenile justice. It is a process cutting across agency and interest group constituencies and responsibilities and is not directed toward the maintenance of any particular organization.

3.2 Agency planning.

  A. Agency planning should be employed by all juveniles' service agencies, regional planning units, and local boards, though it will be the dominant mode of planning only in the juveniles' services agency.
  B. Agency planning should be recognized as inherently designed to reconcile the need for agency stability with the need for constant change and should be employed only as a part of a broader planning network.
  C. Agency planning should be organized to elicit continuous response from service providers and clients and should modify its goals, allocation decisions, and programs in such ways as to ensure the highest quality of services.
  D. Agency planning should be visible and accessible to those who are not mandated to participate. All documents generated by the agency planning process should be available to the public. All meetings at which the formulation or modification of announced plans of the agency are to be discussed should be announced and open to the public. Agency staff and representatives of recognizable interest groups should be informed of plans and of meetings in which plans are to be discussed.
  E. The agency planning process should be closely linked to the principal operating decision makers of the agency, especially those responsible for the following areas of policy determination: budget development, personnel selection and training, operating policy selection, and legislative liaison.
  F. Agency planning should be limited to decisions which clearly fall within the agency's power to implement.
  G. Planners responsible for agency planning should have direct access to all data generated within the agency, subject to safeguards necessary to protect the privacy of individual juveniles.

3.3 Advocacy planning.

  A. Advocacy planning should be incorporated into the planning responsibilities of juveniles' services agencies, regional planning units, and local juvenile justice boards, as a legitimate but informal element of the overall planning process.

B. The task of advocacy planning should be divided among juvenile justice agencies according to the following criteria:
1. the juveniles' services agency should have primary responsibility for constituency building with the governor, legislature, and other state agencies;
2. regional planning units should maintain day-to-day contact with direct service providers and other service agencies closely related to juvenile justice;
3. local juvenile justice boards should regard it as their primary mandate to create support for juveniles' services through direct contact with citizens and with other juvenile advocacy groups.

3.4 Program planning.

A. Program planning should be the responsibility of the juveniles' services agency and should be accomplished through the establishment of temporary task forces, special project teams, or commissions composed of officials and private citizens representative of those most immediately concerned with a programmatic issue under study.
B. Programmatic issues to be studied and developed by task forces or special commissions should generally be proposed by the juveniles' services agency, while the task force or commission itself should be appointed at the legislative, state executive, or federal level.
C. The specific agency and level of government which appoints program planners and to which the planners report should be determined by the specific programmatic issues to be addressed. The enabling body should have authority to generate and implement policy concerning the issues the program planners will examine.
D. Program planning should be employed as the principal vehicle for centrally proposed innovation in the juvenile justice system. Fiscal incentives should be available to local boards and private groups to conduct their own periodic studies and experiments.

3.5 Plans.

A. "Plans" is employed in this volume to refer to the result of the planning process, whether or not it is formally promulgated, documented, or otherwise given a fixed shape.
B. Plans should adhere to the following characteristics:
1. Simplicity. Plans should limit the number of changes proposed,

the complexity of the process required for implementation, and the number of people whose participation or cooperation is needed for the plan to be accomplished.

2. Focus. Plans should be limited in topic and clear in the procedures required for implementation.
3. Flexibility. Plans should be subject to continuous review and revision throughout the planning and implementation processes.

C. Guidelines intended to elicit plans which will enable the transfer of funds from one layer of government to another should specify only general themes to be developed in the plan. This standard applies especially to guidelines disseminated by federal agencies to states and localities, specifying the nature of plans for the allocation of federal funds.

PART IV: ROLES FOR EXTERNAL PARTICIPANTS IN THE JUVENILE JUSTICE PLANNING PROCESS

4.1 The federal role.

A. Federal policy in juvenile justice should be concentrated in two areas: the development of new ideas, both in the form of basic research and through the process of evaluating reform strategies; and the funding of states, localities, and private agencies in support of programs oriented toward innovation.

B. Federal policy concerning juvenile justice should be planned through a process which provides maximum opportunity for participation by the states and which reflects, insofar as possible, the needs of the states.

C. Federal programs directed to the development of new ideas should include at least the following:[1]

---

1. The role of federal policy in juvenile justice should be concerned with the areas as outlined: the development of new ideas and the funding of public and private agencies to support innovative programs. However, federal policy should not be limited to these areas alone. It should accept responsibility for defining and monitoring minimum standards to safeguard the welfare of juveniles in all programs which it funds. The past failure to monitor and evaluate programs funded by federal grants reflects the failure of the federal government during recent years not only to achieve accountability for the use of tax funds but to confront its responsibility for establishing minimal standards as a condition to making grants on which such monitoring and evaluation can be consistently based.—Hon. Justine Wise Polier

1. a national research institute;
2. a continuing program of monitoring and evaluation of all federally funded programs in juvenile justice;
3. appointment of commissions and task forces to address salient issues in juvenile justice as they arise.

D. Federal funds in direct support of juvenile justice agencies and programs should be administered and distributed by a single federal agency; other funds available to juveniles in the juvenile justice system should be planned and coordinated by that agency.

E. Federal juvenile justice policy should encourage reduction of the number of agencies in each jurisdiction, innovation in services and organizational structure, and new approaches to decision-making. Federal funding for juvenile justice should be allocated in such a way as to give incentives to states, localities, and private agencies to pursue these purposes.

F. Federal funds for juvenile justice planning and service delivery should be allocated to an agency having authority to perform the function for which the funds are designated, consistent with the mandate of the juveniles' services agency.

G. Federal funds should include money directly allocated for agency and program planning, and indirectly allocated to support advocacy planning through the funding of professional staff.

H. Priority for federal funding in the juvenile justice system should be placed in the following areas: planning and personnel to support planning, demonstration or pilot projects, and incentive awards for agencies to upgrade services or adopt innovations.

I. Federal funds allocated to state, local, and private agencies of juvenile justice should be allocated in support of locally planned and defined programs which respond to more general federally defined policy themes.

4.2 State executive leadership.

A. Governors should employ the authority and influence of their offices to work toward improvements in the quality of juvenile justice planning, such as those outlined in these standards.

B. Governors concerned with improving the juvenile justice planning process and organization need to discharge a variety of roles, which include the following: advocate legislation supporting organizational changes proposed in these standards; act as appointing authority for commissions and task forces; restructure lines of authority within their branch of government to conform to these standards; and exercise their overall budgetary control to ensure that adequate and appropriate resources are available for juvenile justice.

4.3 Legislators and the legislative process.

    A. Legislatures, both the Congress and those in the states and localities, should assign responsibility for administrative aspects and funding of juvenile justice to a single committee or subcommittee.

    B. Planners in the juvenile justice system should develop a three-part legislative strategy, including the following steps: identification of existing legislative support for reform and strategies for the development of broader support, development of legislative proposals, provision of information concerning the findings and research on which their proposals are based, and support of legislative and public coalitions for change in juvenile justice.

4.4 The courts.

STANDARDS RELATING TO POLICE HANDLING OF JUVENILE PROBLEMS

Egon Bittner and Sheldon Krantz, *Reporters*

PART I: INTRODUCTION

1.1 This volume focuses upon police handling of juvenile problems. Unlike most of the agencies dealt with in other volumes in the *Juvenile Justice Standards* series, police are not exclusively, or even primarily, an institution committed to coping with these problems. Accordingly, whatever is to be said about police dealings with juveniles should be considered in the context of the overall nature of police activity, of which this is an integral part.

1.2 The standards formulated in this volume reflect certain ongoing police reform efforts that are gaining credibility both within and outside police agencies and that hold forth genuine promise of constructive change. This approach may help ensure acceptability of the standards and add weight to currently worthwhile endeavors.

1.3 Most police work consists of inherently provisional procedures. In this work, the police function consists largely of mobilizing remedies for various problems, to be administered by other institutions. It is evident that what police can accomplish in this regard depends largely on what is available to them. Thus, many improvements in police handling of juvenile problems can only result from the availability of more appropriate and effective resources and services, both within and outside of the juvenile justice field, to which police can make referrals. This fact, too, introduces a degree of uncertainty into the formulation of proposed standards for police.

PART II: ROLE OF THE POLICE IN THE HANDLING OF JUVENILE PROBLEMS

2.1 Considerations of race, national origin, religious belief, cultural difference, or economic status should not determine how police exercise their authority.

2.2 Police departments should retain juvenile records only when necessary for investigations or formal referrals to the juvenile or criminal justice systems. Police officers should avoid the stigmatizing effect of juvenile records by retaining only minimal records necessary for investigation and referral in accordance with *Juvenile Records and Information Systems* standards for retention of police records.

2.3 Since other volumes in the Juvenile Justice Standards Project conclude that serious harm can be done to juveniles simply by their being referred into the formal juvenile justice process, police should not make such referrals unless:

A. serious or repeated criminal conduct is involved; or
B. less serious criminal conduct is involved and lesser restrictive alternatives such as those described in Standard 2.4 are not appropriate under the circumstances.

2.4 For juvenile matters involving nuisance, mischievous behavior, minor criminal conduct (e.g., being intoxicated, engaging in minor thefts), or parental misconduct (such as neglect) not involving apparent criminal behavior, police should select the least restrictive alternative from the following courses of action, depending upon the circumstances:

A. nonintervention;
B. temporary assistance to those seeking or obviously needing such assistance (including situations in which the potential of serious physical harm is apparent);
C. short-term mediation and crisis intervention (e.g., resolution of family conflicts);
D. voluntary referral to appropriate community agencies; or
E. mandatory temporary referral to mental or public health agencies under statutory authorization to make such referrals (e.g., to detoxification program).

 In dealing with juvenile problems, police agencies should not attempt to initiate their own deterrence or treatment programs (such as informal probation), but rather should limit their services to short-term intervention and referral.

2.5 In order to stimulate police handling of juvenile problems (both criminal and noncriminal) in ways that are consistent with previous and subsequent standards, the following steps should be taken:

A. Juvenile codes should narrowly limit police authority to utilize the formal juvenile justice process.
B. Juvenile codes should clarify the authority and immunity from civil liability of police to intervene in problems involving juveniles in ways other than through use of their arrest power in

dealing with matters in which the juvenile or criminal courts are to be involved. This means authority and emphasis should be given to the use of summons in lieu of arrest. For matters in which police must act to assist a juvenile in need against his or her will, authority to take a juvenile into protective custody or to make a mandatory temporary referral should be specified and should be properly limited. It should also be specified that a juvenile cannot be detained, even temporarily, in adult detention facilities.

C. Police agencies should formulate administrative policies structuring the discretion of and providing guidance to individual officers in the handling of juvenile problems, particularly those that do not involve serious criminal matters. Such policies should stress:

1. avoiding the formal juvenile justice process unless clearly indicated and unless alternatives do not exist;
2. using the least restrictive alternative in attempting to resolve juvenile problems; and
3. dealing with all classes and races of juveniles in an even-handed manner.

D. Police training programs should give high priority, in both recruit and in-service training, to available and desirable alternatives for handling juvenile problems.

E. Police administrators should work collaboratively with both public and private agencies in ensuring that adequate services are available in various neighborhoods and districts so that referrals can be made to such services, and ensuring that joint policies and common understandings are reached whenever necessary. In addition, police administrators, because of their knowledge of deficiencies in this area, should focus attention on gaps in public and private resources that must be filled in order to meet the needs of juveniles and their families, and on the unwillingness or inability of existing agencies and institutions to respond to the needs.

PART III: THE AUTHORITY OF THE POLICE TO HANDLE JUVENILE DELINQUENCY AND CRIMINAL PROBLEMS

3.1 Serious juvenile crimes require the concern and priority attention of police, as well as other agencies within the criminal and juvenile justice systems and the public at large. Police work in handling such cases should follow patterns similar to those used in the investigation of serious crimes committed by adults.

3.2 Police investigation into criminal matters should be similar whether the suspect is an adult or a juvenile. Juveniles, therefore, should receive at least the same safeguards available to adults in the criminal justice system. This should apply to:

A. preliminary investigations (e.g., stop and frisk);
B. the arrest process;
C. search and seizure;
D. questioning;
E. pretrial identification; and
F. prehearing detention and release.

For some investigative procedures, greater constitutional safeguards are needed because of the vulnerability of juveniles. Juveniles should not be permitted to waive constitutional rights on their own. In certain investigative areas not governed by constitutional guidelines, guidance to police officers should be provided either legislatively or administratively by court rules or through police agency policies.

People v. L.A., 199 Colo. 390, 609 P.2d 116, 118 (1980). It has been suggested that "juveniles should receive at least the same safeguards available to adults in pretrial investigations (*e.g.*, stop and frisk) and in questioning" during police investigations into delinquent activity. (Citing Standard 3.2)

In re J.M., 596 A.2d 961, 972 (D.C. Ct. App. 1991). A consent to search by a juvenile should be subject "to rigorous scrutiny" in light of their lack of sophistication and greater susceptibility to coercion. (Citing Standard 3.2)

B.S. v. State, 548 So.2d 838, 840 (Fla. Dist. Ct. App., 3rd Dist., 1989). Warnings "concerning the right to refuse are required to validate a juvenile's consent [to accompany the police to the station]." (Citing Standard 3.2)

State in the Interest of Dino, 359 So.2d 586, 593–4 (La. 1978). "[I]n order for the State to meet its heavy burden of demonstrating that a waiver is made knowingly and intelligently, it must affirmatively show that the juvenile engaged in a meaningful consultation with an attorney or an informed parent, guardian, or other adult interested in his welfare before he waived his right to counsel and privilege against self-incrimination." (Citing Standard 3.2)

People v. Castro, 118 Misc. 2d 868, 462 N.Y.S.2d 369, 378 (Queen's Co. Supreme Ct. 1983). The failure of the police to make immediate efforts to notify the fourteen-year-old's parents and the juvenile's repeated attempts to contact his parents made the interrogation improper and the statements inadmissible. Juveniles should be given a special preinterrogation warning advising them of their rights to consult with their parents prior to questioning. (Citing Standard 3.2)

Commonwealth v. Henderson, 496 Pa. 349, 437 A.2d 387, 389 (1981). The courts should afford "special protections to juveniles subjected to custodial interrogation," and Pennsylvania has chosen to do so through its "interested-adult rule," requiring consultation with such a person as a matter of state law. (Citing Standard 3.2)

Commonwealth v. Veltre, 492 Pa. 237, 424 A.2d 486, 490 (1981). The juvenile defendant's convictions were affirmed by an equally divided court despite the contention that his inculpatory statements were erroneously admitted without him having the opportunity to consult with an interested adult. A dissenting justice urged that this result undermines the rule without abrogating it. (Dissent cites Standard 3.2)

Jahnke v. State, 692 P.2d 911, 937 (Colo. 1984). Dissenting justice urges that the court adopt a rule requiring that a juvenile suspect *and* his parents or custodians must be advised of the youth's right to counsel before he or she can be interrogated. (Citing Standard 3.2)

3.3 Even if a juvenile is taken into custody under authority other than the arrest power (see Standard 2.5), police should be subject to the same investigative restrictions set forth above in the handling of the juvenile.

3.4 The action by a police officer in filing a complaint against a juvenile either in a juvenile or in a criminal court should be subject to review by a prosecutor (to determine legal sufficiency) and by probation or intake staff (to determine if formal action is appropriate under the surrounding circumstances).

PART IV: IMPLICATIONS OF THE POLICE ROLE FOR POLICE ORGANIZATION AND PERSONNEL

4.1 All police departments should establish a unit or officer specifically trained for work with juveniles. The nature of the allocation must necessarily vary from department to department.

A. In departments where small size, the nature of community needs, or other considerations do not justify the assignment of even one officer to work with juveniles on a full-time basis, one officer should nevertheless be explicitly assigned the principal responsibility for the task, even while he or she might be expected to work in other areas.

B. Wherever resources permit even minimal specialization of function, the full-time appointment of a juvenile officer should receive highest priority.

C. Departments capable of staffing bureaus specializing in work with juveniles should consider the adequate staffing of them as a matter of highest priority.

D. A formalized network of connection for the communication of information and the transfer of cases between the juvenile bureau (or the juvenile officer) and other segments of the department should be established.

E. A formalized network of connection for the communication of information and the transfer of cases between the juvenile bureau (or the juvenile officer) and analogues in departments of adjoining jurisdiction should be established.

4.2 The juvenile officer or the supervising officer of a juvenile bureau should, in conjunction with the chief administrator of the department and other relevant juvenile justice agencies, formulate policies and training relative to police work with juveniles, implement established policies, and oversee their implementation throughout the department.

A. Juvenile officers should be selected from among officers who have mastered the craft of basic police work, and who have acquired, beyond that, the skill and knowledge their specialization calls for.

B. In departments having juvenile bureaus, the supervising officer should be of sufficiently high rank to convey the importance of both the position and the area of responsibility.

C. The juvenile officer or the supervising officer of a juvenile bureau should have the principal responsibility for the development and maintenance of relations within the department, with other agencies within the juvenile justice process, such as the court, the prosecutor, and intake staff, and with other community youth-serving agencies. He or she should have the principal responsibility for the development and maintenance of relations across jurisdictional boundaries with other departments.

D. The juvenile officer or members of juvenile bureaus should represent the police department in most matters connected with juveniles, vis-a-vis other institutions. In situations where such representation calls for the participation of other officers, juvenile officers should supervise or assist in such representations, depending on circumstances, and they should receive information about all representations that take place without their knowledge at the earliest possible opportunity.

E. Juvenile officers should take charge of all cases that go beyond an initial and informal handling that might have been administered by other officers. When the primary responsibility falls upon other segments of the department, as in cases involving serious crimes, juvenile officers should participate in investigations and prosecutions.

F. In cases that have gone beyond the initial and informal treatment accorded to them by other officers, but are judged upon investigation not to require referrals to other institutions, juvenile officers should be responsible for all counseling, guidance, and advice that might be incidentally required to reach a disposition of the case.

4.3 Since most juvenile cases begin by interventions of the uniformed patrol and a large share of these do not go beyond the initial intervention, standard police practices should be planned and instituted for patrol officers along lines of policies developed by the juvenile officers or the juvenile bureau.

A. As a rule, members of the uniformed patrol should assume full responsibility for the handling of all problems and disturbances subject to on-site abatement. In this capacity, they are to employ the least coercive measures of control, and they should avail themselves of the aid of such nonpolice resources as are directly available in the context of the problem or disturbance.

B. While it is in the nature of patrol that all uniformed officers are expected to deal with any problem they encounter, at least provisionally, every patrol unit should contain at least one officer to whom the handling of problems involving juveniles will be assigned, to the fullest extent possible. This officer should remain under the administrative control of his or her patrol unit and should function as a formal link between the unit and the juvenile officer or the juvenile bureau.

C. Police should transfer cases in which further work is indicated to juvenile officers. When circumstances make it mandatory that a juvenile be arrested, detained, placed, or referred to an outside institution, the juvenile officer or the juvenile bureau should be notified without delay about the action taken and the reasons for taking it.

4.4 The principal task of police policy making concerning juveniles should be to maintain flexible response readiness toward actually existing and emerging service and control needs in the community, and an assurance of maximum possible availability of alternative remedial resources to which problem cases can be referred for further care.

A. The juvenile officer or the supervising officer of the juvenile bureau should formulate policy in close coordination with the community relations officer or the community relations unit of the department.
B. Policy formulation should include recognition of the role of the uniformed patrol in police work involving juveniles, and orientation of its potential effectiveness to the proper aims of service and control.
C. The juvenile officer or the supervising officer of the juvenile bureau should formulate procedures and set standards for the transfer of cases from the uniformed patrol to the juvenile bureau; set limits for counseling, advice, and guidance provided by the juvenile unit; and provide guidance for the transfer of cases from the police to other institutions.
D. The basic principle of police policy concerning juveniles should be to rely on least coercive measures of control while maintaining full regard for considerations of legality, equity, and practical effectiveness.

4.5 Adequate staffing of programs for policing juveniles should be a matter of overriding significance.

A. Officers should be selected and appointed to work with juveniles as patrol officers and as juvenile officers on the basis of demonstrated aptitude and expressed interest.
B. To qualify for appointments as juvenile officers, officers should be fully competent members of the police and possess an educational background equivalent to graduation from college. The educational background standard should not be applied retroactively.
C. The initial assignment should be on a probationary basis during

which the officers work under supervision and with restricted decision-making authority, and are given in-service training that should include internship placements in several institutions, the juvenile courts, schools, and social service agencies among them.

D. In the selection of patrol officers to work with juveniles, and of juvenile officers, first consideration should be given to otherwise eligible officers who share the racial, ethnic, and social background of the juveniles with whom they will work.

E. The practice of appointing responsible and interested young people to function in the role of paraprofessional aids in police work with juveniles should be encouraged.

PART V: THE NEED FOR INCENTIVES AND ACCOUNTABILITY: DIRECTIONS FOR NEEDED IMPROVEMENTS AND FURTHER RESEARCH

5.1 Police agencies should establish positive incentives to encourage their personnel to support the thrust of these and other standards in the *Juvenile Justice Standards* series. These incentives should include:

A. appropriate status and recognition for the juvenile bureau and juvenile officers, given the importance of their task;

B. formulation of policy guidelines in the juvenile area that assist officers in handling juvenile problems, both criminal and noncriminal in nature;

C. provision of creative recruit, in-service, and promotional training that explores both juvenile policy guidelines and the philosophy behind them;

D. establishment of criteria for measuring effectiveness in handling juvenile problems that are consistent with departmental policy guidelines and with these standards; and

E. use in promotional examinations of material relating to the role of police in handling juvenile problems.

5.2 Police policies should be developed with appropriate input from other juvenile justice agencies, community social service programs, youth service agencies, schools, and citizens. Each year, police agencies should issue a report describing their handling of juvenile problems, the alternative approaches they have used, and the problems encountered in complying with departmental policies on the handling of juvenile problems.

5.3 High priority should be given to ensuring that police officers are made fully accountable to their police administrator and to the public for their handling of juvenile problems. This will require effective community involvement in police programs, administrative sanctions and procedures, and remedies for citizens whenever warranted. The need for research on and development of sanctions and remedies is particularly acute at this time.

In addition, juvenile bureaus and juvenile officers should periodically monitor the effectiveness of juvenile policies and the extent of compliance with them. Further, they should learn from the juvenile court, from other agencies, and from the public about any problems that may be arising with departmental policies or with their execution. Information obtained from these and other sources should be used for policy review and the development of new or modified training efforts.

STANDARDS RELATING TO PRETRIAL COURT PROCEEDINGS

Stanley Z. Fisher, Reporter

PART I: REPORT, PETITION, AND SUMMONS

1.1 Reports.

No delinquency petition should be filed unless a report in the matter has first been filed with the intake department and the prescribed procedures for intake and prosecution screening have been complied with. A delinquency report is a sworn written statement of the essential facts constituting the grounds of a juvenile's alleged delinquency. Where feasible, it should be signed by a person who has personal knowledge of the facts; otherwise it may be made by a person who is informed of the facts and believes that they are true.

1.2 Functions of petition and summons.

A. The petition should serve the following purposes:
  1. assist the parties to prepare adequately for trial and reduce surprise or disadvantage to the respondent;
  2. provide a record of the allegations tried for purposes of the double jeopardy protection; and
  3. enable the court to conduct an orderly and directed fact-finding hearing.
B. The summons should serve the following purposes:
  1. ensure the presence of all essential participants at the initial hearing and at all later stages of the proceedings; and
  2. advise the parties of the contents of the petition.
C. A statement advising the parties and other participants of their legal rights should be included in or appended to either the petition or the summons.

1.3 Contents of the petition.

A. The petition should set forth with particularity all factual and other allegations relied upon in asserting that the juvenile is within the juvenile court's jurisdiction, including:
  1. the name, address, and date of birth of the juvenile;
  2. the name and address of the juvenile's parents or guardian and, if the juvenile is in the custody of some other person, such custodian;

   3. the date, time, manner, and place of the acts alleged as the basis
      of the court's jurisdiction;
   4. a citation to the section and subdivision of the juvenile court
      act relied upon for jurisdiction; and
   5. a citation to the federal, state, or local law or ordinance, if any,
      allegedly violated by the juvenile.
B. The petition should state the kinds of dispositions to which the
   respondent could be subjected if the allegations of the petition
   were proven, such as transfer for criminal prosecution,[1] probation, or removal from the home.

1.4 Filing and signing of the petition.

Petitions alleging delinquency should be prepared and filed by the
prosecuting attorney and should bear the prosecuting attorney's signature to certify that he or she has read the petition and that to the best
of his or her knowledge, information, and belief, there is good ground
to support it.

1.5 The summons; subpoenas.
   A. Upon the filing of a petition, the clerk should issue a summons.
   B. The summons should direct the parties to appear before the court
      at a specified time and place for an initial appearance on the
      petition. A copy of the petition should be attached to the sum-
      mons.
   C. A copy of the summons should be served by mail or in person.
   D. The summons should be served upon the following persons:
      1. the juvenile;
      2. the juvenile's parents and/or guardian, and, if the juvenile is
         in custody of some other person whose knowledge or partici-
         pation in the proceedings would be appropriate, such custo-
         dian;
      3. the attorney[s] for the juvenile and parents, if the identity of
         the attorney[s] is known; and
      4. any other persons who appear to the court to be necessary or
         proper parties to the proceedings.
   E. No bench warrant should issue against a respondent unless it
      appears to the judge from the delinquency report, or from an
      affidavit or affidavits filed with the report, that there is probable

---

1. These standards were drafted before the Supreme Court's decision in *Breed v. Jones*,
421 U.S. 519 (1975).

cause to believe that the court has jurisdiction over the respondent, and:

1. the respondent fails to appear in response to a summons; or
2. the prosecuting attorney demonstrates to the court that issuance or service of a summons will result in the respondent's flight; or
3. a summons having issued, it is shown that reasonable efforts to serve the respondent, both personally and by mail, have failed.

F. [Upon application of a party, the clerk of the court should issue, and the court on its own motion should have the power to issue, subpoenas requiring attendance and testimony of witnesses and production of records, documents, and other tangible objects at any hearing.] Without prejudice to the court's power to quash any subpoena for cause shown, the respondent's ability to subpoena public officials and records of the respondent's involvement with law enforcement, judicial, welfare, school, or other public agencies, including any reports or records, whether or not made in connection with the particular case, should not be impaired.

1.6 Multilingual notices.

Courts serving populations containing significant numbers of persons whose dominant language is not English should attempt to send petitions, summonses, and notifications of rights in English and in the dominant language of such persons. Such courts should take appropriate precautions to ensure that non-English-speaking recipients of court notices receive actual notice of the nature of the document sent.

1.7 Waiver of service of summons and petition.

A. The respondent in a delinquency proceeding should be permitted to waive service of the summons and petition as provided in Standards 6.1 through 6.4. If a respondent accompanied by counsel appears and knowingly submits to the proceedings without objecting to improper or defective service, such conduct should constitute waiver of those objections.

B. Parents of respondents and other adults should be permitted to waive their rights to service of the summons and petition as provided in Standard 6.10. A parent's voluntary and knowing appearance and submission to the court should constitute waiver of such rights.

PART II: NOTIFICATION OF RIGHTS; INITIAL APPEARANCE

2.1 Notification of rights.

At every stage in the proceedings at which these standards require the giving of notice of rights, the following requirements should be satisfied:

A. notification of the juvenile's rights should always be given to both the juvenile and the parent and/or guardian or custodian who is present at the proceedings;
B. the notice should be in writing but should be explained to the recipient by the judge personally in open court at the regularly scheduled hearing, in all circumstances where notice is given in the recipient's presence;
C. notification should be given in simple language calculated to ensure the recipient's understanding;
D. in bilingual and multilingual communities, notification should be given in English and in the dominant language of the recipient; and
E. the official record of the proceedings should record the fact that such notice was given and the contents of the notice.

2.2 Initial appearance.

A. The initial appearance of a delinquency respondent before a judge of the juvenile court should be not later than [five] days after the petition has been filed.
B. At the first appearance in court, the juvenile should be notified by the judge of the contents of the petition and of his or her rights, including:
   1. the right to counsel as provided in Standard 5.2;
   2. the right to have parents present at all stages of the proceedings;
   3. the right to a probable cause hearing;
   4. the right to a trial by jury;
   5. the right to confrontation and cross-examination of witnesses; and
   6. the privilege against self-incrimination.
C. At the initial appearance, counsel should be appointed if necessary, and a date should be set for the fact-finding hearing.

2.3 Multilingual communications.

In bilingual and multilingual communities, the court and counsel should take appropriate steps to ensure that language barriers do not deprive the respondent, parents, and other appropriate persons of the ability to understand and effectively participate in all stages of the proceedings. Such steps should include the provision of interpreters at all stages of the proceedings, at public expense.

PART III: DISCOVERY

Introductory

3.1 Scope of discovery.

In order to provide adequate information for informed intake screening, diversion, and pleas in delinquency cases, and to expedite trials, minimize surprise, afford opportunity for effective cross-examination, and meet the requirements of due process, discovery prior to trial and other judicial hearings should be as full and free as possible consistent with protection of persons and effectuation of the goals of the juvenile justice system.

3.2 Responsibilities of the trial court and of counsel.

A. The trial court should encourage effective and timely discovery, conducted voluntarily and informally between counsel, and should supervise the exercise of discovery to the extent necessary to ensure that it proceeds properly, expeditiously, and with a minimum of imposition on the time and energies of the persons concerned.

B. Counsel for the petitioner and respondent should take the initiative and conduct required discovery willingly and expeditiously, with a minimum of imposition on the time and energies of the persons concerned.

Disclosure to the Respondent

3.3 Petitioner's obligations.

A. Except as otherwise provided as to matters not subject to disclosure (Standard 3.8) and protective orders (Standard 3.17), the petitioner should disclose to respondent's counsel the following material and information within his or her possession or control:

247

1. the names and addresses of persons whom the petitioner intends to call as witnesses at the hearing or trial, together with their relevant written or recorded statements;
2. any written or recorded statements and the substance of any oral statements made by the respondent, or made by a co-respondent if the trial is to be a joint one;
3. any reports or statements of experts, made in connection with the particular case, including scientific tests, experiments or comparisons, and results of physical or mental examinations, behavioral observations, and investigations of the respondent's school, social, or family background;
4. any reports or records, whether or not made in connection with the particular case, of the respondent's involvement with law enforcement, judicial, welfare, school, or other public agencies, which might assist counsel in representing the respondent before the court at any stage of the proceedings;
5. any books, papers, records, documents, photographs, or tangible objects which the petitioner intends to use in the hearing or trial or which were obtained from or belong to the respondent;
6. any record of prior criminal convictions of persons whom the petitioner intends to call as witnesses at the hearing or trial; and
7. those portions of grand jury minutes containing testimony of the respondent and relevant testimony of persons whom the petitioner intends to call as witnesses at the hearing or trial.

B. Subject to Standards 3.8 and 3.17, the respondent should have the right to obtain discovery by way of deposition.

C. The petitioner should inform respondent's counsel:
   1. whether there is any relevant recorded grand jury testimony which has not been transcribed; and
   2. whether there has been any electronic surveillance (including wiretapping) of conversations to which the respondent was a party or of the respondent's premises.

D. Subject to Standard 3.17, the petitioner should disclose to respondent's counsel any material or information within his or her possession or control which tends to negate the allegations of the petition or would tend to mitigate the seriousness thereof.

E. The petitioner's obligations under this standard extend to material and information in the possession or control of members of the petitioner's staff and of any others who have participated in the screening, investigation, or evaluation of the case and who either regularly report, or who have reported with reference to the particular case, to the petitioner's office.

3.4 Petitioner's performance of obligations.

A. The petitioner should perform the obligations set forth in Standard 3.3 as soon as practicable following the filing of a petition in respect of the respondent.

B. The petitioner may perform these obligations in any manner mutually agreeable to petitioner and counsel for the respondent, or by:

1. notifying counsel for the respondent that material and information described in general terms may be inspected, obtained, tested, copied, or photographed during specified, reasonable times; and

2. making available to respondent's counsel, at the time specified, such material and information, and providing suitable facilities or other arrangements for inspection, testing, copying, and photographing of such material and information.

C. The petitioner should ensure that a flow of information is maintained between the various investigative personnel and petitioner's office sufficient to place within his or her possession or control all material and information relevant to the respondent and the allegations of the petition.

3.5 Additional disclosures upon request and specification.

Subject to Standards 3.8 and 3.17, the petitioner should, upon request of the respondent, disclose and permit inspection, testing, copying, and photographing of any relevant material and information regarding:

A. specified searches and seizures;

B. the acquisition of specified statements from the respondent; and

C. the relationship, if any, of specified persons to the petitioning authority.

3.6 Material held by other governmental personnel.

Upon the request of respondent's counsel and designation of material or information that would be discoverable if in the possession or control of the petitioner, and that is in the possession or control of other governmental personnel, the petitioner should use diligent good faith efforts to cause such material to be made available to respondent's counsel; if the petitioner's efforts are unsuccessful and such material or other governmental personnel are subject to the jurisdiction of the court, the court should issue suitable subpoenas or orders to cause such material to be made available to respondent's counsel.

3.7 Discretionary disclosures.

    A. Upon a showing of materiality to the preparation of the respondent's case and if the request is reasonable, the court, in its discretion, may require disclosure to respondent's counsel of relevant material and information not covered by Standards 3.3, 3.5, and 3.6.

    B. The court may deny disclosure authorized by this standard if it finds that there is a substantial risk to any person of physical harm, intimidation, bribery, economic reprisals, or unnecessary annoyance or embarrassment resulting from such disclosure which outweighs any usefulness of the disclosure to respondent's counsel.

3.8 Matters not subject to disclosure.

    A. Disclosure should not be required of legal research or of records, correspondence, reports or memoranda to the extent that they contain the opinions, theories, or conclusions of the petitioner's attorney or members of petitioner's legal staff.

    B. Disclosure of an informant's identity should not be required where the identity is a prosecution secret and a failure to disclose will not infringe the constitutional rights of the respondent. Disclosure should not be denied hereunder of the identity of witnesses to be produced at a hearing or trial.

3.9 Discovery at intake screening stage.

Upon the request of counsel for a juvenile who has been referred for intake screening on a delinquency report, the intake unit should give the juvenile's counsel access to all documents, reports, and records within its possession or control which concern the juvenile or the alleged offense.

Disclosure to the Petitioner

3.10 Medical and scientific reports.

Subject to constitutional limitations, the trial court may require that the petitioner be informed of and permitted to inspect and copy or photograph any reports or statements of experts made in connection with and intended to be introduced in evidence in the particular case, including results of physical or mental examinations and of scientific tests, experiments, or comparisons.

3.11 Nature of defense.

Subject to constitutional limitations, the trial court may require that the petitioner be informed of the nature of any defense which respondent's counsel intends to use at trial and the names and addresses of persons whom respondent's counsel intends to call as witnesses in support thereof.

3.12 Depositions.

Subject to Standards 3.8 and 3.17, the petitioner should have the right to obtain discovery by way of deposition, except that the petitioner should not have the right to depose the respondent without the respondent's consent.

Regulation of Discovery

3.13 Investigations not to be impeded.

Subject to Standards 3.8 and 3.17, neither the counsel for the parties nor others officially involved in the case should advise persons having relevant material or information (except the respondent) to refrain from discussing the case with opposing counsel or showing opposing counsel any relevant material, nor should they otherwise impede opposing counsel's investigation of the case.

3.14 Deposition procedures.

Depositions in delinquency proceedings should be governed by the rules governing depositions in criminal proceedings in jurisdictions which have such rules. In other jurisdictions, special rules to govern depositions in delinquency proceedings should be adopted.

3.15 Continuing duty to disclose.

If, subsequent to compliance with these standards or orders pursuant thereto, a party discovers additional material or information which is subject to disclosure, such party should promptly notify the other party or opposing counsel of the existence of such additional material, and if the additional material or information is discovered during trial, the court should also be notified.

3.16 Custody of materials.

Any materials furnished to an attorney pursuant to these standards should remain in the exclusive custody of such attorney and be used only for the purposes of conducting the case and should be subject to such other terms and conditions as the court may provide. In the discretion of counsel for the respondent, the contents of furnished material may be disclosed to the respondent and, subject to a mature juvenile's consent under Standard 6.5 A.2, to the respondent's parent or guardian *ad litem.* Counsel should exercise utmost caution before doing so if disclosure might cause injury or embarrassment to the respondent or any other person and if disclosure is not necessary to protect the respondent's interests in the proceedings.

3.17 Protective orders.

Upon a showing of cause, the court may at any time order that specified disclosures be restricted or deferred or make such other order as is appropriate, provided that all material and information to which a party is entitled under these standards must be disclosed in time to permit counsel to make beneficial use thereof.

3.18 Excision.

When some parts of certain material are discoverable under these standards and other parts not discoverable, as much of the material should be disclosed as is consistent with the standards. Excision of certain material and disclosure of the balance is preferable to withholding the whole. Material excised pursuant to judicial order should be sealed and preserved in the records of the court, to be made available to the appellate court in the event of an appeal.

3.19 *In camera* proceedings.

Upon request of any person, the court may permit any showing of cause for denial or regulation of disclosures or portion of such showing to be made *in camera.* A record should be made of such proceedings. If the court enters an order granting relief following a showing *in camera,* the entire record of such showing should be sealed and preserved in the records of the court, to be made available to the appellate court in the event of an appeal. A judicial officer who is exposed in an *ex parte* proceeding under this standard to material which might be prejudicial to the absent party should be excused from further involvement in the case.

3.20 Sanctions.

    A. If at any time during the course of the proceedings it is brought to the attention of the court that a party has failed to comply with an applicable discovery rule or an order issued pursuant thereto, the court may order such party to permit the discovery of material and information not previously disclosed, grant a continuance, or enter such other order as it deems just under the circumstances.

B. Willful violation by counsel of an applicable discovery rule or an order issued pursuant thereto may subject counsel to appropriate sanctions by the court.

PART IV: THE RIGHT TO A PROBABLE CAUSE HEARING

4.1 The right to a probable cause hearing.

A. In all delinquency proceedings, the respondent should have the right to a judicial determination of probable cause, unless the adjudicatory hearing is held within [five] days after the filing of the petition if the juvenile is detained and within [fifteen] days if the juvenile is not detained. Unless it appears from the evidence that there is probable cause to believe that an offense has been committed and that the respondent committed it, the petition should be dismissed.

B. Unless there has been a prior judicial determination of probable cause, detention and transfer hearings should commence with consideration of that issue.

4.2 The conduct of a probable cause hearing.

A. The probable cause hearing should be held before a judge of the juvenile court. The judge should inform the juvenile of his or her rights as provided by Standard 2.2 B.

B. The prosecutor should be required to present evidence of probable cause as to every element of the offense and as to the respondent's identity as the perpetrator. The finding of probable cause should not be based upon hearsay in whole or in part. The respondent should have the opportunity to cross-examine witnesses and to introduce evidence and witnesses on his or her own behalf.

PART V: RESPONDENT'S RIGHT TO COUNSEL

5.1 Scope of the juvenile's right to counsel.

A. In delinquency cases, the juvenile should have the effective assistance of counsel at all stages of the proceeding.
B. The right to counsel should attach as soon as the juvenile is taken into custody by an agent of the state, when a petition is filed against the juvenile, or when the juvenile appears personally at an intake conference, whichever occurs first. The police and other detention authorities should have the duty to ascertain whether a juvenile in custody has counsel and, if not, to facilitate the retention or provision of counsel without delay.
C. Unless waived by counsel, the statements of a juvenile or other information or evidence derived directly or indirectly from such statements made to the intake officer or social service worker during the process of the case, including statements made during intake, a predisposition study, or consent decree, should not be admissible in evidence prior to a determination of the petition's allegations in a delinquency case, or prior to conviction in a criminal proceeding.

In the Interest of Jane Doe, 77 Haw. 46, 881 P.2d 533, 536 (1994). The court rejects the Standard's view that the "right to counsel can never be validly waived," and reaffirmed the view that such a waiver can be sustained based on the totality of the circumstances. (Citing Standard 5.1; the more specific prohibition against the waiver of the right to counsel is found in Standard 6.1 A)

5.2 Notification of the juvenile's right to counsel.

As soon as a juvenile's right to counsel attaches under Standard 5.1 B, the authorities should advise the juvenile that representation by counsel is mandatory, that there is a right to employ private counsel, and that if private counsel is not retained, counsel will be provided without cost.

5.3 Juvenile's eligibility for court-appointed counsel; parent-juvenile conflicts.

A. In any delinquency proceeding, if counsel has not been retained for the juvenile, and if it does not appear that counsel will be retained, the court should appoint counsel. No reimbursement should be sought from the parent or the juvenile for the cost of court-appointed counsel for the juvenile, regardless of the parent's or juvenile's financial resources.
B. At the earliest feasible stage of a delinquency proceeding, the intake department should determine whether a conflict of interest

exists between the juvenile and the parent and should notify the court and the parties of any finding that a conflict exists.

C. If a parent has retained counsel for a juvenile and it appears to the court that the parent's interest in the case conflicts with the juvenile's interest, the court should caution both the parent and counsel as to counsel's duty of loyalty to the juvenile's interests. If the parent's dominant language is not English, the court's caution should be communicated in a language understood by the parent.

PART VI: WAIVER OF THE JUVENILE'S RIGHTS; THE ROLE OF PARENTS AND GUARDIANS *AD LITEM* IN THE DELINQUENCY PROCEEDINGS

Waiver of the Juvenile's Rights

6.1 Waiver of the juvenile's rights: in general.

A. Any right accorded to the respondent in a delinquency case by these standards or by federal, state, or local law may be waived in the manner described below. A juvenile's right to counsel may not be waived.

B. For purposes of this part:
1. A "mature respondent" is one who is capable of adequately comprehending and participating in the proceedings;
2. An "immature respondent" is one who is incapable of adequately comprehending and participating in the proceedings because of youth or inexperience. This part does not apply to determining a juvenile's incapacity to stand trial or otherwise participate in delinquency proceedings by reason of mental disease or defect.

In re Lisa G., **127 N.H. 585, 504 A.2d 1, 4 (1986). If a juvenile client is "immature," counsel should request the appointment of a guardian** *ad litem* **to "act as a substitute decision maker for the juvenile." (Citing Standard 6.1 B.2.)**

C. Counsel for the juvenile bears primary responsibility for deciding whether the juvenile is mature or immature. If counsel believes the juvenile is immature, counsel should request the court to appoint a guardian *ad litem* for the juvenile.

D. A mature respondent should have the power to waive rights on his or her own behalf, in accordance with Standard 6.2. Subject to Standard 6.3, the rights of an immature respondent may be waived on his or her behalf by the guardian *ad litem*.

***In the Interest of N.E.*, 122 Wis. 2d 198, 361 N.W.2d 693, 698 (1985). The juvenile's withdrawal of a jury demand must be knowing and voluntary, and should take place in open court with the advice of counsel. (Citing Standards 6.1, 6.2, 6.4)**

6.2 Waiver of the rights of mature respondents.

    A. A respondent considered by counsel to be mature should be permitted to act through counsel in the proceedings. However the juvenile may not personally waive any right:

        1. except in the presence of and after consultation with counsel; and

        2. unless a parent has first been afforded a reasonable opportunity to consult with the juvenile and the juvenile's counsel regarding the decision. If the parent requires an interpreter for this purpose, the court should provide one.

    B. The decision to waive a mature juvenile's privilege against self-incrimination; the right to be tried as a juvenile or as an adult where the respondent has that choice; the right to trial, with or without a jury; and the right to appeal or to seek other post-adjudication relief should be made by the juvenile. Counsel may decide, after consulting with the juvenile, whether to waive other rights of the juvenile.

***In the Interest of N.E.*, 122 Wis. 2d 198, 361 N.W.2d 693, 698 (1985). The juvenile's withdrawal of a jury demand must be knowing and voluntary, and should take place in open court with the advice of counsel. Certain decisions are tactical decisions which may be made by the lawyer, but not that regarding a jury. (Citing Standards 6.1, 6.2, 6.4)**

***In the Interest of T.R.B.*, 109 Wis. 2d 119, 325 N.W.2d 329, 338 (1982). The decision not to contest a prosecutor's petition for waiver or transfer is akin to those tactical decisions to be made by the lawyer, as opposed to the decision by the juvenile to seek waiver of the juvenile court's jurisdiction himself. (Citing Standard 6.2)**

6.3 Waiver of the rights of immature respondents.

    A. A respondent considered by counsel to be immature should not be permitted to act through counsel, nor should a plea on behalf of an immature respondent admitting the allegations of the petition be accepted. The court may adjudicate an immature respondent delinquent only if the petition is proven at trial.

B. The decision to waive the following rights of an immature respondent should be made by the guardian *ad litem,* after consultation with the respondent and counsel: the privilege against self-incrimination; the right to be tried as a juvenile or as an adult, where the respondent has that choice; the right to a jury trial; and the right to appeal or seek other postadjudication relief. Subject to subsection A of this standard, other rights of an immature respondent should be waivable by counsel after consultation with the juvenile's guardian *ad litem.*

6.4 Recording.

A. Express waivers should be executed in writing and recorded. When administering a waiver of the juvenile's right, the judge or other official should:
   1. ascertain whether the waiver is being made by the juvenile or by the guardian *ad litem* on the juvenile's behalf;
   2. if the juvenile is waiving a right on his or her own behalf, require counsel to affirm belief in the juvenile's capacity to do so, and affirm that counsel has otherwise complied with the requirements of this part, and
   3. ascertain that the juvenile or guardian *ad litem,* as the case may be, is voluntarily and intelligently waiving the right in the presence of and after advice of counsel.

B. Waivers should be executed in the dominant language of the waiving party or, if executed in English and the waiving party's dominant language is not English, should be accompanied by a translator's affidavit certifying that he or she has faithfully and accurately translated all conversations between the juvenile, parent[s], guardian *ad litem,* counsel, and the court with respect to the waiver decision. The affidavit should be recorded.

In the Interest of N.E., **122 Wis. 2d 198, 361 N.W.2d 693, 698 (1985). The juvenile's withdrawal of a jury demand must be knowing and voluntary, and should take place in open court with the advice of counsel. (Citing Standards 6.1, 6.2, 6.4)**

The Role of Parents and Guardians **Ad Litem**
in the Delinquency Proceedings

6.5 The role of parents.

A. Except as provided in subsection B,
   1. the parent of a delinquency respondent should have the right to notice, to be present, and to make representations to the court either *pro se* or through counsel at all stages of the proceedings;
   2. parents should be encouraged by counsel, the judge, and other officials to take an active interest in the juvenile's case. Their proper functions include consultation with the juvenile and the juvenile's counsel at all stages of the proceedings concerning decisions made by the juvenile or by counsel on the juvenile's behalf, presence at all hearings, and participation in the planning of dispositional alternatives. Subject to the consent of the mature juvenile, parents should have access to all records in the case. If the juvenile does not consent, the court should nevertheless grant the parent access to records if they are not otherwise privileged, and if the court determines, *in camera*, that disclosure is necessary to protect the parent's interests.
B. The court should have the power, in its discretion, to exclude or restrict the participation of a parent whose interests the court has determined are adverse to those of the respondent, if the court finds that the parent's presence or participation will adversely affect the interests of the respondent.
C. Parents should be provided with necessary interpreter services at all stages of the proceedings.

People in the Interest of J.F.C., 660 P.2d 7 (Colo. App. 1982). **The presence of the juvenile's parent or parents is of "critical significance" to the knowing and intelligent waiver of a constitutional right of the juvenile. (Citing Standard 6.5)**

6.6 "Parent" defined.

The term "parent" as used in this part includes:
A. the juvenile's natural or adoptive parents, unless their parental rights have been terminated;
B. if the juvenile is a ward of any person other than a parent, the guardian of the juvenile;
C. if the juvenile is in the custody of some person other than a parent, such custodian, unless the custodian's knowledge of or participation in the proceedings would be detrimental to the juvenile; and
D. separated and divorced parents, even if deprived by judicial decree of the respondent juvenile's custody.

6.7 Appointment of guardian *ad litem.*

A. The court should appoint a guardian *ad litem* for a juvenile on the request of any party, a parent, or upon the court's own motion:
1. if the juvenile is immature as defined in Standard 6.1 B.2;
2. if no parent, guardian, or custodian appears with the juvenile;
3. if a conflict of interest appears to exist between the juvenile and the parents; or
4. if the juvenile's interest otherwise requires it.
B. The appointment should be made at the earliest feasible time after it appears that representation by a guardian *ad litem* is necessary. At the time of appointment, the court should ensure that the guardian *ad litem* is advised of the responsibilities and powers contained in these standards.
C. The function of a guardian *ad litem* is to act toward the juvenile in the proceedings as would a concerned parent. If the juvenile is immature, the guardian *ad litem* should also instruct the juvenile's counsel in the conduct of the case and may waive rights on behalf of the juvenile as provided in Standard 6.3. A guardian *ad litem* should have all the procedural rights accorded to parents under these standards.
D. The following persons should not be appointed as a guardian *ad litem:*
1. the juvenile's parent, if the parent's interest and the juvenile's interest in the proceedings appear to conflict;
2. the agent, counsel, or employee of a party to the proceedings, or of a public or private institution having custody or guardianship of the juvenile; and
3. an employee of the court or of the intake agency.

In re Lisa G., **127 N.H. 585, 505 A.2d 1, 5 (1986). The role of the guardian *ad litem* cannot be performed by "employees of the court or of other institutions with custody of the juvenile" because of their possibly adverse interests. (Citing Standard 6.7 D)**

E. Courts should experiment with the use of qualified and trained nonattorney guardians *ad litem,* recruited from concerned individuals and organizations in the community on a paid or volunteer basis.

6.8 The parent's right to counsel.

A. A parent should receive notice of the right to counsel when he or she receives the petition or the summons, and also, if the parent appears without counsel, at the start of all judicial hearings. The notice should state that the juvenile's counsel represents the juvenile rather than the parent, that if the parent wishes, he or she has a right to be advised and represented by his or her own counsel, to the extent permitted by Standard 6.5, and that a parent who is unable to pay for legal assistance may have it provided without cost, to the extent permitted by Standard 6.5.

B. A parent's counsel may be present at all delinquency proceedings but should have no greater right to participate than a parent does under Standard 6.5.

6.9 Appointment of counsel for parent unable to pay.

A. The court may appoint counsel for a respondent's parent who does not waive that right and who is unable to obtain adequate representation without substantial hardship to the parent or family.

B. A preliminary determination of the parent's eligibility for court-appointed counsel should be made at the earliest feasible time after the parent's right to appointed counsel arises. The final determination should be made by the judge or an officer of the court selected by the judge. A questionnaire should be used to determine the nature and extent of the financial resources available for obtaining representation. If at any subsequent stage of the proceedings new information concerning eligibility becomes available, eligibility should be redetermined.

C. The ability to pay part of the cost of adequate representation should not preclude eligibility. The court may appoint counsel on the condition that the recipient make some reasonable payment in accordance with financial capabilities.

6.10 Waiver of the parent's rights.

A. Any right accorded to a parent by these standards or under federal, state, or local law may be waived. A parent may effectively waive a right only if the parent is fully informed of the right and voluntarily and intelligently waives it. The failure of a parent who has the right to counsel to request counsel should not of itself be construed to constitute a waiver of that right.

B. A parent's waiver of counsel should not be accepted unless it is in writing and recorded. If the waiving party's dominant language is not English, the safeguards described in Standard 6.4 B of this part should apply.

PART VII: JUVENILE COURT CALENDARING

7.1 Priorities in scheduling juvenile court cases.

    A. To effectuate the right of juveniles to a speedy resolution of disputes involving them and the public interest in prompt disposition of such disputes, juvenile court cases should always be processed without unnecessary delay.

    B. Insofar as is practicable, hearing priorities should favor the following categories:

        1. young, immature, and emotionally troubled juveniles;

        2. juveniles who are detained or otherwise removed from their usual home environment; and

        3. juveniles whose pretrial liberty appears to present unusual risks to themselves or the community.

P.V. v. District Court In and For Tenth Judicial District, **199 Colo. 357, 609 P.2d 110, 112 (1980). Speedy trial rules and considerations are more significant for juveniles than for adults and the court endorses the concerns expressed in the commentary to Standard 7.1.**

In re Russell C., **120 N.H. 260, 414 A.2d 934, 938 (1980). The statutory right to a "speedy trial" is a substantive right for which noncompliance may compel the court to forfeit jurisdiction. (Citing Gilman, "IJA/ABA Juvenile Justice Standards Project," 57 Boston University Law Review 617 (1977), for the tension between the "treatment orientation" of the court and due process)**

7.2 Court control; duty to report.

Control over the juvenile court calendar should be vested in the court. The official charged with representing petitioners should be required to file periodic reports with the court setting forth the reasons for delay as to each case for which no trial has been requested within a prescribed time following the filing of the petition. Such official should also advise the court of facts relevant in determining the order of cases on the calendar.

7.3 Calendaring aims and methods.

    A. The court should endeavor by control of the calendar to ensure a regular and efficient flow of cases through the court.

    B. Every reasonable effort should be made to ensure that the same judge who presides at the adjudication hearing presides at all postadjudication proceedings.

    C. Calendaring should be designed, insofar as is practicable, to avoid having a judge preside at the adjudication hearing who has had earlier prejudicial contacts with the case.

7.4 Calendaring of pretrial motions; pretrial conference.

A. Motions in civil or criminal proceedings that are ordinarily in writing should also be made in writing in delinquency proceedings.

B. In appropriate cases the court should hold an omnibus hearing prior to adjudication, in order to:
1. ascertain whether the parties have completed the discovery authorized in Part III and, if not, make appropriate orders to expedite completion;
2. make rulings on any motions or other requests then pending, and ascertain whether any additional motions or requests will be made at the hearing;
3. ascertain whether there are any procedural or constitutional issues which should be considered before trial; and
4. ensure compliance with the standards regarding provision of counsel.

C. Whenever proceedings at trial are likely to be protracted or unusually complicated, or upon request by agreement of counsel, the court should hold one or more pretrial conferences, with counsel present, to consider such matters as will promote fair and expeditious proceedings.

STANDARDS RELATING TO PROSECUTION

James P. Manak, Reporter

PART I: GENERAL STANDARDS

1.1 The role of the juvenile prosecutor.

A. An attorney for the state, hereinafter referred to as the juvenile prosecutor, should participate in every proceeding of every stage of every case subject to the jurisdiction of the family court, in which the state has an interest.

B. The primary duty of the juvenile prosecutor is to seek justice: to fully and faithfully represent the interests of the state, without losing sight of the philosophy and purpose of the family court.

1.2 Conflicts of interest.

Juvenile prosecutors should avoid the appearance or reality of a conflict of interest with respect to their official duties. In some instances their failure to do so will constitute unprofessional conduct.

1.3 Public statements.

The juvenile prosecutor should avoid exploiting his or her office by means of personal publicity connected with a case before trial, during trial, or thereafter.

1.4 The relationship of the juvenile prosecutor to the community.

Juvenile prosecutors should take an active role in their community in preventing delinquency and in protecting the rights of juveniles. They should work to initiate programs within their community and to improve existing programs designed to deal with the problems of juveniles.

PART II: ORGANIZATION OF THE JUVENILE PROSECUTOR'S OFFICE AND QUALIFICATIONS OF THE JUVENILE PROSECUTOR AND HIS OR HER STAFF

2.1 The juvenile prosecutor's office as a separate prosecutorial unit.

A. Where population and caseload warrant, in each prosecutor's office in which there are at least six attorneys, there should be a separate unit or attorney devoted to the representation of the state in family court. The attorney in charge of this unit should be known as the juvenile prosecutor.

B. The juvenile prosecutor should have a professional staff adequate to handle all family court cases in his or her jurisdiction, as well as clerical workers, paralegal workers, law student interns, investigators, and police liaison officers. Such staff should be separate and distinct from persons in the prosecutor's office who handle adult criminal cases.

2.2 The full-time nature of the juvenile prosecutor's office; salary.

A. The juvenile prosecutor should, if possible, be employed on a full-time basis. It is preferred that assistant juvenile prosecutors also be employed on a full-time basis. The clerical staff should, if possible, be employed on a full-time basis. Paralegal workers and law student interns may be employed on a part-time basis.

B. The salary of the juvenile prosecutor and his or her professional staff should be commensurate with that paid to other government attorneys and staff members of similar qualification, experience, and responsibility in the community.

2.3 Methods and criteria for selection of the juvenile prosecutor.

A. The juvenile prosecutor should be an assistant prosecutor, appointed by and responsible to the local prosecutor.

B. The juvenile prosecutor should be an attorney, selected on the basis of interest, education, experience, and competence. He or she should have prior criminal prosecution or other trial experience.

2.4 Methods and criteria for the selection of the professional staff of the juvenile prosecutor's office; minority representation.

A. The professional staff of the juvenile prosecutor's office should be appointed by the local prosecutor, using the same criteria considered in selecting the juvenile prosecutor.

B. The staff should represent, as much as possible, a cross section of the community, including minority groups.

2.5 Training programs.

A. There should be an orientation and training program for the juvenile prosecutor and for every new assistant before each assumes his or her office or duties.

B. There should be a program of ongoing, in-service, interdisciplinary training of both professional and nonprofessional staff in the philosophy and intent of the family court, the problems of juveniles, the problems and conflicts within the community, and the resources available in the community.

2.6 Statewide organization of juvenile prosecutors.

Within each statewide organization of prosecuting attorneys, there should be a division whose membership is composed of juvenile prosecutors within the state.

    A. This division should coordinate training programs and establish and maintain uniform standards for the adjudication and disposition of family court cases.

    B. This division should also establish an advisory council of juvenile prosecutors, which should provide prompt guidance and advice to juvenile prosecutors seeking assistance in their efforts to comply with standards of professional conduct.

PART III: RELATIONSHIPS OF THE JUVENILE PROSECUTOR WITH OTHER PARTICIPANTS IN THE JUVENILE JUSTICE SYSTEM

3.1 With counsel for the juvenile.

There should be maintained at all times an atmosphere of detachment between the juvenile prosecutor and counsel for the juvenile. The appearance as well as reality of collusion should be zealously avoided.

3.2 With the court.

There should be maintained at all times an atmosphere of detachment between the juvenile prosecutor and the court.

3.3 With jurors.

    A. The juvenile prosecutor must not communicate privately with any person once that person is summoned for jury duty or impaneled as a juror in a case.

    B. The juvenile prosecutor should treat jurors with deference and respect, avoiding the reality or appearance of currying favor by a show of undue solicitude for their comfort or convenience.

    C. After verdict, the juvenile prosecutor should not make comments to or ask questions of a juror for the purpose of harassing or embarrassing the juror in any way which will tend to influence judgment in future jury service.

3.4 With prospective nonexpert witnesses.

A. Juvenile prosecutors must not compensate a nonexpert witness. They may, however, request permission from the family court to reimburse a nonexpert witness for the reasonable expenses of attending court, including transportation and loss of income.

B. In interviewing an adult prospective witness, it is proper but not mandatory for juvenile prosecutors or their investigators to caution the witness concerning possible self-incrimination and his or her possible need for counsel. However, if the prospective witness is a juvenile, such cautions are mandatory and should be extended in the presence of the juvenile's parents or guardian. Where a parent or guardian is not available, the family court may, in the exercise of its discretion, appoint a guardian *ad litem* or independent counsel for the juvenile witness to be present at the giving of such cautions.

3.5 With expert witnesses.

A. A juvenile prosecutor who engages an expert for an opinion should respect the independence of the expert and should not seek to dictate the formation of the expert's opinion on the subject. To the extent necessary, the juvenile prosecutor should explain to the expert his or her role in the trial, as an impartial expert called to aid the fact finders, and the manner in which the examination of witnesses is conducted.

B. The juvenile prosecutor must not pay an excessive fee for the purpose of influencing the expert's testimony or make the fee contingent upon the testimony he or she will give or the result in the case.

3.6 With the police.

A. There should be maintained at all times an atmosphere of mutual respect and cooperation between the juvenile prosecutor's office and the police.

B. The juvenile prosecutor should strive to establish an effective line of communication with the police.

C. The juvenile prosecutor should provide legal advice to the police concerning police functions and duties in juvenile matters.

D. The juvenile prosecutor should cooperate with the police in providing the services of his or her staff to aid in training the police in the performance of their duties in juvenile matters.

3.7 With intake officers, probation officers, and social workers.

An atmosphere of mutual respect and trust should exist among the juvenile prosecutor and intake officers, probation officers, and social workers. He or she should be available to advise them concerning any matters relevant to their functions.

PART IV: THE PREADJUDICATION PHASE

4.1 Responsibilities of the juvenile prosecutor and intake officer at the intake stage.

  A. The juvenile prosecutor should be available to advise the intake officer whether the facts alleged by a complainant are legally sufficient to file a petition of delinquency.

  B. If the intake officer determines that a petition should be filed, he or she should submit a written report requesting that a petition be filed to the juvenile prosecutor. The intake officer should also submit a written statement of the decision and the reasons therefor to the juvenile and his or her parents or legal guardian. All petitions should be countersigned and filed by the juvenile prosecutor. The juvenile prosecutor may refuse the request of the intake officer to file a petition. Any determination by the prosecutor that a petition should not be filed should be final and not appealable to the family court.

  C. If the intake officer determines that a petition should not be filed, the officer should notify the complainant of the decision and of the reasons therefor and should advise the complainant that he or she may submit the complaint to the juvenile prosecutor for review. Upon receiving a request for review, the juvenile prosecutor should consider the facts presented by the complainant, consult with the intake officer who made the initial decision, and then make the final determination as to whether a petition should be filed.

  D. In the absence of a complainant's request for a review of the intake officer's determination that a petition should not be filed, the intake officer should notify the juvenile prosecutor of a determination that a petition should not be filed. The juvenile prosecutor then has the right, after consultation with the intake officer, to file a petition.

4.2 Withdrawal of petition upon a subsequent finding of lack of legal sufficiency.

If, subsequent to the filing of a petition with the family court, the juvenile prosecutor determines that there is insufficient evidence admissible in a court of law under the rules of evidence to establish the legal sufficiency of the petition, he or she should move to withdraw the petition.

4.3 Investigation: proper subject for family court jurisdiction.

A. The juvenile prosecutor should determine, by investigating the juvenile's past record with the police and the court, whether he or she is a proper subject for family court jurisdiction.

   1. Where the juvenile prosecutor's inquiry into the conduct alleged and the juvenile's circumstances warrant it, the complaint may be transferred to the intake agency for a pre-adjudication disposition.

   2. If the juvenile prosecutor determines that the state's interest requires the formal adjudicative process of the family court, a petition should be filed as soon as possible with the family court.

   3. A motion to transfer the case to the criminal court may be filed with the petition if the youth is at least fifteen years of age but under the age of eighteen at the time of the conduct alleged in the petition, and if there is clear and convincing evidence that

      a. the alleged conduct would constitute a class one or class two juvenile offense, and

      b. the juvenile alleged to have committed a class two offense has a prior record of adjudicated delinquency involving the infliction or threat of significant bodily injury, and

      c. previous dispositions of the juvenile have demonstrated the likely inefficacy of the dispositions available to the family court, and

      d. the services and dispositional alternatives available in the criminal justice system are more appropriate for dealing with the juvenile's problems and are, in fact, available.

B. If a petition is filed, the information obtained in the course of this investigation should be made available to the juvenile or to the counsel for the juvenile.

4.4 Speedy decision.

A. If the juvenile is in custody pending the filing of a petition, the juvenile prosecutor should file a petition within [forty-eight] hours after the juvenile has been taken into custody.

B. If the juvenile is not in custody pending the filing of a petition, the juvenile prosecutor should file a petition within [five] days of the time that he or she receives the recommendation of the intake officer.

4.5 Power over dismissal of petition.

A. Once a petition has been filed with the family court it should not be dismissed, except by the court on its own motion or on motion of the juvenile in furtherance of justice, without the consent of the juvenile prosecutor.

B. Once a petition has been filed with the family court, a nonjudicial disposition should not be effected without the consent of the juvenile prosecutor, the juvenile, the juvenile's parents or guardian, and the juvenile's attorney.

4.6 Judicial determination of probable cause at the first appearance of the juvenile in family court.

Whether it be a detention hearing, a hearing on a motion to waive family court jurisdiction, or other preliminary hearing, the juvenile prosecutor should present evidence to establish probable cause that the acts alleged in the petition were committed by the juvenile, at the first appearance of the juvenile in family court.

4.7 Disclosure of evidence by the juvenile prosecutor.

The juvenile prosecutor is under the same duty to disclose evidence favorable to the juvenile in family court proceedings as is the prosecuting attorney in adult criminal proceedings.

PART V: UNCONTESTED ADJUDICATION PROCEEDINGS

5.1 Propriety of plea agreements.

A. A plea agreement concerning the petition or petitions that may be filed against a juvenile may properly be entered into by the juvenile prosecutor.

B. Plea agreements should be entered into with both the interests of the state and those of the juvenile in mind, although the primary concern of the juvenile prosecutor should be the protection of the public interest, as determined in the exercise of traditional prosecutorial discretion.

5.2 Plea discussions when a juvenile maintains factual innocence.

The juvenile prosecutor should neither initiate nor continue plea discussions if he or she is aware that the juvenile maintains factual innocence.

5.3 Independent evidence in the record.

A plea agreement should not be entered into by the juvenile prosecutor without the presentation on the record of the family court of independent evidence indicating that the juvenile has committed the acts alleged in the petition.

5.4 Fulfillment of plea agreements.

If juvenile prosecutors find that they are unable to fulfill a plea agreement, they should promptly give notice to the juvenile and cooperate in securing leave of court for the withdrawal of the admission and take such other steps as may be appropriate and effective to restore the juvenile to the position he or she was in before the plea was entered.

PART VI: THE ADJUDICATORY PHASE

6.1 Speedy adjudication.
   A. When the juvenile prosecutor has decided to seek a formal adjudication of a complaint against a juvenile, he or she should proceed to an adjudicatory hearing as quickly as possible. Detention cases should be given priority treatment.
   B. Control over the trial calendar should be exercised by the family court.

6.2 Assumption of traditional adversary role.

At the adjudicatory hearing, the juvenile prosecutor should assume the traditional adversary position of a prosecutor.

6.3 Standard of proof; rules of evidence.
   A. The juvenile prosecutor has the burden of proving the allegations in the petition beyond a reasonable doubt.
   B. The rules of evidence employed in the trial of criminal cases in the jurisdiction of the juvenile prosecutor should be applicable to family court cases involving delinquency petitions.

6.4 Selection of jurors.
   A. If juvenile prosecutors are in a jurisdiction affording a juvenile a statutory right to jury trial in family court proceedings, they should prepare themselves prior to the adjudicatory hearing to

effectively discharge their function in the selection of the jury and the exercise of challenges for cause and peremptory challenges.

B. If juvenile prosecutors investigate the background of prospective jurors, they should use only investigatory methods which minimize the risk of causing harassment, embarrassment, or invasion of privacy.

C. If juvenile prosecutors are in a jurisdiction that allows them to personally examine jurors on *voir dire,* they should limit their questions solely to those designed to elicit information relevant to the intelligent exercise of challenges. They should not expose the jury to evidence which they know will be inadmissible, nor should they argue the case to it.

6.5 Opening statement.

In their opening statements, juvenile prosecutors should confine their remarks to evidence they intend to offer which they believe in good faith will be available and admissible and a brief statement of the issues in the case.

6.6 Presentation of evidence.

A. Juvenile prosecutors should never knowingly offer false evidence in any form. If they subsequently discover the falsity of any evidence that they have introduced, they must immediately seek its withdrawal.

B. The juvenile prosecutor should never knowingly offer inadmissible evidence, ask legally objectionable questions, or make impermissible comments in the presence of the judge or jury.

C. The juvenile prosecutor should never permit any tangible evidence to be displayed in the view of the judge or the jury which would tend to prejudice fair consideration of the issues by the judge or jury, until such time as a good faith tender of such evidence is made.

D. The juvenile prosecutor should never tender tangible evidence in the view of the judge or jury if it would tend to prejudice fair consideration by the judge or jury unless there is a reasonable basis for its admission in evidence. When there is any doubt about the admissibility of such evidence, it should be tendered by an offer of proof and a ruling obtained.

6.7 Examination of witnesses.

A. The interrogation of witnesses should be conducted fairly, objectively, and with proper regard for the dignity and privacy of the witness, and without seeking to intimidate or humiliate the witness. When examining a youthful witness, the juvenile prosecutor should exercise special care to comply with this standard.

B. Juvenile prosecutors should not call a witness whom they know will claim a valid privilege not to testify, for the purpose of impressing upon the fact finder the claim of privilege.

C. Juvenile prosecutors should not ask a question which implies the existence of a factual predicate which they cannot support by evidence.

6.8 Closing argument.

A. Juvenile prosecutors may argue all reasonable inferences from the evidence in the record, but they should not intentionally misstate the evidence or mislead the fact finder as to the inferences that may be drawn.

B. The juvenile prosecutor should never intentionally refer to or argue on the basis of facts outside the record, unless such facts are matters of common public knowledge based upon ordinary human experience or matters of which the court may take judicial notice.

C. The juvenile prosecutor should never express his or her personal belief or opinion as to the truth or falsity of any evidence or testimony, or the guilt of the juvenile.

D. The juvenile prosecutor should not use arguments solely calculated to inflame the passions or prejudices of the fact finder.

E. The juvenile prosecutor should refrain from argument which would divert the fact finder from his or her duty to decide the case on the evidence, by injecting issues broader than the guilt or innocence of the juvenile under the controlling law, or by making predictions of the consequences of the fact finder's decision.

6.9 Comment by the juvenile prosecutor after decision.

The juvenile prosecutor should not make public comments concerning a finding or decision, by whomever rendered, at any stage of the juvenile justice system, from intake through postdisposition proceedings.

PART VII: DISPOSITIONAL PHASE

7.1 Permissibility of taking an active role.

A. Juvenile prosecutors may take an active role in the dispositional hearing. If they choose to do so, they should make their own, independent recommendation for disposition, after reviewing the reports prepared by their own staff, the probation department, and others.

B. While the safety and welfare of the community is their paramount concern, juvenile prosecutors should consider alternative modes of disposition which more closely satisfy the interests and needs of the juvenile without jeopardizing that concern.

7.2 Duty to monitor the effectiveness of various modes of disposition.

A. Juvenile prosecutors should undertake their own periodic evaluation of the success of particular dispositional programs that are used in their jurisdiction, from the standpoint of the interests of both the state and the juvenile.

B. If juvenile prosecutors discover that a juvenile or class of juveniles is not receiving the care and treatment contemplated by the family court in making its dispositions, they should inform the family court of this fact.

PART VIII: POSTDISPOSITION PROCEEDINGS

8.1 Subsequent proceedings to be handled by the juvenile prosecutor's office.

The juvenile prosecutor may represent the state's interest in appeals from decisions rendered by the family court, hearings concerning the revocation of probation, petitions for a modification of disposition, and collateral proceedings attacking the orders of the family court.

8.2 Expediting subsequent litigation.

A. If juvenile prosecutors become aware of the possibility that a juvenile is violating the terms of a probation order, they should investigate the matter promptly and decide as quickly as possible whether they will seek a revocation of probation status.

B. If a juvenile files an appeal, or seeks a modification of the disposition that has been rendered in his or her case, the juvenile prosecutor should decide, as quickly as possible, what his or her position will be in response to the juvenile's action, and then act as quickly as possible to effectuate that decision.

8.3 Facts outside record in postdisposition proceedings.

The juvenile prosecutor must not intentionally refer to or argue on the basis of facts outside the record on appeal, or in other postdisposition proceedings, unless such facts are matters of common public knowledge based upon ordinary human experience or matters of which the appellate court may take judicial notice, or the taking of new evidence is otherwise appropriate in the proceeding.

STANDARDS RELATING TO RIGHTS OF MINORS

Barry Feld and Robert J. Levy, Reporters

PART I: AGE OF MAJORITY

1.1 Age of majority.

All persons who have attained the age of eighteen years should be regarded as adults for all legal purposes.

PART II: EMANCIPATION

2.1 A new approach to emancipation.

  A. The legal issues traditionally resolved by reference to the emancipation doctrine should be resolved legislatively as aspects of the substantive doctrines which govern legal relationships between child and parent, between parent and parent, between child and nonmembers of the family, and between parents and nonmembers of the family.

  B. Legislatively created, narrowly drawn doctrines which obviate the need for relying upon the vague criteria of the traditional emancipation doctrine should include the following principles:

    1. A parent should not be permitted to recover from the child's employer wages due or paid by the employer to the child;

    2. A child should be permitted to sue his or her parent and the parent should be permitted to sue the child for damages arising from intentional or negligent tortious behavior so long as the behavior is not related to the exercise of family functions.

  C. Because legal disputes concerning the activities and needs of children will inevitably arise—between child and parent, between parent and parent, between child and nonmembers of the family, and between parents and nonmembers of the family—and the disputes will arise in contexts and present legal issues which cannot be forecast legislatively, the legislature should also enact an emancipation doctrine of general applicability.

    1. The doctrine should not permit emancipation by judicial decree.

    2. The doctrine should be explicitly limited to issues not addressed by other standards of this volume and should authorize a finding of emancipation when a child, prior to the age

of majority, has established a residence separate from that of his or her family, whether or not with parental consent or consent of a person responsible for his or her care, and is managing his or her own financial affairs.

Gore v. Stowe, **186 Cal. App. 3d 283, 243 Cal. Rptr. 224, 747 P.2d 1152, 1156 (Ct. App., 2d Dist. 1987). The disabilities of minority are eliminated to the extent that statutes, case law or a court decision provide.**

PART III: SUPPORT

3.1 Who is obligated to support.

A child entitled to support is entitled to support from each of his or her parents, natural or adopted, whether or not they are married.

3.2 Scope of support.

A child is entitled to such support from a person obligated to support as will permit the child to live in a manner commensurate with that person's means.

3.3 Enforcement of support obligations.

The obligation to support a child may be enforced:
A. by a suit brought by the child or on behalf of the child;
B. by a parent who has custody of the child;
C. by a nonparent who has custody of the child pursuant to an order of a court with guardianship, neglect, or delinquency jurisdiction;
D. by a nonmember of the family, in a proceeding brought against either parent of the child to recover the price or the fair market value of any goods or services provided to the child, if the goods or services so provided are either essential to preserve the life of the child or reasonably appear to the provider to be suitable to the child's or the family's economic situation;
  1. a parent obligated to support the child is not liable to a nonmember of the family who has provided the child with goods or services if the parent obligated to support does not have custody of the child and, if subject to a court decree ordering payments in the child's behalf, has fully complied with the financial terms of the decree;
E. by criminal prosecution, if a proceeding could be maintained under subsection A and if the parent obligated to support a child under the age of [sixteen] persistently fails to provide support

which the parent can provide and which the parent knows he or she is legally obligated to provide to the child.

3.4 Duration of the obligation to support.

    A. The obligation to support a child should terminate when the child reaches the age of majority.

    B. The obligation to support a child should terminate prior to his or her reaching the age of majority:

        1. if and for so long as the child is married or if the child is managing his or her own financial affairs and is living separate and apart from a custodial parent or a nonparent who has custody of the child pursuant to an order of a court with guardianship, neglect, or delinquency jurisdiction, except when the child is living in a separate residence in connection with a judicial finding of endangerment;

        2. when the parental rights of a parent obligated to support are terminated by a juvenile court pursuant to the *Abuse and Neglect* volume.

    C. The obligation to support a child should not terminate when the person obligated to support dies.

PART IV: MEDICAL CARE

4.1 Prior parental consent.

    A. No medical procedures, services, or treatment should be provided to a minor without prior parental consent, except as specified in Standards 4.4-4.9.

    B. Circumstances where parents refuse to consent to treatment are governed by the *Abuse and Neglect* volume.

4.2 Notification of treatment.

    A. Where prior parental consent is not required to provide medical services or treatment to a minor, the provider should promptly notify the parent or responsible custodian of such treatment and obtain his or her consent to further treatment, except as hereinafter specified.

    B. Where the medical services provided are for the treatment of chemical dependency, Standard 4.7, or venereal disease, contraception, and pregnancy, Standard 4.8, the physician should first seek and obtain the minor's permission to notify the parent of such treatments.

1. If the minor-patient objects to notification of the parent, the physician should not notify the parent that treatment was or is being provided unless he or she concludes that failing to inform the parent could seriously jeopardize the health of the minor, taking into consideration:
   a. the impact that such notification could have on the course of treatment;
   b. the medical considerations which require such notification;
   c. the nature, basis, and strength of the minor's objections;
   d. the extent to which parental involvement in the course of treatment is required or desirable.
2. A physician who concludes that notification of the parent is medically required should:
   a. indicate the medical justifications in the minor-patient's file; and
   b. inform the parent only after making all reasonable efforts to persuade the minor to consent to notification of the parent.

C. Where the medical services provided are for the treatment of a mental or emotional disorder pursuant to Standard 4.9, after three sessions the provider should notify the parent of such treatment and obtain his or her consent to further treatment.

4.3 Financial liability.

A. A parent should be financially liable to persons providing medical treatment to his or her minor child if the parent consents to such services, or if the services are provided under emergency circumstances pursuant to Standard 4.5.

B. A minor who consents to his or her own medical treatment under Standards 4.6-4.9 should be financially liable for payment for such services and should not disaffirm the financial obligation on account of minority.

C. A public or private health insurance policy or plan under which a minor is a beneficiary should allow a minor who consents to medical services or treatment to file claims and receive benefits, regardless of whether the parent has consented to the treatment.

D. A public or private health insurer should not inform a parent or policy holder that a minor has filed a claim or received a benefit under a health insurance policy or plan of which the minor is a beneficiary, unless the physician has previously notified the parent of the treatment for which the claim is submitted.

4.4 Emancipated minor.

  A. An emancipated minor who is living separate and apart from his or her parent and who is managing his or her own financial affairs may consent to medical treatment on the same terms and conditions as an adult. Accordingly, parental consent should not be required, nor should there be subsequent notification of the parent, or financial liability.

    1. If a physician treats a minor who is not actually emancipated, it should be a defense to a suit basing liability on lack of parental consent, that he or she relied in good faith on the minor's representations of emancipation.

4.5 Emergency treatment.

  A. Under emergency circumstances, a minor may receive medical services or treatment without prior parental consent.

    1. Emergency circumstances exist when delaying treatment to first secure parental consent would endanger the life or health of the minor.

    2. It should be a defense to an action basing liability on lack of parental consent, that the medical services were provided under emergency circumstances.

  B. Where medical services or treatment are provided under emergency circumstances, the parent should be notified as promptly as possible, and his or her consent should be obtained for further treatment.

  C. A parent should be financially liable to persons providing emergency medical treatment.

  D. Where the emergency medical services are for treatment of chemical dependency (Standard 4.7); venereal disease, contraception, or pregnancy (Standard 4.8); or mental or emotional disorder (Standard 4.9), questions of notification of the parent and financial liability are governed by those provisions and Standards 4.2 B, 4.2 C, and 4.3.

4.6 Mature minor.

  A. A minor of [sixteen] or older who has sufficient capacity to understand the nature and consequences of a proposed medical treatment for his or her benefit may consent to that treatment on the same terms and conditions as an adult.

  B. The treating physician should notify the minor's parent of any medical treatment provided under this standard, subject to the provisions of Standard 4.2 B.

4.7 Chemical dependency.

A. A minor of any age may consent to medical services, treatment, or therapy for problems or conditions related to alcohol or drug abuse or addiction.

B. If the minor objects to notification of the parent, the person or agency providing treatment under this standard should notify the parent of such treatment only if he or she concludes that failing to inform the parent would seriously jeopardize the health of the minor and complies with the provisions of Standard 4.2.

4.8 Venereal disease, contraception, and pregnancy.

A. A minor of any age may consent to medical services, therapy, or counseling for:
   1. treatment of venereal disease;
   2. family planning, contraception, or birth control other than a procedure which results in sterilization; or
   3. treatment related to pregnancy, including abortion.

B. If the minor objects to notification of the parent, the person or agency providing treatment under this standard should notify the parent of such treatment only if he or she concludes that failing to inform the parent would seriously jeopardize the health of the minor, and complies with the provisions of Standard 4.2.

4.9 Mental or emotional disorder.

A. A minor of fourteen or older who has or professes to suffer from a mental or emotional disorder may consent to three sessions with a psychotherapist or counselor for diagnosis and consultation.

B. Following three sessions for crisis intervention and/or diagnosis, the provider should notify the parent of such sessions and obtain his or her consent to further treatment.

PART V: YOUTH EMPLOYMENT

5.1 Employment during school.

A. No minor below the age of sixteen who is required to attend school should be employed during the hours in which he or she is required to be in school, as indicated on the work permit. See Standard 5.4.

1. This prohibition should not apply to a minor employed during school hours in a school sanctioned work-study, vocational training, or apprenticeship program.

5.2 Minimum age of employment.

A. No minor below twelve years of age should be employed in any occupation, trade, service, or business:

1. except that, with the consent of the minor's parent, no minimum age limitations or restrictions should apply to a minor employed:

   a. by his or her parent in nonhazardous occupations, as defined in Standard 5.3; or

   b. by third parties in domestic service, casual labor, or as a youthful performer, provided that such exempt services should not be performed by a minor required to attend school during hours in which the school is in session. See Standard 5.1.

5.3 Employment in hazardous activities.

A. No minor below sixteen years of age should be employed in any occupation determined to be hazardous.

B. The secretary of labor [or state labor commissioner] should promulgate specific standards and regulations defining what occupations are hazardous.

1. The secretary should regularly review and investigate to determine if a particular occupation or employment should be added to or deleted from the list of those which are hazardous.

C. The prohibition on employing minors in hazardous activities does not apply to a minor fourteen or older who is employed in or supervised under a state or federal apprentice training or work-study program in which the minor receives training and supervision.

5.4 Work permit as proof of eligibility of employment.

A. No minor below sixteen years of age should be employed without presenting to an employer or prospective employer a permit to work, which is the sole basis by which eligibility to work should be established.

B. A work permit should be issued by or under the authority of the school superintendent of the district or county in which the minor resides, upon request by a minor, and upon a showing that the minor is at least twelve years of age, as established by a birth certificate or other reliable proof of age including the oath or affirmation of a parent.

C. The work permit should contain the following information:
 1. the name, address, and description or picture of the minor;
 2. the date of birth of the minor;
 3. the name, address, and position of the issuing officer;
 4. the date of issuance of the permit;
 5. the hours during which the minor is required to attend school, and when his or her employment is thereby prohibited; and
 6. a statement that no minor under sixteen years of age may work during school hours, or in hazardous activities, except as part of a recognized work-study or apprentice program.

D. Every employer should require a minor employee or prospective employee to furnish a work permit as proof of age and authorization to be employed.
 1. Every employer should obtain a copy of the work permit from the issuing officer and retain it in his or her possession. An employer of a minor is entitled to rely upon such permit as evidence of age and legal hours of employment.

5.5 Enforcement of child labor laws.

Enforcement of the provisions of Standards 5.1–5.4 should be by civil fines.

5.6 Restrictions on hours of employment.

Adult and minor employees should be subject to the same restrictions on the total number of hours per day, or per week, or the actual hours during which they may be employed.

5.7 Compensation and minimum wage.

A. State and federal minimum wage laws should apply equally to minors and adults, without wage variations or differentials on the basis of age.

B. Persons performing similar work should receive similar compensation without regard to the age of the worker.

5.8 Workmen's compensation.

All minors, whether or not lawfully employed under the provisions of these standards, should be subject to the same rights and remedies as adults under applicable workmen's compensation laws.

PART VI: MINORS' CONTRACTS

6.1 Minors' contracts.

The validity of contracts of minors, other than those governed by other standards of this volume, should be governed by the following principles:

A. The contract of a minor who is at least twelve years of age should be valid and enforceable by and against the minor, as long as such a contract of an adult would be valid and enforceable, if:
   1. the minor's parent or duly constituted guardian consented in writing to the contract; or
   2. the minor represented to the other party that he or she was at least eighteen years of age and a reasonable person under the circumstances would have believed the representation; or
   3. the minor was a purchaser and is unable to return the goods to the seller in substantially the condition they were in when purchased because the minor lost or caused them to be damaged, the minor consumed them, or the minor gave them away.

B. The contract of a minor who has not reached the age of twelve should be void.

C. Release of a tort claim by a minor should be valid, if an adult's release would be valid under the same circumstances:
   1. if the minor is at least twelve years of age, if the release is approved by the minor, the minor's parent, and, if suit is pending, by the court; or
   2. if the minor has not reached the age of twelve, if the release is approved by the minor's parent, and, if suit is pending, by the court.

STANDARDS RELATING TO TRANSFER BETWEEN COURTS

Charles Whitebread, Reporter

PART I: JURISDICTION

1.1 Age limits.

    A. The juvenile court should have jurisdiction in any proceeding against any person whose alleged conduct would constitute an offense on which a juvenile court adjudication could be based if at the time the offense is alleged to have occurred such person was not more than seventeen years of age.

    B. No criminal court should have jurisdiction in any proceeding against any person whose alleged conduct would constitute an offense on which a juvenile court adjudication could be based if at the time the offense is alleged to have occurred such person was not more than fourteen years of age.

    C. No criminal court should have jurisdiction in any proceeding against any person whose alleged conduct would constitute an offense on which a juvenile court adjudication could be based if at the time the offense is alleged to have occurred such person was fifteen, sixteen, or seventeen years of age, unless the juvenile court has waived its jurisdiction over that person.

In the Matter of C.S., 384 A.2d 407, 412 (D.C. Ct. App. 1977). **Only a few states at the decision of this case automatically conferred jurisdiction on adult criminal courts over certain juveniles. (Citing Whitebread & Batey, "Transfer Between Courts: Proposals of the Juvenile Justice Standards Project," 63** *Va. L. Rev.* **221 (1977))**

State v. R.G.D., 108 N.J. 1, 527 A.2d 834, 836 (1987). **It is difficult and inherently arbitrary to draw lines for the transfer of juveniles between courts. (Citing** *Standards Relating to Transfer Between Courts* **generally)**

In the Matter of B.C., 749 P.2d 542, 548 (Okla. 1988). **The term "waiver" in national jurisprudence generally refers to the transfer of jurisdiction from the juvenile court to the adult court or vice versa. (Citing** *Standards Relating to Transfer Between Courts* **generally)**

1.2 Other limits.

    A. No juvenile court disposition, however modified, resulting from a single transaction or episode, should exceed [thirty-six] months.

B. The juvenile court should retain jurisdiction to administer or modify its disposition of any person. The juvenile court should not have jurisdiction to adjudicate subsequent conduct of any person subject to such continuing jurisdiction if at the time the subsequent criminal offense is alleged to have occurred such person was more than seventeen years of age.

1.3 Limitations period.

No juvenile court adjudication or waiver decision should be based on an offense alleged to have occurred more than three years prior to the filing of a petition alleging such offense, unless such offense would not be subject to a statute of limitations if committed by an adult. If the statute of limitations applicable to adult criminal proceedings for such offense is less than three years, such shorter period should apply to juvenile court criminal proceedings.

PART II: WAIVER

2.1 Time requirements.

A. Within [two] court days of the filing of any petition alleging conduct which constitutes a class one or class two juvenile offense against a person who was fifteen, sixteen, or seventeen years of age when the alleged offense occurred, the clerk of the juvenile court should give the prosecuting attorney written notice of the possibility of waiver.

B. Within [three] court days of the filing of any petition alleging conduct which constitutes a class one or class two juvenile offense against a person who was fifteen, sixteen, or seventeen years of age when the alleged offense occurred, the prosecuting attorney should give such person written notice, multilingual if appropriate, of the possibility of waiver.

C. Within [seven] court days of the filing of any petition alleging conduct which constitutes a class one or class two juvenile offense against a person who was fifteen, sixteen, or seventeen years of age when the alleged offense occurred, the prosecuting attorney may request by written motion that the juvenile court waive its jurisdiction over the juvenile. The prosecuting attorney should deliver a signed, acknowledged copy of the waiver motion to the juvenile and counsel for the juvenile within [twenty-four] hours after the filing of such motion in the juvenile court.

D. The juvenile court should initiate a hearing on waiver within [ten] court days of the filing of the waiver motion or, if the juvenile seeks to suspend this requirement, within a reasonable time thereafter.

E. The juvenile court should issue a written decision setting forth its findings and the reasons therefor, including a statement of the evidence relied on in reaching the decision, within [ten] court days after conclusion of the waiver hearing.

F. No waiver notice should be given, no waiver motion should be accepted for filing, no waiver hearing should be initiated, and no waiver decision should be issued relating to any juvenile court petition after commencement of any adjudicatory hearing relating to any transaction or episode alleged in that petition.

2.2 Necessary findings.

A. The juvenile court should waive its jurisdiction only upon finding:

1. that probable cause exists to believe that the juvenile has committed the class one or class two juvenile offense alleged in the petition; and

Wolf v. State, **99 Idaho 476, 583 P.2d 1011, 1014, 1026 (1978). A finding of probable cause is a necessary finding in a transfer proceeding. (Citing Standard 2.2 A.1)**

2. that by clear and convincing evidence, the juvenile is not a proper person to be handled by the juvenile court.

In the Matter of the Appeal in Maricopa Co. Juvenile Action No. J-93117, **134 Ariz. 105, 654 P.2d 39, 46 (1982). Dissenting judge would adopt the clear and convincing evidence standard for juvenile transfer hearings. (Citing the Standards Summary volume)**

People v. A.D.G., **895 P.2d 1067, 1071 (Colo. Ct. App. 1994). Transfer decisions in Colorado are subject to a preponderance of the evidence burden of the proof rather than clear and convincing evidence standard. (Citing and rejecting the *Standards Relating to Transfer*)**

In the Interest of T.R.B., **109 Wis. 2d 119, 325 N.W.2d 329, 333 (1982). The statutory requirement that "prosecutive merit" be found in a transfer hearing is analogous to probable cause. (Citing the *Standards Relating to Transfer Between Courts* generally)**

B. A finding of probable cause to believe that a juvenile has committed a class one or class two juvenile offense should be based solely on evidence admissible in an adjudicatory hearing of the juvenile court.

In the Interest of J.G., **119 Wis. 2d 748, 350 N.W.2d 668, 677 (1984).
Where a juvenile asserted that his confession was involuntary, without more, the juvenile court is not required to conduct a hearing on
the confession but may independently assess the reliability of the
statement during the transfer hearing. (Concurring justice cited Standard 2.2 B)**

    C. A finding that a juvenile is not a proper person to be handled by
       the juvenile court must include determinations, by clear and convincing evidence, of:

        1. the seriousness of the alleged class one or class two juvenile
           offense;

State v. G.L.P., **590 P.2d 65, 70 (Alaska 1979). The seriousness of the
offense is a significant factor in the transfer decision. (Citing Whitebread & Batey, "Transfer Between Courts: Proposals of the Juvenile
Justice Standards Project," 63** *Va. L. Rev.* **221 (1977))**

        2. a prior record of adjudicated delinquency involving the infliction or threat of significant bodily injury, if the juvenile is alleged to have committed a class two juvenile offense;

A Juvenile v. Commonwealth, **380 Mass. 552, 405 N.E.2d 143, 149 (1980).
Without necessarily endorsing the view, in general "transfer to adult
prosecution should not be ordered for juvenile first offenders." (Citing Standard 2.2 C.2)**

State ex rel. Coats v. Johnson, **597 P.2d 328, 334 (Okla. Crim. App.
1979). Justice concurring specially in the court's opinion holding the
state's transfer statute unconstitutionally vague, and suggesting factors that could be incorporated in a new statute. (Citing** *Standards
Relating to Transfer Between Courts,* **particularly as to consideration
of prior adjudications as a factor)**

        3. the likely inefficacy of the dispositions available to the juvenile
           court as demonstrated by previous dispositions of the juvenile;
           and

        4. the appropriateness of the services and dispositional alternatives available in the criminal justice system for dealing with
the juvenile's problems and whether they are, in fact, available.
Expert opinion should be considered in assessing the likely
efficacy of the dispositions available to the juvenile court. A
finding that a juvenile is not a proper person to be handled by
the juvenile court should be based solely on evidence admis-

sible in a disposition hearing of the juvenile court and should be in writing, as provided in Standard 2.1 E.

State v. Wright, 456 N.W.2d 661, 663 (Iowa 1990). **Juvenile had no right to confrontation during the hearing to waive the juvenile court's jurisdiction. (Citing Standard 2.2 C as equating such a proceeding with a disposition hearing)**

People v. Williams, 111 Mich. App. 818, 314 N.W.2d 769, 772 (Mich. Ct. App. 1982). **Phase 2 of waiver hearings is comparable to a disposition hearing "with respect to evidentiary questions." (Citing Standard 2.2 C)**

In the Matter of the Welfare of T.D.S., 289 N.W.2d 137, 140 (Minn. 1980). **"Reference proceedings" are like "dispositional proceedings with respect to evidentiary questions." (Citing Standard 2.2 C)**

In the Matter of Seven Minors, 99 Nev. 427, 664 P.2d 947, 951 (1983). **Transfer hearings focus on the public interest in determining whether juveniles should be placed within the jurisdiction of adult criminal courts. However, this view "is not in harmony with the rules commonly seen in operation throughout the juvenile justice system." (Citing Standard 2.2 C)**

D. A finding of probable cause to believe that a juvenile has committed a class one or class two juvenile offense may be substituted for a probable cause determination relating to that offense (or a lesser included offense) required in any subsequent juvenile court proceeding. Such a finding should not be substituted for any finding of probable cause required in any subsequent criminal proceeding.

State v. Buelow, 155 Vt. 537, 587 A.2d 948, 953–4 (1991). **The absence of specific statutory standards governing juvenile transfer decisions does not constitute a denial of due process, and the court declines the invitation to "adopt as mandatory the ABA Juvenile Justice Standards."**

2.3 The hearing.

In re E.H., 166 W.Va. 615, 276 S.E.2d 557, 562 (1981). **The general right to demand a jury trial in the West Virginia Code does not apply to a juvenile transfer hearing, and no commentator has suggested that a jury is the appropriate decision maker in such a proceeding. (Citing *Standard Relating to Transfer Between Courts* generally)**

A. The juvenile should be represented by counsel at the waiver hearing. The clerk of the juvenile court should give written notice to the juvenile, multilingual if appropriate, of this requirement at least [five] court days before commencement of the waiver hearing.

B. The juvenile court should appoint counsel to represent any juvenile unable to afford representation by counsel at the waiver hearing. The clerk of the juvenile court should give written notice to the juvenile, multilingual if appropriate, of this right at least [five] court days before commencement of the waiver hearing.

C. The juvenile court should pay the reasonable fees and expenses of an expert witness for the juvenile if the juvenile desires, but is unable to afford, the services of such an expert witness at the waiver hearing, unless the presiding officer determines that the expert witness is not necessary.

D. The juvenile should have access to all evidence available to the juvenile court which could be used either to support or contest the waiver motion.

E. The prosecuting attorney should bear the burden of proving that probable cause exists to believe that the juvenile has committed a class one or class two juvenile offense and that the juvenile is not a proper person to be handled by the juvenile court.

F. The juvenile may contest the waiver motion by challenging, or producing evidence tending to challenge, the evidence of the prosecuting attorney.

G. The juvenile may examine any person who prepared any report concerning the juvenile which is presented at the waiver hearing.

H. All evidence presented at the waiver hearing should be under oath and subject to cross-examination.

Wolf v. State, 99 Idaho 476, 583 P.2d 1011, 1014, 1026 (1978). Dissent urges that Standard 2.2 [sic] E through H define criteria that should be necessary findings in a transfer hearing.

I. The juvenile may remain silent at the waiver hearing. No admission by the juvenile during the waiver hearing should be admissible to establish guilt or to impeach testimony in any subsequent proceeding, except a perjury proceeding.

J. The juvenile may disqualify the presiding officer at the waiver hearing from presiding at any subsequent criminal trial or juvenile court adjudicatory hearing relating to any transaction or episode alleged in the petition initiating juvenile court proceedings.

Perotti v. State, 806 P.2d 325, 329 (Alaska Ct. App. 1991). Judge who

presided as transfer hearing should not have conducted the juvenile's trial in disregard of the youth's motion that he recuse himself. (Citing Standard 2.3 J)

2.4 Appeal.

    A. The juvenile or the prosecuting attorney may file an appeal of the waiver decision with the court authorized to hear appeals from final judgments of the juvenile court within [seven] court days of the decision of the juvenile court.

In the Matter of the Welfare of Hartung, 304 N.W.2d 621, 624 (Minn. 1981). Juvenile court judge did not err in staying the certification order and placing juvenile in treatment program pending immediate appeal of certification or in relying on conduct subsequent to the initial transfer hearing in a new transfer hearing after earlier order was remanded. A reconstructed reference hearing is seldom satisfactory as it ignores present conditions. (Citing commentary to Standard 2.4 A)

    B. The appellate court should render its decision expeditiously, according the findings of the juvenile court the same weight given the findings of the highest court of general trial jurisdiction.

    C. No criminal court should have jurisdiction in any proceeding relating to any transaction or episode alleged in the juvenile court petition as to which a waiver motion was made, against any person over whom the juvenile court has waived jurisdiction, until the time for filing an appeal from that determination has passed or, if such an appeal has been filed, until the final decision of the appellate court has been issued.

People of the Territory of Guam v. Kingsbury, 649 F.2d 740, 742 (9th Cir. 1981). The decision of the federal district court affirming the Guam juvenile court's action transferring the juvenile for trial as an adult was a final decision and was appealable. (Citing Standard 2.4)

United States v. C.G., 736 F.2d 1474, 1477 (11th Cir. 1984). District court's order denying juvenile's motion to strike certification and granting the government's motion to transfer juvenile for trial as an adult was a collateral order that was immediately appealable. (Citing Standard 2.4)

In re Juvenile Appeal (85-AB), 195 Conn. 303, 488 A.2d 778, 785 (1985). Dissent urges that transfer decision was a final order that was appealable prior to trial in the criminal court. (Citing Standard 2.4)

State in the Interest of R.L., 202 N.J. Super. 410, 495 A.2d 172, 175 (N.J. Super. 1985). Waiver of the juvenile court's jurisdiction and referral of a case for criminal prosecution is an interlocutory order appealable only by leave. (Quoting the commentary to Standard 2.4 as supporting appeal as of right)

In re J.G., 627 A.2d 362, 365 (Vt. 1993). Appeal of a decision granting transfer to the criminal court is discretionary but should have been granted in this case. (Citing Standard 2.4)

State v. Lafayette, 532 A.2d 560, 562 (Vt. 1987). Where injustice would result if a juvenile defendant were erroneously tried as an adult after transfer, an immediate appeal should be allowed. (Citing Standard 2.4)

STANDARDS RELATING TO YOUTH SERVICE AGENCIES

Judith Areen, Reporter

PART I: ESTABLISHMENT OF YOUTH SERVICE AGENCIES

1.1 Enabling legislation.

Jurisdictions should by statute require the development of community-based youth service agencies that would focus on the special problems of juveniles in the community. The statutes should permit each local agency to be structured in accordance with the character and needs of the community, both initially and over time as experience is gained from working with juveniles and families in the community, provided that each such agency functions in a manner consistent with the following standards, which are designed to protect the rights of participants and to ensure that services are provided to juveniles diverted from the formal court system, as well as to improve the delivery of needed services for all juveniles and their families.

PART II: OBJECTIVES

2.1 Service provision.

The primary objective of a youth service agency should be to ensure the delivery of needed services to juveniles in the community and their families, including juveniles diverted to the agency from the formal court system. Several approaches may be pursued to accomplish this objective. At a minimum, the agency should be responsible for developing and administering needed resources to provide effective services to juveniles. Once such services exist, the agency should develop:

A. an up-to-date listing of available community services for juveniles and their families;
B. a community-wide self-referral system for juveniles and families in need of services;
C. a comprehensive service system oriented to diagnose participant needs and to ensure the delivery of services to juveniles and families through existing resources by such means as coordination, advocacy, or purchase of services; and
D. an effective monitoring system.

PART III: DECISION STRUCTURE

3.1 Control.

The managing board of the youth service agency should contain juveniles, parents, concerned community residents, and representatives of schools, agencies, and service organizations operating in the community. The most appropriate mix of decision makers should depend on the character and needs of the local community, but in no case should the youth service agency be under the control of any component of the formal juvenile justice system.

PART IV: ACCESS TO THE YOUTH SERVICE AGENCY

Informal Referrals

4.1 Self-referrals and outreach.

The youth service agency should develop outreach programs designed to contact juveniles and families in the community who are in need of their services. The aim of such programs should be to encourage self-referrals to the youth service agency before court intervention is necessary.

4.2 Parental referrals for noncriminal misbehavior.

Parents who previously would have reported their children to the juvenile court for noncriminal misbehavior should be encouraged to utilize the resources of the youth service agency. Such referrals should never be used as an excuse for abdication of parental responsibility, however, so parents who make referrals should be prepared to become active participants in the juvenile's program.

4.3 Citizen, agency, and school referrals.

All community residents, agencies, and schools should be encouraged to refer juveniles and their families who are in need of services to the youth service agency in lieu of the court. Every citizen, agency, or school that refers a juvenile or family for conduct that could be referred to the juvenile court should be encouraged to sign a waiver of complaint so as to ensure that participation by the juvenile in the agency program is voluntary.

Formal Referrals of Juveniles by Police and Courts

4.4 Police referrals.

The police should become a prime source of formal referrals to the youth service agency in order to ensure early diversion. To encourage such referrals:

A. Police should be included in the planning and administration of the youth service agency;

B. Diversion to the youth service agency should be made an official policy of the department;

C. Written guidelines should be promulgated to ensure that diversion occurs in appropriate cases (see Standard 4.5);

D. Every referral to the juvenile court should be accompanied by a written statement of the referring officer explaining why the juvenile was not diverted to the youth service agency.

4.5 Police diversion standards.

Police diversion should be made pursuant to guidelines in order to avoid discrimination based on race, color, religion, national origin, sex, or income. At a minimum, the following standards should be observed:

A. No juvenile who comes to the attention of the police [or court] should be formally referred to the youth service agency if, prior to the existence of the diversionary alternative, that juvenile would have been released with a warning. Such juveniles should, however, be informed of the existence of the program, the services available, and their eligibility for such services through a voluntary self-referral.

B. In keeping with Standard 1.1 of the *Noncriminal Misbehavior* volume eliminating the jurisdiction of the juvenile court over juveniles for acts of misbehavior, ungovernability, or unruliness that do not violate the criminal law, such juveniles should not be formally referred to the youth service agency.

C. All juveniles accused of class four or five offenses (as defined in Standard 5.2 of the *Juvenile Delinquency and Sanctions* volume) who have no prior convictions or formal referrals should be formally referred to the youth service agency rather than to the juvenile court.

D. All other juveniles accused of class four or five offenses who have been free of involvement with the juvenile court for the preceding twelve months should be formally referred to the youth service agency rather than to the juvenile court.

E. Serious consideration should be given to the formal diversion of all other apprehended juveniles, taking into account the following factors:

1. prosecution toward conviction might cause serious harm to the juvenile or exacerbate the social problems that led to his or her criminal acts;
2. services to meet the juvenile's needs and problems may be unavailable within the court system or may be provided more effectively by the youth service agency;
3. the nature of the alleged offense;
4. the age and circumstances of the alleged offender;
5. the alleged offender's record, if any;
6. recommendations for diversion made by the complainant or victim

4.6 Police liaison.

If representatives of the police are not on the managing board of the youth service agency, and no police staff are active in the agency itself, the police should assign a staff person to oversee productive relations with the agency and to encourage diversion.

4.7 Court referrals.

No juvenile should be petitioned to the court without an independent determination by the court intake official that diversion is not appropriate, pursuant to the guidelines of Standard 4.8. Every decision to petition should be accompanied by a written statement of the intake official as to why the juvenile is not diverted.

4.8 Court diversion guidelines.

Court intake guidelines, at a minimum, should contain the same diversion standards set forth in Standard 4.5 above. If it is determined that the apprehended juvenile is an active participant in a youth service agency program, the decision on whether to petition may be deferred up to twenty-four hours beyond the normal time limit in order to obtain a report from the youth service agency on the juvenile's progress in the program.

4.9 Minority review.

Each court intake staff should include a minority rights advocate who keeps records on which juveniles are diverted in order to ensure that the referral guidelines are being applied without regard to race, color, religion, national origin, sex, or income.

4.10 Court review.

Decisions by the court intake official (1) not to divert a juvenile, or (2) in the case of a previously diverted juvenile, to require the signing of a participation agreement (see Standards 5.3 and 5.4) as a condition of diversion, or (3) to resume proceedings against a juvenile who has allegedly violated the terms of a participation agreement, may be appealed by motion of the juvenile by his or her attorney to the juvenile court at any time prior to the fact-finding hearing. A judge who hears such a motion should not also preside at the fact-finding hearing(s) for that juvenile.

4.11 Legal consequences of diversion to YSA.

Formal referral to a youth service agency should represent an alternative to prosecution; such referral therefore should be accompanied by a formal termination of all legal proceedings against the juvenile which were the subject of the referral, except as provided in Standard 5.1. Mere suspension or deferral of prosecution pending participation in a youth service program is inconsistent with the concept of a youth service agency as a voluntary option. Referral in exchange for a guilty plea is inconsistent with the goal of stigma avoidance.

4.12 Confidentiality.

To encourage full participation by juveniles and their families in youth service agency programs, any statements made during participation in a youth service agency program to intake, counseling, and supervisory personnel in the agency should be confidential and privileged. Appropriate legislation should prohibit their use in subsequent civil or criminal proceedings involving the juvenile or family or their divulgence to anyone without the written permission of the juvenile.

4.13 Right to refuse diversion.

Any juvenile should have the right at any time to request processing by the juvenile court in lieu of formal diversion to a youth service agency. Before a juvenile can be required to elect diversion to a YSA or to sign a participation agreement as a condition of diversion (see Standards 5.3 and 5.4), the juvenile and his or her parents or guardian should be advised that the juvenile has a right to first consult with an attorney, who, among other things, may appeal the requirement of a participation agreement to the court (see Standard 4.10).

PART V: THE SERVICE SYSTEM

5.1 Voluntarism.

A fundamental premise in the administration of a youth service agency program should be that participation by the juveniles should be voluntary. In the case of formal referrals, therefore, juveniles should only be required to attend two program planning sessions. Such attendance should be ensured by allowing further juvenile court proceedings in the event of nonattendance. Except as provided in Standard 5.3, the youth service agency should not have the authority to refer juveniles back to the court on the ground of nonparticipation after the initial planning sessions. Juveniles and families who are informally referred to the youth service agency should be free to drop out of the program without penalty at any time.

5.2 Initial planning sessions.

A key purpose of the initial planning sessions should be to inform the juvenile and his or her family of the voluntary nature of continued participation in the program. If the juvenile has been formally referred, such assurance may properly be coupled with a realistic appraisal of the effect nonparticipation could have in the event of subsequent apprehension.

5.3 Refusal by the juvenile to participate.

If a formally referred juvenile refuses to participate in a service program after the initial planning sessions, the youth service agency should have the authority to file a recommendation with the police and the court that the juvenile not be diverted if apprehended subsequently unless the juvenile enters into a written agreement for services of a specified duration (termed a participation agreement), which should also specify that failure to abide by the agreement will allow referral back to the court. The youth service agency should make use of the nondiversion recommendation only in exceptional circumstances. The juvenile should be informed of the existence and meaning of the agency action.

5.4 Limits on formal participation.

No formally-referred juvenile who has attended an agency program for one year should be penalized by the filing of a recommendation against future diversion pursuant to Standard 5.3. Similarly, no participation agreement should require a juvenile to agree to participate in a youth service agency program for more than one year.

5.5 Resource evaluation.

The development of service priorities should be preceded in the planning stage by a complete and realistic evaluation of existing community resources and of the availability of such services to juveniles and families.

5.6 Service development.

When the resource evaluation indicates the absence of a needed service, such as a drug rehabilitation program, the youth service agency should establish and administer or provide support for the establishment of the service in the community.

5.7 Service provision.

The youth service agency should ensure the receipt of a mix of services rather than specializing in only one. The priorities will vary in each community; however, at a minimum the following should probably be available:

A. individual and marital counseling;
B. individual and family therapy;
C. residential facilities;
D. job training and placement;
E. medical services;
F. psychiatric services;
G. educational programs;
H. legal services;
I. recreational and athletic programs;
J. day care;
K. crisis intervention services that are available twenty-four hours a day;
L. bilingual services in communities with non-English-speaking residents.

The agency should, as an objective, honor personal preferences in selecting the services to be received by a particular individual or in developing new ones. Services should always be distributed in a manner that evidences respect for the participants and enhances the ability of participants to direct their own lives.

PART VI: MONITORING AND ASSESSMENT SYSTEM

6.1 Management accountability.

Each youth service agency should keep accurate case records designed to monitor agency input, process, and output. Specifically, each agency should establish a case filing system that includes intake records, records of contact with each client, and termination records. From this data each agency should periodically profile the volume and character of clients at intake, sources of referral, length of service provided, character of termination, and degree of defined success or failure. While such profiles should generally conform to national standards (see Standard 6.4), each agency should seek technical assistance in developing the profile design and maintenance system that best meets the needs of that agency and the community.

6.2 Client safeguards.

Every case file should be confidential. Access to files should be limited to the project director and a few designated agency staff. Under no circumstances should any information be released from the file to other than authorized agency staff members or the participant's lawyer without the express written consent of the program participant. At no time should program participants be denied access to their own personal case files. Upon termination of a client's participation, the relevant data necessary for monitoring should be recorded and the case file sealed permanently unless the individual is referred again to the youth service agency. (Standards on confidentiality and access to records are set forth in the *Juvenile Records and Information Systems* volume, Standards 5.1 to 5.8.)

6.3 Agency review.

Each youth service agency should be examined by outside persons or agencies. This assessment process should provide funding agencies with periodic statements that include supporting data as well as a complete annual report. The continued funding of a youth service agency should be contingent upon following this accountability procedure. While conforming generally with national standards (see Standard 6.4), each assessment system should be designed to adequately meet the needs of the youth service agency and its funding agencies. The persons or agencies who carry out the assessment should work closely with both the youth service agency and the primary funding agency in developing a research design that includes, at a minimum, input from the youth service agency, the clients and their families, local law enforcement and court agencies, related social service agencies, and local government officials.

6.4 Central clearinghouse.

A central clearinghouse should be established at the national level to collect and analyze data from youth service agencies, to disseminate descriptions of exemplary programs, and to establish suggested guidelines for standardizing categories of evaluation data and methods of collection.

PART VII: ORGANIZATION AND ADMINISTRATION

7.1 Planning.

Planning is a continuing process. No agency should begin operations without at least three months of preliminary planning. During this preliminary planning period, the organizational structure should be developed and attention given to:

A. service priorities;
B. service mix;
C. community resources.

Thereafter the process of assessment described in Standard 6.3 should be used to guide planning.

7.2 Location.

The youth service agency should be in a location or locations sufficiently close to the major sources of informal and formal referrals to ensure easy access, but in no event should the agency be housed in the court or police buildings.

7.3 Access.

The youth service agency should be available to receive formal referrals on a twenty-four-hour, seven-day-a-week basis so that no juvenile will be detained or have diversion deferred simply because of the time of apprehension.

7.4 Staff.

The staff of the youth service agency should represent a broad range of background and experience, but every effort should be made to include, to as great an extent as possible, both community residents and former agency participants. Staff should be responsible for each of the following:

A. community-agency relations;
B. service brokerage;
C. resource development and coordination;
D. volunteer services;

E. professional services;
F. police, court, and school liaison;
G. self-referrals and outreach;
H. staff selection and training;
I. program evaluation.

7.5 Volunteers.

Community volunteers should be used whenever appropriate either as part-time staff or as supplemental staff for special projects. In addition, community residents should be actively encouraged to "sponsor" agency participants by volunteering to provide jobs, counseling, or companionship.

CASES CITING TENTATIVE JUVENILE JUSTICE STANDARDS
VOLUMES THAT WERE NOT APPROVED

Three volumes of *Standards* were issued by the Juvenile Justice Standards Project of the American Bar Association and the Institute of Judicial Administration that were not approved by the House of Delegates of the Association. The *Schools and Education* volume was withdrawn from House of Delegates consideration by the Project because many of the issues raised were too technical for resolution by persons without expertise in education. The *Noncriminal Misbehavior* volume was under great fire from many juvenile and family court judges, and its consideration was tabled after the 1980 House of Delegates meeting as too controversial. The executive committee of the Project ordered that extensive changes be made in the *Abuse and Neglect* volume, and those changes were completed too late for House of Delegates consideration during the life of the Project. None of these three volumes have been submitted subsequently for consideration. Therefore, these three volumes have been distributed under the sponsorship of the Project.

The standards in the twenty volumes of *Standards* approved by the American Bar Association House of Delegates are included in this book. Cases citing the unapproved volumes are listed below.

Abuse and Neglect

Standards Generally. *A.E. v. State*, 743 P.2d 1041, 1050 (Okla. 1987). Parents had a right to a trial by jury in a proceeding for the termination of parental rights. Dissenting Justice cited Flicker, *Standards for Juvenile Justice: A Summary and Analysis* (2d ed. 1982) for a survey of juvenile justice history as a backdrop to the discussion of the right to a jury trial.

Standard 1.1. *State v. Robert H.*, 303 A.2d 1387, 1389 (N.H. 1978). Citing Standard 1.1 as focusing on the specific harm to a child as the sole basis for state intervention as opposed to the actions or neglect of parents.

Standards 1.1, 1.3, 2.1. *In the Matter of Inquiry into J.L.B.*, 594 P.2d 1127, 1133–35 (Mont. 1979). Citing Standards 1.1, 1.3 and 2.1 in determining whether the "unspecific" definitions of abuse and neglect in the Montana statutes are unconstitutionally vague, but concluding that the Standard definitions are not universally accepted and do not establish constitutional parameters.

Standards 1.5, 2.1. *In re Juvenile Appeal (83-CD)*, 189 Conn. 276, 455 A.2d 1313, 1318–21 (1983). Coercive intervention into the family should be minimal, and is justified only when the child or children are significantly endangered. (Citing Standards 1.5, 2.1)

Standard 2.2. *In the Matter of Theresa C.*, 121 Misc. 2d 15, 467 N.Y.S.2d 148, 150, 152 (Monroe Co. Fam. Ct. 1983). Family Court intervention to protect and safeguard maltreated children and to stabilize family life might be counterproductive if these goals cannot be achieved. (Citing Standard 2.2)

Standard 7.4. *In re Brenda H.*, 119 N.H. 382, 402 A.2d 169, 174 (1979). Citing the commentary to Standard 7.4 at pages 140–41 to support the utilization of a "clear and convincing" evidentiary standard in proceedings for the termination of parental rights.

Standard 8. *Champagne v. Welfare Division of the Nevada State Department of Human Resource*, 100 Nev. 640, 691 P.2d 849, 856 (1984). The Nevada definition of abuse and neglect, unfitness and abandonment of children includes a parent's inability or unwillingness to remedy the conditions which resulted in the removal of a child from the home and is derived from Standard 8 of the *Standards Relating to Abuse and Neglect*.

Standard 8.1. *State ex rel. Juvenile Department of Multnomah County v. Habas*, 299 Ore. 177, 700 P.2d 225, 231 (1985). Quoting the commentary to Standard 8.1 at page 149 as recommending an early decision to either return a child home or terminate parental rights in order to secure a permanent home for the child.

Standard 8.3. *In re R.J.M.*, 164 W.Va. 496, 266 S.E.2d 114, 117 (1980). Citing Standard 8.3 for the proposition that the termination of parental rights is more justified for a child under the age of three so as to avoid numerous placements and because foster parents may have difficulty in forming a lasting bond.

Standard 8.4. *Deahl v. Winchester Department of Social Services*, 224 Va. 664, 299 S.E.2d 863, 868 (1983). Citing Standard 8.4 as supporting the right of a child of an age of discretion to block a termination of parental rights.

Standard 9.1. *In the Matter of Theresa C.*, 121 Misc. 2d 15, 467 N.Y.S.2d 148, 150, 152 (Monroe Co. Fam. Ct. 1983). A former boyfriend of a mother whose child was allegedly sexually abused by the man was a proper respondent in a child protection proceeding as a "person legally responsible" for the child. (Quoting the commentary to Standard 9.1 at page 166 as utilizing a narrower definition limited to "'parents' who have a legally recognized right to custody of the child.")

Standards Relating to Noncriminal Misbehavior

Standards Volume Generally. *In re Michael G.*, 44 Cal. 3d 283, 243 Cal. Rptr. 224, 747 P.2d 1152, 1156 (1988). Citing the Standards volume generally in a case concerning the power of a juvenile court to detain a status offender in a secure facility for contempt of court. Opinion points out that the Standards call for the elimination of court jurisdiction over status offenders.

Standards Volume Generally. *W.M. v. State*, 437 N.E.2d 1029, 1030 (Ind. App., 3d Dist., 1982). Juvenile cannot be incarcerated for contempt of court where underlying act was a status offense. (Citing Standards volume generally to show direction in which Indiana is going through deinstitutionalization)

Standards Volume Generally. *In the Matter of Freeman*, 103 Misc. 2d 649, 426 N.Y.S.2d 948, 952 (Onondaga Fam. Ct. 1980). An alleged person in need of supervision held in a nonsecure agency boarding house was not in detention and cannot be convicted of escape. (Citing the Standards volume generally in dealing with the problems of status offenders.)

Standards Volume Generally. *In the Matter of Price*, 94 Misc. 2d 345, 404 N.Y.S.2d 821, 823 (Monroe Co. Fam. Ct. 1978). Element of conscious intent is required to prove that a juvenile is a person in need of supervision. The court acknowledges that there is a debate as to whether status offenders should be subject to court jurisdiction, and this debate is generated in part by the *Juvenile Justice Standards*.

Standards 1.1, 5.2. *State ex rel. L.E.A. v. Hammergren*, 294 N.W.2d 705, 707 (Minn. 1980). In coming into compliance with the Juvenile Justice and Delinquency Prevention Act of 1974 by removing status offenders from secure detention facilities, Minnesota moved in the direction of the *Standards Relating to Noncriminal Misbehavior*. (Citing Standards 1.1 and 5.2)

INDEX TO THE
ABA-IJA JUVENILE JUSTICE STANDARDS

The following index is derived from the one developed by Alaire Bretz Rieffel for the 1983 American Bar Association publication, *The Juvenile Justice Standards Handbook,* and it is intended to facilitate the use of the *American Bar Association/Institute of Judicial Administration Juvenile Justice Standards.* It is not an exhaustive index, but rather attempts to anticipate the needs of the user by providing references to relevant sections, without burdening the user with references to every use of a particular word anywhere in the text of the Standards. Only the twenty ABA House of Delegate approved volumes are included:

Abbreviations used in the index:

Adjudication	Adjudication
Appeals and Collateral Review	Appeals
Architecture of Facilities	Architecture
Corrections Administration	Corrections
Counsel for Private Parties	Counsel
Court Organization and Administration	Court Organization
Dispositional Procedures	Dispositional Procedures
Dispositions	Dispositions
Interim Status	Interim
Juvenile Delinquency and Sanctions	Delinquency
The Juvenile Probation Function	Probation
Juvenile Records and Information Systems	Records
Monitoring	Monitoring
Planning for Juvenile Justice	Planning
Police Handling of Juvenile Problems	Police
Pretrial Court Proceedings	Pretrial
Prosecution	Prosecution
Rights of Minors	Rights
Transfer Between Courts	Transfer
Youth Services Agencies	Agencies

Standards Relating to:

A

Abuse, removal pending appeal   *Appeals,* 5.4

Access to attorney   *Corrections,* 7.6N

Access to information   *Records,* 1.6, 1.7, 1.8, Part IV

Access to information for monitoring purposes   *Monitoring,* 1.6, 9.1

Access to juvenile records   *Records,* Part XV

Access to youth services agencies   *Agencies,* Part IV, 7.3

Accountability   *Interim,* page 14; *Corrections,* 9.1

Accountability in administration of juvenile corrections   *Corrections,* 1.2D, Part IX

Accountability of police   *Police,* Part V

Adaptive architecture   *Architecture,* 3.3

Adequacy of treatment   *Appeals,* 6.4

Adequate resources for detention   *Interim,* 3.6

Adjudication decision   *Adjudication,* Part V

Adjudication, requirement of   *Adjudication,* 5.1

Adjudication, role of counsel   *Counsel,* 7.1, 7.2, 7.3b

Administration of investigative services   *Prosecution,* Part IV

Administrative data, retention of   *Records,* 4.4

Administrative sanctions for misuse of records   *Records,* 2.5

Administrative standards for detention facilities   *Interim,* Part XI

Admissibility of juvenile records   *Records,* 18.4

Admissibility of statements   *Pretrial,* 5.1C

Admission of allegations   *Adjudication,* 2.5

Admonitions—before accepting plea   *Adjudication,* 3.2

Adoption proceedings, role of counsel in   *Counsel,* 2.3(b)

Adult criminal courts   *Transfer,* 2.2A,B

Adult jails prohibited   *Interim,* 10.2

Adversity of interests   *Counsel,* 3.2

Advising client   *Counsel,* Parts III, IV, V

Advisory committees   *Corrections,* 4.2

Advisory councils   *Monitoring,* 5.1

Advocacy groups   *Monitoring,* 8.2

Advocacy planning   *Planning,* 3.3

Affirmative action in corrections employment   *Corrections,* 3.2F

Affirmative defense of lack of *mens rea*   *Delinquency,* 3.1

Age of juvenile court jurisdiction   *Delinquency,* 2.1

Age limits, appeals — *Appeals*, 1.4

Age limits, informed consent to behavior modification — *Dispositions*, 4.3

Age limits, use of secure facility as disposition — *Dispositions*, 3.3E

Age limits, transfer to adult court — *Transfer*, 1.1

Age—minimum for employment — *Rights*, 5.2

Agencies, detention of juveniles — *Interim*, Part XI

Agencies, general principles for — *Planning*, Part I

Agency, access to records — *Records*, 5.3

Agency, juvenile — *Records*, 1.1; *Planning*, 2.1

Agency planning — *Planning*, 3.2

Agency, referrals to youth service agencies — *Agencies*, 4.3

Agency review — *Agencies*, 6.3

Agency, statewide — *Interim*, 11.1

Age of majority — *Rights*, 1.1

Alternative programs — *Corrections*, 2.5, Part VI, 7.10

Alternatives to detention — *Interim*, 11.4

Anticipated unlawful conduct — *Counsel*, 3.4

Annual statement, corrections programs — *Corrections*, 4.7, 9.3F

Apartment settings as disposition — *Corrections*, 7.10D

Appeal of detention decision — *Interim*, 7.12–7.14

Appeal, parties to — *Appeals*, 2.2

Appeal, right to — *Appeals*, 4.2

Appeals, age limits — *Appeals*, 1.4

Appeals from waiver or transfer hearings — *Transfer*, 2.4

Appeals, role of counsel — *Counsel*, 10.3, 10.4

Appeals, role of prosecutor — *Prosecution*, Part VIII

Appearance, initial — *Pretrial*, 2.2

Appearance of group homes — *Architecture*, 4.8

Appearance of secure corrections facilities — *Architecture*, 5.2

Appellate courts — *Appeals*, 1.1

Appellate process, as monitoring resource — *Monitoring*, 9.3

Appellate review — *Appeals*, 2

Appellate review, goals of — *Appeals*, 1.1

Appellate review of detention decision — *Interim*, 7.12–7.14

Application forms — *Records*, 18.2

Appointment of counsel for indigent parents — *Pretrial*, 6.9

Architectural program, definition of — *Architecture*, 1.7

Architectural programs — *Architecture,* 3.1
Argument, rules governing — *Counsel,* 7.10
Arrest, definitions — *Interim,* 2.2
Arrest process — *Police,* 3.2
Arrest warrant — *Interim,* 7.1–7.5
Assessment of five youth service programs — *Agencies,* Appendix A

Assessment of youth service agencies — *Agencies,* Part VI
Attorney, access to — *Corrections,* 7.6N
Attorney-client privilege — *Counsel,* 3.3
Attorney, juveniles in detention — *Interim,* 10.7
Attorney, role in detention decision — *Interim,* 6.5C, Part VIII

Attorneys — *Counsel* (see generally)

Attorneys, effectiveness of — *Adjudication,* 3.6, 3.8a 2a

Attorneys, presence of — *Adjudication,* 1.2
Attorneys, telephone calls to — *Corrections,* 7.6B
Audits, control of records — *Records,* 2.6

B
Bail — *Interim,* 4.7
Bar Association, role in monitoring — *Monitoring,* 3.2
Behavior modification, limits on use — *Corrections,* 4.10G; *Dispositions,* 4.3

Best interests of community — *Prosecution,* 1.1, 1.4
Boards, juvenile justice — *Planning,* 2.4
Boarding schools, as disposition — *Corrections,* 7.10D
Burden of proof, at adjudication — *Adjudication,* 4.3; *Delinquency,* 1.2

Burden of proof, pretrial restraints — *Interim,* 4.2
Burden of proof, transfer hearing — *Transfer,* 2.3E

C
Calendar—of juvenile court — *Pretrial,* Part VII
Capacity of detention facilities — *Architecture,* 6.2, 6.3
Capacity of group homes — *Architecture,* 4.2
Capacity of secure corrections facilities — *Architecture,* 5.3
Capacity to appreciate criminality of conduct — *Delinquency,* 3.5
Capacity to plead — *Adjudication,* 3.1

Case decision making — *Court Organization,* 3.2

Case files — *Records,* 13.3, 15.2

Case indexes — *Records,* 13.2

Case processing time standards — *Court Organization,* 3.3

Censorship of radio, television in secure facilities, prohibited — *Corrections,* 7.6G

Centralized information system, definition — *Records,* 1.11

Centralized recordkeeping — *Records,* 4.7

Central national clearinghouse — *Agencies,* 6.4

Certification of group homes — *Architecture,* 4.3

Certification of secure detention facilities — *Architecture,* 6.6

Chapels in detention facilities — *Architecture,* 6.15

Chemical dependency — *Rights,* 4.7

Chemical restraints in secure facilities — *Corrections,* 7.8B

Child labor laws — *Rights,* Part V

Citation, definition — *Interim,* 2.13

Citizen referrals to youth service agencies — *Agencies,* 4.3

Civil remedy for misuse of juvenile records — *Records,* 2.3

Classes of juvenile offenses — *Delinquency,* 4.2

Clear and convincing evidence in waiver hearing — *Transfer,* 2.2

Client safeguards — *Agencies,* 6.2

Clients' interest — *Counsel,* 3.1, 3.2 (see generally)

Closing argument — *Prosecution,* 6.8

Clothing in secure facilities — *Corrections,* 7.6J

Code, juvenile delinquency — *Delinquency* (see generally)

Code of conduct, corrections personnel — *Corrections,* 3.4

Codes, architectural — *Architecture,* 3.5; *Corrections,* 7.6

Coeducational programs, presumption in favor of — *Corrections,* 7.5

Coercive dispositions — *Dispositions,* 1.2

Collateral disabilities prohibited — *Dispositions,* 1.21

Collection of information — *Records,* Part III

Commission of new offense — *Dispositions,* 5.4D

Commission on juvenile advocacy — *Monitoring,* Part IV

Committee, privacy — *Records,* 2.1

Community

Community activities of juveniles in secure programs

Community advisory councils

Community agency referral

Community based facilities, as purpose

Community, best interests of in intake decision

Community, definition of

Community norms, consideration of in planning facilities

Community relations, function of juvenile court

Community, relationship of prosecutor to

Community service, as a program

Community service, as a disposition

Community services

Community setting, definition of

Community supervision, as a program

Community supervision, as disposition

Compensation of juveniles

Complaint, definition

Compliance, enforcement powers

Compulsory process for disposition hearing

Computers, use in information keeping

Conditional dispositions

Conditional release

Conditional sanctions

Confidentiality

Confidentiality, disclosure of respondents' identity

Confidentiality of record of adjudication proceedings

Confidentiality of youth service agency programs

Conflicts of interest, attorney

Architecture, 1.2, 1.3, 2.6

Corrections, 7.11D

Monitoring, Part V

Probation, 2.4C

Architecture, 2.2

Probation, 2.8

Architecture, 1.2

Architecture, 2.6

Court Organization, 3.5

Prosecution, 1.4

Corrections, 6.3

Dispositions, 3.2B3

Agencies, 2.1

Architecture, 1.2, 1.3

Corrections, 6.2

Dispositions, 3.2C1

Rights, 5.7

Probation, 2.7, 2.10

Monitoring, 1.7

Dispositional Procedures, 6.2

Records, 4.6

Dispositions, 3.2

Interim, 6.6

Delinquency, 4.1B

Counsel, 3.3; *Probation,* 3.3; *Records* (see generally)

Adjudication, 6.3

Adjudication, 2.1B, 5.3

Agencies, 4.12

Interim, 8.1

Conflicts of interest, parents — *Pretrial,* 5.3
Conflicts of interest, prosecutors — *Prosecution,* 1.2
Consent decree — *Probation,* 2.5
Consent, informed — *Dispositions,* 4.3; *Interim,* 4.5
Consent of victim — *Delinquency,* 3.3
Consent to preparation of history — *Records,* 7.1, 7.2
Construction of detention facilities — *Interim,* 11.3
Construction of group homes — *Architecture,* 4.9
Continuing detention review — *Interim,* 7.9
Contraception — *Rights,* 4.8
Contracts of minors — *Rights,* 6.1
Control centers in detention facilities — *Architecture,* 6.9
Control centers in secure corrections facilities — *Architecture,* 5.6
Control, definition — *Interim,* 2.6
Control, in corrections — *Corrections,* 1.2A
Control of accused juvenile — *Interim,* 3.2, 3.3
Control of court calendar — *Pretrial,* 7.2
Control, youth service agencies — *Agencies,* 3.1
Coordination of services — *Planning,* 1.2
Corporal punishment prohibited — *Corrections,* 4.8
Correctional personnel — *Corrections,* 3.2
Correction of illegal disposition — *Dispositional Procedures,* 7.1B
Correction of juvenile records — *Records,* Part XVI
Correction of police records — *Records,* Part XXI
Correction of records — *Records,* 2.6, Parts XVI, XXI
Corrections, Department of — *Corrections,* Parts II–III
Corrections, federal role — *Corrections,* 2.4
Corrections, general principles — *Corrections,* Part I
Corrections, state department of — *Corrections,* 2.1, 9.3
Councils, advisory — *Monitoring,* 5.1
Counsel, after disposition hearing — *Counsel,* 9.5
Counsel, at disposition hearing — *Counsel,* 9.4
Counsel, challenge to effectiveness — *Counsel,* 10.7
Counsel, consent to predisposition investigation — *Probation,* 3.4
Counsel for parent — *Counsel,* 3.1
Counsel, general standards — *Counsel,* 1.1, 1.2

Counsel in juvenile proceedings (see also "Attorney") — *Counsel,* (see generally)

Counsel, on appeal — *Counsel,* 10.3

Counsel, Prosecutor's relationship with — *Prosecution,* 3.1

Counsel, right to — *Appeals,* 3.1

Counsel, waiver hearings — *Transfer,* 2.3

Court administrators — *Court Organization,* 2.3

Court-appointed Counsel — *Pretrial,* 5.3A

Court control — *Pretrial,* 7.2

Court diversions — *Agencies,* 4.8

Court functions — *Court Organization,* Part III

Court, monitoring by — *Monitoring,* Part IX

Court, prosecutor's relationship with — *Prosecution,* 3.2, 3.7

Court referrals to youth services agencies — *Agencies,* 4.7

Court review — *Agencies,* 4.10

Court, role in planning — *Planning,* 4.4

Courts — *Court Organization,* (see generally)

Criminal court jurisdiction — *Transfer,* (see generally)

Criminal penalties for misuse of records — *Records,* 2.4

Criteria for intake dispositional decisions — *Probation,* 2.6–2.8

Custodial dispositions — *Dispositions,* 3.3

Custodial dispositions, presumption against — *Dispositions,* 3.3B

Custodial sanctions — *Delinquency,* 4.1A

Custody, definition — *Interim,* 2.3

Custody, levels of — *Dispositions,* 3.3E

Custody of materials — *Pretrial,* 3.16

Custody proceedings, role of counsel in — *Counsel,* 2.3

Custody, protective — *Interim,* 5.7

D

Database — *Architecture,* 3.2

Day custody as a corrections program — *Corrections,* 6.3A

Day custody as a disposition — *Dispositions,* 3.2C

Decree, consent — *Probation,* 2.5

Defense attorney (see also "Counsel" and "Attorney") — *Interim,* Part VIII; *Counsel* (see generally)

Defenses to delinquency allegations   *Delinquency,* Part III
Delay, reduced   *Interim,* p. 11
Delinquency proceedings, role of counsel in   *Counsel,* 2.3
Denial, effect of   *Adjudication,* 2.6
Depositions   *Pretrial,* 3.12, 3.14
Destruction of juvenile records   *Records,* Part XVII
Destruction of police records   *Records,* Part XXII
Destruction of records, rules providing for   *Records,* 5.8
Destruction of social histories   *Records,* Part X
Detention   *Counsel,* 6.4
Detention criteria   *Interim,* p. 5,
   Appendices A–B
Detention, definition of   *Architecture,* 1.11;
   Interim, 3.2
Detention facilities, secure   *Architecture,* Part VI;
   Interim, 2.10–2.12
Detention inventory   *Interim,* 10.8
Detention, protective   *Interim,* 6.7
Detention review   *Interim,* 7.9
Detention, role of counsel   *Counsel,* 6.4
Detention services   *Court Organization,*
   1.2
Direct access to records   *Records,* 1.6, 5.1
Directors of programs   *Corrections,* 4.2
Disciplinary Board   *Corrections,* 8.8
Disciplinary procedures   *Corrections,* 8.9
Discipline   *Corrections,* Part VIII
Discipline, in correctional setting   *Corrections,* 7.9, Part VIII
Disclosure of police records   *Records,* 20.3
Disclosure of record retention   *Records,* 4.3
Disclosure of respondent's identity   *Adjudication,* 6.3
Disclosure, secondary   *Records,* 15.6
Disclosure to petitioners   *Pretrial,* 3.10–3.12
Disclosure to respondent of information   *Pretrial,* 3.3–3.9
Discovery   *Pretrial,* Part III
Discovery, counsel's role in   *Counsel,* 7.3a
Discretionary decisions, in monitoring   *Monitoring,* 2.1
Discretionary dismissal   *Delinquency,* 1.3
Discretionary release of juvenile   *Interim,* 6.6C

Dismissal of complaint — *Delinquency,* 1.3; *Probation,* 2.3

Dispositional alternatives at intake — *Probation,* 2.2–2.5
Dispositional authority — *Dispositional Procedures,* 1.1

Dispositional conferences — *Probation,* 2.14
Dispositional criteria at intake — *Probation,* 2.2–2.5
Disposition agreement — *Dispositional Procedures,* 5.3

Disposition hearing — *Dispositional Procedures,* Part VI

Disposition, modification of — *Corrections,* Part V; *Dispositions,* Part V

Disposition, procedures — *Dispositional Procedures* (see generally)

Disposition, role of counsel — *Counsel,* Part IX
Disposition, role of prosecutor — *Prosecution,* Part VII
Dispositions — *Dispositions* (see generally)

Dispositions, early, role of counsel — *Counsel,* 6.3
Dispositions, noncompliance — *Corrections,* 5.2
Dispositions, purpose of — *Dispositions,* Part I
Dispositions, reduction of — *Corrections,* 5.1
Disposition, stay of — *Appeals,* Part V
Dispute resolution — *Disposition Procedures,* Part V

Disruption of court proceedings — *Adjudication,* 6.2
Dissemination of information — *Records,* 1.9, Part V
Distractions from court proceedings — *Adjudication,* 6.2D
Diversion — *Agencies,* Part IV
Diversion, definition — *Interim,* 2.19
Doctrine of inherent powers — *Court Organization,* 4.1

Double jeopardy — *Adjudication,* 2.3
Drug addiction — *Rights,* 4.7
Drugs, limitations on use — *Corrections,* 4.1OF
Due Process in alteration of status of juvenile under correctional supervision — *Corrections,* 4.5

Duplication of services — *Planning,* 1.3
Duties of prosecutor — *Interim,* 9.1

Duty of counsel to keep client informed — *Counsel,* 3.5
Duty of police to account for release of records — *Records,* 19.5
Duty of police to keep records — *Records,* 19.2
Duty to account for security — *Records,* 8.1
Duty to destroy social history — *Records,* 10.1
Duty to disclose existence of information — *Pretrial,* 3.15
Duty to inform of probation investigation — *Records,* 7.1, 14.4
Duty to keep records — *Records,* Part XII
Duty to regulate information practices of outside agencies — *Records,* 14.6
Duty to report — *Pretrial,* 7.2
Duty to review probation report — *Records,* 14.5

E
Early dispositions — *Counsel,* 6.3
Education in detention facilities — *Interim,* 10.6
Education of intake and investigative personnel — *Probation,* 5.3
Effectiveness of representation by attorney — *Adjudication,* 3.6; *Counsel,* 10.7
Emancipated minor, medical care of — *Rights,* 4.4
Emancipation of minors — *Rights,* Part II
Emergency medical treatment of minor — *Rights,* 4.5
Emotional disorder — *Rights,* 4.9
Employment of youth — *Rights,* Part V
Enforcement of disposition — *Dispositions,* 5.4
Enforcement of support obligations — *Rights,* 3.3
Entrances of detention facilities — *Architecture,* 6.8
Equality of treatment — *Interim,* 3.5D
Ethics of attorney — *Counsel,* (see generally)
Evaluation — *Corrections,* 9.4B
Evaluation, access to — *Records,* 15.5
Evaluation, access to information for the purpose of — *Records,* 5.6
Evaluation, information for — *Records,* 3.5
Evaluation of corrections programs — *Corrections,* 9.4B
Evaluation of facilities — *Architecture,* 4.5
Evidence — *Adjudication,* 4.2, 4.3
Evidence of adjudication — *Prosecution,* 6.3, 6.6

Evidence, disclosure by prosecutor — *Prosecution,* 4.7

Evidence at disposition — *Dispositional Procedures,* 2.5, 6.3B

Evidence at waiver hearing — *Transfer,* 2.2, 2.3

Evidence, disclosure — *Counsel,* 7.7

Evidence—discovery, disclosure — *Pretrial,* Part III

Evidence, independent — *Prosecution,* 5.3

Evidence, presentation by counsel — *Counsel,* 7.7, 9.2, 9.4

Evidence, rules of at dispositional hearing — *Dispositional Procedures,* 2.5

Examination of witnesses — *Counsel,* 7.8; *Prosecution,* 6.7

Excision of material — *Pretrial,* 3.18

Expedited appeals — *Appeals,* 4.1

Experimentation — *Interim,* 11.4

Expungement of the record — *Adjudication,* 2.1C

F

Facts found by juvenile court — *Appeals,* 1.3

Fairness, in programs for adjudicated juveniles — *Corrections,* 1.2C

Family court — *Court Administration,* 1.1

Federal government — *Corrections,* 2.4

Federal role, generally — *Planning,* 4.1

Federal role, in corrections — *Corrections,* 2.4

Federal role in planning — *Planning,* 4.1

Final disposition, definition — *Interim,* 2.18

Final order, definition of — *Appeals,* 2.1

Financial liability for medical care — *Rights,* 4.3

Financing of investigative services — *Probation,* 4.4

Findings, of dispositional hearings — *Dispositional Procedures,* 7.1

Findings, in waiver hearing — *Transfer,* 2.2

Findings of judge of appropriate disposition — *Dispositional Procedures,* 7.1

Fines as disposition — *Dispositions,* 3.2B

Fingerprints — *Records,* 19.6

Fixtures in detention facilities — *Architecture,* 6.17

Fixtures of secure corrections facilities — *Architecture,* 5.12

Flexibility of design, as value — *Architecture*, 2.3
Force, use on juvenile in detention — *Interim*, 10.7
Foster homes as disposition — *Corrections*, 7.10B
Funding — *Interim*, 11.2
Funding, federal, of corrections — *Corrections*, 2.4

G
Goals of monitoring — *Counsel*, 3.1;
Monitoring, 1.2
Good-time credit — *Corrections*, 7.9
Governing body of group homes — *Architecture*, 4.6
Governor's role in planning — *Planning*, 4.2
Grievance mechanisms in corrections — *Corrections*, 9.2
Group homes, as disposition — *Corrections*, 7.10C
Group homes, generally — *Architecture*, Part IV
Guardian *ad litem* — *Pretrial*, 6.1C, D, 6.7;
Adjudication, 1.4C

H
Hazardous activities in employment of youth — *Rights*, 5.3
Hearing, release — *Interim*, 7.6
Hearing, probable cause — *Pretrial*, Part IV
Hearing, transfer to criminal court — *Transfer*, Part II
Homes, links with — *Corrections*, 7.3
Hours of employment of juveniles — *Rights*, 5.6

I
"Immature respondent" for purpose of waiver — *Pretrial*, 6.1, 6.3
Imminent danger to juvenile — *Appeals*, 5.4
In camera proceedings — *Pretrial*, 3.19, 6.5
Incentives for police — *Police*, Part V
Independent research — *Monitoring*, 8.1
Indigency, determination of, party appealing (see also "Right to Counsel") — *Appeals*, 3.1, 3.3;
Pretrial, 6.9
Indirect access to juvenile records — *Records*, 1.8
Information access, use in monitoring — *Monitoring*, 1.6
Information base — *Monitoring*, 2.5;
Dispositional Procedures, 2.3
Information base in monitoring — *Monitoring*, 2.5

Information, collection of · *Records,* Part III
Information, dissemination of · *Records,* Part V
Information for dispositions · *Dispositional Procedures,* Part II

Information, retention of · *Records,* Part IV
Informed consent to certain programs · *Dispositions,* 4.3
Initial appearance · *Pretrial,* 2.2
Inquiries about juvenile records · *Records,* 18.3
Inquiries for police records · *Records,* 20.5
Inspection of juvenile facilities · *Architecture,* 6.6
Intake, definition · *Interim,* 11.2
Intake interviews · *Probation,* 2.14
Intake officer · *Probation,* 2.16
Intake officer, definition · *Probation,* 1.1H
Intake personnel · *Prosecution,* 3.7, Part IV

Intake procedures · *Interim,* Part VI; *Probation,* 2.9–2.15; *Court Organization,* 1.1C

Intake, role of counsel · *Counsel,* 6.1, 6.2; *Court Organization* 1.2

Intake services, definition · *Probation,* 1.1F
Interests of community · *Probation,* 2.8
Interest of juvenile · *Probation,* 2.8
Interim detention · *Appeals,* 6.4
Interim period, definition · *Interim,* 2.1
Interim status agency, definition of · *Architecture,* 1.15
Interim status, change in · *Interim,* 7.11
Interim status of juveniles · *Interim,* (see generally)

Interlocutory orders, appeals from · *Appeals,* 2.3
Internal organization of detention facilities · *Architecture,* 6.7
Interpreters · *Adjudication,* 2.7; *Interim,* 5.3; *Pretrial,* 1.6, 2.3, 6.10; *Transfer,* 2.3; *Agencies,* 5.7

Interview of client · *Counsel,* 4.2
Interview rooms in detention facilities · *Architecture,* 6.14

Inventory of detention facilities — *Interim,* 10.8
Investigation, intake — *Probation,* 2.11
Investigation of case, proceedings to transfer to adult court — *Counsel,* 4.3
Investigation officer, definition — *Probation,* 1.1L
Investigation, predisposition — *Prosecution,* 4.3; *Probation,* 3.1–3.4
Investigations — *Pretrial,* 3.13
Investigations, police — *Police,* 3.2
Investigative personnel — *Probation,* Part V
Investigative services — *Probation,* 3.1
Investigative services, definition — *Probation,* 1.11
Isolation rooms in detention facilities — *Architecture,* 6.13
Isolation rooms in secure correction facilities — *Architecture,* 5.10; *Corrections,* 7.11

J
Jails, adult — *Interim,* 10.2
Judgement, stay of — *Appeals,* 5.5
Judges — *Court Organization* (see generally, especially, 2.1)
Judge's authority to determine disposition — *Dispositional Procedures,* 1.1
Judges, responsibility of with respect to plea agreements — *Adjudication,* 3.3
Judicial access to information — *Records,* 5.7
Judicial administration of investigative services — *Probation,* 4.2
Judicial approval of disposition agreements — *Dispositional Procedures,* 5.3
Judicial disposition of complaint — *Probation,* 2.2
Judicial officers, use of — *Court Organization,* 2.2
Judicial probation, definition — *Probation,* 1.1N
Jurisdiction, appeal of finding — *Appeals,* 2.2; 2.3
Jurisdiction of criminal court — *Transfer,* (see generally)
Jurisdiction of juvenile court — *Court Organization,* 1.1; *Delinquency,* Part II; *Transfer* (see generally)

Jurors, counsel's selection of and relation with — *Counsel*, 7.6

Juror selection — *Prosecution*, 6.4

Jurors, prosecutors' relationship with — *Prosecution*, 3.3

Jury trial — *Adjudication*, 4.1

Juvenile agency, definition — *Records*, 1.1

Juvenile court calendar — *Pretrial*, Part VII

Juvenile courts — *Court Organization* (see generally)

Juvenile courts, standards for — *Interim*, Part VII

Juvenile, definition — *Records*, 1.2

Juvenile detention facilities, standards for — *Interim*, Part X

Juvenile facility intake official, standards for — *Interim*, Part VI

Juvenile justice agencies, self-monitoring — *Monitoring*, Part X

Juvenile justice boards — *Planning*, 2.4

Juvenile offenses — *Delinquency*, 2.3

Juvenile probation, definition — *Probation*, 1.1A

Juvenile probation officer, definition — *Probation*, 1.1C

Juvenile probation services, definition — *Probation*, 1.1B

Juvenile record, definition — *Records*, 1.3

Juvenile records, admissibility of — *Records*, 5.7

Juvenile services agencies — *Planning*, 2.1

K–L

Labels, use in information keeping — *Records*, 4.5

Law Enforcement, access to information for purpose of — *Records*, 5.7

Lawyer-client relationship — *Counsel*, Part III; *Counsel* (see generally)

Lawyers (see entries under "Attorney," "Counsel") — *Counsel*, (see generally)

Lawyers' committee, role in monitoring — *Monitoring*, 3.2, 3.3

Least intrusive alternative — *Interim*, 3.4; *Dispositions*, 2.1

Least restrictive environment — *Dispositions*, 2.1; *Corrections*, 1.2B

Leave to appeal — *Appeals*, 2.2, 5.2

Legal consequences of adjudication — *Adjudication*, 5.3; *Corrections*, 4.3

Legal consequences of diversion — *Agencies*, 4.11

Legal services, organizations of, generally   *Counsel,* 2.1, 2.2
Legal sufficiency of complaint   *Probation,* 2.7;
    Adjudication, 1.1
Legislation concerning juvenile court records   *Records,* Part XI
Legislation—establishing youth service   *Agencies,* 1.1
   agencies
Legislative committees, role in monitoring   *Monitoring,* Part VI
Legislators' role in planning   *Planning,* 4.3
Legislature, monitoring by   *Monitoring,* Part VI
Length of intake process   *Probation,* 2. 15
Liability, general principles of   *Delinquency,* Part III
Limitations period   *Transfer,* 1.3
Limitations on sanctions   *Delinquency,* 5.2

M
Minority review   *Agencies,* 4.9
Misrepresentation of factual propositions or   *Counsel,* 1.3
   legal authority
Mixing of accused offenders with other   *Interim,* 10.4
   juveniles
Modification of disposition   *Dispositions,* Part V;
    Appeals, 6.2
Modification of orders by court   *Appeals,* 6.1
Money bail, prohibition against   *Interim,* 4.7
Monitoring   *Monitoring,* (see
    generally)
Monitoring mechanisms, definition   *Monitoring,* 1.1B
Monitoring mechanisms   *Monitoring,* 1.3
Monitoring of correction programs   *Corrections,* 9.3C, 9.4
Monitoring of youth services agencies   *Agencies,* 6.1, (see VI
    generally)
Monitoring process, definition   *Monitoring,* 1.1A
Moratorium on construction of detention   *Interim,* 11.3
   facilities
Motion for continuance   *Adjudication,* 1.5B
Motion for withdrawal of plea   *Adjudication,* 3.8
Motion practice, counsel's role in   *Counsel,* 7.3
Multilingual communications   *Pretrial,* 1.6, 2.3
Multilingual notices   *Pretrial,* 1.6, 2.3;
    Transfer, 2.3A,B
Multiple juvenile offenses   *Delinquency,* 5.3

N

Needs and desires of juveniles — *Disposition*, 2.2
Neglect, removal pending appeal — *Appeals*, 5.4
News media, access to proceedings — *Adjudiction*, Part VI
Night custody as sanction — *Dispositions*, 3.3D
Nominal dispositions — *Dispositions*, 3.1; *Counsel*, 1.6

Nominal sanctions — *Delinquency*, 4.1C
Noncriminal offenses — *Interim*, p. 4
Nondisclosure agreement — *Records*, 15.8, 20.4
Nonjudicial probation — *Probation*, 2.4D
Nonresidential programs — *Corrections*, Part VI
Nonsecure alternatives — *Interim*, 10.3; *Dispositions*, 3.3E1

Nonsecure detention facility, definition — *Interim*, 2.11
Nonsecure facilities — *Corrections*, 7.1
Nonsecure residential programs — *Corrections*, 7.10
Nonsecure setting, definition — *Architecture*, 1.13
Normal growth and development — *Corrections*, 1.2A
Normalization as purpose — *Architecture*, 2.1
Normalization, definition of — *Architecture*, 1.1
Notice of charges — *Adjudication*, I.IA
Notification of parents of minor's medical treatment — *Rights*, 4.2

Notification of rights — *Pretrial*, 2.1
Notification of right to counsel — *Pretrial*, 5.2

O

Objectives of youth service agencies — *Agencies*, Part II
Offense, as requirement of jurisdiction — *Delinquency*, 2.2
Office of the prosecutor — *Prosecution*, Part II
Ombudsman, in monitoring — *Monitoring*, Part VII
Opening statement — *Prosecution*, 6.5
Operating conditions of group homes — *Architecture*, 4.10
Operational functions, monitoring of — *Monitoring*, 2.4
Operational programs, definition of — *Architecture*, 1.8
Opportunity to prepare for adjudication proceeding — *Adjudication*, 1.5, 2.2B

Order of disposition, non-compliance with — *Corrections*, 5.2
Orders, compliance with, counsel's role — *Counsel*, 7.4
Orders imposing sanctions — *Delinquency*, 5.1

Orders, modification of   *Appeals,* 6.1, 6.2, 6.3
Organizational functions, monitoring of   *Monitoring,* 2.4
Organization of corrections administration   *Corrections,* 3.1
Organization of intake, investigative,
and predisposition services   *Probation,* Part IV
Organization of juvenile court   *Court Organization,*
    Part I

Organization of planning network   *Planning,* Part II
Organization of prosecutor's office   *Prosecution,* Part II
Organization of secure corrections facilities   *Architecture,* 5.5
Orientation, definition of   *Architecture,* 1.10
Out-of-state programs for adjudicated   *Corrections,* 7.4
    juveniles
Overcrowding, generally   *Architecture,* 2.5, 7.11

P
Paraprofessionals, use to assist intake and
investigative officers   *Probation,* 5.6
Parent   *Probation,* 1.1
Parental authority as defense   *Delinquency,* 3.4
Parental consent to medical care   *Rights,* 4.1
Parental referrals to youth service agencies   *Agencies,* 4.2
Parent, definition   *Pretrial,* 6.6; *Interim,*
    2.17; *Records,* 1.4
Parent-juvenile conflicts   *Pretrial,* 5.3
Parents, access to records   *Records,* 5.2
Parents, consent to decree   *Probation,* 2.5;
    Records, 1.4
Parents of respondent, presence at hearing   *Adjudication,* 1.4
Parents, obligation to support   *Rights,* Part III
Parents, role in contested pleadings   *Adjudication,* 4.5
Parents, role in delinquency proceedings   *Pretrial,* 6.5–6.10
Parents, role in detention decision   *Interim,* 3.3B, 5.3, 6.5
Parole revocation, role of counsel   *Counsel,* 10.6
Parties in disposition proceedings   *Dispositional*
    Procedures, 3.1
Parties to appeal   *Appeals,* 2.2
Permanent probation files   *Records,* 14.3
Permissible control or detention   *Interim,* 3.2
Personal information, collection of   *Records,* 3.6
Personal space, provision of in secure setting   *Architecture,* 2.7

Personnel, intake and investigative — *Probation*, Part V
Personnel training, in corrections — *Corrections*, 3.3
Petition — *Adjudication*, 1.1
Petition, amendment of — *Adjudication*, 2.2
Petition, definition — *Probation*, 1.1E
Petition, dismissal — *Prosecution*, 4.5
Petition, filing of — *Pretrial*, Part I
Petitions concerning adequacy of treatment — *Appeals*, 6.4
Petition, withdrawal of — *Prosecution*, 4.2
Photographs of juvenile by police — *Records*, 19.6D, E
Physical force to control juveniles — *Corrections*, 4.8; *Interim*, 10.7E

Physical harm, unreasonable risk of — *Dispositions*, 1.2H
Physical health, prevention of harm to — *Dispositions*, 4.2B; *Interim*, 3.5B

Physical requirements of detention facilities — *Architecture*, 6.16
Physical requirements of secure corrections facilities — *Architecture*, 5.11
Planners, juvenile justice — *Planning*, Part III
Planning — *Planning* (see generally)

Planning, agency — *Planning*, 3.2
Planning, definition — *Planning*, 1.1
Planning for interim status — *Interim*, 11.2
Planning modes, definitions of — *Planning*, 3.1
Planning, network — *Planning*, Part II
Planning of corrections programs — *Corrections*, 9.3E
Planning of youth service agencies — *Agencies*, 7.1
Plans, characteristics of — *Planning*, 3.5
Plea, accuracy of — *Adjudication*, 3.5
Plea agreements — *Adjudication*, 3.3; *Prosecution*, Part V

Plea alternatives — *Adjudication*, 2.4
Plea bargaining — *Adjudication*, Alternate, 3.3, 3.4, 3.8

Plea, voluntariness of — *Adjudication*, 3.4
Plea withdrawal — *Adjudication*, 3.8
Police — *Police*, (see generally)
Police, authority of — *Police*, 2.1, 2.5, Part III

Police detention facility — *Interim,* 5.4
Police diversion standards — *Agencies,* 4.5
Police handling of juvenile problems — *Police,* 2.5
Police investigation — *Police,* 3.2
Police liaison to youth service agencies — *Agencies,* 4.6
Police organization of juvenile matters — *Police,* Part IV
Police, prosecutor's relationship with — *Prosecution,* 3.6
Police records, access to — *Records,* Part XX
Police records, disclosure of — *Records,* 20.3
Police records, generally — *Records,* Section IV; *Police,* 2.2
Police referrals to youth service agencies — *Agencies,* 4.4
Police, role in detention — *Interim,* Part V
Police, role of — *Police,* Part II
Policy favoring release — *Interim,* 3.1, 5.1
Population limits of detention facilities — *Interim,* 10.5
Population limits of secure programs — *Corrections,* 7.11A
Postdisposition proceedings — *Counsel,* 10.2; *Prosecution,* Part VIII
Preadjudication programs — *Adjudication,* 5.1A
Preadjudication, role of prosecutor — *Prosecution,* Part IV
Predisposition conferences — *Dispositional Procedures,* 5.1
Predisposition investigation, definition — *Probation,* 1.1J
Predisposition report and investigation — *Probation,* 3.1–3.4
Predisposition report, definition — *Probation,* 1.1K
Pregnancy — *Rights,* 4.8
Prehearing detention and release — *Police,* 3.2
Preparation of case — *Counsel,* 4.3; *Adjudication,* 1.5
Preparation of social, psychological histories — *Records,* Part VII
Pretrial conference — *Pretrial,* 7.4
Pretrial identification — *Police,* 3.2
Pretrial motions — *Pretrial,* 7.4
Pretrial motions, calendaring of — *Pretrial,* 7.4
Pretrial release — *Interim,* p. 4
Principles for monitoring systems — *Monitoring,* 1.4
Privacy Committee — *Records,* 2.1, 19.8
Privacy in detention — *Interim,* 10.7A
Privacy in secure facilities — *Corrections,* 7.6C, J, K

Private sector programs   *Corrections,* 2.5
Private sector, role in monitoring   *Monitoring,* Part VIII
Privilege against self-incrimination   *Probation,* 2.12
Probable cause, as condition for waiver   *Transfer,* 2.2, 2.3E
Probable cause hearings   *Prosecution,* 4.6;
                                                   Pretrial, Part IV
Probation   *Probation,* (see
                                                   generally); *Court
                                                   Organization,* 1.1,
                                                   1.2
Probation officer, definition   *Probation,* 1.1C
Probation records   *Records,* Part XIV
Probation revocation, role of counsel   *Counsel,* 10.6
Probation services, definition   *Probation,* 1.1B
Probation supervision services, definition   *Probation,* 1.1M
Probation workers, counsel's relationship   *Counsel,* 1.4
   with
Program planning   *Planning,* 3.4
Programs for adjudicated juveniles   *Corrections,* Part IV–
                                                   VII
Programs of secure facilities   *Corrections,* 7.11
Programs, selection of   *Corrections,* 4.11
Prohibited control or detention   *Interim,* 3.3
Promotion of intake, investigative personnel   *Probation,* 5.2
Proof   *Prosecution,* 6.3
Proof, burden of   *Adjudication,* 4.3
Prosecution   *Prosecution,* (see
                                                   generally)
Prosecutor   *Adjudication,* 1.2
Prosecutor, role in detention   *Interim,* Part IX
Prosecutor's office   *Prosecution,* Part II
Prosecutor's relationship with others   *Prosecution,* Part III
Protective custody   *Interim,* 5.7
Protective detention   *Interim,* 6.7
Protective orders   *Pretrial,* 3.17
Provision of counsel, stages & types of   *Counsel,* 2.3., 2.4
   proceedings
Psychiatric and psychological histories   *Records,* Parts VI–X
Public, protection of   *Corrections,* 1.2A
Public statements by prosecutor   *Prosecution,* 1.3, 6.9
Public statements of counsel   *Counsel,* 1.6

Public trial, right to	*Adjudication*, Part VI
Punctuality of counsel	*Counsel*, 1.5
Punishment in corrections programs	*Corrections*, 4.8
Purchase of services	*Dispositions*, 4.1B; *Architecture*, 4.4
Purchase of services system	*Planning*, 2.3
Purposes of juvenile delinquency code	*Delinquency*, 1.1
Purposive duplication of services	*Planning*, 1.3

Q

Qualifications of intake, investigative personnel	*Probation*, 5.1
Questioning by police	*Police*, 3.2

R

Reasonable doubt	*Adjudication*, 3.2B, 4.3
Reasonableness defense	*Delinquency*, 3.2
Recording of adjudication proceedings	*Adjudication*, 2.1
Recording, waiver of juvenile's rights	*Pretrial*, 6.4
Records	*Records* (see generally)
Records, as bases in monitoring	*Monitoring*, 2.5
Records, confidentiality of records of Department of Corrections	*Corrections*, 4.15
Records, correction of	*Records*, 2.6
Records in group homes	*Architecture*, 4.14
Records in secure corrections facilities	*Architecture*, 5.8
Records of detention facilities	*Architecture*, 6.11
Records of juvenile courts	*Records*, Parts XII–XIII
Records of waiver	*Pretrial*, 6.4
Records, probation	*Records*, Part XIV
Reduction of disposition	*Dispositions*, 5.1–5.3
Referees, use of	*Court Organization*, 2.2
Referrals to youth service agencies	*Agencies*, Part IV
Refusal of juvenile to participate	*Agencies*, 5.3
Regional detention facility, definition	*Interim*, 2.12
Regional juvenile services agencies	*Planning*, 2.2
Regional, definition of	*Architecture*, 1.4
Regulations	*Records*, 2.2

Regulations, corrections program   *Corrections,* 4.6
Relaxation of interim status   *Interim,* 7.11
Release   *Interim,* (see
     generally);
     Appeals, 5.2, 5.6
Release awaiting disposition   *Dispositional
     Procedures,* 4.1
Release conditions, violation of   *Interim,* 4.6
Release, definition   *Interim,* 2.5
Release hearing   *Interim,* 7.6
Release, mandatory   *Interim,* 6.6A
Release on conditions, definition   *Interim,* 2.7
Release pending appeal   *Appeals,* Part V
Release, policy encouraging   *Interim,* 3.1, 5.1, 9.2
Release, pretrial   *Interim* (see
     generally)
Release under supervision, definition   *Interim,* 2.8
Religious services, in secure facilities   *Corrections,* 7.6F
Remedial enforcement powers   *Monitoring,* 1.7
Remedial programs as dispositions   *Dispositions,* 3.2D
Report, predisposition   *Probation,* 3.4
Reports, filing with intake   *Pretrial,* 1.1
Reprimand and release as disposition   *Disposition,* 3.1
Reserch, access to information for   *Records,* 5.6, 15.5
     purposes of research
Research, access to information of   *Records,* Part V
Research planning, corrections department   *Corrections,* 9.3
Researchers, privileged information   *Records,* 2.8
Research, information for   *Records,* 3.5
Research programs   *Corrections,* Part VII
Resource evaluation, youth services   *Agencies,* 5.5
Resources, adequate for program   *Interim,* 3.6
Respondent, presence of   *Adjudication,* 1.3
Respondent's testimony   *Counsel,* 7.9
Responsibility for records   *Records,* 19.3
Responsibility, lack of as defense   *Delinquency,* 3.5
Restitution as disposition   *Dispositions,* 3.2B
Restraints, limitations on use   *Corrections,* 7.8
Restrictive detention criteria   *Interim,* page 5
Retention of information   *Records,* Part IV
Retention of records   *Records,* 19.4

Retention of social histories — *Records,* Part VIII

Review of court orders — *Appeals,* 6.3

Review of court proceedings — *Interim,* 4.3

Right of adjudicated juveniles — *Corrections,* 4.4, 4.5

Rights of juveniles in detention — *Interim,* 10.7

Rights, monitoring of compliance — *Monitoring,* 2.2

Rights, notification of — *Pretrial,* 2.1

Right to a hearing — *Adjudication,* 3.2B

Right to appeal — *Appeals,* 4.2; *Adjudication,* 3.2D

Right to a probable cause hearing — *Pretrial,* 4.1

Right to be present — *Adjudication,* 1.3

Right to compensation and minimum wage — *Rights,* 5.7

Right to copy of transcript — *Appeals,* 3.2, 4.2

Right to counsel — *Interim,* 5.3; *Probation,* 2.5, 2.13

Right to counsel, at intake — *Probation,* 2.13

Right to counsel, generally — *Pretrial,* 2.2, Part V

Right to counsel on appeal — *Appeals,* 3.1, 4.2

Right to counsel, parents' — *Pretrial,* 6.8

Right to public trial — *Adjudication,* 6.1

Right to refuse diversion — *Agencies,* 4.13

Right to refuse services — *Dispositions,* 4.2

Right to remain silent — *Adjudication,* 3.2C; *Interim,* 5.3

Right to services — *Dispositions,* 4.1

Right to testify — *Adjudication,* 3.2C

Right to treatment — *Counsel,* 10.5; *Dispositions,* 4.1D, 5

Right to trial by jury — *Adjudication,* 3.2E, 4.1

Rule making — *Court Organization,* 3.1

Rules concerning records — *Records,* 2.2, Part III

Rules of evidence — *Adjudication,* 4.2; *Dispositional Procedures,* 2.5; *Prosecution,* 6.3

Rules relating to disposition — *Dispositional Procedures,* 5.4

Rural programs as disposition

Corrections, 12A, D, 4.9

S

Safe, human, caring environment

Corrections, 12.A, D, 4.9

Salary of intake & investigative personnel

Probation, 5.4

Sanctions

Delinquency, Part IV, V (see generally)

Sanctions, administrative

Records, 2.5

Sanctions related to discovery

Pretrial, 3.20

Sanctions, result of discipline in secure programs

Corrections, 8.7

Scandinavia, youth service programs in

Agencies, Appendix B

Scheduling of juvenile court

Pretrial, Part VII

School, employment during

Rights, 5.1

School referrals to youth service agencies

Agencies, 4.3

Scientific reports

Pretrial, 3.10

Search and seizure

Police, 3.2

Searches in secure facilities

Corrections, 7.6K

Secondary disclosure

Records, 15.6

Secure corrections facilities

Corrections, 7.1; *Architecture,* Part V

Secure detention, decision

Interim, 6.6

Secure detention facilities, definition

Interim, 2.10

Secure facility as disposition

Dispositions, 3.3E

Secure programs

Corrections, 7.11

Secure setting, definition

Architecture, 1.12; *Corrections,* 7.1

Secure settings, values

Architecture, 2.4

Security measures, definition of

Architecture, 1.5

Security of corrections facilities

Architecture, 5.1; *Corrections,* 7.11

Security of detention facilities

Architecture, 6.2

Security of records in corrections facilities

Architecture, 5.8

Security of records in detention facilities

Architecture, 6.11

Security of records in group homes

Architecture, 4.14

Self-incrimination, privilege against

Probation, 2.12

Self-monitoring by juvenile justice agencies

Monitoring, 10.1

Self-referrals to youth service agencies

Agencies, 4.1

Service agencies

Planning, 2.1, 2.2

Service development — *Agencies,* 5.6
Service provision — *Agencies,* 5.7
Services, duration of — *Corrections,* 4.13
Services, intake — *Prosecution,* Part II
Services, provision by corrections department — *Corrections,* 4.10
Services, provision by youth service agencies — *Agencies,* 2.1
Services, right to — *Dispositions,* 4.1
Services, right to refuse — *Dispositions,* 4.2
Simultaneous sanctions — *Dispositions,* 3.3C
Size of residential facilities — *Corrections,* 7.2
Social histories — *Records,* Section 11; *Counsel,* 9.2; *Interim,* 4.4; *Records,* VI–X

Social information at adjudication — *Adjudication,* 4.4
Social workers, counsel's relations with — *Counsel,* 1.4
Soft architecture, definition of — *Architecture,* 1.9
Special juvenile unit of police department — *Interim,* 5.2
Speed adjudication — *Prosecution,* 6.1
Speedy appeal — *Interim,* 7.14
Speedy decision — *Prosecution,* 4.4, 6.1
Speedy trial — *Interim,* 7.10
Staff living quarters in detention facilities — *Architecture,* 6.10
Staff office in group homes — *Architecture,* 4.13
Staff offices in detention facilities — *Architecture,* 6.12
Staff offices in corrections facilities — *Architecture,* 5.9
Staff of youth service agencies — *Agencies,* 7.4
Staff quarters in group homes — *Architecture,* 4.12
Staff quarters in secure corrections facilities — *Architecture,* 5.7
Staff ratios of intake, investigative personnel — *Probation,* 5.5
Standard of proof — *Prosecution,* 6.3
Standards in juvenile proceedings — *Counsel,* 1.2
State administration of investigative services — *Probation,* 4.3
State commission on juvenile advocacy — *Monitoring,* Part IV
State executive's role in planning — *Planning,* 4.2
Statewide agency — *Interim,* 6.1
Statewide organization of prosecutors — *Prosecution,* 2.6
Statistical reports — *Records,* 13.4
Statistical reports by police — *Records,* 13.4, 19.7
Status decision — *Interim,* 5.5, 5.6, 6.4, 6.6

Status decision, definition   *Interim,* 2.4
Status during appeal   *Appeals,* 5.3
Stay and release   *Appeals,* 5.2
Stay of order   *Appeals,* Part V
Stigmatization of juvenile   *Interim,* 3.5
Stipulated statement   *Appeals,* 4.3
Stipulated statement for appeal   *Appeals,* 4.3
Stop and frisk   *Police,* 3.2
Subpoenas   *Pretrial,* 1.5
Summary records   *Records,* 13.1
Summary records, access to   *Records,* 1.53
Summary records, maintenance of   *Records,* 13.1
Summons   *Interim,* 7.1–7.5;
                                           Pretrial, Part I
Summons, definition   *Interim,* 2.14
Summons, for dispositional proceedings   *Dispositional
                                           Procedures,* 3.2
Support, obligation to   *Rights,* 3.1
Support of minors   *Rights,* Part IV
Surrogate parent, definition   *Records,* 1.5
Surveillance in secure programs   *Corrections,* 7.11
Suspended adjudication   *Adjudication,* 5.2
Suspended sentence as disposition   *Dispositions,* 3.2A

T
Telephone, access to in detention   *Interim,* 10.8
Temporary probation files   *Records,* 14.2
Tenure of intake, investigative personnel *Probation,* 5.2
Termination of orders imposing sanctions *Delinquency,* 5.4
Testimony, by respondent   *Counsel,* 7.9
Testing, definition   *Interim,* 2.16
Testing, limitations on   *Interim,* 4.5
Therapy, limitations on use of   *Corrections,* 4.10F, G,
                                           H
Third person access to records   *Records,* 5.4
Third person, definition   *Records,* 1.10
Time requirements, waiver to adult court *Transfer,* 2.1
Time standards for case processing   *Court Organization,*
                                           3.3; *Interim,* 1.1
Time standards for intake process   *Probation,* 2.15
Training of corrections personnel   *Corrections,* 3.3

Training of intake personnel — *Probation,* 5.3
Training of prosecutors — *Prosecution,* 2.5
Training programs — *Records,* 2.7
Training, use of records — *Records,* 2.8
Transcript — *Appeals,* 3.2
Transcript for subsequent proceedings — *Adjudication,* 2.1C; *Appeals,* 3.2

Transfers, between programs — *Corrections,* 7.7
Transfer to adult corrections prohibited — *Corrections,* 2.2B
Transfer to adult court — *Transfer* (see generally); *Counsel,* Part VII

Transportation to detention facility — *Interim,* 5.3
Treatment, adequacy of — *Appeals,* 6.4
Treatment, as a purpose of detention — *Interim,* 3.3
Treatment, definition — *Interim,* 2.15
Treatment, limitations on — *Interim,* 4.5
Treatment of minors — *Rights,* Part IV
Treatment, provision by agencies — *Agencies,* 5.7
Treatment, right to — *Counsel,* 10.5; *Corrections,* 2.3D; *Prosecution,* 7.2

Trial, speedy timetable — *Interim,* 7.10

U
Unconditional dismissal of complaint — *Probation,* 2.3
Unconditional release — *Interim,* 6.6
Uncontested adjudication proceedings — *Adjudication,* Part III
Unlawful conduct, anticipated — *Counsel,* 3.4
Urban police — *Police,* Appendix A
Use of juvenile records — *Records,* Part XVIII
User participation in monitoring — *Monitoring,* 2.6

V
Values in detention decision — *Interim,* 3.5
Vandalism, juvenile facilities — *Architecture,* 3.4
Victim, consent of — *Delinquency,* 3.3
Victims, consultation with concerning restitution — *Dispositions,* 3.2B
Victims, family members — *Delinquency,* 1.3
Victim, role in detention decision — *Interim,* 3.3

Violation of release conditions — *Interim,* 4.6
Visitors, juvenile in detention — *Interim,* 10.7
Visits to detention facilities — *Interim,* 8.3
Visits to secure detention facilities — *Corrections,* 7.6D
Vocational training in detention facilities — *Architecture,* 6.15
Volunteers — *Agencies,* 5.1, 7.5; *Probation,* 5.6

Volunteers in corrections programs — *Corrections,* 3.6

W
Wages of minors — *Rights,* 5.7
Waiting rooms of detention facilities — *Architecture,* 6.8
Waiver of confidentiality of records — *Records,* 15.7; *Transfer,* Part II

Waiver, of juvenile's rights — *Pretrial,* Part VI
Waiver, of parents' right to counsel — *Pretrial,* 6.10
Waiver of right to counsel prohibited — *Pretrial,* 6.1
Waiver, of service of summons & petition — *Pretrial,* 1.7
"Waiver" to adult court — *Transfer* (see generally); *Counsel,* Part VI

Warnings — *Records,* 20.4
Warrant — *Interim,* 7.1–7.5
Weapons, limitations on use — *Corrections,* 7.8C
Weekend custody as sanction — *Dispositions,* 3.3D
Withdrawal of counsel — *Counsel,* 2.4
Witnesses, examination of by counsel — *Counsel,* 7.8
Witnesses, presence at hearing — *Adjudication,* 1.4D
Witnesses, prosecutor's relationship with — *Prosecution,* 3.4, 3.5
Witnesses, relations with prospective — *Counsel,* 4.4, 9.2
Work by adjudicated juveniles — *Corrections,* 4.14
Workload of intake, investigative personnel — *Probation,* 5.5
Workmen's compensation for juveniles — *Rights,* 5.8
Work permit — *Rights,* 5.4
Written agreements regarding dispositions — *Dispositional Procedures,* 5.3

Written guidelines for intake dispositions — *Probation,* 2.9
Written reasons for detention decisions — *Interim,* 4.3
Written rules concerning information — *Records,* 2.2

JOKER

by Bonnie Highsmith Taylor

Cover and Inside
Illustration: Christine McNamara

For Lennise "Cookie" Thomas

About the Author

Bonnie Highsmith Taylor is a native Oregonian. She loves camping in the Oregon mountains and watching birds and other wildlife. Writing is Ms. Taylor's first love. But she also enjoys going to plays and concerts, collecting antique dolls, and listening to good music.

Text © 1999 by Perfection Learning® Corporation.

Printed in the United States of America. For information, contact
Perfection Learning® Corporation
Phone: 1-800-831-4190
Fax: 1-712-644-2890
1000 North Second Avenue, P.O. Box 500
Logan, Iowa 51546-1099.

Paperback ISBN 0-7891-2931-0
Cover Craft® ISBN 0-7807-8961-X
Printed in the U.S.A.

Contents

1. In Trouble Again! 5

2. What's in a Name? 10

3. What a Horse! 17

4. Tiptoeing in the Tulips 24

5. A Sticky Situation 32

6. Not Your Average Horse 40

7. Out of Chances 47

8. Joker or Hero? 55

1

In Trouble Again!

At first I thought it was a siren going off. Right in my bedroom. Gol, was the house on fire?

Then I realized it was Mom. She was standing right over me. She was screeching bloody murder right in my ear.

"Scott! Get out of that bed! Right now!" Mom yelled, nearly breaking my eardrums.

Boy, she was mad about something!

In the back of my mind, I knew right away what it was. But I hated to admit it.

It had to be about Joker. It always was.

The whole family—Mom, Dad, and my brother—had been in an uproar ever since I'd gotten him. That had been last fall—for my twelfth birthday. What a great birthday present!

I loved that little black pony more than anything in the world. All my life I'd wanted a horse of my own. My brother had had his own horse for three years.

"We can't afford to get two horses right now," Dad had said when he bought Wayne's horse. "Maybe later. Why don't you boys share him?"

Well, in the first place, Wayne wasn't into sharing. Besides, it was his birthday present.

"Anyway," Wayne argued, "a horse isn't something you can share."

I agreed. A horse should belong to just one person.

So Mom and Dad had decided I'd have to wait. Until I was older, and they could afford it.

I'd gotten Joker nearly five months ago. And—well—things hadn't been going very well. That's really putting it mildly too. It had been total chaos!

The siren went off again—louder.

"I mean it, Scott! Get up out of that bed! Immediately!" Mom screeched.

She emphasized every word with a stomp of her foot. The bed was shaking.

"But, Mom," I groaned. I squinched my eyes closed as tight as I could. "It's Saturday."

I scooted down in the bed and pulled the covers over my head. Mom jerked them off. "Get up!" she demanded.

I drew my knees up to my chin. "Aw, Mom!"

I was wishing I knew how to look pitiful. That had worked so well when I was five and six. But it didn't work when you were twelve. And a guy at that.

It probably worked for girls—no matter how old they were.

Oh, well. It probably wouldn't work on Mom now anyway. Not as mad as she was.

Through the window I could hear my brother. He was laughing like an idiot. He sounded like a giraffe gargling. If giraffes gargled.

Wayne is three years older than I am. He thinks that that makes him more important. He's about as important as crust on bread. And I hate crust.

Mom walked over to the window. She raised the blind and looked out.

"I'm glad your brother thinks it's funny," she said. "Because I don't."

She turned back toward me. "And neither will you," she said. "Especially when you see what your precious pony just did."

I sat up in bed. I took a deep breath to prepare myself for whatever. I dreaded looking out that window.

"Because," Mom went on, "you are going to rewash the entire laundry."

"Huh!" I gasped. I flew to the window.

Oh, no!

All of Mom's clean laundry was on the ground. Or the fence. Or blowing across the road.

Except for Mom's skimpy pink nightie. It was draped across Joker's nose.

Wayne was leading Joker back through the gate. Joker had kicked it open again. My brother was laughing. Loud! So loud he was nearly drowning out Joker's whinny.

Oh, why couldn't Mom use her clothes dryer? The way other people did.

Mom picked up my jeans and T-shirt off the floor. She threw them at me.

"Dress!" she ordered. "You have five minutes."

I made it in three.

I ran around the yard. I picked up towels, shirts, socks, and undies. They were filthy.

Wayne handed me the nightie he'd taken off Joker's nose. "Wonder if this looks as good on Mom as it looks on that stupid horse," he snickered.

I jerked it away from him. It was wet with horse slobber. I crammed it into the basket with the rest of the stuff.

"Don't forget those things," Wayne said. He pointed across the road. "The things that blew into

Mrs. Carter's yard."

I hurried over to our neighbor's yard. I hoped no one would see me. But Mrs. Carter seldom missed anything. Sure enough—her door opened, and there she was.

"What are you doing, dear?" she called from her porch.

I smiled up at her. "Just picking up my dad's undershorts," I answered.

2

What's in a Name?

It was almost noon before I finished the laundry. Mom ended up helping me.

I was putting Dad's jeans in the washer when Mom let out a howl. "No!" she screeched.

I jumped three feet. "What?" I asked.

"Don't put the jeans in with the underwear," she said.

She pulled the jeans out of the washer. She slopped water all over the floor—and me.

"Why not?" I asked.

"You just don't," she snapped.

Well, how was I supposed to know? I'd never done laundry.

Mom finished the rest of the laundry. But she made me mop up the water she'd slopped.

I had a feeling this was going to be a sad Saturday.

Dad wasn't home when Joker broke out. He was helping his friend fix his car. Dad's a mechanic. His friends are always getting him to work on their cars.

Dad didn't see the mess my pony made. But he heard about it—all through lunch. And mostly from Wayne.

"You should have seen him, Dad," Wayne said. "It was a riot! Joker scattered clothes and stuff all over. Even across the road. Your shorts ended up on Mrs. Carter's lawn!"

"Oh, great," Dad groaned.

He took a swallow of coffee. Then he turned to me. "He's not working out, Scott," Dad said. "I think we'd better find another home for him."

"But, Dad—" I began.

"I've told you before, Scott," Dad interrupted. "We can't keep an animal that acts the way Joker does."

Dad took a couple of bites of salad. Mom and Wayne went right on eating. I couldn't believe it. I couldn't swallow a bite. And they were stuffing their faces. Just as though nothing was wrong. As though Dad hadn't just said I'd have to get rid of Joker.

I'd die without Joker. I loved him so much.

Then Mom started. "Do you realize how much trouble that horse has caused?" she asked. "He's destroyed the flower bed twice. Knocked down my rose trellis. And nearly killed your father."

That set Wayne off. He really roared. He laughed so hard he urped up an olive. A whole olive. It landed in his chocolate pudding. The smart mouth.

Joker's incident with Dad was something I wanted to forget. But of course, I couldn't. It hadn't really been Joker's fault though. At least I didn't think so.

I had spent the morning riding with my friend Tyler. When I rode into our drive, Dad was on a ladder. He was painting Mom's rose trellis. He had just built it the day before. He was painting it green.

I got off Joker by the pasture gate near the drive.

Dad called out to us. "Hi, Scott," he'd said. "Did you guys have a nice ride?"

"Sure did," I answered. "We rode across Tyler's pasture and over to the pond."

Tyler and I hadn't ridden very far. His mare was due to foal soon.

Then Dad spoke to Joker. "Hi, fella. How ya doing?"

He shouldn't have said anything to Joker. Joker got all excited. He always did when someone spoke to him.

He ran over to Dad and greeted him with a friendly nicker. When he nodded his head up and down, his head hit the ladder. The bucket of paint came down right on top of Joker's head. Dad went flying through the air. He landed on top of Mom's favorite rosebush. The one we'd bought her for Mother's Day.

What a mess!

Mom took Dad to the doctor. He came home with his ankle bandaged. And man, was he mad! I'm not sure about some of the words he used. Mom kept putting her hand over his mouth. They must have been pretty bad.

Dad was determined to sell Joker right then and there.

"That darned horse!" he mumbled through Mom's fingers. "I've had it with him. He's been nothing but trouble since the day he came."

I pleaded for all I was worth. "Please, please, please, Dad!" I begged. "You can't sell him. I'd just die."

Dad didn't budge.

"Maybe he'll get better," I said, fumbling for words—the right words. "After he's been here a little longer."

I turned to Mom for help. But she was nearly as mad as Dad.

13

And Wayne was no help at all. Actually he made things worse. He wouldn't quit laughing.

"Dad!" I was yelling now. "I'll do anything! Anything!"

I knew I wasn't making any sense. What the heck could I do?

At last, Dad gave in. "One more time," he said. "Just one more time. And that's final."

Mom spent the rest of the day picking rose thorns out of Dad. Wayne and I didn't watch, but we were pretty sure where most of them were.

It took over two weeks to get all the green paint off Joker. It took nearly that long for Dad's sprained ankle to heal.

And now, once again, Dad was mad.

"We can't keep a horse that acts the way he does, Scott," Dad said. "I've never heard of a horse that does such crazy things. I think that's why his owners sold him. They had to get rid of him."

"And that's why he was so cheap," Mom added. "A good horse should have cost twice that much. King cost a lot more."

Then Wayne started in. "Well, one thing's for sure," he said. "His name is perfect for him. What a Joker!"

I couldn't argue about that. I knew he was probably right.

The pony had already been named when we got him. Dad said we should keep his name. That way, we wouldn't confuse him.

"And he's confused enough as it is," my smart-mouthed brother said.

I hate calling my horse Joker. Sometimes I secretly call him Beauty, or Midnight, or Champion.

Sometimes, when I ride him at full gallop across the pasture, I'm Alexander the Great. And he's Bucephalus, the wonder horse of the world.

I ride swiftly into battle with my sword held tightly in my outstretched hand. "Charge, oh mighty mount!" I roar. "On to victory!"

Joker loves it. The louder I yell, the faster he goes. He holds his head high and lifts his tail in the wind.

It's our favorite game. We play it a lot.

But I've never told anyone about it. Not even my very best friend, Tyler Flemming.

Tyler's horse is a pretty little buckskin mare. Her name is Misty.

Tyler feels bad when Joker gets in trouble, the same as I do. He's given me lots of advice. But so far nothing has worked.

Dad pushed his chair back. He got up from the table. "I'm not kidding, Scott," he said. "The very next time Joker does something nutty, I'll put an ad in the paper and sell him. We can't keep a horse like that."

I swallowed hard to keep from sniffling.

"It can't be helped, honey," Mom said. "He's a real problem. We may as well own a goat."

"You never see King acting that way," Wayne gloated. "He's a perfect horse."

How right he was.

King was Wayne's beautiful sorrel. He had won all kinds of prizes and ribbons. He was a model of good conduct.

Everyone was always comparing Joker to King. That just made Joker look even worse.

But it didn't make me love him any less.

3

What a Horse!

My friend Tyler was really excited Monday morning. He jumped on the bus and flopped down next to me.

"Guess what, Scott!" Tyler exclaimed. "Misty had her foal last night! A filly. It looks just like Misty." He was all out of breath. "She's really pretty. I named her Dash."

"Cool," I answered.

I felt guilty. I'd been waiting for him. I wanted to talk to him. I needed someone to tell my troubles to. Someone who could understand how I felt. And Tyler was always a good listener. He always gave me the support I needed.

Now I hated to spoil his good news with my bad news.

"Gol—" I tried to sound cheerful. "That's neat, Tyler. I'll stop by after school and see her. Okay?"

"Sure," he answered. "You're going to love her."

Lucky Tyler. He had a nice, well-behaved horse. And now a foal of his very own. And no big brother with a smart mouth.

Tyler knows me pretty well. So well that he guessed something was wrong.

"You okay, Scott?" he asked.

So I told him all about the awful weekend.

"Oh, man," he groaned. "Not again."

I tried to swallow. I had a lump in my throat.

"Dad says he's—he's putting an ad in the paper," I said. "He's going to—to sell Joker." I had to swallow the lump again. "If he does one more thing." My voice was shaking. "And—and I'm pretty sure he will."

Tyler slugged me on the shoulder. "That's rough, Scott," he said. "But, well, maybe it won't happen."

Tyler was a special friend. He always felt the same as I did about everything. No matter what. Tyler and I had been friends since kindergarten.

The bus pulled up in front of school. Tyler and I were in the same class this year. We headed toward Miss Lee's room. Every Monday started the same. Miss Lee asked us to share a story with the class.

"About anything that has happened to you," she explained. "Or to someone you know."

She always said, "Try to make it interesting to the rest of the class."

Well, Joker's laundry stunt would be interesting. The class would love it. But no way was I telling it.

I'd already learned my lesson. Once, I told the class about one of Joker's antics. They danced around the whole day singing "Tiptoe Through the Tulips."

We were just sitting down to breakfast—Mom, Dad, Wayne, and me. All of a sudden, there was Joker in the window. Right over Mom's flower bed. He was nodding his head back and forth—with a tulip in his teeth.

Mom let out a scream. Wayne guffawed. Dad swore. I tried not to giggle, but I couldn't help it.

That is, until I followed Mom outside. We looked at her flower bed. And it wasn't so funny anymore.

That wasn't the only thing I got teased about. Stacy Robbins' father was a doctor. The doctor who treated Dad's sprained ankle. So the class knew about the paint incident.

I got pretty tired of kids calling Joker a dumb horse.

Miss Lee was standing in the front of the room. "I hope you have some interesting stories to share this morning," she said.

I didn't.

Miss Lee called on us alphabetically. With Yates as a last name, I had a little time to come up with something.

Bryce Adams was first. He told about buying baseball cards at the new card shop. As if anybody cared.

Kate Bowman's great-aunt Milly came to visit. All the way from London. Whoop-de-do.

Ron Davis bought a hamster. That was cool.

Some of the kids told about movies they'd seen. Most of them had seen the same one.

Then Tyler told about Misty's new foal. The kids asked a lot of questions. Some of them were kind of dumb.

"Did you watch it being born?" "How big is it?" "Is it her first baby?" "Is it your very own?" "When can you ride it?"

Miss Lee finally said, "Let's move on now."

Beth Garret shared a fishing story. She'd gone fishing with her father and caught a ten-inch trout. So she said.

I guess maybe I was a little jealous of Tyler. He was getting a lot of attention over Misty.

Tyler and I were the only kids in the class who had horses. And I didn't talk about mine anymore.

But right then I made up my mind I was going to talk about Joker. I was sick of everyone laughing at him. I'd make him a hero. I'd make him the greatest horse that ever lived!

At last, Alex Wells finished his dopey story about his piano recital.

I was ready. I crossed my fingers behind my back. Hard. I felt my knuckles crack. I took a deep breath.

"It was Saturday afternoon," I started. "I was riding my big black horse alongside the highway."

Bryce Adams snickered.

Miss Lee stared at him.

I was careful not to say Joker's name. That would made everyone laugh.

"I'd taught my horse to prance " I said. "To raise his knees up to his chest—just like show horses do."

Alex yawned. Loudly.

"My horse learned fast," I went on. "My brother wants me to teach his horse how to prance. But I'm not sure I can."

Stacy picked up a pencil and started doodling on her notebook.

I gritted my teeth, then continued. "He was stepping along with his head held high," I demonstrated.

The picture unfolded in my mind. The story got better and better.

"There was a lot of traffic. Drivers were slowing down. They were looking at us in amazement."

Bryce snickered again. So did some other kids.

"Then—ah—all of a sudden—uh—" Think fast, I told myself.

"A tiny child toddled onto the highway," I said. I drew in my breath. "I couldn't believe my eyes. A truck was coming fast. Too fast to stop in time."

I sucked in more air.

Then I sucked in more air.

"Then, my brave, fearless horse gave a screeching whinny. He dashed into the traffic and snatched up the child with his teeth. By his T-shirt!"

I paused. My mouth was so dry I had to swallow three times.

"Then my horse dropped the kid on the ground just off the highway. Just as the truck reached the very spot where the little kid had been."

My mind raced. Oh, yes—the parents.

"Suddenly, the child's parents came running toward us. They were so happy and grateful. They were surprised at how brave my horse was."

More snickers.

"The father tried to pay me. He tried to give me—uh—one hundred dollars," I said. "Of course, I couldn't take it. Jok—my horse had only done what his strong, brave heart had told him to do."

I figured that was a good place to stop. So I did.

22

I looked around the room. Bryce was shaking his head and rolling his eyes. Alex was yawning. Stacy was reading a book. Two kids had their heads on their desks.

"What a nice—story," Miss Lee said.

So what if no one believed me. It was the best story of all.

For a long time, I stood there feeling foolish.

Then, of all things, Tyler started clapping. I felt more foolish than ever. Leave it to Tyler to be on my side.

I stopped at Tyler's after school to see Misty's foal. Boy, was she ever cute. Stumbling around on her long, wobbly legs.

I stayed for almost an hour. Not once did Tyler say anything about my stupid story. Neither did I.

4

Tiptoeing in the Tulips

By Wednesday, things at home had cooled down a little. Nobody said much about Joker.

Until Wayne spoke up. "Mom, where's the mate to my blue sock?" he asked.

I held my breath. Some of the mates to my socks were missing too. They'd come up missing after Saturday.

Mom looked right at me. "I'll give you three guesses," she said.

"Huh!" Wayne snorted, looking dumb.

"Oh, yeah," he said when he caught on. "That crazy horse probably ate it."

I changed the subject fast—to baseball standings. Dad and I were really into baseball.

Mom made peanut butter waffles and crisp bacon. Cool! My favorite. I decided right then it was going to be a great day.

To top it off, I had new shoes. When I got to school, six kids said they liked them.

One of them was Erica Stanfield! The girl I had liked since last fall. She'd been new in the class.

Erica Stanfield was like no girl I'd ever liked. And I had liked a few.

In kindergarten and first grade, it was Angie Pope. She could make the best clay snakes. But she moved away.

In second grade, it was Katie Mills. Until she gave me a black eye—just for giving my tuna fish sandwich to Lisa Brown. Katie didn't even like tuna fish.

In third and fourth grades, I didn't like girls too much. I liked horses.

That was when Tyler got Misty. I spent all my time at his place. I helped him curry Misty. And we rode double. That was when Wayne got King too. But Wayne wouldn't let me around him. Once in a while, he'd let me ride double with him. But just around the pasture.

Next, I really liked Jessica Lowe. She was something else. She still was, but now she was a foot taller than me. Now Tyler liked her. He didn't care how tall she was. Jessica was the first girl he'd ever liked.

Erica Stanfield was really something too. Even more than Jessica. She had long blonde hair. Jessica's hair was brown and short.

Erica had never even looked at me until that morning. She was on her way to the pencil sharpener when suddenly she tripped over my foot. It was sticking out in the aisle.

"Gol!" I exclaimed. "I'm sorry."

She regained her balance. She looked down at my shoes. Then she looked straight into my eyes. "Cool shoes," she said.

My heart jumped right up into my throat. She liked me! She liked me!

Wonderful Wednesday!

So far, anyway. How could the day possibly get any better?

Wednesday was pizza day. I traded my salad to Kyle Martin for his serving. I couldn't believe that anyone in the world would like salad better than pizza. Especially salad with celery in it. Yuck! Kyle's whole family was into health food. Kyle ate some really weird stuff.

After lunch, Miss Lee started to hand back our graded history reports. She didn't look at all pleased. "I'm sorry to say that most of your reports are not acceptable," she said. "They will have to be done over."

I groaned along with the rest of the class.

"Some of these," Miss Lee said, "have been copied straight from the encyclopedia."

Not mine! Mom made sure I never copied word for word. I don't have to anyway. I have a way with words. Everyone says so.

I know words that Wayne doesn't know. And he's in high school.

Miss Lee went on. "Most of them have not been researched at all."

Mine had! I used three sources. The encyclopedia and two history books. Just the way Dad told me to.

Miss Lee had said to pick someone and do a 200-word report.

"It should be about someone who really interests you," she said. "Someone in history."

That had been the difficult part. I'd had a hard time deciding. Lots of historical people interested me.

First I'd picked Christopher Columbus. He interested me. I'd figured if he hadn't discovered America, I wouldn't even be here. But then I'd decided that if he hadn't, someone else would've.

Probably Thomas Edison. He discovered a lot of things. Or maybe he invented them.

27

I'd thought about doing Dr. Martin Luther King. But I'd found out that Tyler was doing him. I liked George Washington, John Paul Jones, and Daniel Boone.

I had almost decided on Paul Revere. Then I came across this picture in a history book. A picture of a handsome man on a beautiful black horse. A horse that looked like Joker.

It was General Ulysses S. Grant. He was a general in the Civil War. He later became the eighteenth president of the United States. He served two terms, so he must have been a good president.

He'd interested me a lot. So I did a 300-word report on him and his beautiful horse.

And now Miss Lee was saying that it was not acceptable?

But, how could she?

"However," Miss Lee was saying. "One student turned in a very interesting report." She was smiling now.

She motioned to me. "Scott Yates," she said. "Will you please read this out loud to the class?"

Needless to say, the class was impressed. So was I. It was even better than I'd thought. And I did a great job of reading it.

Miss Lee said my report was especially well-written.

My great day continued. I got a perfect grade in

spelling. In PE, we played baseball, and I hit a super home run.

I could hardly wait to get home and tell Mom about the history report, the spelling grade, and the home run. I wouldn't tell her about trading my salad for pizza. I didn't think she'd be interested in that.

I wouldn't tell her that I'd found out that Erica Stanfield liked me either. She'd tell Dad and Wayne. Dad might not tease me, but Wayne would. In his dumb way.

It was exactly 3:35 p.m. when my wonderful day ended. That's when I stepped off the bus in front of my house.

Mom was in the yard. She was standing beside the flower bed she'd been working on so hard. Or rather— what used to be a flower bed. Now it was only a mess of trampled plants.

Joker was sprinting back and forth in his pasture along the fence by the driveway. He was shaking his head and whinnying in snorts. He always did that when he got put back in the pasture—after he'd gotten loose.

The pasture gate was tied with a rope. The big metal clasp was lying on the ground.

Daffodils, tulips, and pansies were scattered all over. The ones that weren't smashed in the ground.

This was the third time.

Oh, Joker. I choked back tears as I walked toward Mom.

"Hi, Mom," I half whispered. "I—I'm awful—awful sorry."

"Sorry!" Mom snorted. "Hah! What good is sorry?"

Joker was bobbing his head up and down, happy to see me. I tried not to look at him.

Mom turned toward Joker. She was glaring. "Hah!" she snorted again.

She sounded almost like Joker when she snorted like that. So much that he answered with a snort of his own.

Mom threw a tulip at him—bulb and all. It fell short by a mile.

I could see King out in the pasture, calmly grazing. He was being a perfect model horse.

I began to plead with Mom. "Please don't tell Dad, Mom," I begged. "He'll put an ad in the paper and sell Joker."

"Right!" she answered. "That's exactly what he'll do. And it's about time."

"But, Mom! I'd just—just die without him," I moaned.

"Well, I won't!" Mom spat. She spread her hands out over the flower bed. "Look at that! Look!"

I looked. It was pretty bad. Some of Joker's tracks were almost a foot deep.

"But—but, Mom," I began. Quick! Think of something, I told myself. "The—the cat does worse things than that in your flower bed. And you wouldn't sell her. Not for anything."

Mom threw her head back. She put her hands on her hips. "For your information, young man, Joker did that too. Only he didn't cover it up."

I looked again. Mom was right. Gol! It had wiped out at least six pansy plants. And did it ever smell!

I wanted to ask her if it wasn't good fertilizer. But I decided I'd better not.

I got the shovel out of the barn and cleaned it up. I was glad Wayne wasn't home. I could just hear him.

I helped Mom fix the flower bed. I didn't talk the whole time I was working. I just sniffed a lot and tried my best to look pitiful.

Oh, how I hoped it would work.

5

A Sticky Situation

Mom didn't say anything to me either—the whole time we were working. I gathered up all the tulips I could. And the daffodils. They were okay. But most of the pansies were destroyed. Mom and I replanted everything.

I wanted so bad to tell Mom about my history report. About the nice things Miss Lee had said about it. And about the perfect spelling grade and the terrific home run I'd hit.

But at the moment, it didn't seem like a good idea. Mom was stabbing the ground with her trowel and grunting with every stab. I took that to mean she was very angry. I guess I couldn't really blame her. If I didn't love Joker so much, I'd be mad at him too. Because he got me in so much trouble.

Right now, though, I wanted to concentrate on being sorry and pitiful.

When we finished the job, Mom stood up. She scraped the mud off her knees with her trowel. We were both pretty dirty.

"I'm going to take a shower," she said.

She didn't even notice how sad I was looking.

"I think I'll take Joker for a ride," I said. "To calm him down."

"A little late for that," Mom answered. "Besides, that horse doesn't calm down. Ever."

Now I felt worse than ever. I had to get away. To be alone with Joker.

I had an idea.

"Mom," I said. "Would you help me saddle Joker, please?"

"Why?" she asked. "You've never had to have help before."

"I—I have a—a blister on my finger," I said. "From all the digging I did."

It wasn't a fib. I really did have a tiny blister. I thought if Mom helped me, Joker might win her over just a little bit. She did like him. At least she always had before.

She helped me saddle him. Joker nuzzled her neck. Mom just glared at him. How could she resist him? I wondered. He was so lovable. He nuzzled her again. She pushed his nose away.

"Keep your nasty slobber to yourself," she said.

But I could see a smile—a very little smile.

I mounted my horse, and I started down the drive.

"Don't be gone too long," Mom called. "I want you here when your father gets home. Understand?"

"Yes, Mom," I said, swallowing hard.

I rode Joker down the gravel road to an old logging road. Then we went up to a wooded area. Flynn Butte was about a mile from home. It was a great place to ride.

My eyes were blurred as I rode along. It was so hard to keep from crying. I thought how awful it would be if they sold my pony. How could I live without him?

I reached forward and scratched Joker's ears. He nickered and bobbed his head up and down to let me know how much he liked it.

I thought of how much fun we'd had together. How neat it was the day I got him for my birthday. And what a surprise. The last thing I'd expected was a horse of my very own.

I was so sure I was going to get a TV for my room. That would have been good too. But compared to a horse! Of my very own! Nothing could be better than Joker.

Even Wayne was in on the big surprise.

My birthday had been on a Saturday. When I walked into the kitchen, Mom was putting breakfast on the table. She'd fixed French toast and ham. Dad stuck a lighted candle into my French toast. Then they all sang "Happy Birthday." I looked around, but I didn't see any packages.

After we ate, Wayne jumped up. "Hey, shrimp. Want to help me feed King?" he asked. "I'll take you for a run across the pasture."

"Sure," I answered.

I was a little surprised. But sometimes he did let me ride double with him. And it was my birthday. I guess he figured that was sort of a present.

I put on my jacket and baseball cap. Then I followed Wayne to the barn. Wayne kept King in the barn at night sometimes. Like when it was cold or rainy.

I could hear a nicker from inside.

"King must be eager to get out," I said.

"I guess so," Wayne answered.

He opened the barn door and there was Joker. He was bobbing his head up and down, nickering.

I was speechless. "Is—is it mine?" I gasped.

Wayne said, "Happy Birthday, shrimp."

The first thing Joker did was pull my cap off with his teeth.

Wayne guffawed.

Suddenly, Mom and Dad were standing in the doorway. "Meet Joker, Scott," said Dad.

Mom really laughed when she saw Joker waving my cap back and forth in his teeth.

It was the greatest feeling! The greatest feeling in the world! A horse of my very own!

Joker nickered when I stopped scratching his ears.

"You're spoiled," I laughed.

Joker shook his head.

"Gol, Joker," I said. "I wish you wouldn't get in so much trouble. Why can't you be like King?"

Joker flicked his ears.

"I wouldn't want you to be just like King," I explained. I didn't want to hurt his feelings. "I love you more than I could ever love King—or any other horse."

We came to the log bridge. It spanned a gulf that ran through the valley below. Across the bridge was a good riding trail. Tyler and I had ridden it a lot. Wayne and his friends went there to hunt for agates. They were into rock collecting. Tyler and I collected some too.

But today, I didn't want to ride the trail. So I dismounted and flopped down on the soft, cool grass.

My pony grazed. He was so contented. He didn't have the slightest idea he'd done anything wrong. He never did.

It was terrible having people hate and laugh at your pet. A pet you loved more than anything in the world.

How could I stand to lose him? The last six months had been so wonderful. Except when he was in trouble, of course. And that was a lot.

But I loved him so much. I couldn't hold it back any longer. I rolled over on my stomach and cried until I couldn't cry anymore.

A loud nicker from Joker made me sit up. I looked around. My pony was walking very slowly toward the bridge. His head was down and his ears were flattened.

"What is it, Joker?" I called. "What do you see?"

I stood up and rubbed my eyes with my fists.

As I moved closer, I saw what Joker was looking at. A big, fat porcupine. It was sitting on the bridge, chewing on a limb.

Oh, no, I thought. I panicked. "You'd better stay back!" I yelled. "If you know what's good for you!"

Joker edged closer. Hearing my voice only made him braver.

"No, Joker! No!" I yelled. "Get back!"

It was no use. Joker wouldn't obey me. I ran to him, but I was too late. Joker let out a scream of pain. And he reared high into the air.

"Joker! Joker!" I cried.

Joker galloped off through the woods, still neighing wildly. I thought he must have been out of his mind with pain and fear.

I finally found him standing in a thicket. He was whimpering and trembling all over. His coat was covered with foamy lather. There were four quills in his nose.

"Poor boy," I soothed. I patted Joker's neck. "Come on, Joker. I'll take you home."

I felt sorry for him.

I led him out of the woods and started home. I could hardly see where I was going, my eyes were so full of tears. I walked as fast as I could. Joker trembled all the way.

Luckily, I got him into the barn without being seen. I got Dad's pliers and pulled out the quills. Joker didn't move a muscle. He seemed almost in shock from the awful thing that had happened to him. I put salve on his swollen nose. Then I took off his saddle and rubbed him down. When I gave him a big kiss—right on his nose—he just stood dead still.

Moments later, I walked into the kitchen.

"It's about time," Wayne said. "I was just going to look for you."

I must have gasped. "Why?" I asked at last.

"Mom said to," Wayne answered. "She was afraid something might have happened to you." Wayne laughed his dumb laugh. He smacked me on the back.

"After all, you were on that kooky horse of yours."

"Very funny!" I snapped.

I sucked in my breath. I hoped I didn't look different. Oh, please, please, I prayed. Don't let anyone ever find out about the porcupine.

We were almost finished with dinner before I realized something. Mom hadn't said a word about the flower bed. I studied her face, but it didn't tell me anything.

Gol, was it possible that my pitiful act had worked? I thought so.

Just before I dozed off that night, she tiptoed into my room. She kissed me on the cheek. She didn't know I was awake. I made a little sobbing sound. She kissed me again.

6

Not Your Average Horse

It took about three days for the swelling on Joker's nose to go down. No one had noticed it. But they noticed something else.

Joker was different. He was quieter and calmer—not like himself at all.

"I wonder if we should have the vet look at him," Dad suggested. "There may be something wrong."

Dad was serious.

"I—I think he's okay," I stammered. "He's just—just getting more used to being here."

"After six months?" Wayne said. "Are you kidding?"

Wayne didn't believe Joker had changed. "He's just plotting something," Wayne said. "That horse will never change."

"Let's not give up hope," said Mom.

Gol, was she on Joker's side?

But then she said, "Though I'm not sure there is any hope for him. He's not your average horse, after all."

"Well—well—who wants an average horse?" I asked. But I wished right away I hadn't said that.

"We do!" Mom, Dad, and Wayne exclaimed.

For over a week, nothing happened. Joker was behaving almost as well as King.

I reminded everyone of it every day. Mom and Dad were really pleased. So was I.

But Wayne said, "Just wait. He'll do something. You know how dumb he is."

"Joker is not dumb," I insisted. "He's just—just high-spirited. And a little curious at times."

"And dumb," Wayne retorted. "You don't see King doing the things Joker does."

"That's because King has no personality," I blurted. "He's dull—with a capital D."

What the heck made me say that?

But then I thought maybe I was right. Maybe that was the difference. King had no personality and Joker did. King might be a big, prize-winning, well-behaved horse. But he was dull. And no one could say that Joker was dull.

One day, Mom was baking apple pies. She discovered she was out of cinnamon. "I don't want to stop now and go to the store," she said. She was peeling apples. "Would one of you go for me?"

There was a little store not far away.

"I'll go," Wayne offered. "I'll ride King."

"I'll go too," I said. "I'll ride Joker."

"No way!" exclaimed Wayne. "I'll go by myself. I'm not going to be embarrassed by that stupid horse."

He went on and on until Mom told him to knock it off. "Both of you go," she said.

We were riding down the road when we heard a motorcycle coming. And it was coming fast. I tensed a little. Traffic made Joker nervous. Especially something as loud as a motorcycle.

"Hold him firm, Scott," Wayne said. "Raise his head—like this. And talk to him. Keep talking to him."

I watched Wayne hold the reins close to King's neck. King raised his head—just a little.

Then I tried it. I held the reins against Joker's neck the way Wayne did. "Steady, boy," I said. "Steady now."

I kept talking to him gently as the motorcycle raced past. Joker didn't even flinch. That had never happened before.

"Not bad," Wayne grinned at me. "For a horse who is—uh—high-spirited."

That was something coming from Wayne. It was close to a compliment.

But the very next day, Wayne was making fun of Joker the same as always.

Joker was chasing a raven around the pasture. It was one of his favorite pastimes. The raven would cry, "Caw! Caw!" And Joker would whinny.

Sometimes Joker would chase the ravens until he wore himself out. Dad said he thought the ravens enjoyed it as much as Joker did.

"Get a load of that dumb nag!" Wayne roared. "What a nerd!"

I didn't mind him laughing. I thought it was really funny too. But I hated it when he called Joker a dumb nag.

I spent a lot of time at Tyler's, seeing the new foal. She was so cute. She had long skinny legs and a head that looked too big for the rest of her.

"I can't believe how fast she's growing," Tyler said.

I told him how well Joker was behaving. "He hasn't been in trouble for ages," I said. "Even Wayne said something good about him."

Tyler was as happy and proud as I was.

I had finally told Tyler about the porcupine. He'd promised not to tell anyone.

"I don't want anyone making fun of him either," he'd said. "Don't worry, Scott. You can depend on me."

I knew that. I'd counted on Tyler since we were five years old. I told him all my secrets. I couldn't count all the times he'd covered for me.

But I could count the times I'd covered for him. Zero. I couldn't remember Tyler ever doing much of anything wrong. Tyler was just about perfect.

In the back of my mind, I giggled. Like King, I thought. Perfect. But he was still my best friend.

I rode over to Tyler's one day to see Dash—the new foal.

"It's really weird," I told Tyler. "But since that porcupine slapped Joker, he's been acting so much different. So well behaved."

I took Joker's saddle off so he could run around the pasture.

Tyler got two sodas from his mother. We climbed on the top rail of the corral and watched the horses. Joker and Misty always got along fine. But she was a little nervous since foaling. She even nipped toward Joker. He must have thought she was playing. He ran around in circles kicking up his hind legs.

Tyler laughed. "I don't know, Scott," he said. "He acts the same as always to me."

"But he is different," I insisted. "A lot. He hasn't broken out for a long time. And you know how he hates being in that pasture."

"I guess it could be because of the porcupine," Tyler said. "Maybe it did calm him down a little."

I hoped so. But if it was that, it had been a hard lesson.

Joker was crazy about the foal. He followed it around, sniffing at it. Misty nickered a gentle warning now and then. After a while she seemed to understand that Joker wouldn't harm her baby. So she relaxed.

When it was time to go, Joker came right to me. Usually he made a game of it. Bobbing his head up and down. Stepping to one side as I was about to catch him.

Wayne had told me it was my own fault for letting him get away with it. But I didn't know how to make him stop.

On the way home from Tyler's, a noisy sports car sped by. I held Joker's reins the way Wayne had shown me. And I talked to him. "It's all right, Joker. It's all right."

Joker paid no attention to the car.

Tyler started riding Misty again. We rode together in her pasture. Dash would follow along behind. I thought Joker might act up, but he didn't. He did nicker a little at the foal, like he was saying, "Come on, slowpoke."

Joker always came to me when I called him now. No more games of tag.

"Oh, Joker I'm so proud of you," I told him. He pushed his cold nose against my neck. "And I love you so much."

I was sure that everything was going to be all right from now on.

But Wayne wasn't.

"Okay," Wayne said. "So he's acting a little better lately. I wouldn't count on it to last." He smirked. "After all, he's got a name to live up to."

I didn't care what my brother thought. I knew that Joker had given up his bad habits.

Everything would be fine. Joker was mine for keeps.

7

Out of Chances

I was so excited over the way things were turning out. Joker had finally settled down. He was being the kind of horse people couldn't make fun of.

Well—most of the time. He still did things that some people might think were a little weird.

There was a small birch tree in the pasture that Joker used for a rump-scratching post.

"We should put a grass skirt on him," Dad said. "He looks like he's doing the hula."

The problem was the tree was so small it always bent. So Joker always ended up sitting on the ground with a surprised look on his face.

That always cracked up Dad and Wayne.

One time, Dad brought some of his friends home to watch it. It was really embarrassing. They said rude things about Joker.

"That horse must have been brain damaged at birth," said one.

"Is that what you call horse sense?" laughed another.

Very funny.

Wayne declared, "If it was any other horse but Joker, he would have figured it out by now."

"Maybe he does it on purpose," I suggested. "Because he knows it makes people laugh."

"Yeah, sure," said Wayne.

Joker loved apples. He did something that some people, like Mom, thought was gross. He'd chew up the apple, swallow, then blow out his lips. Apple juice, bits of peelings, and seeds would fly out. Right in the face of whoever had given him the apple.

That cracked my brother up too. Until he was the one who got it in the face.

But these things were just part of Joker's neat personality. They weren't things that caused trouble.

No more kicking down the gate. No more destroying things. No more running away.

Ever since I'd gotten Joker, he'd tried to be friends with King. But King would have nothing to do with him.

"It's because Joker is not as good as King," Wayne tried to tell me. "King won't have anything to do with a horse who isn't his equal."

"It's because he's stuck-up," I replied. "Just like you."

My brother laughed in my face. "Whoever heard of a stuck-up horse?" he asked. "He's simply smart enough to realize that your pony isn't bright. He wants nothing to do with him."

At times, King actually had been mean to Joker. And all Joker wanted was to be friends. Twice King had kicked Joker. And once he'd bitten him bad enough that it bled.

So I was really surprised when, one morning, I saw King rubbing his long nose against Joker's neck.

For a moment, I thought he was going to bite my pony again. Then I realized he was being friendly. When Joker nickered softly, King answered. Just like he was saying, "Let's be friends."

Wayne's school bus left before mine, so he didn't see it. But just wait till he finds out, I thought. He'll eat his words.

I could barely wait to tell Tyler. Not just about that,

but about how well Joker was behaving. How smoothly things were going at home.

Tyler was as pleased as I was. "Hey, Scott, that's great," he said. "You don't have to worry anymore about your parents selling him."

It looked like the start of another great day. I hoped this one would last longer than the last one had.

Miss Lee chose a really good book for read-aloud time. Oh, sweet bliss! It was a horse story. About a wild stallion named Whitey. I loved it, and so did the rest of the class.

I got a B+ on a social studies test—my most hated subject.

And the best part of the whole day was—Erica ate lunch with me!

Tyler and Jessica sat with us. But I only had eyes for Erica. Ever since the day she'd finally noticed me, she'd gotten prettier and prettier. If that was possible.

She and Tyler had been the only kids in the class who hadn't sneered or laughed at my story. The one about Joker saving the little kid. Even Jessica had snickered a little.

It was plain to see that Jessica had gotten over me. It was Tyler all the way now. But that was okay.

After school, Wayne's smart mouth was the same as always. He explained why King was making friends with Joker. "He feels sorry for your pony," Wayne said. "He knows how terrible it must be to be so dumb."

Then he said something really rotten. "After all, sometimes I even treat you nice—out of pity."

"You couldn't be nice if you tried," I snapped.

Wayne was ready with a smart reply, but Mom stepped in. "One more word out of either of you, and you'll go without TV for a week. Maybe a month."

She didn't sound like she meant it though. Seconds later, she poured two glasses of milk for us. And she put a plate of cookies, warm from the oven, on the table.

Chocolate chip!

My mom made the best cookies. And pies, and cakes, and pizzas!

I was on my fifth cookie when a loud neigh and a crashing sound almost made me spill my milk.

"It's Joker!" Wayne shouted. "It's got to be!"

We all ran into the yard. Wayne was right. The gate was hanging by one hinge. And Joker was tearing across the lawn toward the road.

A big farm truck, filled with sheep, was going by the house.

Wayne scratched his head. "What's that crazy horse doing?"

"Joker! Joker!" I shouted. "Come back here!" I even whistled as hard as I could.

But he was chasing the truckload of sheep, neighing with every breath he took. I'd never seen him run like that.

I could have died. I'd been so sure that Joker had changed. That he was mine for keeps. I knew now that this was the end of everything. Mom and Dad wouldn't give him another chance. And I guess I couldn't really blame them. All I could do was stand there being miserable.

Until Wayne jerked my arm. "Come on," he ordered. "Get your bike. We have to catch that fool horse before he really gets into trouble."

I never pedaled so fast in my life. But as fast as I was going, Wayne was way ahead of me.

"Hurry up, Scott," he kept shouting.

"I—I—am," I panted. My chest hurt. My eyes were burning. I had a pain in my side.

I could still see the truck ahead with my pony close behind. I didn't think the truck driver knew he was being chased by a horse. But it sounded as though the sheep did. I could hear the bleating from as far back as I was.

When we reached town, we caught up with the truck at a red light. We yelled at the top of our lungs at Joker. He wouldn't pay any attention.

Joker reared high in the air. He pawed at the back of the truck. The poor sheep were nearly trampling one another to death.

Suddenly, there was the truck driver, yelling his bald head off. "What's going on?" he shouted. "Get that harebrained horse out of here." He used some pretty strong language.

Then a policeman came.

What a commotion!

Hundreds of bleating sheep. A whinnying horse. And at least two dozen people lined up on the sidewalk—laughing themselves sick.

A man brought us a rope. While the policeman wrote stuff down in his book, the man tied the rope around Joker's neck.

Wayne rode off and left me behind. I had to pedal home, leading my horse by the rope. All by myself. Joker was so tired he kept stopping. "Come on, Joker," I begged. I was hoarse from yelling so much.

It was the most embarrassing thing that had ever happened to me in my whole life.

Dinner that night was a disaster. I felt so rotten. I could hardly see my plate. And I could hardly swallow. I think it was liver and lima beans, which I hate anyway.

My head ached from Mom and Dad hollering.

"I knew we should have gotten rid of that horse the first time he got out and trampled my flower bed," Mom said.

I didn't know anyone could chew as fast as Mom was chewing and talk at the same time.

The policeman had been there when Dad got home from work. He gave Dad a ticket. "For allowing an animal to run at large," the policeman explained.

"I don't allow this animal to run at large!" Dad had shouted. "I absolutely forbid him to run at large!"

The policeman had grinned and walked away.

"I hope you understand, Scott," Dad said, his face bright red. "This fine is coming out of your allowance."

I didn't care about my allowance. I didn't care about anything. I could just die, I felt so awful.

Wayne wasn't saying anything. He was hunched over the table stirring the food around his plate.

It was probably my imagination, but he looked like he felt awful too.

Right after the policeman left, Dad called the newspaper office and placed a for-sale ad.

8

Joker or Hero?

The next morning, I walked downstairs to breakfast. The newspaper was lying on the kitchen table.

There was a picture of Joker on the front page. He was pawing at the truck. The caption read HORSE MAKES EWE-TURN ON MAIN STREET.

I didn't turn to the page with the for-sale ad. I couldn't stand to see it.

I don't remember ever having such a terrible day.

Bryce Adams followed me around all day. He kept saying, "Baa! Baa!"

The whole class was in hysterics. Except Tyler and Erica. They felt as bad as I did.

I think even Miss Lee was trying to keep from laughing. Although she kept telling the class it wasn't nice.

And it started raining that morning right after school started. It really poured all day. We couldn't go out for recess. I found a quiet corner in the library and pretended to read a book.

When I got off the school bus that afternoon, the roads were full of deep puddles. I didn't even glance toward the pasture when I heard Joker nickering a greeting. I couldn't stand to look at him. Especially knowing that in a short time he'd be gone.

No matter what he'd done, I still loved him more than anything in the world. I'd be so lost without him.

Mom had pretzels and orange juice for my snack. Any other time that was one of my favorite snacks. I liked to dip the pretzels in the orange juice. But not today.

I wondered if anyone had called about the ad. But I didn't want to ask.

"I know how bad you feel, honey," Mom said. "But you've got to understand. Sooner or later, Joker could cause serious trouble." She sighed. "He's already cost us a lot of money. Putting in new plants twice. Dad's doctor bill for his sprained ankle. And now a fifty-dollar ticket."

Then she added something I wished everyone had forgotten. "And what about the money we had to pay to have the car repaired?"

I hate to tell this, it's so awful. Joker actually attacked the car. Dad had just finished polishing it. It was really shiny. I think Joker saw his reflection in the fender. First he nickered at it. Then he slobbered all over it.

"Hey, knock it off!" Dad had thundered.

But it was too late. Joker reared in the air and came down on the fender with his front feet. It was a mess. I'm not sure why he did it. But I'm sure he had a good reason. A good reason for a horse anyway.

Mom went on. "We've spent so much money for the damage Joker has done. More than what we paid for him to begin with."

I didn't say anything. There wasn't anything to say. It was all true.

"Maybe someday we'll get you another horse," Mom said.

"I don't want another horse!" I cried. "I don't ever want another horse!"

Then Wayne came home from school in a bad mood. "Stupid rain," he grumbled. "If this keeps up, the Saturday trip will be ruined."

"What trip?" I asked.

"Matt Sills, Rob Jones, Tony Martinez, and I planned to go on a ride," Wayne answered. "We're riding up the old logging road to Flynn Butte. We're going to hunt for rocks.

"Matt found a neat carnelian there last week," Wayne continued. "Up the trail on the other side of the bridge where we find the agates."

It sounded like fun. I guess I envied Wayne and his friends. They all had well-behaved horses. Horses that never got in trouble.

Without thinking, I sighed. "I wish I could go with you," I mumbled.

"Are you kidding?" Wayne blurted. "No way can that stu—that horse go with us."

Wayne had been a little nicer since Joker's recent adventure with the sheep truck. Almost as though he felt bad for me. He'd even stopped saying mean things about my horse.

I couldn't help thinking about Wayne's trip. And how nice it would be to have one last day with Joker.

"Please, Wayne," I begged. "It—it'll be the last time."

Wayne looked like he was in agony. "Aw, Scott. You know how he is. He'll be a nuisance. And—and the guys will be there."

Wayne took a deep breath. Then just like that, he stopped being sorry. "That dumb horse isn't going. And that's final. So let it drop."

I did.

There was no school Friday because of the rain. The roads were so bad that the buses couldn't get through.

Wayne and I moped around all day. Wayne because he figured his trip was off. And me because of knowing I was losing Joker.

"If you want me to, Scott, I'll feed Joker until—" he offered.

He didn't finish. But I knew what he meant.

"Thanks," I whispered.

Saturday morning we woke to a beautiful sunny day. Wayne was in a wonderful mood. He even sang at the breakfast table while Mom packed his lunch for the trip.

I wanted so much to go I decided to swallow my pride and give it one more try. I begged and pleaded for all I was worth.

Then Mom joined in. "It would be a nice thing to do, Wayne," she said. "And it'll be Scott's last time with Joker."

Wayne finally gave in. "But I'm warning you," he said as he shook his finger right in my face. "If that crazy horse causes any trouble—"

Wayne's friends had a lot of fun teasing me about Joker. But I wasn't going to let it bother me. I was going to enjoy this last day with my pony in spite of their teasing.

Joker stepped along nicely as I rode along behind Wayne and the other boys. A couple of times he shook his head in protest against the tightly held reins. But he was behaving pretty well.

It was beautiful in the woods. And it smelled good from the rain. Some places on the trail were soft and muddy. So we had to detour around them. When we got close to the bridge, it was really muddy.

"We better go pretty slow up the trail," said Rob. "It's awful steep. And as soft as the ground is, the horses could slip and fall."

"Why don't we just stop at the bridge?" suggested Tony.

"Because the best agates are up on the flat," said Wayne. "That's where we found them before. By the waterfall."

"Yeah, right," Tony replied. "We'll just ride slow."

"Come on," said Wayne, taking the lead.

Joker started to follow. Then suddenly, with no warning, he bucked. He threw me off. And I landed on the ground with a thud.

With an ear-splitting whinny, Joker began running around and around in circles. He kicked his hind legs like mad.

The boys struggled to control their horses. Tony's horse bucked him off. So the other boys dismounted.

Wayne was furious. "That crazy horse of yours has gone loco!" he yelled. "I knew we shouldn't have let him come."

I lay on the ground staring in wonder. What was wrong with Joker? He'd never bucked me off before. Sure, he'd done a lot of strange things. But he was acting as though he'd lost his mind completely.

He was bucking wildly, and his whinnies were deafening. He had a wild look in his eyes. I'd never seen him look like that. Except the time—

All at once it hit me! I knew what was wrong with my pony. The porcupine! He was remembering the awful thing that had happened to him on the bridge. And he was terrified.

I jumped to my feet and ran to him. "Steady, Joker, steady," I soothed. I grabbed his reins. At last I was able to calm him. "It's all right, boy," I said. "It's all right."

"Oh, sure, it's all right!" Wayne howled. "It's fine to go off your rocker. For no reason at all. Even if it endangers lives."

The boys were all glaring at me. And at Joker.

I just stood there and said nothing. I couldn't let them know. I couldn't let them laugh at Joker anymore. I'd rather have them mad at him than making fun of him.

I fumbled for some excuse—some reason—for his actions. "Maybe—maybe something was hurting him," I said. "Maybe he had a pain—"

"He is a pain," grumbled Matt.

Wayne looked at me. He was really mad. "You take that stupid horse home!" he snapped. "I should've known better than to give in and let you bring him."

All the boys mounted their horses.

They started again on the road toward the bridge. But all of a sudden, Wayne's friend, Rob, pulled his horse to a stop. So hard that the horse reared a little.

"What's wrong?" asked Matt.

"I'm not sure," Rob said. He got off his horse. He knelt down on one knee. "Hey, you guys!" he hollered. "Holy cow! Come here!"

The other boys moved closer.

"Look here!" said Rob. "The heavy rain has washed the ground away from those timbers. Look!"

"I think you're right," Wayne gasped. "That bridge is ready to cave in."

Matt and Tony picked up a small log lying close by. With all their might, they threw it on the bridge.

In horror, we watched as the old timbers broke loose from the ground. Seconds later, they crashed at the bottom of the gulch.

"Wow!" they all exclaimed together.

Wayne turned toward me. His face was dead white. His eyes looked like they were about to pop out.

"How—how—" Wayne stammered. "How could Joker have known?"

"But he must have known," said Rob. "That's why he was acting so strangely."

"Man!" cried Matt. "He was warning us not to go on the bridge."

Wayne walked over to where I was standing with my mouth hanging open.

"Scott," Wayne said, "I take back everything I ever said about that dumb—uh—that wonderful horse."

"That goes for me too," Matt said. "If it hadn't been for him, we'd all be at the bottom of that gulch."

"Joker saved our lives," Tony said. "What a horse!"

"Wait till we tell Mom and Dad," said Wayne. He gave me a big hug. "No way will they ever sell Joker."

I think I was in shock. I couldn't believe what I was hearing. They actually thought Joker was a hero.

Oh, sweet bliss! For the first time, Joker was being praised instead of made fun of.

I had a terrible time trying to keep a straight face. What if Wayne and his friends knew the real reason for Joker's behavior? I thought. What a laugh they would have. I would never live it down. Never.

But they'd never laugh at Joker again now. He was a hero—even if it was by accident.

And another thing. I decided to change his name. Let's see—maybe Rex. Or Gallant. Or Dandy.

Or maybe—maybe I'd name him Hero.